S0-CQS-363

St. Louis Community College

Library

5801 Wilson Avenue
St. Louis, Missouri 63110

INSIDE
PUBLIC RELATIONS

Ronald P. Lovell

Oregon State University

ALLYN AND BACON, INC.
Boston London Sydney Toronto

Photos on pages 2, 16, 70, 86, 104, 130, 144, 156, 168, 188, 218, 232, 272, 290, 302, 318, 332, 342, 354, 372, and 386 courtesy Talbot Lovering.
Photo on page 50 courtesy Talbot Lovering and McKinney/New England.
Photo on page 34 courtesy Ejay/Freelance Photographer's Guild.

Library of Congress Cataloging in Publication Data

Lovell, Ronald P.
  Inside public relations.

  Bibliography: p.
  Includes index.
  1. Public relations—United States. I. Title.
HM263.L595   659.2   81–15065
ISBN 0–205–07741–2   AACR2

Series Editor: Michael Meehan

Printed in the United States of America.

10 9 8 7 6 5 4 3 2 1   87 86 85 84 83 82

To my father

Contents

Preface

Inside Public Relations has a number of distinctive features that make it useful to both student and professor.

As the title implies, the book attempts to get "inside" a complicated and varied industry by using the opinions and experiences of working public relations practitioners. These people tell what they do every day as they conduct their business, whether it be in an agency, a corporate PR department, or a public information office at a nonprofit organization.

Their descriptions should help students interested in the profession understand what they will be getting into and give them a feel for the job. Some of the opinions are candid and critical of public relations. This honesty is necessary in a field that is much maligned and much misunderstood. The same approach should help instructors of public relations, too, by augmenting their own thoughts and experiences.

The book is directed at two audiences: journalism students and business students. Journalism has long been the academic home for PR courses. Recently, however, business schools have begun to teach PR, as a result of which there are dual assignments at the ends of chapters. This approach should help both sides when they have to face each other as either PR professionals or managers deciding whether to support suggested programs.

At various points in the book I have included sections that illuminate the subject of that particular chapter. These are called "PR Focus" if they deal with a company or an issue and "PR Bio" if they deal with a person. An analysis follows each to tie the information into the overall discussion.

The first half of the book gives readers a philosophical and an informational base for public relations. Section I explains public relations, gives a brief history of it, and talks about PR today. Section II discusses the various segments of the profession: agency, corporate, and public information, and tells how to conduct a PR campaign. Section III contains material on financial public relations, dealing with management, working with agency clients, and working with the government.

The second half of the book shows readers how to do the various tasks needed in public relations and includes a number of illustrations: chapters on writing news releases, preparing brochures and press kits, preparing annual reports and company magazines, using TV and radio, setting up external events, and using advertisements. The chapters in Section V discuss how to deal with the various publics: the press, other parts of the company, and the general public. The last part, Section VI, considers certain outside elements related to public relations: how to conduct a public opinion survey and how to avoid legal and ethical problems. The last chapter discusses public relations as a career.

Because it discusses public relations through the words and deeds of people working in various aspects of that profession, this book would not have been possible without the help and cooperation of a great number of individuals. I contacted old friends in both public relations and the working press for help, either as interview subjects or as conduits to other professionals I did not know.

I am very grateful for the help and encouragement of these old friends and co-workers: Barbara Lamb of McGraw-Hill World News; Jim Roscow, a freelance financial journalist; Vic Pesqueira of Xerox; Kemp Anderson of McGraw-Hill; Mike Murphy, an old friend and former colleague; Peter Britton, a New York freelance writer; Joan Dolph, a friend and former PR executive; Rosemary Stroer, a New York freelance writer; Sandra Atchison of *Business Week;* Bob Henkel of *Business Week;* Bill Cushing, a Seattle business journalist; Nichole Vick, a technical editor; Dick Floyd, an Oregon State University editor; Tom McLaughlin, a Colorado public information man; Gwil Evans, an OSU extension service chairman; Allen Wong, an OSU art professor; Marilyn Holsinger, a University of Missouri art professor; Bob Mason of the OSU Survey Research Center; Jeff Clausen, a Portland public relations man; Ken Niehans, former public information director at the University of Oregon Medical School; Dianne Sichel, a Portland magazine editor; and Judy Carlson, a freelance publicist.

The help of a number of other professionals I met during the course of this book was invaluable and I thank them: John Pihas, The Pihas, Schmidt, Westerdahl Company; James Lamb, Joseph M. Cahalen, Homer Schoen, and Carol Zimmerman of Xerox Corporation; Bob Neale of Chrysler Corporation;

George Hobgood of Hill and Knowlton; Regis McKenna of Regis McKenna Public Relations; William Brown of Trans World Airlines; Otto Glade and Downs Matthews of Exxon; John DeMilia of Carl Byoir; Robert Hostetter of the Bureau of Land Management; Henry Rogers of Rogers and Cowan; Ted Weber and Don Rubin of McGraw-Hill; Craig Lewis of Earl Newsom; Tom Nunan of Burson-Marsteller; Mickey Parr of Atlantic Richfield; Ted Michel of Levi Strauss; Bill Jones, Charles Michals, Dale Basye, and Walter Morris of Standard Oil of California; the Public Relations Society of America; the International Association of Business Communicators; and the John R. O'Dwyer Company.

I appreciate very much the valuable suggestions of Professor Harold Davis of Georgia State University, which I used in revising the original manuscript. Judith Gimple and her co-workers at Bywater Production Services deserve my gratitude and praise for their excellent design and editing work. This project could not have been completed without the willingness of Michael Meehan, my editor at Allyn and Bacon, to stick with me throughout. I also appreciate the work of Jack Rochester, a former editor at Allyn and Bacon, in offering me a contract in the first place.

To my typist, Glenda Monroe, and my tireless proofreader, Verna Lovell, my gratitude for jobs well done.

Ronald P. Lovell

SECTION I

Introduction to Public Relations

...**ic prose/cutor,** an officer charged with the conduct of criminal prosecution in the interest of the public.

pub/lic rela/tions, 1. the actions of a corporation, store, government, individual, etc., in promoting good will between itself and the public, the community, employees, customers, etc. 2. the art or technique of promoting such good will.

pub/lic school, 1. (in the U.S.) a school that is maintained at public expense for the education of the children of a community or district and that constitutes a part of a system of free public education commonly in...2. (in England...

CHAPTER **1**

What is public relations?

Public relations has become one of the most all-encompassing phrases of our time — assigned by people to activities as varied as selling real estate and seeking publicity for a local club. To some, it is nothing more than "free" advertising, that is, stories printed in publications or broadcast over television or radio that extol the virtues of a product or an idea in the same unobjective manner as in a paid advertisement. In politics, thanks in large part to members of the Nixon administration, "PR" is tantamount to cover-up, hiding the bad so that only the good comes to public attention.

The real definition of public relations shows it to be quite different from any of these popular views, which are all misconceptions.

PUBLIC RELATIONS DEFINED

Public relations, according to *The Random House Dictionary of the English Language,* comprises "the actions of a corporation, store, government, individual, etc. in promoting good will between itself and the public, the community, employees, customers." That sparse description can be augmented by an explanation from the Public Relations Society of America, an organization that attempts to foster public relations and increase the professionalism of those working within it.

"Public relations is difficult to grasp at first," says a PRSA booklet on *Careers in Public Relations.* "For one thing, the term is used to describe both a way of looking at an organization's performance and a program of activities. . . . Basic to all public relations . . . is communicating. Well thought out, effectively handled communications are increasingly seen as essential to the success and even existence of organizations and causes in today's complex, fast-changing world. Every organization — governmental, business, labor, professional and membership, health, cultural, educational and public service — depends on people. Their attitudes, attention, understanding and motivation can be critical factors in whether an organization or an idea succeeds or fails."

4

According to PRSA, public relations must do more than tell an organization's story to the various publics that might be interested in hearing it. People working in public relations must try to shape the organization itself and the way it performs. By conducting research into the thoughts and concerns of these publics, and by properly evaluating that research, the public-relations person can advise members of management on making necessary changes. "A responsible — and effective — public relations program should be based on the understanding and support of its publics," says the PRSA careers booklet.

PR: DIFFERENT THINGS TO DIFFERENT PEOPLE

The dilemma of finding a precise definition of public relations results from three factors: the many masks PR wears, the many publics it serves, and the various approaches its practitioners take.

Public relations to some companies is "public affairs," while others use that term to describe their lobbying efforts with government. Still other organizations substitute "communications" for PR. Rarely do companies or agencies use the term "publicity" except when applied to new product information. They apparently think that it denotes the desire to see one's name in print for whatever reason, good or bad. Whatever the title, however, the aim is the same: influencing one public or another.

There is more than one "public" in public relations. The general public comes to mind most often, but that broad group is more often divided into more specific publics: members of the print and electronic media, employees, retired employees, customers, stockholders, government officials, and other even more specialized groups. All of them can be possible targets for the work of PR people; it depends on the goals of the sponsoring company or non-profit organization.

The approach taken by PR people varies widely as well. In some company public-relations departments, and in the companies that make up the client list of public-relations agencies, the activity is a passive one — handling day-to-day relations with the public via occasional contacts with the press. In other company PR departments and agencies, the attention to the world outside the door is constant, aggressive, and as varying as the many publics to be reached.

Even experienced public-relations practitioners find it difficult to define precisely the field in which they work. Some see it primarily as communicating an idea, philosophy, or product to an audience interested in such information. Others consider it an educational process where the PR person learns as much as possible about the subject (a company, a research institution), then conveys that information to those who ask about it, as a teacher would do. Public relations can be the main ingredient of the sales effort for a specific product, or the basis for a more indirect and abstract campaign to get people to think well of an entire company.

Many times, the real work of a public-relations person or department is unknown to any of the targeted publics. A good PR practitioner spends much time advising company officials behind the scenes in how to deal with problems that confront them. Very few such problems today escape at least a peripheral connection to one public or another "out there," in the outside world beyond the doors of the organization.

JOBS

The work done by people in public relations falls into a number of categories, according to PRSA:

1. *Programming* — analyzing problems and opportunities, defining goals and publics, and recommending programs.
2. *Relationships with others* — gathering information from management, from others in the organization, and from external sources, and evaluating it to develop recommendations.
3. *Writing and editing* — using the printed word to reach various publics through such devices as press releases, booklets, reports, speeches, film scripts, trade magazine articles, product information and technical material, employee publications, newsletters, reports to shareholders, and other management communications.
4. *Information* — setting up the mechanism to disseminate material to the appropriate editors at newspapers, broadcasting stations, and general and trade publication magazines, and to interest those editors in publishing the organization's views.
5. *Production* — having a general knowledge of designing, laying out, writing the copy for, and selecting the appropriate art, photographs, and typography for brochures, special reports, and films.
6. *Special events* — planning and coordinating news conferences, convention exhibits and special displays, new facility openings, anniversary celebrations, and contest and awards programs and tours.
7. *Speaking* — giving speeches about the organization to large and small groups of people, and writing speeches for others to deliver.
8. *Research and evaluation* — gathering facts for use in public-relations programs by personal interviews, review of library materials, and informal conversations; hiring and evaluating the work of public-opinion research firms; developing workable programs based on the results of either the fact gathering or the more sophisticated polling.

STRUCTURE

If the jobs to be done in public relations vary, the same can be said for the kinds of organizations that need to communicate with the large numbers of publics.

Corporate Public-Relations Departments

More people work in this segment of the profession than in any other, especially in small and medium companies with one- or two-person PR departments. Companies have a particular point of view to put across, and they do not mind spending money to do so. Public-relations activities within large corporations and smaller companies usually involve giving advice to management on the organization's public statements and attitudes; maintaining regular contact with reporters and editors; keeping in touch with diverse publics like employees, customers, shareholders, and members of the board of directors; and preparing printed and broadcast materials to support the first two activities. The scope of the work is limited only by the budget for the department and the number of people employed. A growing and important segment of corporate public relations is investor relations or financial public relations. Here the publics are shareholders, security analysts, and financial reporters; and the information is limited strictly to a company's profits and losses.

Public-Relations Agencies

The 1,500 agencies in the United States do many of the same things as their counterparts in corporate public-relations departments, but with one big difference: they do what they do for more than one corporation, collectively called *accounts* or *clients* in the agency business. The employees of an agency carry out writing and editing chores; advise company management on approaches to goal-setting and communication with the outside world; and help their accounts communicate with their various publics.

The challenge and the hectic atmosphere of an agency come from dealing with the problems of more than one company at once. Often, a large corporation will have both an internal public-relations department and a public-relations agency at work on its problems, with the two entities vying for the attention of management. Many public-relations agencies are part of advertising agencies, although the two sides are kept separate in the better organizations.

Public-Information Departments

Nonprofit organizations like government agencies, trade associations, colleges and universities, and volunteer agencies usually contact the outside world through public-*information* departments rather than public-*relations* departments. Because of the nature of their "product," for example, research findings or educational information, these organizations have no need to sell in the same way that companies do. Often, such institutions present their material as a responsibility and in a more objective way than would a company, including at times the presentation of bad news. At least that is the theoretical definition of public information.

Most public-information people are just as anxious to avoid negative news as their counterparts in corporate PR. The federal government, for example, sometimes has trouble getting out all the negative facts on a given subject. Public information is public relations without a distinct product other than the work or service of the organization involved. Such organizations depend on the public for support, however, even if not to buy products. People must still support legislation, pay association dues, and agree to public funding. They will do so after they have been given the proper amount of information.

Miscellaneous Publicity-Seeking

The most unorganized and most unprofessional part of the business is that which seeks publicity for its own sake. The people working in this segment are after "ink" — stories — in printed publications or air time from broadcast stations. Their clients range from "I don't care what you say as long as you spell my name right" actors and actresses to small community groups with causes to push. Such publicists are usually untrained, except in the attempted manipulation of reporters and editors. On the small-town level, the lack of training manifests itself in the naive belief of publicity chairmen of local boards, clubs, and committees, often volunteer nonprofessionals, that the world is anxious to hear even the most insignificant details about the organization.

A "TYPICAL" DAY

When he got the call at 8:15 A.M., Dale Basye knew that it was going to be a bad day.

The vice president for public affairs was on the line to tell him that he had got the word from management that Saudi Arabia was increasing its crude-oil prices. Basye, a media-relations man in the public-affairs department at Standard Oil of California, would need to know. Members of the press would be calling him soon.

The vice president had worked with members of top management to develop a statement on the company's response to the increase; it was raising gasoline prices. Basye took it down quickly, listening intently to the vice president's instructions for him to give the statement only if the press inquired. It would not be an official company *news release,* that is, a story written from an official point of view and sent out — released — to names of people on a carefully prepared mailing list.

"Effective December 14, Chevron USA is increasing the wholesale price of gasoline, diesel, and jet fuel by blank cents per gallon," he read it back to his boss, leaving out for the time being the precise amount of the price rise. That was still being worked out by the financial people upstairs. "The current price increase reflects higher costs that Chevron now is incurring, primarily due to the recent increase in the price of Saudi Arabian crude."

That sounded fine to both men and Basye sat back to wait for the phone to ring. Because of its size, Standard was the authority for the whole industry on the West Coast so the inquiries would come from members of the press outside San Francisco, the city in which the headquarters is located.

As always, Basye knew how he would handle each call. After reading the prepared statement, he would put the reporter in touch with people in the company who were specialists in the areas of interest to the reporter.

"The best media relations happen if you get the press through to the person with the answer," he says. "It saves the reporter time, it saves the spokesman time. It is almost impossible to anticipate all the questions the press will ask. If you get them directly with an expert, he or she can answer questions on the spot. The press would rather quote experts than public-affairs people."

The first call was from an Associated Press reporter who wanted to hear the statement. He also asked the price of gasoline now and when the price was last raised. Basye transferred the call to a good source in the controller's office for the precise answers.

As the morning wore on, Basye got a number of other calls, all on the price increase. By prearrangement, the company telephone operators assign the calls to the public-affairs people who specialize in the various activities of the corporation.

In an average day, Basye gets fifteen to twenty such calls. In between, he must work on other duties: covering his "beat," that is, the area of the company about which he is expected to be knowledgeable: exploration and production. To do this he keeps in touch with company experts in that area and reports what he finds out twice a month to his public affairs co-workers.

He will know, for example, that Indonesia has also hiked the price of its crude oil, that Chevron had exchanged Iranian crude with Exxon, that a new gas-treatment plant will open soon, and what tariff and quota systems are for oil-import control, or the answers to many other questions about the company's business. He found out some of this information as the result of questions from reporters, some on his own in an effort to keep up with many corporate activities.

Some of the information will be filed away — figuratively in his mind or literally in a report kept in a drawer — for future use as answers to inquiries or as the basis for news releases or stories for one of the many corporate magazines or newsletters, or for the newspapers.

Whatever the day brings, the routine is never the same. "If you're in the oil business," says Basye, "it's never dull, since the energy shortage reared its head."

Up the Pacific Coast in Portland, Oregon, Jeff Clausen is doing something similar, but for more than one company. As director of public relations for Marx, Knoll & Mangells, an advertising and public-relations agency, Clausen has to juggle the problems and solutions for a number of accounts simultaneously. He does not have the luxury of working on one activity for one company in the way Dale Basye does at Standard Oil.

"A typical day? I never know when I have one," says Clausen. "In an average day I'm in the office five hours and outside three, including lunch. I might write a news release or work on a speech. But I have to maintain personal, face-to-face contact with the press, primarily business editors, so two days a week I go to the newspaper offices and deliver a release."

Because he works for a small agency, Clausen must also look for new business and tell prospective accounts why they should sign him up. "You pitch from the counseling point of view, 'you hire me on a consulting basis at a set fee — let's say $1,000 a month,'" he continues. "After agreeing on the price and the goals, you do research to get to know the company, its people and products. You find out its weaknesses and strengths."

This research is carried out by the agency itself or by an outside polling firm. "Based on that determination — the strengths and weaknesses — you propose a program with specific things to be done, an employee magazine, a periodic meeting, or bulletin boards, if the problem involves poor employee communication for example," he says.

"We carry out the program for $1,000 a month and other costs. The client is essentially hiring a $30,000-a-year PR person for $12,000 and getting the same kind of service. There is a lot of dead time in a company. Why pay someone to draw a blank half the time? Another advantage to an agency is that you get outside objectivity. A company employee tends to get tunnel vision."

The agency's public-relations clients include Coldwell, Banker, a real-estate investment company for which it writes news releases and prepares brochures and newsletters for sales purposes and annual reports; the Dairy Farmers of Oregon, for which it writes news releases in support of a successful advertising campaign extolling the virtues of drinking milk; and Shaw Surgical Company, for which it organized a geriatric lecture series and wrote the news releases and prepared a newsletter to publicize it.

Dick Floyd's professional life is more well-ordered than are those of Basye or Clausen. As editor of the Oregon State University Agricultural Experiment Station, Floyd usually knows in advance what he will be doing on a given day.

He is responsible for getting out information about the research activities of the many scientists working on the OSU campus or at the farflung research stations around the state. Floyd and his two assistant editors gather material from the scientists, either in person or on the telephone, and prepare it for distribution in one of several forms: as a news release, an article in the quarterly magazine *Oregon's Agricultural Progress,* a "filmed" release for television, a public-service announcement for radio, or a combination of two or more of these means.

Floyd is also charged with editing technical manuscripts for the station scientists, either for submission to a number of specialized journals or for one of several publications put out by the university as an aid to other researchers and farmers.

So Floyd sorts out his many hats and wears more than one for various parts of the day. He may begin his day by editing an article on a crop disease that is especially tough going. The scientist-author obviously knows little about writing and it is Floyd's job to help him say what he means in simple, understandable language that retains the technical precision needed for the intended audience.

A trip to a field station at mid-day may save him from his boredom. Another researcher there is working on wild-horse nutrition and Floyd thinks it will make a good story. His broadcast assistant is going with him to take some film footage for a simultaneous release for television stations.

Although he began his day at his desk on the OSU campus, Dick Floyd will end it watching wild horses gallop about on the plains of eastern Oregon. No matter where he is, he has definite ideas about what he does. "Public information presents material as a responsibility and gives it to people in a form they can use," he says. "You're not selling anything. PR to me is a little bit of the salesman and not all that objective. We present material that doesn't always make us look good. If there is a negative story to be told, we tell it. We pride ourselves in that."

The public relations process outlined in the maze of boxes and arrows in Figure 1.1 might remain a maze without an explanation of its various parts and the role these parts play in achieving success for the whole. Every public-relations task, no matter if it is carried out by an agency, a company **PR** department, or the public-information office of a nonprofit organization, must go through a series of five parts, the **DOING** system:

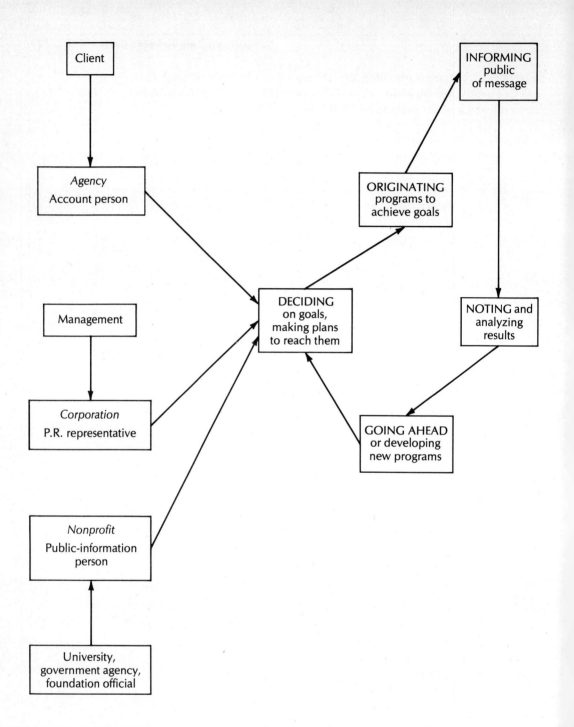

Figure 1.1
The DOING system of public relations.

1. Deciding on goals and making plans to reach them;
2. Originating programs to achieve the goals;
3. Informing the publics of the message;
4. Noting and analyzing results;
5. Going ahead or developing new programs.

This book is divided into sections that correspond with the parts of the DOING system. After giving a background to public relations in the chapters of Section I, Introduction to Public Relations, the book discusses the various Segments of Public Relations in Section II. The delineation of the DOING system begins in the chapters in Section III, Deciding on Goals. Section IV, Originating Programs, is the largest in the book because it covers the many ways to reach PR goals and to build successful programs. The chapters in Section V, Informing the Publics, spell out how to deal with the various publics, while Section VI covers the last two parts of DOING, Noting and Analyzing Results, and Going Ahead or Developing New Programs. This section also brings the book full circle by going through a hypothetical PR campaign and by discussing the legal and ethical aspects of public relations that pervade the profession as a whole.

SUMMARY

Public relations comprises the actions of a corporation, a small business, a government, or an individual in promoting good will between itself or himself and the public. The "publics" at which public relations directs its activities can be many and varied: the general public, members of the press, customers, stockholders, employees, government officials. Jobs in public relations fall into such categories as programming, relationships with others in the organization, writing and editing, figuring out how best to disseminate information, producing printed material and films, setting up special events, giving speeches, researching and evaluating all other activities. Public relations is organized into corporate PR, agency PR, public information for nonprofit organizations, and miscellaneous publicity seeking. The public-relations process begins when an agency or a corporate or public-information person receives instruction from a client or official about what that client or official wants help to accomplish. The PR person does the necessary planning and goal setting, and then decides what means will be used to reach the publics determined in the planning state. He or she develops the program to reach the desired public, actually reaches the public with the programs, and then analyzes the results with the client or organization official. If the program worked, it will probably be continued. If not, the PR person will have to develop a new one.

REVIEW QUESTIONS

1. Does the definition of public relations given on the first page of this chapter fit your own preconceived ideas about the profession? How do your ideas differ from the definition? Why?

2. Which of the various public-relations jobs seem most creative, and which ones are more suited to influencing public opinion?

3. What are the various parts of the PR business?

4. In the four-part structure of the public-relations profession detailed earlier in this chapter, what kind of organization seems the most flexible and most likely to reach its goals? Why?

5. What part of the public-relations process noted in this chapter seems the most important? Why?

CHAPTER 2

A brief history

Public relations as a technique for persuading the American people of the validity of a certain point of view was first used in the United States during the Colonial period and the Revolutionary War that followed it.

THE COLONIAL PERIOD

Samuel Adams and other patriots developed ways to gain public support for American independence from England. Adams organized committees of correspondence to write letters against English rule and held public meetings to protest colonial status. He wrote articles for newspapers about major events like the Boston Massacre (1770) and the Boston Tea Party (1773). He and others wrote and distributed pamphlets that conveyed the arguments for nationhood.

John Dickinson also articulated the colonial position well in his 1765 Declaration of Rights and Petition to the King, and "The Letters from a Farmer in Pennsylvania," published serially in the *Pennsylvania Chronicle* in 1767 and 1768. He discussed American foreign policy and attacked the natural rights theory of politics in a series of letters reprinted in twenty-one of the twenty-five newspapers then published in the colonies. These letters were later issued as pamphlets.

Thomas Paine added his abilities to the struggle in 1774, when he founded *Pennsylvania Magazine*. In "Common Sense," a pamphlet published in January 1776, he argued forcefully for separation from England and the establishment of an independent country. Eventually, after being reprinted by newspapers, this publication reached 120,000 people, a large number for that time.

Independence brought Adams, Paine, and their fellow conspirators a legitimate framework in which to work. The Constitution and Bill of Rights established freedom of the press, of speech, of petition, and of assembly. Whether they knew it or not, the framers of these documents had opened the way for the public-relations business of today.

In the decades that followed American independence, men in positions of power used similar techniques — newspapers, magazines, pamphlets, speeches, public meetings, demonstrations, even songs and plays — to change public opinion concerning various national political issues.

They were aided in their work by a series of inventions that would also prove invaluable to people working in public relations for years ahead: a way to make cheaper paper (1799), a means to manufacture newsprint from ground wood pulp (1844), the telegraph (1844), and the ability to print on both sides of a sheet of paper (1863).

THE PENNY PRESS AND P. T. BARNUM

The rise in importance of the penny press helped hasten the use of techniques that would later be called public relations. While the content of earlier newspapers had been aimed only at upper-class readers because of a high price, the new penny newspapers like the *Philadelphia Cent* (1830) and the *New York Sun* (1834) reached great numbers of people of the big cities for the first time. Now this larger mass of readers could be influenced in a way not possible before.

One of the earliest men to see the advantages of the new, cheap newspaper was P. T. Barnum. Soon after he purchased a circus museum in 1842, Barnum displayed a keen ability to pick what would interest the public and publicize it in the pages of the penny press. "Educated dogs, industrious fleas, automatons, jugglers, ventriloquists, living statuary, tableaux, gypsies, albinos, fat boys, giants, dwarfs" and other attractions were extolled by Barnum in a succession of stories and advertisements.

Barnum used the penny press to publicize the appearance of Joice Heth, a 160-year-old former slave who, he said, had been George Washington's nurse. When Heth died and an autopsy placed her age at about 80, Barnum said he had been tricked along with everybody else.

Barnum's greatest creation was "General Tom Thumb," a two-foot-tall, sixteen-pound five-year-old named Charles Stratton before Barnum met him. The publicist changed his name and put him to work at $3 a week. Thumb accompanied Barnum and the rest of his bizarre entourage on a European tour in 1844. The trip included an audience with Queen Victoria. When Thumb got married, Barnum invited 2,000 people. President Abraham Lincoln later asked the Thumbs and Barnum to the White House. All of these events were carefully chronicled in the penny press.

Although Barnum is credited with saying, "There is a sucker born every minute," a remark he later denied, another utterance is closer to his true belief: "The public is wiser than many imagine."

In spite of attempts to enhance his image in recent years, however, he remains the ultimate in early manipulators of the American public. "To the egress," read one sign he placed in his museum. He then stood and watched happily as gullible people paid their money and walked through a door, only to find themselves quickly back on the street.

TEMPERANCE AND SLAVERY

As the country moved through the first half of the nineteenth century toward the Civil War, public-relations techniques were used on both sides of the two great issues of the day — temperance and slavery.

In temperance, the "drys" had great success as they warned of the perils of demon rum in magazines, pamphlets, and books, and in a series of local societies where reformed drunks and others talked to interested audiences. The campaign worked: farmers stopped furnishing liquor to laborers, for example, and the Baltimore and Ohio Railroad refused even to sell liquor on its trains.

Public-relations techniques had a similar effect on the slavery issue. William Lloyd Garrison organized the New England Anti-Slavery Society and founded *The Liberator* in 1831. Through the pages of this newspaper and in other newspapers, pamphlets, and books, Garrison and others called for ending the practice that had become the basis for the economy of the southern part of the United States.

The techniques Garrison and other abolitionists employed have been used in countless campaigns in recent years to influence public opinion. They did their work in a sophisticated way and on many levels of society.

By uniting local antislavery societies in a national organization, the abolitionists were able to organize a boycott of cotton and goods made from cotton, a move that cut heavily into the southern economy. They strengthened their point by opening shops to sell what they called "free" goods, that is, anything produced by a non-slave-supported economic system.

This national organization also enabled the abolitionists to circulate thousands of petitions denouncing slavery. When they were forwarded to members of Congress, these petitions helped force debate on the slavery issue. Members of these societies also pressured state legislators to enact laws favoring the abolition of slavery.

The members of the antislavery organizations also prepared and distributed nationally papers and pamphlets on the issue. They saw to it that phrases calling for the abolition of slavery were inserted into textbooks. Finally, abolitionists organized a system of "underground railroads" to help slaves escape their bondage and journey north by staying in a series of houses and barns at strategic locations.

The South tried to counteract this increasingly effective campaign, but to no avail. The campaign continued, and successfully.

The slavery issue reached its peak in the election of 1860. The Republican Party spread abolitionist ideas, but also used what public-relations practitioner and historian Edward Bernays calls the "segmental approach." It appealed to different publics in different ways. Where feeling against slavery was strong, the Republican candidates emphasized the party's antislavery stance. Where the feeling was weak, they talked about other issues.

Their campaign worked nationally: Abraham Lincoln was elected president. Soon after, however, the Civil War began, and state after state in the South seceded from the Union.

THE CIVIL WAR PERIOD

Attempts to influence public opinion at home and abroad continued. Both sides tried to gain favorable reaction overseas by sending emissaries to European countries.

Lincoln understood immediately the need to capture favorable public reaction to the Union side. He sanctioned government efforts in this regard, as exemplified by his support for the bond-selling drive by the New York brokerage firm Jay Cooke & Company to finance the war. The drive was a large-scale, high-pressure national effort that was copied in the Liberty Bond campaign during World War I. Aggressive salesmen sold bonds through local banks, but their efforts were helped by favorable editorials and stories by editors and reporters carefully cultivated by Cooke himself.

Cooke later became a close adviser to Lincoln and got the president to remove General George McClellan as commander of the Army of the Potomac, the main Union Army post, because the general's defeats were affecting bond sales.

The many government and private public-relations techniques used by both sides in the war were helped by the increase in numbers of newspapers and by a clear distinction for the first time between editorial matter and advertising. According to Bernays, the free "puffery" of advertising stopped appearing in news columns as soon as newspapers began to rely on staff-written stories instead of the contributed — and often biased — material of the past.

The war left the country torn apart, but industrial expansion helped heal the wounds. Slavery no longer existed as a major national issue. Industrial growth and the acquisition of money took over. Big business grew, particularly in fields like oil, iron, steel, railroads, and later, electricity. The growth of companies in these fields changed the country and, because of the attitude of the small group of men who controlled these companies, the need for public-relations people grew.

THE "ROBBER BARONS"

Commodore William Vanderbilt of the New York Central Railroad exemplified the era. "The public be damned," he said when reporters asked him why he was taking off a fast New York-to-Chicago passenger train. "I am working for my stockholders; if the public wants the train, why don't they pay for it?"

Other businessmen adopted a similar attitude, and soon public outrage caught the attention of government. The New York Legislature's Hepburn Committee, for example, revealed a secret agreement between railroads and oil refiners. Because Vanderbilt owned eighty-seven percent of stock in the New York Central, he got the criticism when the committee alleged that Vanderbilt himself was getting a kickback on all milk shipped on his railroad. Later, he and financier Jay Gould bribed legislators regularly.

Vanderbilt's lawyer, Chauncey DePew, advised him to sell some of his holdings to ease the outcry. Vanderbilt did so and some of the public wrath lessened. But his image and, indirectly, the image of all leaders of big business suffered from his "public be damned" remark.

By the 1880s the press was leading the attack against such businessmen, and government was feeling the pressure. Beginning in 1883, Joseph Pulitzer of the *St. Louis Post-Dispatch* and *The New York World* urged more public information to end business secrecy and arrogance. Articles in magazines caused sympathy for the workers, especially women and children, who were increasingly emerging as the victims of a small group of money-mad industrialists and financiers.

As both sides — industrialists and reformers — saw the effect that publicity had on their causes, they began to use the press to win support. According to Bernays, they were using the techniques of public relations without knowing it.

Newspapers themselves were not beyond reproach. Publishers still "killed" articles that were detrimental to the interests of their advertisers. And, because of a hunger for sensational news, editors were still likely to run stories resulting from publicity stunts or that were not really newsworthy, at least in today's definition of the word. Businessmen, in the meantime, put out the occasional brushfires of criticism but continued to make money and generally ignore critics.

THE MUCKRAKERS

As the twentieth century began, a group of magazine writers focused attention on the real evils of bigness that had only been hinted at before. The "muckrakers" worked first for *McClure's, Cosmopolitan,* and *Munsey's* magazines, later for other publications, systematically exposing the evil sides of business and government — the exploitation of women, children, and blacks, the underside of religion, politics, and the judicial system — in a way not seen before.

Although circulation of these magazines was at first small, the effect of the articles within their pages was great because many of their readers were influential. Soon, however, the three reduced their prices to a dime and the number of readers increased. *Ladies' Home Journal, Collier's, Everybody's* and the *Saturday Evening Post* then joined them in a crusade to right the wrongs of society.

In 1906 President Theodore Roosevelt assured the reputations of these magazines by attacking them in public. "In Bunyan's *Pilgrim's Progress,*" he said at the annual Gridiron Club dinner, "you may recall the description of the Man with the Muck-Rake, the man who could look no way but downward with the Muck-Rake in his hand, who was offered a celestial crown for his Muck-Rake, but would neither look up nor regard the crown he was offered, but continued to rake to himself the filth of the floor."

Although newspapers eagerly began to use these words, criticism against their archrivals, the magazines, the epithet "muckrakers" was borne by the writers it was aimed at as a badge of honor.

Most of the articles by the muckrakers had great effect on the specific area of life at which they were aimed. Ida M. Tarbell's *History of the Standard Oil Company,* which appeared in a series of installments in *McClure's* from late 1902 to 1904, had the most dramatic effect on big business and, indirectly, influenced public relations. In minute detail and a straightforward writing style, the skilled biographer exposed the unfair business practices John D. Rockefeller had employed to put his competitors in the oil industry out of business.

"The truth is," Tarbell wrote, "blackmail and every other business vice is the natural result of the peculiar business practices of the Standard. . . . The Standard men as a body have nothing to do with public affairs except as it is necessary to manipulate them for the 'good of the oil business.' "

These articles and those by other writers, appearing as they did month after month throughout the early years of this century, had a telling effect on the public, which soon began to demand change. For its part, big business belatedly saw the need to change its image when it could no longer ignore reports of its outrageous behavior or cover it up.

The time was now right for the emergence of public-relations practitioners to alter the public view of these large corporations, which more often than not were called "robber barons" or "malefactors of great wealth." Publicity men, many of the same type as P. T. Barnum, had been at work for years vying for space for "puff" pieces that amounted to little more than free advertising in news columns. But they gave no thought to planning programs or developing techniques to alter an organization's relations with the public it was serving or selling products to.

THE RISE OF IVY LEE

The role of planner would now be filled by an easygoing Georgian and Princeton graduate, Ivy Lee, who is called the father of public relations because of the professional attitude he took toward the work of the press agent, then held in almost the same low esteem that businessmen were. When Lee had worked as a financial reporter for the *New York Times,* the *New York Journal,* and the *New York World,* he had noted that businessmen and reporters seldom got along. He thought that the two would get along better if businessmen told their story more openly.

He entered the publicity business in 1903 determined to change the old approach to publicity. In his "Declaration of Principles" he espoused the main theme of his life's work in public relations: "This is not a secret press bureau. All our work is done in the open. We aim to supply news. This is not an advertising agency, if you think any of our matter ought properly to go to your business office, do not use it. Our matter is accurate. . . ."

In 1906, Lee was retained by the first of a long list of prestigious clients that added to his fame, the anthracite coal-mine operators and the Pennsylvania Railroad.

His novel approach was tested later that year after a railroad accident at Gap, Pennsylvania. Company officials tried to suppress information about the crash. Lee talked them into taking reporters to the scene at the railroad's expense, where he had arranged for facilities to be set up to help their reporting and the taking of photographs. Lee and his assistants also offered the facts to the reporters without their asking for them, something unheard of until then. When that story had run its course in the pages of newspapers, the railroad emerged with a better reputation.

At about the same time, after a reporter had inaccurately reported another train wreck, Lee sent a letter to Melville Stone, the general manager of the Associated Press, offering to gather the facts of future accidents and give them to the AP. "If you ever find the company is not candid, you are asked to disregard the arrangement; but until then you are asked to accept no report as authentic unless the company corroborates it." Stone at first declined Lee's offer but later accepted it.

Gradually, Lee added Armour & Company, Bethlehem Steel, Chrysler, Portland Cement, the Guggenheim interests, and American Cuban Sugar to his list of clients. His next noteworthy association was with the Rockefeller family (see PR Bio).

Smarting from the image his father had gained after Ida Tarbell's articles in *McClure's,* John D. Rockefeller, Jr. hired Lee to change the public perception of the country's wealthiest family. Except for the *McClure's* muckraking articles, most of the material about the Rockefellers appeared on the financial pages. Lee met the two principal Rockefellers and found them warm and human. Even though they had given $100 million to charity by this time, however, little of their "good" side had been reported.

Lee set out to change this situation. Contrary to popular belief, however, he did not convince the John D. Rockefellers to give dimes away. They were already doing that. Lee talked the family into letting him talk about it.

He got the old man to agree to be interviewed for feature stories and photographed for the first time. Even Ida Tarbell met him and was reportedly charmed. Throughout his dealings with reporters on behalf of the Rockefeller family, Lee had one firm rule: he never granted exclusives. If one reporter got information, all reporters got it.

At about this same time, corporations were finding out about the value of in-house public-relations offices. Theodore N. Vail, president of American Telephone and Telegraph Company, saw the need for such a department and even used the term *public relations* for the first time in the company annual report for 1908.

WORLD WAR I

World War I brought an increased use of public-relations people and techniques as the federal government realized the importance of public opinion with the organization of the Committee on Public Information under the direction of George Creel, a former newspaperman.

The main tasks of this government organization were to disseminate facts about the war, to coordinate government propaganda efforts, and to act as the government's link with the press. It also prepared and administered a voluntary code of censorship designed to prevent the publication of material that would aid the enemy. The CPI helped Washington reporters cover government agencies and issued press releases that were remarkable in their accuracy and absence of exaggeration.

Creel also proved to be a master organizer of talent to aid the war effort. At his direction, such diverse professionals as advertising men, painters, sculptors, illustrators, cartoonists, photographers, writers, musicians, public lecturers, and movie actors contributed their talents in such varied activities as motion pictures, war exhibits, and street rallies.

Two young men, trained by Creel at the CPI, helped public relations develop more as they used the lessons of war to help business clients in the 1920s. Both Edward L. Bernays and Carl Byoir prospered along with the large companies they helped.

EDWARD BERNAYS, PR COUNSEL

Bernays, a 1912 graduate of Cornell Agricultural College, began his career as a medical journalist. He soon switched to entertainment publicity and began writing "puffs" for singer Enrico Caruso and actors Henry Miller and Otis Skinner.

Bernays gravitated toward the new field of public relations after the war, trying to avoid the taint of publicity but unsure of what even to call his new area of work. "Press agent" had bad connotations and "publicity" was too in-definite. He decided to call it "publicity director" because "director gave dig-nity and emphasized planning and direction." As the scope of his work broad-ened, he called himself a "counsel on public relations."

One of his first clients was the War Department, which was trying to help returning servicemen fit into civilian life. Bernays decided to tie this goal into an appeal from the Kansas City Chamber of Commerce for people to harvest the wheat crop. He prepared a statement calling attention to em-ployment opportunities in Kansas, and this was carried as an Associated Press dispatch. The city got its harvesters.

Bernays also appealed to the pride of American businessmen by empha-sizing the duty and honor of hiring ex-servicemen. He arranged for the prepa-ration of a citation signed by the War and Navy department secretaries to be displayed in the shop windows of the business hiring the ex-servicemen. This campaign was also successful.

Another early client was the Hotel Association of New York, which feared a drop in business because of nationwide concern over a crime wave in New York City. A survey commissioned by Bernays, however, revealed that the decline in customers had been caused by a widespread feeling that the city was cold and inhospitable. At Bernays' urging, civic and social groups in New York formed a "Welcome Stranger" Committee whose friendly, hospitable aims were broadcast around the country. Business soon went back up.

Some of Bernays' early public-relations efforts were aimed at increasing sales. For a hair-net company, for example, Bernays pushed the idea that loose hair is a health and safety hazard. This caused state legislatures to enact laws requiring factory workers and waitresses to wear nets. For the golden jubilee of the electric light in 1929, Bernays arranged for Thomas Edison to reenact his discovery, an event attended by President Herbert Hoover and sponsored by Henry Ford.

In 1923, Bernays wrote *Crystallizing Public Opinion,* the first book on the new field of public relations and how it worked. "His [the PR man's] primary function now," he wrote, "is not to bring his clients by chance to the public's attention, nor to extricate them from difficulties into which they have already drifted, but to advise his clients how positive results can be accomplished in the field of public relations and to keep them from drifting inadvertently into unfortunate or harmful situations."

To Bernays, the public-relations man was a "special pleader" with two big hurdles to overcome: (1) the public's reluctance to acknowledge a depen-dence on people or groups, and (2) the establishment of the profession itself.

ENTER THE PR AGENCY

As Bernays prospered, so did his old co-worker at the Committee on Public Information, Carl Byoir, who set up an agency in 1930. John Hill also became a public-relations pioneer when he set up an agency in New York with a partner, Don Knowlton, specifically to handle work for the American Iron and Steel Institute. Earl Newsom followed in 1935 as did Ben Sonnenberg, a successful press agent in the 1920s who turned to corporate PR in the 1930s and 1940s.

Hill had worked first as a newspaperman in Cleveland in the 1920s. He developed his credo with that experience in mind. "I had learned," he wrote in a later autobiography, "by practice supported by instinct, that newspapers would accept and print stories about client companies only if they felt assured that the stories were true. . . . The result was that my office had worked hard to build up from the very start a reputation for reliability."

As the prosperity of the 1920s gave way to the Depression of the 1930s, an increasing number of companies were realizing the value of sound public-relations advice. Bethlehem Steel set up its own public-relations department in 1930, followed quickly by General Motors in 1931, U.S. Steel in 1936, International Harvester in 1937, and the New York Central Railroad in 1939.

Two industry-wide efforts in this period were harbingers for similar programs later. In 1922, sixty motion-picture companies hired the postmaster general, Will Hays, to improve the wage of that industry. Hays' office screened films before they were shown publicly, and the quality of these films gradually improved. In 1924, the oil industry spent $100,000 — a great deal of money for that time — to tell the story of oil by distributing facts to the public through the public-relations committee of the American Peroleum Institute.

As the Depression wore on, business, education, and the press seemed to recognize the importance of public relations and to distinguish it from the press agentry of old. The economic system and the contributions of big business to it would need to be explained, in addition to selling products. If not, the system itself might be overturned.

President Franklin D. Roosevelt proved to be a genius at public relations. On March 12, 1933, he gave the first of a series of what were called "Fireside Chats." Seated in front of microphones of the National, Columbia, and Mutual radio networks near a fireplace in the Diplomatic Reception Room of the White House, Roosevelt sought to explain the bank holiday in simple terms. The idea worked and the president used it on a number of other occasions to talk about other subjects.

As the Roosevelt administration launched the programs to end the Depression, techniques similar to those used by Creel in World War I were used to gain public support for the plethora of agencies and programs designed to put the country back on its feet.

WORLD WAR II

World War II lifted the country out of the financial abyss and increased the sophistication of tools used to influence public opinion and to sell the war.

Radio and sound film were used by government — and private public-relations people — to augment the older print means. People also began to travel by airplane, which speeded communication considerably.

The Office of War Information, run by CBS commentator Elmer Davis, resembled the old CPI in its commitment to truth. The organization coordinated the release of all war news, trying, whenever possible, to keep government officials from hiding bad news and overplaying good news.

THE GRAY FLANNEL SUIT

After the war, more and more companies realized the value of public relations. Company executives had seen how the federal government had successfully manipulated American public opinion, from Roosevelt's various activities with the press to Davis' more all-encompassing OWI. These officials were now more willing to spend the money needed to open public-relations departments and pay the fees of public-relations agencies. More important, they were ready to take advice from public-relations people.

The trend that had begun in the 1930s with the organization of company public-relations departments and public-relations agencies continued unabated throughout the rest of the 1940s and into the 1950s. Public relations became an accepted part of American business — and a much sought-after career. The phrase "Madison Avenue approach" entered the national vernacular, after the street in New York City on which most advertising and public-relations agencies came to be located.

Hollywood entered the fray in 1956 with the film version of Sloan Wilson's novel, *The Man in the Gray Flannel Suit.* This fictionalized story of a man in the public-relations business in New York caught the fancy of the public, and the title was soon being used to describe the public-relations business as a whole.

The professionals were not completely impressed, however. "You carefully blend seven clichés and produce a stereotype," said an editorial in the June 1956 issue of *PR Journal,* the publication of PRSA. " 'Gray Flannel' brings us a new classic in the public relations man — a classic to rank with the stone-hearted banker, the conniving lawyer, the drunken newspaperman who wears hats in the house, the kindly old family doctor. Hollywood has taken note of our business and catalogued it for posterity in celluloid clichés. . . . It is entirely possible that real public relations men and women will be able to survive the 'Gray Flannel' treatment. . . ."

SUMMARY

Public relations as a technique of persuasion was first used in the United States during the pre-Revolutionary War period. Samuel Adams, Thomas Paine, and other patriots developed new ways to gain public support for

American independence from England. After independence, the techniques of public relations regularly reappeared during wartime, when the government needed to rally the American people to a cause. Similar national efforts worked well in the temperance and the antislavery movements. Technological advances in paper-making, printing, and telegraphic communication helped expand the growing field of public relations, as did the rise of the penny press and the expansion of the population due to immigration.

As the country expanded industrially, the ruthless practices of the small group of men who controlled the large companies were exposed by journalists. These industrialists then saw the need to hire men in the new field of public relations to help them get the public to understand better their points of view. Ivy Lee and Edward Bernays were the first of a group of public-relations men whose work formed the basis of the profession as it is today. These two men and others advised clients and formed PR agencies in a way that turned the molding of public opinion into an art.

PR BIO: IVY LEE AND THE ROCKEFELLERS

The Rockefeller family had owned an interest in Colorado Fuel and Iron since early in the twentieth century. Within a few years, John D. Rockefeller, Jr. decided to increase this investment to $20 million, which gave him control of the coal-mining company. Day-to-day operations were carried out by company officials at the scene, and Rockefeller probably knew little about their policies and methods, although everything was done in his name.

These policies dictated a particularly harsh life for the miners who worked in the coal mines of southern Colorado and their families, who lived in drab mining camps haphazardly scattered around the entrances to the mine shafts. The miners got $1.68 a day for their hard work, an amount given in scrip redeemable only at the company-owned store, where prices were high. The men and their families lived in small two-room shacks owned by the company, which charged high rents. The company also hired ministers for local churches and even controlled the schools and libraries.

The company employed detectives and mine guards to keep camp residents cut off from the organizers of the United Mine Workers of America, a union that was trying to ease the plight of miners in Colorado and elsewhere.

On September 23, 1913, 9,000 miners had had enough. They walked out of the mining camps, taking their families with them into tent camps established by the United Mine Workers. For the next few months, the miners and the guards clashed repeatedly — and violently. Gunfire, including that from machine guns on the company side, was exchanged. The governor of Colorado called out the National Guard to restore order. Soon the guardsmen were openly aiding the company by escorting strikebreakers through the picket lines into the mines.

On April 20, 1914, the tensions of the previous seven months exploded at the mining camp of Ludlow. A company of guardsmen took positions overlooking the tents. After one shot was fired from the camp, the men on the high ground opened fire with a machine gun, beginning a battle that continued all day. By nightfall, the tent town had been burned to the ground and forty people were dead, including two women and eleven children who had suffocated in a cellar dug beneath one tent. The "Ludlow Massacre" sparked further clashes in the area, and the trouble did not end until President Woodrow Wilson sent in federal troops.

At first, the Rockefellers denied responsibility for an event happening so far away from their New York headquarters at 20 Broadway. Eventually, however, advisers to John D. Rockefeller, Jr. convinced him that something had to be done to erase this dark image on the family's name. Rockefeller turned to two men for help: Ivy Lee, then working in public relations for the Pennsylvania Railroad, and Mackenzie King, a Canadian politician and labor expert.

Rockefeller called Lee to headquarters in May 1914 and told him that he and his father were misunderstood by the press. "I should like to know what your advice would be on how to make our position clear," he told him.

Initially Lee published a bulletin series about the situation in Colorado and sent them to a mailing list of what he called "opinion makers" around the country. He included in his bulletins newspaper stories, the opinions of important people, and other miscellaneous material. The aims of the bulletins were to play down the bad aspects of the company's actions at Ludlow and the other tent camps, and to make the union look bad.

At times, Lee stretched a bit too far to make his points, doing further damage to the Rockefeller case in the process. One of his bulletins, for example, contained a statement by a local official that the deaths of the women and children resulted from their carelessness in turning over a stove and not from the gunfire.

After going to Colorado himself in August, Lee counseled a more moderate view than Rockefeller was getting from his other advisers. Lee urged the industrialist to publicize his entire holdings in Colorado Fuel and Iron. He also told Rockefeller that company officials had been too rigid in their reactions to union grievances. He urged the posting of signs on company property noting the company's willingness to hear complaints, and the establishment of a policy to compensate grievances.

After hearing these suggestions, Rockefeller turned to King to carry them out. The Canadian then developed a plan to bring the company and the miners together.

Later, after John D. Rockefeller, Jr., had been ordered to explain Ludlow and the general labor unrest before the Federal Industrial Relations Commission, King convinced him to go to Colorado to see conditions for himself. King was also counting on Rockefeller's gentle manner to help quiet the criticism.

Over a year after Ludlow, the Rockefeller party arrived in Colorado in

September 1915, with the massacre site their first stop. They got out of their cars and stood quietly before a makeshift cross placed there in honor of the dead. For the next few days, Rockefeller talked to the miners and their families in the camps. He ate with them and discussed their problems with them in their humble houses. He also went into the mines.

At the end of the two-week visit, Rockefeller was the guest of honor at a social gathering in the schoolhouse in Cameron. He talked to the group for a time and then suggested that the evening end with a dance. The orchestra began to play and John D. Rockefeller, Jr., one of the richest and most powerful men in the country, spent the remainder of the evening dancing with the wives of miners. No public relations man — even Ivy Lee at his best — could have planned an incident to help heal the terrible wounds of Ludlow. The company cared after all, and was not as heartless as so many people thought.

After he returned to New York, Rockefeller bought a bandstand and dance pavilion for the town and signed a plan to give the miners a better life.

Analysis

Sometimes a simple gesture — like Rockefeller's visit to the mining camps and his personal kindness later — can mean more than all the elaborate public-relations programs in the world. The elusive nature of public relations, however, makes such instances highly ephemeral. They are there only once, to be used accordingly. And this use must not be overdone or it will have a reverse effect. If the action taken by the client or company official is genuine — like Rockefeller's improving employment conditions for his company's miners — it will speak for itself.

REVIEW QUESTIONS

1. Would the techniques used by the Revolutionary War propagandists be successful in influencing public opinion on a major issue today? Why and for what issue?
2. Would the techniques of a P. T. Barnum work today? Are people as gullible? Are there similar men trying to influence the American public today?
3. What major public issue today resembles slavery in its impact on the United States? Has that issue been exploited through use of public-relations techniques? How?
4. Does big business have the same image problems it had in the era of the robber barons and the muckrakers? How can public relations help change the public perception of business?

5. Given the influence of novels like *The Man in the Gray Flannel Suit,* how often have fiction and film changed the public perception of professions like public relations? Consider your own views about the field. How were they shaped by popular books and motion pictures?

ASSIGNMENTS

For Journalism Students

1. Research the techniques used by one of the propagandists of the American Revolution (Samuel Adams, Thomas Paine, John Dickinson). How might these approaches be used by public-relations people to solve the problems of corporations today?
2. Do a research paper on one of the muckrakers and his or her exposé of an unsavory business practice.
3. Do a research paper on one of the robber barons attacked by the muckrakers, and develop a rough public-relations plan to improve that businessman's image.
4. Research the major technological developments that have helped public-relations people do their jobs over the years.
5. Write an essay on the subject, "American Business Would Be Nothing Without the Help of Public Relations." Cite historical examples.

For Business Students

1. Put yourself in the shoes of one of the businessmen attacked by the muckrakers and devise a public-relations plan to counter their attack on you.
2. Write a research paper on instances in the business history of this country where business needed, but did not have, public-relations help. How would public relations have improved things?
3. Write an essay on the subject, "American Business Has Always Needed the Help of Public Relations."

CHAPTER **3**

Public relations today

"In public relations you are dealing with ideas, abstracts, people, emotions, attitudes. You are not dealing with things you can put your hands on. Communication is the most difficult aspect of man's life — wars are caused by it, homes break up over it, so many things relate to it. We take it so for granted and think we've known all about it since we were two. It isn't that simple. People think communication is its form. Because you know how to write good English, however, doesn't let you communicate."

Regis McKenna, the president of his own public-relations and advertising agency in Palo Alto, California, is talking about the key element to successful public relations: the ability to communicate. Both agencies and in-house public-relations and public-information departments have as their main aim the successful communication of information and ideas about their organizations to one or more publics interested in receiving the information and ideas.

CONVEYORS OF INFORMATION

Public-relations people are the conveyors of information, from one entity (a company or nonprofit organization) to another (the publics). Although the form may vary, the aim is the same: successful communication. Because so few people in business and other large organizations are totally effective as communicators, the role of the public-relations person has grown in importance in recent years. Companies and other organizations that fail to communicate effectively often find their products not selling and their messages unheeded by the public.

Because of this basic desire and need to communicate, public relations has grown steadily in importance over the past twenty-five years. Some agencies are larger in income and number of employees than their clients. All large corporations employ public-relations people. Public relations is a multimillion-dollar business employing over 100,000 people by some estimates.

The organization set up in 1948 to increase professionalism in the field, the Public Relations Society of America, found in a recent survey that 42 percent of respondents worked for corporations, 33 percent worked for government agencies or foundations, and 23 percent worked in public-relations agencies or as one-person public-relations counselors.

A recent trend in the business is the acquisition of major public-relations agencies by advertising firms. In 1980, Hill and Knowlton, the largest public-relations firm, was acquired by J. Walter Thompson, the second largest advertising agency. During 1979, Carl Byoir and Associates, the nation's third largest public-relations firm, became a subsidiary of Foote, Cone & Belding, the ninth largest advertising agency. Burson-Marsteller, the number two public-relations organization, is now part of Young & Rubicam, another of the largest advertising firms. Manning, Selvage & Lee, the seventh largest in the public-relations business, was taken over by Benton & Bowles, the fourteenth largest advertising agency.

These moves alarm some industry observers, who fear that the independence of public-relations practitioners will be compromised by close association with organizations whose primary purpose is to sell the products of clients. They are forgetting the fact that most public-relations agencies have themselves long been a part of advertising agencies or have had advertising departments. The two disciplines have always been linked in the goals for which they strive for their clients. Public relations may be less blatant in approach and may use more sophisticated and subtle techniques than advertising, but the ultimate aim is selling products directly, or creating an image of excellence within which an indirect sales effort can later be made.

HOW PUBLIC RELATIONS IS VIEWED

More worrisome to the profession are the longstanding questions about its ethics and the overall esteem in which public relations is held by the two main groups that form its reason for existence, the press and the public. Because people in public relations are hired to put the best public face possible on information released publicly about the companies and agency clients they work for, that which does come out is sometimes suspect.

"It seems to me," says Barbara Lamb, bureau chief for McGraw-Hill World News in Los Angeles, "the name of the game today is to keep it secret. I don't think there's a flow of material out from companies, especially on the touchier subjects, like utility companies talking about nuclear plants. If something happens in the plant, no matter how significant, in the old days they would have written a press release; now they have a press release by the phone. If you call in, they'll read it to you.

"Watergate was the start of all this hesitancy. There's a definite distrust of the press. Almost everybody wants to see copy, some people want to see pictures, or read the story in proof to see it as it's going into the book. They've obviously had orders. I've had PR people tell me their main objective is to keep information from going out."

While all PR people do not go this far, Watergate did have a great influence on public-relations people and the press and public they serve. The Nixon tape transcripts are riddled with references to "PR." In this case, the term was usually a code word for cover-up. The problem existed in the fact that reporters and the readers and viewers they serve only belatedly realized the extent of the high level of obfuscation.

Richard Nixon in 1968 had relied upon similarly contrived methods: town meetings before handpicked friendly audiences, asking soft questions, infrequent and controlled press conferences, and staff members who seldom offered the press anything that resembled true information. What must be remembered is that most of the people doing the covering up, however, were lawyers, not trained public-relations professionals.

The long series of revelations about illegal corporate contributions and payoffs that followed the Nixon transgressions only deepened the distrust of businessmen for the press. No matter that some of their members had been caught breaking the law. It was somehow the fault of the press for uncovering it and the public for reading about it and viewing it.

CRISIS PUBLIC RELATIONS

Recently, this gap has widened because of a series of calamitous events that have befallen whole industries and the companies within those industries. Beginning with the Santa Barbara oil spill in 1969 and continuing since the 1973 oil embargo and resultant shortages and increased fuel prices, oil companies have come under increasingly sharp attack. The problems with the reactor core at the Three Mile Island, Pennsylvania nuclear power plant have heightened distrust of an energy source that government and industry officials were relying on in the future. A series of crashes of DC–10 airplanes and the subsequently revealed faulty construction and maintenance of that aircraft and government supervision of both has worried the public.

For the corporations involved in those and other catastrophic and ruinous events, the stakes have been enormous. For the members of their public-relations staffs the challenges and the pressures have been constant. They have had to operate in what the *Wall Street Journal* (1979) has termed, " 'crisis PR,' the term that public relations practitioners apply to the handling of disasters. When a nuclear plant fails, an airliner crashes, a car turns up with a dangerous flaw or a supertanker sinks, the company involved is placed on trial in the press and in the public mind long before regulators or juries get around to finding legal fault. And, many PR veterans say, how the company reacts in this period can mean the difference between a temporary loss of public good will and the permanent loss of business."

This response often hinges upon the recommendations that public-relations people make to the management of their companies, and the willingness of those officials to follow the recommendations.

"Part of the job of a communications person is to educate top management about the importance of always telling the truth," says Gwil Evans, chairman of communication of the Oregon State University Extension Service. "If you educate managers day-to-day and they do it routinely, these managers get accustomed to it so that when something bad comes along they've seen that the truth works and they trust in PR. You also have to develop a plan of how to respond, of what your objectives are, of who your audiences are, and get some agreement. Having done all that, when a crisis comes along with management and audiences oriented to the truth, they'll think, 'the truth is what we deal in, it isn't so painful as we otherwise might have thought.' "

Adds John Pihas, a Portland, Oregon agency president: "If a crisis comes up and you have an emergency plan, you'll be better off. We advise our clients to be honest, but not necessarily to tell everything, which is a difficult line to try and walk."

William Jones, manager of corporate communications for Standard Oil of California, has seen how a changed philosophy has helped his company weather its frequent crises. "Prior to 1973, we wouldn't answer many charges," he says. "The feeling was, 'Don't dignify *that* with a reply.' In 1973 it became absolutely essential. At the time of the Arab oil embargo and long gas lines, there were wild charges like that we had full tankers waiting off the coast for prices to go up and that tanks at abandoned service stations were being used for storage. The charges were coming so fast you had to select that day what to tackle."

After months of using what Jones calls "the-charge-and-response approach" of preparing regular written statements that gave company answers to complaints and issuing them to the press and to employees of the company around the world, things had improved. "Using sort of a wet finger in the wind method of getting feedback, I was satisfied that things were better," he says. "That's our function, developing information that people need to know. It's been a guiding philosophy since. Who needs to know what, when, and how. You apply that internally as well as externally."

Crisis or mundane event, the basic concern for people in public relations is the way in which members of the press and, through them, the public view them and their companies and clients.

WORKING WITH THE PRESS

"Honesty is the most important quality for people in any business," says Robert Henkel, senior editor of *Business Week*. "You have nothing if you don't have that. All that PR people really have to offer me is their credibility. Without it, they've cut me off permanently."

For Henkel, part of this credibility comes from how often public-relations people contact him — and what they have to offer when they do so. "In New York, publications are inundated with PR people. There are thousands of them and lots of devious ones trying to get the attention of editors. On a typical day, excluding internal calls, I could get thirty to forty calls, many from PR people. They should not call cold into a national publication. But they do. I have an editorial assistant who stops them. Anyone interested in 'selling' a story to a business journalist normally should not call unless he or she has written a letter in advance proposing a subject for discussion or unless it's about important news. To call to sell an innocuous, timeless feature — all it does is infuriate the journalist. What PR people don't understand is that the time pressures are fierce."

The relationship of PR people with their own New York management will often determine how successful they are with the press. Adds James Roscow, a New York freelance financial journalist: "The success of PR people depends on how their role is structured, whether it be corporate PR or agency PR. If they are permitted the run of the company and access throughout the company, and if they are blessed by top management with support, they can be very useful. If a PR manager is down the line of hierarchy and shielded from top management, it doesn't work. That's a company that's on the defensive. It tends to tell us as little of itself as it can get away with. A good PR person will get out and go someplace else. A lot of good journalists have gone into PR and pulled it over them like a blanket. You get nothing from them. They are nothing but job protectors. A good PR program starts with top management."

ETHICS

Beyond the structure of PR and the question of whether information will be forthcoming in good times and bad, the success or failure of public relations hinges upon its ethics as a profession, both as practiced by people within its ranks and as that practice is perceived by people outside.

But ethics is evasive and ephemeral. If it is instilled early enough within the hearts and souls of the people who go into public relations as a career, there is no problem. They will resist temptations to lie, cheat, and hide the truth — even if their clients or company superiors ask them to. If people in public relations do not take to such high principles early on, however, they and the profession will suffer the consequences.

And no high tribunal guards against transgressors, drumming the unethical out of the ranks in a formal way. Word will get around in time and the people who cut corners and are willing to disregard ethical standards will eventually be unable to find jobs. But that will take time and some damage will be done.

Ethics begins — and ends — with everyone in the public-relations business and the corporate executives and clients they work for. Says John Pihas: "A code of ethics is really good judgment."

The Public Relations Society of America has attempted to set high professional standards from its founding in 1948. Since 1954 it has issued and followed a Declaration of Principles. As revised in 1959, 1963, and 1977, the declaration sets the standard by which PRSA thinks people in public relations should follow.

Members of the Public Relations Society of America base their professional principles on the fundamental value and dignity of the individual, holding that the free exercise of human rights, especially freedom of speech, freedom of assembly, and freedom of the press, is essential to the practice of public relations.

In serving the interests of clients and employers, we dedicate ourselves to the goals of better communication, understanding, and cooperation among the diverse individuals, groups, and institutions of society.

We pledge:

To conduct ourselves professionally, with truth, accuracy, fairness, and responsibility to the public;

To improve our individual competence and advance the knowledge and proficiency of the profession through continuing research and education;

And to adhere to the articles of the Code of Professional Standards for the Practice of Public Relations as adopted by the governing Assembly of the Society.

Code of Professional Standards for the Practice of Public Relations

These articles have been adopted by the Public Relations Society of America to promote and maintain high standards of public service and ethical conduct among its members.

1. A member shall deal fairly with clients or employers past and present, with fellow practitioners, and the general public.
2. A member shall conduct his or her professional life in accord with the public interest.
3. A member shall adhere to truth and accuracy and to generally accepted standards of good taste.
4. A member shall not represent conflicting or competing interests without the express consent of those involved, given after a full disclosure of the facts; nor place himself or herself in a position where the member's interest is or may be in conflict with a duty to a client, or others, without a full disclosure of such interests to all involved.
5. A member shall safeguard the confidence of both present and former clients or employers and shall not accept retainers or employment which may involve the disclosure or use of these confidences to the disadvantage or prejudice of such clients or employers.
6. A member shall not engage in any practice which tends to corrupt the integrity of channels of communication or the processes of government.

7. A member shall not intentionally communicate false or misleading information and is obligated to use care to avoid communication of false or misleading information.

8. A member shall be prepared to identify publicly the name of the client or employer on whose behalf any public communication is made.

9. A member shall not make use of any individual or organization purporting to serve or represent an announced cause, or purporting to be independent or unbiased, but actually serving an undisclosed special or private interest of a member, client, or employer.

10. A member shall not intentionally injure the professional reputation or practice of another practitioner. However, if a member has evidence that another member has been guilty of unethical, illegal, or unfair practices, including those in violation of this Code, the member shall present the information promptly to the proper authorities of the Society for action in accordance with the procedure set forth in Article XIII of the Bylaws.

11. A member called as a witness in a proceeding for the enforcement of this Code shall be bound to appear, unless excused for sufficient reason by the Judicial Panel.

12. A member, performing services for a client or employer, shall not accept fees, commissions, or any other valuable consideration from anyone other than the client or employer in connection with those services without the express consent of the client or employer, given after a full disclosure of the facts.

13. A member shall not guarantee the achievement of specified results beyond the member's direct control.

14. A member shall, as soon as possible, sever relations with any organization or individual if such relationship requires conduct contrary to the articles of this Code.

ACCREDITATION

PRSA has also tried to improve the public-relations profession in another direct way. Since 1965 it has administered a voluntary accreditation program that gives members the opportunity to take written and oral examinations to demonstrate their knowledge and competence in public relations. The purpose of PRSA accreditation is to help raise professional standards and to improve the practice of public relations. The accreditation program is directed by a board of members appointed for one-year terms.

Candidates are judged by a jury of their peers, that is, fellow public-relations practitioners who are already accredited. Each person seeking accreditation must pass a written examination and an oral examination administered by a three-person team of examiners. To apply for accreditation, a person must have at least five years of experience in the practice or teaching of public relations.

Both examinations are designed to determine the practitioner's knowledge of the principles and practice of public relations. Section one of the written exam includes questions on the general principles of public relations. Section two consists of six different public-relations situations and presents a detailed program for dealing effectively with a chosen situation. Each of these six questions deals with one or more specific areas of public-relations practice — corporate, nonprofit, for example — so that candidates can find at least one to parallel their own area of practice and experience. In the one-hour oral examination, candidates respond to a series of structured questions in a discussion with the three oral examiners.

Areas covered in the examination include the background and basic premises of public relations; publics and opinion; public-relations practice; communications; ethics, laws, and regulations affecting public relations; professional public relations; and public-relations firms.

Success in the examination allows members to use their accreditation in business contacts — APR, PRSA Accredited, or Accredited by the Public Relations Society of America, and/or the official accreditation shield in connection with his or her name on letterheads or other printed material. Many public-relations people proudly display the accreditation certificate on their office walls, just as many others deride the examinations as demeaning and laugh at the whole program as futile and unnecessary.

The fact remains, however, that PRSA and its work in the accreditation program and in raising ethical standards form the only large-scale effort of upgrading a profession that has had many lapses in ethics and training among individuals working within it in the past.

SUMMARY

Both public-relations agencies and in-house public-relations and public-information departments have as their main aim the successful communication of information and ideas about their organizations to one or more publics interested in receiving that information and those ideas. As such, they are conveyors of information from one entity (a company or nonprofit organization) to another (the publics). In recent years, however, a number of factors have developed that impede this process: a general questioning of the ethics of public-relations people and their ways of doing business, the need for PR people to deal with major recent national crises that often defy attempts to solve them, and a general hostility by members of the press toward the public-relations profession and the people who work within it. One organization is attempting to solve some of the problems of the public-relations profession. Since 1948, the Public Relations Society of America has tried to raise ethical standards through the issuance of a tough Code of Professional Standards for the Practice of Public Relations and to certify professional competence through its accreditation program.

PR FOCUS: HANDLING AN ICE STORM

It was the second night of the ice storm. Like almost everyone else in his neighborhood in Portland, Oregon, John Pihas had been without lights since big shards of ice had sent power lines plummeting to the ground two days before.

But Pihas had concerns beyond his immediate discomfort as he sat in his darkened house in 1979 bundled up in a heavy sweater. What could he do to help Pacific Power & Light Company out of the negative public-relations situation in which the storm had placed it? PP&L, one of the clients of Pihas' public-relations firm, Pihas, Schmidt, Westerdahl, was sure to get a lot of the blame for the long delay in restoring power.

Suddenly, Pihas recalled that help was on the way for PP&L from power companies in Washington state and Montana. Because the trucks were arriving in a caravan, Pihas decided to contact the newspapers and television stations in Portland to alert them to their arrival time at the bridge that runs over the Columbia River between Washington and Oregon.

"I thought it would make a good visual and offset all the negative," says Pihas. "People would think the utility was trying to do something." He was right. The arrival of the trucks got front-page play in both daily newspapers and prominent television coverage the next day.

The internal public-relations staff at PP&L augmented his efforts later with publications mailed to the members of the press and other interested publics, including a special pictorial issue of the employee newspaper that detailed how the company had coped with the storm.

The next morning, Pihas was able to wend his way to work over the remaining ice patches knowing that he had done what he could to help a client solve a bad public-relations problem. He had used a rather simple technique to accentuate the positive in a generally negative situation.

Analysis

There are times when a simple idea can help turn a negative situation around. For a little time and no money, John Pihas conveyed the information that Pacific Power & Light was trying to help its customers, even if they were still sitting in their homes without heat or lights. Such simple ideas must be thought through, however, to make sure that no negative connotations result.

PR FOCUS: HELPING A BELEAGUERED AUTO MAKER

Robert Neale had a problem. How could Chrysler Corporation indicate to important members of the press the fact that it was a company worth saving?

Neale, the company's eastern public-relations representative, pondered the thought in the fall of 1979 as Congress was considering a billion-dollar loan package for the ailing auto maker. The company had said all along that it would introduce smaller but efficient cars in the early 1980s that would sell better than the medium to large "gas guzzlers" it was offering in the late 1970s. The challenge was to survive long enough to reach the 1980s.

Neale eventually decided what to do. With the approval of the senior executives of the company, he arranged for a display of full-size prototypes of all models of cars to be introduced through 1986 to be set up in the Grand Ballroom of the Waldorf-Astoria Hotel in New York. He then held dinners for two groups of people important to the company.

First, 42 of the most influential members of the press, including Tom Brokaw of NBC's *Today Show*, Barbara Walters of ABC, and print journalists from *Time, Newsweek, Business Week, Fortune,* and the Associated Press and United Press International agencies, were invited to dine with board chairman Lee Iacocca and other senior executives. The officials were seated among the guests so that points about the company's future could be made informally. Later, the prototypes were shown to the journalists. The next day, the same group of officials met in a similar way with 140 security analysts, the people who analyze and recommend stock purchases to investors.

Although the results of the expensive — and off-the-record — event may never be known, a climate of hope emerged. Chrysler might be worth saving after all. A kind word here in conversation and a favorable sentence there in print and things were soon looking better.

"We communicated with two very important publics," says Neale, "that we do have something very special down the road competing with General Motors and Ford. They could ask questions, make comments, kick the tires of the cars, and find out about our problems and how we were settling them."

Analysis

If a company has a problem but cannot really talk about it openly, there are times when a special event for one or two special publics helps speed the solution. In Chrysler's case, the two publics were highly influential members of the New York-based national press and security analysts. But, they were also extremely sophisticated. A heavy-handed approach in which members of both groups were told how great and strong the company is would not work. The creation of the means for a more subtle exchange of information and ideas — the dinner and the showing of automobile prototypes — probably helped. In the sometimes vague world of public relations, a definite answer to that question may never be known. You try to do what you can — and hope for the best.

REVIEW QUESTIONS

1. Why has public relations increased in importance over the past twenty-five years?
2. How serious a problem do the mergers of public-relations agencies with advertising agencies pose for the independence and credibility of the PR profession?
3. Does public relations have a role to play in solving the various crises in existence today? If so, what should that role be? If not, why not?
4. Does public relations as a profession rely too much on help from the press? Is there any way around this cooperation?
5. How important is ethics to public relations? Is it unrealistic to expect people in PR to be ethical in everything they do?
6. How workable is the accreditation program of the Public Relations Society of America? Is it a futile exercise or a step in the right direction to raise standards?

ASSIGNMENTS

For Journalism Students

1. Interview a public-relations person in your town and write a paper that explains what he or she does and how he or she does it.
2. Interview a local reporter and ask him or her to assess the public-relations people he or she knows. Write a paper that details what the reporter told you.
3. Write an essay on the subject, "Public Relations Is an Ethical Profession."
4. Analyze the PRSA Declaration of Principles. How practical and usable are its major parts?
5. Select a current problem in the business of a specific corporation and devise a rough public-relations plan that helps solve the problem.

For Business Students

1. Interview a business executive in your town and write a paper that presents his or her views on public relations.

2. Interview a business executive and ask him or her to tell you about the biggest company problems during the coming year. Put yourself in the chair of that executive and decide how your public-relations staff might solve those problems.

3. Write an essay on the subject, "Public Relations Can Solve My Business Problems."

SECTION II

The Segments of Public Relations

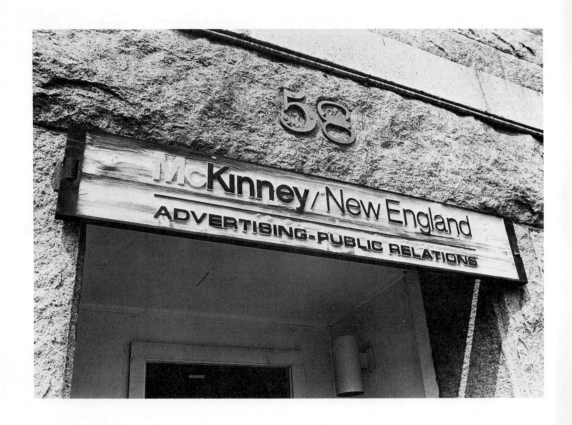

CHAPTER **4**

Inside agency public relations

For clients, large and small, public-relations agencies work to solve special problems or to devise long-range plans. The work of agencies is often carried out while an internal public-relations staff handles the day-to-day needs of the company.

"You do the same thing but you do it for different clients," says Jeff Clausen of Marx, Knoll & Mangells in Portland, Oregon. Clausen used to work in public relations at Crown Zellerbach, a large forest-products company. "You don't get involved with internal corporate politics. When you have a news release, for example, you clear it with one person and not all the way up the corporate ladder as you have to when you work directly for a corporation. There's one contact point and it's much easier."

Adds George Hobgood, vice president of Hill and Knowlton, the largest public-relations firm in the United States: "Every day is totally different. I hate routine. I was once on a corporate PR staff and it was boring. You have more time to do your work but you don't get the stimulation from many different projects. Agency PR is very exhausting. I can be in the middle of something and another client will call. I have to act like I've thought of nothing else all day."

THE WORK OF AN AGENCY

The typical agency consists of *senior executives,* who run the company as they would any other business; a group of *account executives,* who actually make contact with the *clients* needing public-relations help, who are also called *accounts;* a group of *creative people* such as *copy writers, artists, photographers,* and *graphic designers,* who prepare materials for the clients such as *news releases* (a client's version of a story sent to the press), *public-service announcements* (a nonprofit organization's prepared announcement sent to television and radio stations), *brochures,* and *annual reports;* the creative people also set up meetings and press conferences, write speeches, and carry out special projects. Agencies also employ secretaries and accountants just as any business does. Figure 4.1 lists the fifty largest U.S. agencies in 1980.

In a typical situation in an agency, the client will come to the account executive handling his or her account with a task to be accomplished. If the client has an internal public-relations staff, the task will probably be of a specialized nature and one that the internal PR staff does not have the time or, in the opinion of the client, the ability to handle. If the client does not have a PR staff, the task might be more routine. The agency will perform the service for the client and charge a *fee* for it.

The client and the account executive meet to discuss what needs to be done and then the account executive returns to the office to plan the actual way the problem will be solved. Often, this will involve a *brainstorming session* during which the account executive and the creative people sit around a table and talk informally about ways to help the client. Out of such sessions a *public-relations plan* generally emerges that the account executive will take back to the client for approval. Often, the agency will first conduct an *audit* or survey of the company and its problems by talking to employees, customers, or other groups to find the information it needs to help solve the problem. If the task is complex and large, the account executive will prepare a formal *presentation* of it complete with slides, charts, and other visuals, sample news releases or other printed materials, or broadcast segments, and an estimate of cost. If it is a simpler problem, the account executive will talk it over with the client in a more informal way.

After the client approves the proposal — as it is presented or after changes have been made — the account executive returns to the agency and the creative people get to work, striving to meet a *deadline* worked out in advance with the client.

As this work progresses, the account executive returns periodically to the client to check the wording of the news release, the visual look of the public-service announcement or of the photographs, the text of the annual report, or whatever else is being done.

After it is finished, the work is distributed depending on its form. News releases, for example, are sent out to a *mailing list* of newspapers, magazines, and television and radio stations prepared in advance to accomplish the goals of the client (for example, all the newspapers in the headquarters city of the company or in all the cities where plants are located). Public-service announcements would go to a similarly developed list of television and radio stations. Annual reports, on the other hand, would go to employees of the company, shareholders of the company, security analysts who recommend purchase of the stock, and financial editors, but not to the general public.

Later, the agency will review the job done for the client to see how its program has succeeded: how many newspapers used the news release (a *clipping service* will send copies of stories in newspapers or magazines), how many

Figure 4.1
*The 50 largest public-relations operations, independent and ad agency affiliated.
(Reprinted with permission. Copyright 1981 by the J. R. O'Dwyer Company.)*

	1980 net fee income	Total employees	% change from 1979 income
1. Hill and Knowlton*	$34,773,564	800	+22.8
2. Burson-Marsteller*	31,580,000	839	+23.1
3. Carl Byoir & Associates*	15,700,000	423	+13.7
4. Ruder & Finn	9,095,000	250	+12.2
5. Daniel J. Edelman	7,739,639	173	+32.3
6. Harshe-Rotman & Druck	6,073,000	150	−5.0
7. Manning, Selvage & Lee*	5,893,666	129	+16.1
8. Doremus & Company*	5,282,352	137	+12.1
9. The Rowland Company	5,231,918	116	+40.8
10. Ketchum, MacLeod & Grove PR*	5,040,000	124	+25.5
11. Booke and Company	4,867,083	99	+18.6
12. The Communications Board	4,388,859	109	+25.6
13. Rogers & Cowan	4,200,850	87	+11.8
14. Bozell & Jacobs PR*	4,150,000	101	+16.5
15. Robert Marston and Associates	3,880,000	55	+27.0
16. Creamer Dickson Basford*	3,495,000	96	+27.8
17. Sydney S. Baron & Company	3,439,000	43	−9.8
18. Fleishman-Hillard	2,745,346	58	+47.8
19. Dudley-Anderson-Yutzy PR	2,693,290	67	+19.6
20. Underwood, Jordan Associates	2,575,000	46	+12.1
21. ICPR	2,189,546	55	+ 4.3
22. Aaron D. Cushman and Associates	2,106,720	47	+14.0
23. Golin/Harris Communications	2,009,619	51	+25.6
24. Hank Meyer Associates	2,058,766	21	+18.5
25. The Rockey Company	1,828,600	45	+13.7
26. Gibbs & Soell	1,708,442	40	+12.5
27. Peter Martin Associates	1,689,422	41	+12.6
28. Ayer Communications Services*	—	40	—
29. Newsome & Company[1]	1,641,831	35	—
30. Lobsenz & Stevens	1,452,000	31	+ 7.2
31. Anthony M. Franco	1,450,000	34	+19.9
32. Padilla and Speer	1,403,960	29	−8.3
33. Edward Howard & Company	1,321,409	28	−1.1
34. Kanan, Corbin, Schupak & Aronow	1,255,145	30	+30.0
35. Fraser/Associates	1,206,678	32	+27.4
36. Richard Weiner	1,205,100	34	+19.2
37. Zigman-Joseph-Skeen	1,154,509	41	+46.1
38. Gross and Associates/PR	1,074,000	32	+18.3
39. Barkin, Herman, Solochek & Paulsen	1,044,500	26	+ 2.9

Figure 4.1 (continued).

40. Woody Kepner Associates	947,096	24	+47.8
41. Smith & Harroff	900,000	16	+ 8.4
42. Selz, Seabolt & Associates	883,957	26	+ 8.6
43. Deaver & Hannaford	861,000	23	+22.2
44. Brouillard Communications*[1]	854,124	22	—
45. Porter, Levay & Rose[1]	826,000	12	—
46. Martin E. Janis & Company[1]	795,000	20	—
47. Anna M. Rosenberg Associates	788,000	12	−1.1
48. Dorf/MJH[1]	736,839	34	—
49. Sumner Rider and Associates	732,613	20	+15.6
50. Simon/PR[1]	724,758	20	—

[1] First time in ranking.
* Advertising agency subsidiary.

television and radio stations broadcast the public-service announcement (each of them will provide the information), how the annual report was received (via press comment, the reaction from stockholders). Last, but certainly not least, the account executive will find out how the client liked the work carried out by the agency and whether changes need to be made in any similar work done in the future.

AGENCY PUBLIC-RELATIONS REQUIREMENTS

Agencies are in business to serve their clients and to make money in the process. They accomplish both these goals by providing advice to clients that is not available elsewhere. In the best firms, this advice is similar to counsel given by attorneys. A public-relations agency must fulfill certain basic requirements.

Philosophy

Before any public-relations agency can succeed, it must establish a philosophy about the profession in which it operates. How does it view the PR profession? Does it wish to concentrate on certain kinds of accounts? How closely must the kinds of accounts and the philosophy match? What part will ethics play in the way the agency will operate? Will the agency be prepared to resign an account if it is asked to do something unethical by that account?

Organization

An agency must be large enough — and well staffed enough — to handle the number of accounts it agrees to take on. It must also be staffed properly to assist those accounts in solving their problems. For example, if an agency signs with several electronics companies it must have staff members who understand the technical material on which they are to be working. If the tasks are primarily financial, it must have specialists in that area. The agency staff should include, at a minimum, an executive to set overall philosophy; a series of account executives or account supervisors to work with the clients and the other people in the agency; and a creative group of copy writers, graphic designers, artists, and photographers to prepare the material to be developed for the client. The organized structure should be kept flexible and be easily accessible to clients. Too many levels of authority and clearance encumber the free flow of ideas and recommendations from agency to client.

Fee Structure

The rate at which an agency charges for its services should be realistic but not too low. Companies generally turn to public-relations agencies when other efforts — including those of their own internal public-relations departments — have failed. This expertise should not be given away. Nor should it be so high-priced that clients are driven away.

Time spent on a client's account by, and the knowledge and experience of, agency employees are the principal things being charged for. There are several ways this can be done: by *fixed fee,* in which a certain amount is worked out in advance to cover all work and all other costs; by *fee for services,* which also includes reimbursement for other expenses incurred by agency employees in carrying out their work for the client; or by a *retainer,* a set amount per month paid to the agency for doing the work of the client on a regular basis, plus reimbursement for other expenses. In order to keep proper track of time and expenses, agency employees fill out forms to account for every hour of the day, as much as possible charging this time to a specific job for a specific client.

Working with Clients

Once an account has been acquired, an agency should work with one executive of that client, the higher in the structure the more likely the impact of the agency. Although a client need not take every suggestion made by the agency, the agency should feel free to reassess and possibly cancel the arrangement. If the advice of its professionals is being followed and the relationship with the client has begun with (1) a general discussion with the client about perceived problems, (2) an audit of various publics to support or refute the client's perceptions, and (3) a plan to remedy the problems, such a cancellation will seldom be necessary. Both client and agency have agreed in advance about what has to be done.

A word of caution is necessary in dealing with a client with its own public-relations department. The agency should work as closely as possible with the in-house department in a role of mutual support. One should not undercut the other with members of management, unless one side believes that the other is doing things that are detrimental to the overall good of the client. In the best situations, the outside agency will give advice on overall strategy and make recommendations that the internal public-relations staff will then carry out.

THE DIFFERENCE: AGENCY VS. CORPORATE

Agency public relations is as interesting and challenging as corporate public relations. The two have one big difference: agency life is more hectic than a counterpart position in a large corporation.

"Agency life is never dull," says Thomas Nunan, a vice president of Burson-Marsteller. "You're dealing with five or six clients a day with totally different programs and markets." Adds Regis McKenna, who heads his own agency: "In a PR job at a big company you never learn the whole story. You do one thing. You never interface with the decision makers to see the impact of communication on business."

The hectic life of a PR agency is not as precarious as that in an advertising agency, where the loss of one major account can force the firing of a whole group of people in the agency who are working on the account. "Most firms don't let a client account for more than a few precentage points of their overall business," says Nunan. "The fees range from $50,000 to $500,000 to a million. You're dealing with a different magnitude than a $5 million ad account."

Nevertheless, some element of pressure is always there. "PR is visibility for your clients," says Jeff Clausen of Marx, Knoll & Mangells. "You're either visible or you're out of business. You accept that fact. It's there all the time. People form mental images of a company. You develop and maintain an image of what people have of the company and its products. In PR, all it takes is one bad mistake to blow this image. That's the risky part."

FIVE AGENCIES AND HOW THEY WORK

A close look at five U.S. public-relations agencies of various sizes and organizational structures reveals the diversity present in the agency segment of the PR profession.

Hill and Knowlton

The largest public-relations firm in the world, Hill and Knowlton serves 550 clients with its 725 employees. Its total 1979 fee income was $27.8 million, 45 percent of it from the New York office.

Hill and Knowlton's operating philosophy is based on two major principles: (1) public opinion is the ultimate arbiter of most questions in today's world, and (2) effective public relations must begin with the development of sound management policies in the public interest. The agency uses what it calls the integrated-team approach, each team acting as a small firm responsible for a particular client's interest. The company's operating committee, comprised of senior officers, is in charge of all client operations. One member of management is designated as account supervisor and assures the quality of performance. An account executive is appointed to assist the supervisor in developing specific program recommendations, in maintaining regular contact with the client, and in carrying out approved activities assigned to Hill and Knowlton.

This policy allows management at a number of levels in the agency to become familiar with problems and programs of clients, and provides an informed and interchangeable staff backup capable of handling any emergency.

A Hill and Knowlton account executive acts as a "manager of resources," tapping every sort of expertise within the agency to solve the problems of clients. No set formula is used to fill a company's needs. Each program is carefully designed after long discussion with client officials. A survey of media and other groups often comes next to find out what others think of the client.

As soon as the client approves the program, the account supervisor and account executive put it into effect. As necessary, they call on specialists in the agency for help. The account supervisor and account executive are held responsible for all activities of the account and report regularly to the agency management operating committee and the client. In addition, groups of Hill and Knowlton executives not associated with the account meet regularly to discuss the program in informal "account audits."

Hill and Knowlton charges its clients a standard time charge for actual hours spent on the program, and out-of-pocket expenses like printing, photography, telephone, postage, transportation, and other necessary services. The agency's employees keep track of their expenses on time records submitted semimonthly. Under this system, clients pay only for services rendered, unlike other agencies that charge by the fixed-fee method.

Each of the thirty-five Hill and Knowlton branches in the United States and abroad runs independently of the others. The Los Angeles office exemplifies the way they are organized.

The office serves two kinds of clients: ad hoc, which are clients based in other cities in need of help in Los Angeles, and fifteen to twenty Los Angeles-based companies like Atlantic-Richfield, Security Pacific Bank, Mazda, Home

Savings, Mattel, Caesar's World, Yamaha, and the southern California construction industry.

"What we do for these clients varies from day-to-day publicity to writing their annual reports," says George Hobgood, a senior vice president. "We do a bit of politics on issues, not people, but no personal PR. We do product publicity, marketing, employee communications, and investor relations."

As an example, for Mattel, a diversified corporation best known for its toys, the agency works in financial and industrial relations helping the company maintain contact with security analysts. To this end, account people have arranged a series of meetings and seminars with analysts. "We help select the audience and the place and write the presentation for company officers," says Hobgood. The agency also advises Mattel on publicity, helping members of management, most of whom are wary of the press, decide whom to talk to. "This is a classic case of a company needing PR because of mistakes committed by past management," says Hobgood. "Our job is to help current management restore credibility."

Burson-Marsteller

The second largest public-relations organization in the world, Burson-Marsteller employs more than 700 men and women in sixteen offices on four continents serving about 130 clients. Based in Chicago, its 1978 net fee income was $22.1 million (Figure 4.2).

According to its chairman, Harold Burson, in a speech to the Columbia University Graduate School of Business, Burson-Marsteller has always operated with a philosophy that sees public relations as having four roles: (1) the "early warner," sensing social change and perceiving the mood of society and how it affects the client organization for good or bad; (2) the conscience of the corporation; (3) the communicator, informing audiences internally and externally to bring about understanding; and (4) the monitor, assuring that corporate policies and programs match public expectation.

At the executive level, Burson-Marsteller has three divisions, each headed by a president: Burson-Marsteller domestic, Marsteller domestic, and Marsteller International. Marsteller is the advertising side of the company. Below this are vice-president/general managers who run regional offices and who have the responsibility for groups of accounts and for various account people.

Each Burson-Marsteller client is assigned to an account group that has the primary responsibility for planning and implementing activity and for direct contact with the client. The account group consists of a group manager, account supervisor, and account executives as needed. The account group can then call on more specialized support services within the agency; by discipline (specialists in investor and financial relations, government relations, public affairs, editorial services like speech writing, women's interests, education re-

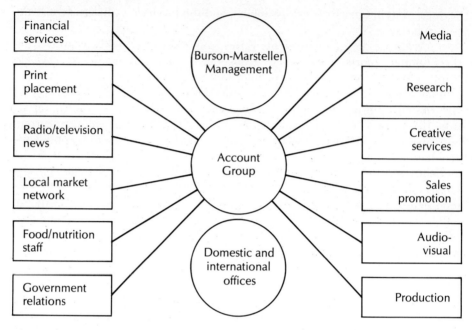

Figure 4.2
The organization chart of Burson-Marsteller. (Reprinted with permission, Burson-Marsteller.)

search, and internal communications), by media (placement teams regularly contact network radio and television, press associations, news and feature syndicates, major business and financial publications), by communications technique (audiovisual, film, graphics, and sales promotion specialists), by geography (people from other offices called in to assist when needed).

The Los Angeles office of Burson-Marsteller exemplifies the way it works as an agency. More than a dozen professionals serve clients. "We rarely put one person on one account," says Thomas E. Nunan, vice president and general manager. "They lose their objectivity if there's a problem. It's not good for the client. The PR discipline has become varied and broad. There are few Renaissance people left who can do everything for a client. Therefore we use different specialists to solve different problems. We rely on people with good capabilities and experience matched to the account backed by these specialists."

One of the Los Angeles Office's major accounts is the Electronic Devices Division of Rockwell International, for which it provides an international program of public relations and marketing in support of that company's marketing effort. The program includes a domestic program, a Japanese program, and an eight-country European program.

"The basic objective is to make engineers potential buyers of Rockwell devices," says Nunan. "We make people aware of what Rockwell offers and communicate with people by getting more detailed."

One element of this approach was a press kit on the company's bubble memory put together for a press conference held at Wescon, an annual western electronics show. The kit contained material that detailed the technical features of the product. Next came a series of technical articles written by a Burson-Marsteller person over the byline of a Rockwell engineer. The series, which appeared in technical publications like *Electronics* and *Electronic Design,* discussed how the bubble memory can be used.

The agency has also become heavily involved in the training af spokespersons at various companies. "It wasn't too long ago that Commodore Vanderbilt's 'public be damned' attitude prevailed," says Nunan. "Things were quiet in the 1950s and companies went out of their way to avoid speaking out. In the 1960s and beyond, this isn't the case. The practice of PR in a crisis is no different. It just requires good preplanning. The airlines have always been masters of this when there is an accident. If you have good solid research and planning up front, you'll know what to do. You've got to have your spokesman identified so outside people know who to communicate with."

This is where Burson-Marsteller's communications training program comes in. In a series of special seminars, managers of corporations likely to be involved in a crisis, like oil companies, are taught how to communicate when a refinery catches fire, for example, or when a tanker runs aground and oil begins to seep out of its damaged hull.

In this program, Burson-Marsteller sets up a panel of people — some from the agency, some who are actors — to simulate a crisis situation and force the company officials who participate to answer questions about what the company is doing to alleviate the problem. The agency also trains company officials in how to communicate with the press in a crisis. They give participants a short introduction to the media and tell them what print and broadcast people expect. Simulated situations are acted out and videotaped so that they can be played back and criticized.

The agency also offers clients training in speechmaking and helps them write speeches and prepare for television appearances on talk shows.

Earl Newsom & Company

This firm, founded in 1935, still bears the name of one of the pioneer public-relations men in the United States. Craig Lewis now heads the New York-based company, which practices a unique and specialized kind of public relations. As a result, it is smaller than the big agencies already covered. The company runs a partnership with four principals and a support staff. It has ten to twelve regular clients, most of them major U.S. corporations.

"We do business on a retainer basis, let's say $2,000 a month to make our services available," says Lewis. "And clients are then charged by the hour for professional services. One of the things you get for your $2,000 is an organization that is ready to go."

Newsom does not have the support services that other agencies offer, like publicity, marketing, or sales promotion. It is basically a consultant. "Most clients have staffs to do those things," says Lewis. "More often than not, we do odd jobs — speech writing, special brochures, special newsletters."

An example of the way the company operates can be seen in the study it did for the Sperry Corporation. "We looked at the organization in New York and the field, talked with management about their needs, and analyzed the current situation," says Lewis. "The whole thing related to improving working relationships between division and corporate headquarters." In another instance the company prepared a Wall Street financial firm to celebrate its one hundredth anniversary by writing a history and helping organize the celebration. "We tend not to do things for people off the street," continues Lewis. "It's not fair to our regular clients who are paying a retainer."

Typically, a job for the agency begins with a preliminary discussion between one of the partners and the client on what the problems are and what needs to be done. The Newsom approach usually begins with an audit. "We are not equipped to make judgments on what we're doing unless we know the public," Lewis continues. "Then we come up with a plan to guide the working relationship that the client can understand and approve."

The Newsom agency has done several audits for electric utilities over the years, for example, where the problems were often public antagonism toward rates, the inability to get rate relief from regulatory agencies, and a bad reputation in the community in terms of public attitude, business attitude, and press relations.

"A fundamental problem was that the executives of these companies would hide behind corporate walls, after rates were increased," says Lewis. "We found out things like the fact that branch managers of various companies were over their budgets by as much as $30,000 annually without warning because of higher electric rates. They and others were mad." The utilities knew nothing about this resentment before the Newsom agency carried out the audit.

After the interviews, the partners involved come back and transcribe their notes, exchange information, and discuss what they have found. Then one of them is assigned to put it all on paper. "We come up with a final product that everyone can stand behind and it is presented to the client," Lewis says.

A typical audit report begins with an introduction that tells what the original assignment was and how the agency went about doing it. Next come the main conclusions, followed by recommendations for change and new ideas. The audits, which range from twenty to forty pages in length, do not fall into any one pattern, according to Lewis. When the client approves the plan, Newsom staff members see that it is carried out.

Regis McKenna Public Relations

A Palo Alto, California, agency, Regis McKenna Public Relations has about thirty clients, all of them in technical fields like electronics, computers, energy, biomedicine, and agribusiness. It had billings over $2 million in 1980 (Figure 4.3).

The agency's work for a client begins with the development of a communications strategy. "We analyze the competition and the strengths and weaknesses of the client," says Regis McKenna, president. "We may do an internal and external audit. We start by doing an audit of editors to find out how the company communicates and if it is viewed as honest." The audit is then compiled and a report presented to the client that tells it what it can do to correct the problems.

"Top management has to be involved in communication," continues McKenna. "They are the character of the company. We show management

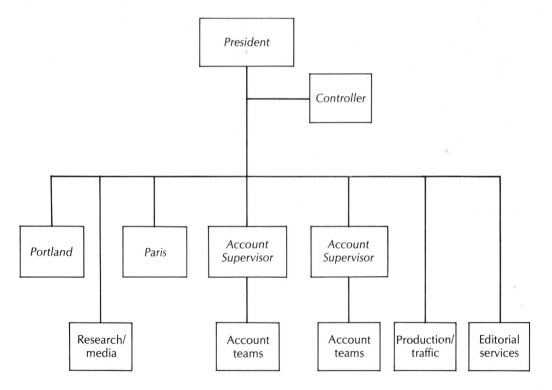

Figure 4.3
The organization chart of Regis McKenna Public Relations. (Reprinted with permission, Regis McKenna Public Relations.)

that PR is not a press release and that they should not sit around and suffer the wording."

McKenna devises a one-year program for the client that includes a strategy for achieving the goals. "The basic elements start with identifying the media you want to educate, generally that's not a lot," he says. "If you are trying to communicate as a major industry in America, if you want to influence, develop, or change attitudes, you have to educate no more than twenty journalists, no less than ten. You don't have to reach a lot of people. Your strategy and rationale and logic have to be well defined."

For Intel Corporation, a California electronics company, McKenna recommended working with only the publications that he deemed would be interested in its products, *Business Week, The Wall Street Journal,* and the electronics trade press.

The agency then organized a one-day seminar in which three Intel managers explained the future of technology and computing to sixty editors. Although the material was presented from one company's viewpoint, there was no attempt to tell or sell one story. "It's not necessary to sell stories when you approach PR as an educational activity," says McKenna. After the seminar, editors began to call Intel engineers for technical information and to look more favorably on writing about its products, according to McKenna.

McKenna thinks of public relations as education — from the practitioner and the client to the publics being reached. "Few people in PR are willing to put in the time and energy to keep abreast of what is going on," he says. "You have to be fairly knowledgeable to be a good PR person. You have to work at it. Too many people fell into PR as an easy field and not a specific discipline."

The Pihas, Schmidt, Westerdahl Company

A Portland, Oregon public-relations and advertising firm, Pihas, Schmidt, Westerdahl has had $6.5 million in total billings since it was organized in 1973. It is the largest public-relations firm in the state, with about thirty major clients.

"A lot of companies get very myopic in talking about PR," says John Pihas, president. "I look at PR as not only placing in the press information that is 'not paid' but as involving advertising. We use a lot of tools. You take a communication problem and determine what would be best to use: a news release, a feature story, a public-service announcement, a paid ad, an external house organ, a dealer organization."

Pihas says the approach varies each time. The small size of Portland also dictates the approach. "In a market like ours you've got to be prepared to do whatever gets the job done," he says. "A lot of purists in both PR and advertising say you shouldn't intermingle the two. We don't have that luxury. The tools are the same. It depends on how you use them." The recommendations the agency made to two clients exemplify how it and other agencies of a similar size operate.

In one case, a small rural county had two hospitals when there were patients to support only one. The officials of the older facility hired the agency to help it fight the tough, aggressive campaign of the other side. The old hospital deserves to stay open, said its proponents, because its soon-to-open new facility will provide good health care for the county.

Enter Pihas, Schmidt, Westerdahl with a plan of action after taking a preliminary look at the situation. The agency recommended a thorough audit of the situation as the first basic step. Following this, the plan suggested as the second basic step the choice of a vehicle through which the hospital could win its fight. "We do know — in advance — what the vehicle is: the opening, occupation, dedication, and operation of the new . . . Medical Center health care complex. . . . We will use the milestone event as the basis for our presence and our action," read the study.

The third basic step was the building of a solid platform for the whole program, the idea that the new facility will provide quality care through the work of a staff that has a great sense of responsibility to the total person and the person's family. The fourth basic step involved the identification of the constituency available to help the hospital through its crisis: opinion leaders, the medical community, the media. From the group, the agency advised the setting up of a public-relations advisory committee. Along with the four basic steps, the agency suggested the preparation of a number of printed materials such as booklets, a tabloid newspaper, and staff newsletters, as well as press releases, features, and photos.

Another agency client was a professional association that was unknown to the public despite the public's reliance on its individual members. Press coverage was nil most of the time and suspicious when there was any at all. Even politicians were negative toward this association. The public perception was negligible as well, especially in the lack of a statewide identity. The agency pointed out in its study that a ballot measure opposed by the professionals in the most recent general election had increased public suspicion.

As it had to the hospital, the agency recommended a public-relations audit as the first step to assess the organization's relationship with the general public, the political leadership, and the media. Because many of the association's members were themselves suspicious about public relations, the agency plan went on to allay some of these fears. "Public relations is the art of making things possible," read the report. "Public relations is a process that seeks to avoid surprises."

Directions that the association might take were limited until the audit had been carried out. The agency did suggest, among other things, that (1) all past and current publications and press releases be assessed, (2) all public-relations mailing and contact lists be examined and updated, (3) special features be written, (4) new broadcast informational programs be developed, (5) automated single-projector or multimedia informational presentations be prepared, (6) speeches of officials be improved, (7) educational programs for schools be considered as a way to reach both children and their parents, and (8) cross-promotional efforts with other public and private agencies be worked out.

SUMMARY

For clients large and small, public-relations agencies work to solve special problems or to devise long-range plans. The work of agencies is often carried out while an internal public-relations staff handles the day-to-day needs of the company. The typical agency consists of senior executives who run the company, a group of account executives who actually make contact with the clients needing public-relations help, and a group of creative people who prepare materials for the clients such as news releases, public-service announcements, brochures, and annual reports.

In a typical situation, the client contacts the account executive with a task to be accomplished. The account executive will give the task to his or her staff to come up with a solution. The staff will "brainstorm" the problem, gather information, and organize a formal presentation of the plan for the client. Once the plan has been approved, the members of the agency will carry out its various parts and analyze how well they worked when they have finished.

Successful public-relations agencies need sound operating philosophies, adequate organizational structures, realistic fee structures, and a good working relationship with clients. Agency public relations differs from corporate public relations because agencies serve more than one client whereas corporation PR people work for only that corporation.

PR BIO: CARL BYOIR AND HOWARD HUGHES

For much of his reclusive life, the late Howard Hughes retained the services of Carl Byoir & Associates, long one of the biggest and best public-relations agencies in the country. The service that the bizarre industrialist got for the undoubtedly large fee he paid the firm was just the reverse of what is usually desired by a client: the Byoir staff kept his name out of the newspapers and held personal publicity about him to a minimum.

An agency vice-president, Richard Hannah, handled Hughes' personal publicity — or lack thereof — for years. He also advised the Hughes organization on public relations. As Hughes became more unavailable to everyone, this service consisted of refusing the many requests for interviews. For a time, it meant the issuance of an occasional press release when a major event involving Hughes occurred. In the end, however, it meant little more than a brief obfuscatory statement about his whereabouts during those years when he moved from one guarded and inaccessible hotel suite to another around the world. "Mr. Hughes is in Vancouver on a business trip," read one in 1972. "There is no indication of the nature of the business or of how long he intends to remain there."

One example of the Byoir approach involving this writer exemplifies the situation for the last twenty-five years of Hughes' life. As a correspondent in the McGraw-Hill World News bureau in Los Angeles in 1964, I was assigned to write an article for *Electronics,* a magazine for electronics engineers, on what my editors and I called the "Hughes Family Tree," that is, all the companies that had been founded by people who left Hughes Aircraft because of the eccentricities of its owner. Among these corporations were Litton Industries and Ramo-Wooldridge (now TRW), two of the biggest in the country.

The story was an exciting one for a young reporter to do. After briefly entertaining, and then abandoning, romantic notions of cornering Hughes in his leased Bel-Air mansion, or at his rented Beverly Hills Hotel bungalow, I settled for an interview with a public-relations man from Byoir, not Hannah.

The tone of our many telephone conversations was never anything but professional and cordial. The Byoir man agreed to meet for lunch and a background-only discussion of Mr. Hughes. The meal and its aftermath lasted until nearly 4 P.M., during which time I got little information beyond what I already knew from other sources — and little of that. All of it was given to me professionally and cordially. I went away resigned to the fact that not only would I not be the first reporter to interview Howard Hughes; I would not be breaking the Byoir wall of protection either.

One request was almost honored. Could the agency furnish a photograph of Howard Hughes for use with the article? "Yes," I was told by the Byoir man. "It's one of him on the runway at Culver City (site of Hughes Aircraft) taken in 1947."

At least, *that* might work out, I mused, with visions of Hughes in an aviator helmet leaning against an experimental plane. Not a bad illustration for the article.

In the end, the photograph did not arrive either. The agency was doing its work well.

The irony here is that at the same time it was helping Hughes avoid publicity at all costs, Byoir was running for his favorite company, Hughes Aircraft, one of the best technical public-relations programs in the business. Throughout the 1960s especially, Byoir, together with NASA and the Jet Propulsion Laboratory at Cal Tech, was publicizing the Surveyor satellite. This Hughes-manufactured satellite was first to achieve a soft landing on the moon, an event which prepared for men to do the same in the Apollo program later in the decade. Other technical advancements at Hughes have been equally well publicized by Byoir.

Another irony of Hughes' reverse public relations was his own superior gift for the field. Beginning with his stint as a Hollywood motion-picture producer in 1930, Hughes showed a flair for knowing what the public liked.

He took "Hell's Angels," a shallow World War I flying story that had cost him an exorbitant $3.8 million, and promoted it into a successful motion picture. For its opening, airplanes buzzed the theater and stunt men descended by parachute onto Hollywood Boulevard. He scheduled the film to open simultaneously at two separate New York theaters. Although the film failed to make back all of the Hughes investment, it established him as "daring, independent, willing to gamble, and blessed with a Midas touch," wrote Donald L. Barlett and James B. Steele, in *Empire: The Life, Legend, and Madness of Howard Hughes* (New York: W. W. Norton, 1979, p. 68).

Hughes would show a similarly canny ability to use the press and manipulate public opinion on a broader scale at other times in his life: during U. S. Senate hearings on war profiteering after World War II, when his control of Trans World Airlines was slipping away because of his neglect, and when he set up a medical institute to keep the aircraft company from being dismembered due to his mismanagement.

Barlett and Steele have an explanation for Hughes' sense of public relations and ability to manipulate the public (p. 622):

From the beginning, Howard Hughes had an overpowering urge to become a legend in his own lifetime. He wanted the world to notice and to marvel at what it saw. He wanted to show others that he was every bit the man his father had been. It was not accident that in his youth he ventured into the two most glamorous fields of the time — movies and aviation — where he could quickly gain notoriety. Repeatedly over the rest of his life he embarked on courses of action that subjected him to intense public curiosity and speculation. His shyness notwithstanding, the public spotlight was his oldest addiction.

Analysis

Carl Byoir & Associates has made millions of dollars in the service of Howard Hughes and the myriad of companies that bear his name. In so doing, however, the company has at times paid a price in its own credibility as an agency, at least in its dealings with Hughes and publicity about Hughes. When an agency is retained by a client, the employees of that agency have to please the client, no matter what, or resign the account. In this case, it meant that Byoir account executives have had to say that black was white — or white was black — repeatedly over the years if that was what Hughes wanted them to say.

REVIEW QUESTIONS

1. What do public-relations agencies do for their clients?
2. Who are the different employees of a public-relations agency?

3. How do agency employees carry out the work to help their clients?
4. What kinds of things are done for clients by the employees of public-relations agencies?
5. What requirements are necessary for a public-relations agency to succeed?
6. What is the difference between agency public relations and corporate PR?

ASSIGNMENTS

For Journalism Students

1. Interview an account executive at a public-relations agency and find out what he or she does. Report your findings to the class.
2. Conduct research and draw the organization chart for an ideal public-relations agency to serve your town.
3. Interview a local businessman and find out his biggest problem. Prepare a series of recommendations to solve that problem as if you were an agency account executive.
4. Howard Hughes was your client and he suddenly changed his mind and decided he wanted publicity; prepare a series of recommendations to alter his image as an eccentric recluse.

For Business Students

1. You are a business executive of a munitions company with high profits but a bad public reputation since one of your plants exploded last month, killing ten children at a nearby school. You are planning to call in a public-relations agency for help. What do you want it to do for you?
2. You are the president of a company that builds nuclear reactors. Your newest reactor nearly overheated and released radiation into the atmosphere. You have a new safety program that your internal public-relations staff can't seem to put across with conventional ideas. You are calling in an outside agency. What do you want it to do for you?
3. You are a corporate executive at a company that uses Canadian baby seal skins for all its products. Environmentalists and the public at large hate the seal killing and your company for using the skins. You have to stay solvent and please your stockholders. What do you want the public-relations agency you are calling in to do for you?
4. Prepare a research paper on an instance in recent business history where a corporation was helped greatly by the work of a public-relations agency.

CHAPTER 5

Corporate public relations

Part of the challenge and the attraction of corporate public relations is its elusiveness. Public-relations practitioners never know for certain that what they are trying to do will work — or know later that it actually has succeeded. The full effect might be felt in increased sales of a product, which is easily measurable. But the goal of the public-relations program might be to regain lost prestige, an almost impossible element to discern.

All that public-relations people and executives in corporations can do is to develop plans to reach their goals, whether they be aimed at attracting more customers or a better feeling about the company.

Corporations employ the largest number of public-relations people in this country. From small departments with one person and a secretary to large staffs including hundreds of specialists, the jobs in corporate public relations are many and varied. They are also increasingly important to corporations.

Business Week noted in a 1979 special report that corporate public relations is enjoying a new boom. Companies are now spending large amounts of money on a great many activities that fit loosely under the label public relations.

The main reason for this upsurge, according to the magazine, is the "pressure cooker" environment faced by many corporations. Because these companies are under attack constantly by consumer, environmental, women's liberation, civil rights, and other activist groups, they are changing their policies on a number of subjects. They are also faced with increasing intervention from federal and state governments. All of these new pressures make necessary a greater reliance upon public relations to explain corporate actions.

ESTABLISHING A PUBLIC-RELATIONS DEPARTMENT

The form of a company's relationship with its publics begins with management. The board chairman, president, and other chief officers usually set the style and tone of the company's public-relations effort by the authority they give to the department director and the budget they provide. They are the ones who decide if the company needs a public-relations department at all.

To what level of management will the public-relations director report? How much power will the director have to set policy on releasing information and working with the press and other external publics? How much money will be provided to hire other staff members? What kind of information can be released? Does the company have a story to tell? The answers to these questions will determine the success or failure of the public-relations program of a company, no matter what the original intention when the department was organized.

"What you do is totally controlled by how the president and chairman view the PR function," says Robert Neale, Eastern area public-relations director for Chrysler. "In a company like ours, the vice president for public affairs reports to the chairman of the board. All of us in PR have no hesitancy to call corporate officers at any time. They know we wouldn't call if it wasn't necessary."

Adds Thomas McLaughlin, who used to be in charge of public relations for Colorado Interstate Gas Company: "In the world of commerce and industry, it is imperative that the management be in tune with public relations and all that it encompasses. If the top man brushes it off as a necessary evil, to be tolerated at the most, then the PR activities will be ineffectual, and the occupant of that particular perch should look for opportunities to move his or her talents elsewhere."

REQUIREMENTS

No matter what their size, companies fund public-relations departments to deal with one main problem: how to keep in touch with various publics while at the same time looking after their specific business interests.

There are as many philosophies of and approaches to public relations as there are corporations in existence. It is impossible to simplify and standardize any examination of corporate public relations. Some minimum requirements are necessary, however, or a company might just as well skip the whole endeavor and leave the perception of itself by employees and outsiders to fate.

Goals

Before any corporate public-relations program can succeed, it must have a set of defined goals. What does the company want to accomplish? Which publics does it want to contact? Does it want to do good in its contact with these publics or does it want to sell products? Are the publics contentious and how can their complaints be countered? How closely will members of management work with the public-relations staff? How much autonomy will public relations have to do its work?

"The first thing is to understand management's problems," says Ted Weber, executive vice president of McGraw-Hill. "You do that by being an executive first, a PR executive second. You have to understand the business plan and the competitive dynamics of the economy at a given time. This leads you to a better appreciation of what management is trying to do. It gives you some positive thing you can do to contribute. If you're not careful, you can do some fruitless and useless things that simply will not complement the organization's aims."

In establishing goals for the public-relations departments he has managed, McLaughlin considers the profession in three parts, "comparable," he says, "to the tines of a fork: (1) good performance by a company and/or organization (2) appreciated and understood by the public (3) because it has been adequately and properly communicated to the targeted public. If one of the tines is missing, the PR program will not succeed."

Organization

There must be some kind of organized structure for it in a company for public relations to succeed. A good department will be headed by a director or manager and have submanagers of as many other units as are necessary to meet the public-relations goals. The organizational structure of the department is thus closely linked with the public-relations goals of the company. Elaborate goals will need an extensive organization in order to be achieved. More modest goals will not take as many staff members to be reached.

No matter what the structure or size of the public-relations department, the director or manager must report directly to the president or chairman of the board if the programs of the PR department are going to help the company. Without this high-level access, the PR director or manager will not have the necessary information to do his or her job, or be able to get decisions made quickly. The result will be slow response to PR concerns and problems, with scant information available to make the response. If a PR director or manager cannot meet regularly with the company president or chairman, the next best thing is to meet regularly with an executive vice president.

Once it has been established, this liaison must be constantly nurtured, with the public-relations director or manager remembering at all times that communication works two ways: from company officials to PR man and in reverse order as well. "Make certain that top management never gets surprised," continues McLaughlin. "As one of my employers once said, 'Just remember, I don't like surprises, particularly unhappy ones.'"

Budget

Even the best organized public-relations department will fail without an adequate budget to hire the people and to put out support material needed to reach the goals set with management. PR directors must be prepared to fight for funds with the heads of other parts of the company. Once an initial amount is established, it should be increased annually by an amount equal to such factors as the inflation rate and the consumer price index, or as close to those amounts as possible. Otherwise, the department will not be able to hire the staff members and pay for the support services needed to carry out the PR goals of the company. "The status of the PR person and department depends to a major extent on the inclinations of top management," says McLaughlin. "And as status goes, so go budgets."

Defined Publics

"Publics depend upon organization," continues McLaughlin. "In the world of commerce and industry, the publics run from 'general public,' the consumer and customer, to the shareholders, the financial community, the press, and employees present and retired." The decisions about which ones to reach relate to the public-relations goals of the corporation. At best, a public-relations department should be organized into a separate unit for each major public with adequate people and resources to get the job done, including the provision for the preparation and mailing of regular publications aimed at each group.

If necessary, a submanager can be added to work on special projects like major company anniversaries, plant openings, or press conferences. This unit might also be responsible for writing the speeches of executives. A research unit could be useful as well to assess the work of the other units. In companies where public relations is closely tied to sales efforts, a unit might be responsible for writing product publicity and technical articles, setting up exhibits at trade shows, and preparing sales literature and sales manuals.

To avoid the "surprises" noted in point 2, public-relations people need to maintain close liaison with the various publics the company serves. One of the best ways to do this is to establish good rapport with the news media, both print and electronic.

A Public-Relations "Product"

Although much of what a corporation public-relations department seeks is intangible and beyond precise measurement, there is a public-relations product that can be prepared, distributed, and assessed. A good public-relations program must include printed materials like external and internal magazines and/or newspapers, news releases, annual reports, brochures, public-service announcements for television and radio, "filmed" news releases, slide and tape programs, company films, and closed-circuit television programs for employees. Every company does not need these PR products to tell the story and reach corporate goals, of course. A careful assessment of a company's publics will indicate the best mix of PR product advisable for the company. Once established, this mix should be reassessed constantly, with parts of it dropped and new ones added as corporation needs change and new problems arise.

PUBLIC RELATIONS AT TWO CORPORATIONS

The best in corporate public relations is exemplified by a close look at two major U.S. companies, Standard Oil Company of California and Xerox Corporation. In these corporations, public relations — or, as Standard Oil calls it, public affairs — has access to executives, some authority of its own, and more than adequate funds on which to operate.

Standard Oil Company of California

As reorganized in January 1977, public affairs is divided between the parent corporation and Chevron USA, its operating company within the United States. The parent company handles stockholder relations, employee publications, planning and research, and special events like the centennial of the company. Chevron's public affairs includes three separate areas: communications, which encompasses traditional public-relations activities like press relations; community affairs, which includes education, institutional advertising, and community involvement; and government affairs, which includes assessment of legislation and the development of company positions on legislation. The annual cost of public affairs to the corporation worldwide is $28 million. Figure 5.1 shows the various departments in public affairs.

"We look at information as a resource and how we can get it across to various constituents," says William H. Jones, manager of corporate communications. "Our approach to public affairs comes from the chairman of the board, the chief operating officer. A number of years ago he decided, in effect, that the corporation could not tolerate the media being told, 'no comment.' We try to be as open as we can and the chairman never turns down a request for an interview. This policy has got him into trouble. He has been manipulated by columnists and freelancers, but he still has the attitude, 'You win some, you lose some.' "

In spite of the openness, Standard Oil still tends to be somewhat conservative in its approach to public relations, somewhere between the combative

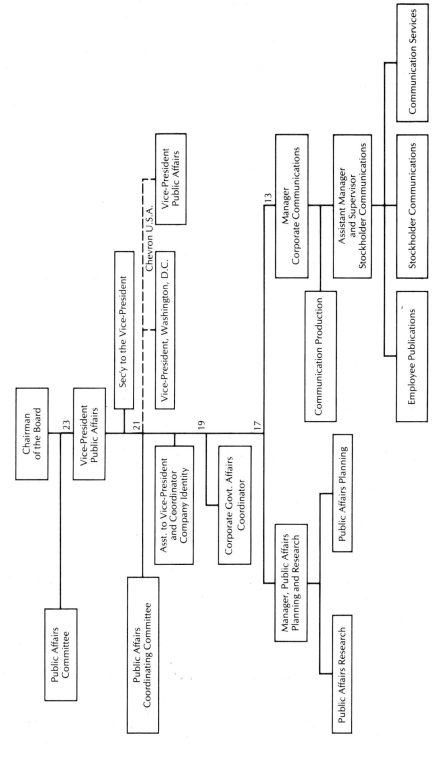

Figure 5.1
Organization chart of the corporate public-affairs department, Standard Oil Company of California. (Reprinted with permission, Standard Oil Company of California.)

Mobil and the reclusive Texaco. "We don't look for media attention," continues Jones. "We prepare statements more often than we issue press releases. We don't take the lead in offering information."

Nor does Standard Oil rely totally on contacts with the print and electronic press. Because of the current oil situation, the press tends to be crisis oriented, according to Jones. "Our approach is influenced by the San Francisco media, which is extremely negative," he continues. "Newspapers and TV here look at us with disdain. On gas lines, for example, the information distortion was so acute that we organized our own press conferences in San Francisco and Los Angeles to get the information out."

Jones says that the crisis atmosphere is heightened by the great number of government regulatory agencies the company has to deal with. "The accusations are so frequent, the constituencies we deal with need current information." Thus, the company cannot rely on the press alone.

What it does rely on is a whole series of sophisticated contacts with diverse publics. For example, Standard Oil keeps in regular touch with its 12,000 retired employees. "We consider them as important as employees and stockholders," says Jones. "These people very clearly represent us. They need some identity when they leave work. They want to defend the company so we keep them informed by sending them the employee magazine *Standard Oiler,* a management newsletter, and a four-page newsletter just for them. To cope with the problems of current issues, we also send them special mailings of news reports."

Another special public the corporation concerns itself with is its stockholders, 270,000 of them. They each get a special quarterly magazine, *Chevron World,* and quarterly stockholder reports. Of this number, 80,000 have been designated "activists," and they receive several letters a year from the chairman and a bimonthly newsletter.

Both these publics as well as current employees, who get a number of magazines and newsletters, are informed so that they can refute what they hear that is derogatory to the company in personal conversation or letters to the editor.

"You can turn a situation around by communicating with people," says Jones. "You blow some because people make errors. The successes are evident in the way the media now handles oil issues. Editorial pages are now taking stances that parallel our own. It has been a long, hard pull of being open and providing information."

Xerox Corporation

A continent away from Standard Oil is the corporate headquarters of Xerox in Stamford, Connecticut. Xerox's problems are less crisis ridden than those of Standard Oil or other oil companies. Although it faces constant litigation and new competition yearly, the company seldom worries about a hostile press in the same way an oil company does. Rather than wondering where the next attack on its high profits will come from, for example, the company frets over the use of its name as a standard part of speech, thus jeopardizing its copyright status as a product name.

"When you talk about the dissemination of information as PR, incoming or outgoing, you have to know, make judgments about what is important and what is trivial if you are any use to management," says James Lamb, director of public relations at Xerox. Given this responsibility from management, "I think you'd better have a policy of always telling the truth. Then you don't have to figure out how to be consistent. Of course you don't have to tell everybody everything you know."

Public relations at Xerox (Figure 5.2) includes such traditional activities as press relations, community relations, internal communication with employees, stockholder relations, speech and feature article writing, as well as a unique corporate responsibility program that is part of the Xerox Foundation and the company's overall philanthropic policy. The urban riots of the 1960s brought big-city and minority problems to the attention of large U.S. corporations like Xerox. These corporations entered the 1970s trying to take seriously their role in society and their obligation to help solve these problems. The response at Xerox was to set up its foundation. Xerox began its involvement in improving the world in 1970 with foundation grants of $2.5 million. In 1979 its annual grants totaled $10 million. One-half of that amount supports higher education and the remainder community affairs both in the United States and abroad. In 1979 it gave about 1 percent of income before taxes, and will eventually move that figure to 5 percent.

The other part of the Xerox program in social responsibility is the company's involvement in community affairs. This involvement takes two forms, one of which is a system of social-service leaves for employees in which any employee of Xerox can apply for a one-year leave of absence to work full-time for an organization in need of his or her services. The project must be a program or activity sponsored or conducted by an existing, functioning, nonprofit, nonpolitical organization. The employee must have worked for Xerox for three years to apply, and must pay all personal expenses, including travel, associated with the project. Since 1971, employees have done everything from working with the handicapped and with drug- and alcohol-abuse programs to service on Indian reservations and in prisons. The program costs about $750,000 a year.

The second community-affairs activity is the Xerox community-involvement program. At a cost of $650,000 annually, the company funds projects in the various communities in which it operates around the country. Employees at any of the 150 branch offices form a location committee to select, plan, and initiate a project or activity to benefit the community. Xerox then gives the committee $5,000 to spend on the project as well as employee time. The project

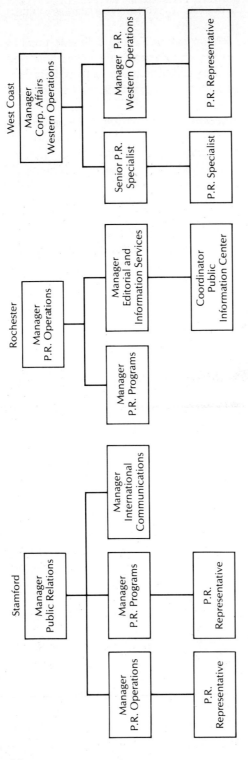

Figure 5.2
Organization chart of the public-relations department of the Xerox Corporation. (Reprinted with permission, Xerox Corporation.)

needs to be innovative and specific enough to have an impact on the community in which it takes place. In one, Xerox employees arranged a job-interview seminar for Cincinnati, Ohio high-school students. In Portland, Oregon, employees organized a center for troubled youths as an alternative to more rigid state-supported institutions.

Xerox has been hesitant to capitalize on its social-responsibility programs from the public-relations standpoint. "It's intangible," says Joseph M. Cahalen, who runs the social-service leave and community-involvement programs, "a dimension of work that's not work, but that builds esprit de corps and company loyalty. We have taken a soft track on publicizing it internally and externally. We're sensitive to appearing to use this as a public-relations vehicle. Much of the publicity comes naturally as a result of the agencies' and our people's involvement."

The Standard Oil and Xerox philosophies of public relations represent two different, but equally effective, approaches to the same problem: how to communicate a point of view effectively both internally and externally. The approaches chosen reflect each company's personality: Standard Oil, aggressive, pugnacious, and ready constantly to do instant battle with every critic; Xerox, more dignified, reserved, and because of its product able to step back from the fray and devote attention to more lofty and unorthodox methods. If these two public-relations philosophies and programs were suddenly reversed, they might fail because the problems and concerns of these two corporations are so different. The same can be said for companies of all sizes and products. That is why the PR requirements noted earlier in this chapter must be fitted carefully to individual companies.

IMAGE

"Image," the way external and internal publics view a company, has always been important in public relations. The term became overused in the years when the public-relations profession was beginning to have a major impact on American life, in the late 1950s and early 1960s. Today, many public-relations practitioners avoid using it for that reason. It does express succinctly the goals of most public-relations programs, however. If corporations care at all about what others inside and outside their organizations think of them, they worry about their image. The time and money spent on public-relations programs are usually approved with the corporate image in mind.

Image is difficult to achieve and measure, however. Some companies have a good image by the nature of their work. They do not even have to try hard to achieve it, although they do try. Xerox is one of those companies. Others, like Standard Oil, have more difficulty achieving the image they want. Again, the nature of their business and forces beyond their control usually influence the image others have of them. But that does not mean that they do not keep trying.

And this quest is what makes corporate public relations so interesting and challenging.

SUMMARY

Part of the challenge and the attraction of corporate public relations is its elusiveness. PR practitioners never know for certain that what they are trying to do will work — or know later that it actually has succeeded. All that PR people and executives in corporations can do is to develop plans to reach their goals. In any corporate public-relations department, the first requirement for success is a smooth relationship with management on as high a level as possible, preferably with the president or chairman of the board.

In addition to a good working relationship with management, certain other requirements need to be met: (1) goals need to be set, (2) the department must be organized and staffed to reach the goals, (3) the budget of the department must be adequate to achieve the desired results, (4) publics need to be defined and contacted regularly, and (5) a public-relations "product" needs to be prepared and distributed to the various publics. Public relations in a company needs to reflect carefully the goals and even personality of that company. What works for one company may not work for another. All PR work in companies — and agencies, for that matter — is aimed at searching for a good "image," the way publics view the company or client. Although overused, the term aptly describes the goals of PR programs. Image is difficult to achieve and measure, but PR practitioners keep trying to achieve a favorable one for their clients.

PR FOCUS: McGRAW-HILL AND CLIFFORD IRVING

On December 7, 1971, McGraw-Hill announced that it had acquired the rights to publish the authorized biography of Howard Hughes, the eccentric and reclusive billionaire whom few people had seen for over fifteen years. The book was to be written by a novelist, Clifford Irving, using material from 100 taping sessions with Hughes. *Life* magazine would run abbreviated versions of the book in three installments. It was a major publishing event.

"Hughes denied the book's authenticity immediately and for ten weeks the controversy was front-page news. By mid-February the truth had come out," says Ted Weber, then director of public affairs for McGraw-Hill, where he has since become an executive vice president.

McGraw-Hill and Time, Inc., the owner of *Life,* were dumbfounded. So was the rest of the world, which had already been startled enough that Hughes had agreed to do a book at all. "We knew at the outset that this was to be a confusing and complex case," continues Weber. "Shelton Fisher, then president of McGraw-Hill, told me at the time, 'Only one person speaks for us and that will be you. You might sometimes say you don't know, but you will never lie.' "

The company immediately began to collect as much information as it could to defend the "biography." Not only were millions of dollars in sales and contracts at stake, but the company's integrity as a publisher was in question as well. And so was its relationship with its authors. "Our authors had to feel that we would not turn our backs on them," says Weber.

After McGraw-Hill got a tip to look at the banks in Zurich, Switzerland, the company sent Lew Young, editor of *Business Week,* and Dan Lacy, senior vice president of the book company, there to gather information on some of Irving's financial arrangements. One night at home, Weber got a call from James Phelan, a California writer. "I can solve this for you," he said. He suggested that Irving had used a manuscript he had prepared on Hughes and another by Noah Dietrich, long-time Hughes chief of staff who had fallen out with the industrialist years before.

Slowly, the pieces of the puzzle began to fall into place for the beleaguered corporation. One bit of information led to another and eventually the entire crooked scheme became apparent. Irving had made up the whole thing, including the documentation.

Neither McGraw-Hill nor Time Inc., had gone into the venture hastily. Irving had already written and published eight books. "He showed us a nine-page handwritten letter from Howard Hughes," says Weber. *Time* had then sent the letter to a handwriting expert, who had authenticated it.

"The corporation came out of this and gained because of the way we handled our public relations," says Weber. "We gained the respect of the press. Before this, McGraw-Hill had not been a big news source. We hadn't had an opportunity to work with it. When we did, they saw that there was no cover-up. If a TV crew showed up with decent warning, we made the conference room available and talked to them. We never gave the press the runaround."

McGraw-Hill eventually got back from an insurance company the advance money it had paid to Irving, from whom the insurance company is still collecting. Irving also spent time in jail.

Today Weber thinks the corporation gained more than it lost in the affair, especially in developing a plan of response in any crisis. "Be available, tell the truth, and have a single spokesman," he says. That approach worked well also early in 1979, when an American Express attempt to seize control of the company was successfully deterred.

Analysis

Surprise, especially when it involves a big company project with high financial stakes, is hard to believe. McGraw-Hill, with all its publishing plans so carefully made and with the thoroughness with which it had investigated the

Irving manuscript and authenticating documentation, could not fathom what was happening. It had to move quickly to get the information needed to tell the full story, no matter what the cost. Once it had the information, the company needed to release it to the public — via the print and electronic media — as quickly as possible. Any attempt to cover up or even delay release of the information to save face would have made matters worse.

REVIEW QUESTIONS

1. Is public relations too elusive to be effective? How can it change the minds of the public about a company or a product that that public views negatively?
2. Is it practical for public-relations directors or managers to deal with high corporate officials? Why is this access important? Can lower-level officials help just as well?
3. How practical are the requirements for a successful corporate public-relations department noted in this chapter? Can goals be set up for something like PR? How can the desired publics be selected? Why is a good public-relations "product" so important?
4. Compare and contrast the Standard Oil philosophy of public relations to that followed by Xerox. How are they the same? How are they different? Why would the approach of one not work for the other?
5. Is "image" an overused term? Does it apply appropriately to the work of public relations?

ASSIGNMENTS

For Journalism Students

1. Select a negative situation in the news involving a corporation, and work out a public-relations approach that will make that situation more positive.
2. You have been selected as the public-relations director for a company. Pick a company and develop an organization chart for that department, keeping in mind the PR requirements noted in this chapter.
3. Analyze the public-relations aspects of the Three Mile Island incident and criticize in a research paper the way things were handled.
4. Write an essay on the subject, "Image Counts for a Lot in Public Relations."

For Business Students

1. Interview a company executive and ask him or her how the company's public-relations department is organized. To whom does the director report? Give your results to the class.
2. Develop an ideal public-relations department by drawing an organization chart that includes the various subdepartments and lines of authority.
3. Analyze the management aspects of the Three Mile Island incident and in a research paper defend the way officials of Metropolitan Edison acted.
4. Write an essay defending or supporting the subject, "PR Is Too Costly a Frill; We Don't Need It."
5. Write an essay on the subject, "Image Means Nothing in Business; We've Got to Make Some Money."

CHAPTER 6

Public information

With public opinion the potent force that it has become in American society, the need for nonprofit groups like government agencies, trade associations, foundations, religious organizations, universities, research organizations, school systems, and hospitals to tell their stories has grown in recent years. These institutions have set up sophisticated and complete public-information departments to help them do so.

THE DIFFERENCE: PUBLIC INFORMATION AND PUBLIC RELATIONS

The major difference between public information and public relations is in the presentation of information.

As Dick Floyd, editor of the OSU Agricultural Experiment Station, pointed out in Chapter 1, public information presents material as a responsibility and a means to inform, not as a way to sell a product.

Gwil Evans, chairman of communication of the OSU Extension Service, augments that definition — and difference. "Public relations is doing something good and getting credit for it," he says. "Public information is different in that it's less to give credit to an organization or institution and more oriented to providing some kind of useful information. The credit is more indirect and incidental."

The differences extend to other parts of the two fields. In addition to technique and goal, as noted, they revolve primarily around staff and budget. A public-information department is usually not as well staffed or as well funded as a corporate public-relations department or a public-relations agency, although that situation is changing.

The federal government alone, by one estimate, spends $400 million a year on public information and employs 19,000 people in various public-information programs. Added to that are the countless public-information people in the other fields already noted. The number of jobs available — and the work to be done — make the public-information segment of the profession an important one in any consideration of career opportunities.

THREE KINDS OF PUBLIC INFORMATION

Federal Government Agencies

All government agencies have a story to tell the public. Because their funding comes from tax dollars, these agencies need to justify the way those funds are spent. The most obvious way is to publicize the work of the agency, as regularly and as skillfully as possible. The public-information people at these agencies must compete for the attention of the press and public with large corporations having their own internal public-relations staffs and able to hire the services of the best PR agencies in the country. Public-information people have to be just as good as the competition or their messages will get lost in the shuffle and wind up unread and unused in the trash cans of newsrooms around the country.

The only way to compete in this unending race for press and public notice is to have an adequate budget to hire people and then let them work on public-information programs. The departments and agencies of the federal government are without peer in getting such funding. For example, in 1979 the Defense Department spent the most on public-information activities of any cabinet agency, about $25 million. The Agriculture Department came next that year with $24 million in annual expenditures.

The *Wall Street Journal* provided a closer look in 1979 at how another federal department, Transportation (DOT) handled its public-information activities with an annual budget of $8.5 million and ninety-three full-time people at work on what the department calls "public affairs." This department and others in the federal government rely less on press releases than in the past. The *Journal* calls the release "a decaying institution in Washington," down 13.7 percent in use since 1971. Still, DOT employs four people to write the twenty-five releases it issues each week. The stiff competition for public attention has caused the department and others like it to turn to more sophisticated tools like television commercials, advertising campaigns, videotape cassettes, full-color brochures, and slick magazines to tell their story.

The brochures have really proliferated in recent years, 102,000 of them published by federal agencies from January 1977 to June 1978, according to a Library of Congress study. The printing of these publications and other government flyers, magazines, catalogues, and other documents costs the federal government about $1.5 billion a year. The federal government operates a central printing plant in Washington and six regional plants, in addition to 300 plants within specific agencies, to turn out the blizzard of material. The remainder come out of 7,000 private printers.

Before federal public-information people use this material, however, they try to reach the public through visual means, like television public-service announcements (called PSAs) that are prepared by the agency concerned and sent free to television stations around the country with the hope that these stations will use them.

One PSA deals with the evils of drunk driving and was produced for DOT's National Highway Safety Administration by a Los Angeles advertising agency. The 30-second spot features actors dressed in the real costumes from *Star Wars* recreating that film's cantina scene. The message is that no one should let a friend drive home drunk. The department's public-information staff sent 900 prints of the commercial to television networks and individual stations around the country.

But federal agencies carry out public-information work regionally and in states as well as in Washington, D.C. All but the most obscure agencies hire people to produce releases, films, brochures, and PSAs for more local consumption. The Bureau of Land Management, for example, employs a public-affairs staff in Portland, Oregon to publicize its programs in Oregon and Washington. "Our goal is to communicate competitively and effectively with the public about our natural-resource programs," says Bob Hostetter, chief of public affairs for the Oregon and Washington region of the bureau, a part of the U.S. Department of the Interior.

The office carries out its work in a variety of ways, some successful, some not. A four-color Oregon recreation guide was very well received, with nearly all 500,000 copies distributed within a few months. Another public-affairs effort by the office was not as successful. In mid-1979, the Bureau of Land Management authorized the use of 2,4–D herbicide in southern Oregon to remove brush from its lands. Many local residents protested the use of 2,4–D. "Those people don't believe that 2,4–D is harmless," says Hostetter, who conducted several public meetings in the area to explain the bureau point of view. "This is not really a good means of communicating with the public. If not carefully handled, the meetings can turn out to be shouting matches." Weeks after the meeting — and a suspension of the spraying — the public was still upset at the agency, and the press coverage of the disturbance resulted in an image that Hostetter had hoped to avoid.

A third program had more pleasing results. The bureau's program to adopt wild horses got generally sympathetic treatment in the press. Later, after a few of the adopted horses were found ill treated or headed for the glue factory, that program was criticized too.

Hostetter worries about handling what he calls "hot potatoes" and constantly prepares material for his headquarters and district staff members on the subject. He also sponsors communications training sessions for his staff. "The most effective public communication is at the district level," he says. "I tell my people not to say anything they don't want to see in print." He directs a staff of five, each of whom specializes in one or more of the research programs of the Bureau of Land Management, for example, wild horses, recreation, allowable cuts of timber. Staff members write press releases and reports and prepare radio and television news releases as well as brochures and specialized publications like the Oregon recreation guide.

Universities and Research Organizations

All universities and research organizations have a story to tell their various publics. The research carried out by their scientists is of interest to any funding agency and to the general public. The public-information people working at those institutions write press releases and special reports and prepare brochures, internal publications, and radio and television public-service announcements. The tone of their work is often more straightforward and subdued than similar materials coming out of a corporate public-relations department. A university or research organization must also do its public-information work with fewer funds than a private public-relations department or agency, or even the public-information arm of a federal agency.

"The aim of public information is to make the general populace aware of how their tax dollars are being spent and to help them understand the nature of the research," says Nichole Vick, technical writer-editor for the Oregon State University (OSU) Forest Research Laboratory. "By nature, research is theoretical and there is a need for someone to help nontechnical people know what is happening. There is a public responsibility, once a program is funded by taxpayers' money, to account for how the money is spent." Vick uses several publication series and technical articles to publicize the work of the laboratory.

Gwil Evans, of the OSU Extension Service, goes back to basic objectives before beginning to produce the materials needed to tell his organization's story to the public. "After figuring out the objectives, the next question is, what is it we want to do, for or with what people? Very often, that's enough to get you started." His office includes several editors to write, edit, and sometimes design the numerous publications put out by the Extension Service every year. Public-information specialists for forestry and agriculture, the marine advisory program, 4–H, home gardening, and radio and television are also in the department.

Dick Floyd's information office for the OSU Agricultural Experiment Station is much smaller and is aimed at a more specialized audience than the extension-service operation down the hall. Two assistant editors and a secretary assist him in telling the research story to the general public and to such specialized publics as state legislators, who provide a large percentage of the funds (the other part comes from federal sources) and organizations like those of dairy farmers or cattlemen that sponsor some of the research.

Floyd writes most of the press releases and edits the texts for the four publications series that highlight the work of the scientists on the Oregon State campus and at eight branch stations around the state. Another editor prepares both radio and television public-service announcements and "filmed" press releases that are also sent free to television stations around the state. The third editor works nearly full time on *Oregon's Agricultural Progress,* a slick magazine that takes the place of an annual report that goes to 6,000 people quarterly. "The goal of the magazine is to tell people in Oregon, particularly urban, about agricultural research in the state," says Floyd. "It's not written for the farmer." The writing style is aimed at the layperson and the design is contemporary. The content is usually balanced between stories about animals and plants, and stories about more cultural things.

Floyd says he gets the feeling quite often that the public-information work of the station pays off. "You feel it most when you go to the legislature," he says, "in the response you get when you're seeking money, when you're appearing personally before groups. The magazine is probably the number one disarmer when we go to talk to people."

But university information work involves more than just reporting research results. Conveying that kind of message to the general public and the legislative public to get more funding is but one part of the job. "In the world of academia, the public includes the students — past and present and potential — parents of students, faculty members, government entities, particularly legislative bodies that control purse strings and staff and administrative personnel," says Tom McLaughlin, public-information officer at the University of Colorado, Colorado Springs.

McLaughlin's is a staff position, reporting to the top administrative officer on campus, the chancellor. The office he heads has responsibilities other than advising the chancellor on public-information matters. It prepares all printed materials like the catalogue, the schedule of classes, and informational brochures. "We label this office 'public information,'" McLaughlin continues, "although the functions of the office include aspects of public relations. This office is primarily one of service to all elements of the university family, and that is where it can achieve its most good."

As with most public-information offices in state-supported institutions, the one McLaughlin runs is always short of funds. "Budgets are so squeezed that in some instances they are almost laughable," says McLaughlin, who used to work for a large corporation. "This becomes quickly apparent to the person who has moved to a state-supported institution from the private sector. There is no such thing as an expense account for entertaining purposes in a state institution. For me to buy your lunch and charge it to the expenses of the office is forbidden."

When he is called upon to give advice to the chancellor and other officials, McLaughlin says he does it quickly and has no regret when his suggestions are not followed. "You offer what you consider your best wisdom and advice, recommend — when the occasion presents itself — courses of action, and carry out directives to the best of your ability," he says. "There will be all too many occasions when top management won't be interested in listening to recommendations and suggestions. That's when you suffer in silence or fly résumés across the landscape."

Most of the time, his job is straightforward: "Service to the university and service to the media interested in campus activities is the best way for the office to do its job," he says.

Hospitals and Medical Centers

Hospitals and medical centers need well-funded, well-organized public-information programs almost more than other nonprofit organizations because their work affects so many people directly. Almost everyone knows someone who has had to go to the hospital. Millions of people are touched at least indirectly by the research that goes on in hospitals and medical centers. Rising health-care costs have been a big political issue for many years, as has the quality of health care and its delivery to more and more people. Federal, state, and local governments have involved themselves increasingly in hospital and health-related affairs.

These reasons for good hospital public-information programs also reveal the many publics that have to be served: patients, visitors, the members of the surrounding community, boards of directors, funding agencies, hospital employees, medical staff members, scientific researchers. Each is unique, but all have to be dealt with through some kind of public-information program.

When Ken Niehans joined the staff on the University of Oregon Medical School as director of information in the 1960s, photographs and names of doctors did not appear in newspapers lest their colleagues and the medical society think them too publicity hungry. When he left that job in 1975, doctors had no such hesitation. This change in the way he did his job is symptomatic of the changed role of hospital public information. "There was always that mystique and doctors could ignore everyone," says Niehans. "When people became more sophisticated, doctors could no longer clam up and hide in the mystique of medicine. Now people 'shop' for a doctor if they don't like what a doctor says. This exemplifies the change in medicine."

Niehans established a program that used print and broadcast methods to reach the many publics of the medical school, the only one in Oregon. External publics include legislators, research groups, federal health officials, civic leaders, boards of directors, the press, and the general public including the neighborhood around the campus. Internal publics are the medical staff, the nursing staff, other employees, medical students, and patients.

The publications varied from an internal typewritten employee newsletter to a slick external magazine used to raise money. A number of educational brochures were developed, to inform patients about their treatments, for example. Regular tours of facilities were held for the general public or for specialized groups. Press releases were issued when there was something newsworthy to discuss. The same held true for press conferences. "We were very selective in holding press conferences," Niehans continues. "We didn't call one unless there was a reason to have it. When we held one, people didn't question what would happen. They came because they knew it was going to be newsworthy."

In Niehans' work at the University of Oregon Medical School, and in all good public information for hospitals, the main ingredient for success is careful preparation.

According to the American Society for Hospital Public Relations of the American Hospital Association, a hospital public-information program consists of seven steps: (1) assessing the current situation about the hospital and any problem areas; (2) defining the problem areas by taking the information gathered about the current situation and designating problems that require PR action; (3) dividing the publics into pertinent "targets"; (4) establishing goals in writing; (5) planning a program that lists each problem, the goals, the public involved, and the means of dealing with the problem; (6) implementing the program by putting the plan into action; and (7) evaluating the PR program periodically by setting review dates upon which to measure progress.

PROBLEMS

The work of public information can be just as frustrating and hectic as that in the biggest agency. It is not without problems, some of them unique to public information, others similar to those in public relations.

Inadequate Budget and Goals

There has to be adequate funding in order for public-information people to be successful in their jobs. As in public relations, good public-information programs begin with the setting of realistic, well-defined goals. What does the organization want to achieve in the relationships with its publics? What are its publics? How can they be reached and in what manner? How much money will it take to hire the people and prepare the materials needed to meet the goals?

Working with Management and Scientists

Universities and research organizations are often headed by technical people who have little or no appreciation of the importance of explaining their work to the public. Presidents and directors can usually be shown the importance of the public contact, especially when public money is funding most of the work going on at the institution.

Scientists often adopt Commodore Vanderbilt's "public be damned" attitude. This stance will not work, however, if any of the funds of the institution come from public sources. Public-information people must insist that the scientists grant interviews and cooperate by providing information for in-house press releases or longer articles. Public-information people have no choice but to keep trying to get scientists to talk to reporters and come out of their laboratories to deal with the outside world. "You go into them and explain what the story is, what you have in mind," says Floyd of the OSU Agricultural Experiment Station. "I go under the assumption that they consider me a blank slate to be filled in. They start out at a low level and very quickly ascend. You have to get them to keep going back to explain. You try to get them to apply their information to the practical side. They don't like to do this so the battle is joined.

"There is a new sense of accountability. Everyone is now stressing it — how they spend their money. It's your job to report this," he concludes. Adds Nichole Vick of the OSU Forest Research Laboratory: "In the future there's going to have to be more accessibility than ever. Scientists are becoming more and more specialized, society more complex. The general public has to rely on public-information people to interpret all of this."

Covering Up Bad News

Nonprofit organizations usually deal with "good" news. No one dies or is robbed in a press release from such an organization. Armies do not march, neither do governments fall. The information released, although often of a highly technical nature, is usually uplifting and commendable. This situation makes both officials and public-information people unable to deal with the occasional "bad" news that comes along to involve their institution. They seem to feel that their image will be irreparably besmirched if the slightest bit of negative information appears in print or is broadcast. As a result, they try to cover up the bad, hoping that it will go away. This never works, except on the most minuscule story. If the story is important enough reporters will double their efforts to get the information they need, and the institution will look worse in the end than if it had done its best to assist reporters in getting the facts.

One case illustrates this point.

From the early days of the manned-space program, the National Aeronautics and Space Administration (NASA) enjoyed a very good press. The field was exciting and new, and the entire country was caught up in the race to beat the Russians to the moon. The original seven astronauts of Project Mercury were instant national heroes when they returned to earth from their suborbital flights. Each told his story to *Life* magazine through an exclusive contract that barred any contact with other reporters. The rest of the press grumbled about this but kept covering the flights.

When the next phase of the program came along, the two-man flights of Project Gemini, the criticism was more open. By this time NASA had geared up for the long haul to the moon by hiring a great many public-information people. At the Manned Spacecraft Center in Houston, the job of these people became little more than telling good news. Officials at the center across the street were simply not available if the story seemed in advance to be the least bit negative. If a reporter got too inquisitive and too pushy, what little access there was could quickly dry up. During flights, the public-information people were unable to explain the reasons for any malfunctions in the space-craft — and unwilling to make available the technical people who could. Harried reporters in the adjacent pressroom relied on a very good public-relations man from the manufacturer of the spacecraft, the McDonnell Company, to use an excellent company-published book on the spacecraft to explain what went wrong and why. Without him, reporters would have been at a loss to determine what was happening.

Officials were made available twice a day after shift changes in the control room, access to which was forbidden to even a few pool reporters. But the time of the press conferences was always limited, and many questions were left unanswered. About the only other information provided officially, except for press releases and flight plans, were the transcripts of air-to-ground communication, which were available several hours later on a continuing basis throughout the flight. Here, however, the public-information people removed anything of a sensitive or controversial nature before the transcript was given to reporters.

The situation reached a low point early in 1966, when the Gemini flight developed trouble and the crew had to return to earth ten to twelve hours away from the nearest pickup point at sea. A live televised press conference was held in prime time to discuss the situation. Reporters, by then very angry over the entire information policy, were quite hostile in their questions. As usual, NASA officials were not forthcoming with any information. In the lively exchanges, the NASA people, by withholding air-to-ground transcripts, left the impression that the astronauts, those valiant heroes whose virtues they worked so hard to extol, had not performed well. When the transcripts came out the next day, they proved that this had not been the case. The fact remains, however, that the tendency of NASA to squelch bad news had backfired badly.

A GOOD PUBLIC-INFORMATION PROGRAM

There is little difference between good public-information programs for public and nonprofit institutions, and good public-relations programs for corporations.

Goals

Nothing can be accomplished without the development of workable, reasonable, well-defined goals for the public-information program. Who are the publics, what should they be told, and in what form should they be told?

Access to Management

As in corporate public relations, access to the officials of the institution is crucial to the development and successful achievement of the goals. " 'Power' is minimal in an academic atmosphere," says Tom McLaughlin, public information officer at the University of Colorado, in Colorado Springs. "With direct access to the chancellor, however, there is opportunity to present plans, suggestions, and ideas about programs that are designed to enhance the image of the university with its various publics. As long as the top man is oriented in that direction, there is a certain amount of power in that the public-information person is able to assist his thinkng."

Adequate Budget

The funding must match the goals. Public-information work is necessarily done in a more understated, simple, and inexpensive way than is public relations. It does no good to a university's image, for example, if the material issued by its public-information office is flashy and expensive looking. Why are they spending our tax dollars on this fancy brochure? the public will ask. Nevertheless, there needs to be adequate money to do the jobs established in the goals.

Adequate Staff

The goals cannot be met without enough people to do the work required. The staff cannot be hired unless there is an adequate budget. The three components are inseparable. A minimum staff is a director and a secretary. Later, others can be hired to do special tasks. If a magazine is the primary means of communication, an editor needs to be hired. If brochures are a key means of a public contact, an editor and a designer need to be brought in. If technical articles, manuals, and reports are important, a technical editor needs to be added. For radio, television, and other visual techniques, another specialist must be brought in. The list goes on, depending on the goals and the budget.

Specified Publics

Who is to be reached with the public-information program? Members of the general public, whose tax dollars are paying the bills? Legislators, who are actually appropriating the money? More specialized publics, who need the research information? An organization must know and work to inform each type of public.

Designated Approaches

Are printed materials the best way to go, or would a good film or videotape serve the targeted public better? Is it best to aim at a technical audience through specialized report series, or would an easy-to-read brochure be best? Is a glossy and expensive quarterly magazine a good way to tell the organization's story, or would a cheap weekly newspaper be more appropriate? The answers to all these questions depend on the goals and the budget.

SUMMARY

As public opinion has grown as a potent force in American society, nonprofit groups have had to set up sophisticated and complete public-information departments to tell their stories to the public. Such public-information departments differ from their counterparts in public-relations departments of companies and PR agencies primarily in the presentation of information, goals, staff, and budget. The federal government, universities and research organizations, and hospitals and medical centers employ most of the public-information people in the United States. Public information has some major problems: (1) inadequate budget, (2) working with management and scientists who have no appreciation of the need to contact the public, and (3) the tendency to cover up bad news. A good public-information program will have well-defined goals, access to management, an adequate budget, an adequate staff, specified publics, and designated approaches to reach those publics.

PR FOCUS: THE DMSO CONTROVERSY

DMSO — dimethylsulfoxide — became known in the early 1960s as a possible treatment for injuries to the muscular and skeletal systems and for chronic diseases of those systems like arthritis. As its success rates became known, its proponents grew. In the opinion of many, DMSO took on the status of a "wonder drug" and a cause to fight for.

The Food and Drug Administration, the federal agency with the power to test and license drugs for production and distribution, was not impressed. The fact that DMSO achieved the status of a wonder drug so quickly caused that agency to be extra cautious in its testing. Initial word of the drug's supposed healing powers spread, multiplying its use greatly: more than 100,000 patients are estimated to have received DMSO during clinical testing in 1964 and 1965. Others who heard about it but could not get it rubbed on their skins the industrial version, used as a solvent of paints and plastics.

Such actions caused the FDA to slow down on testing, a move that caused drug companies to lose interest in financing research. But there were many things about DMSO that were unknown. How can a drug derived from lignin, the cement substance of trees, for as little as thirty-five cents a pint for the crude chemical, be as effective as people claim? Some doctors think that it simply blocks the pain fibers of nerves. They are not completely sure, however.

From the start, the man in the middle of the DMSO controversy has been Dr. Stanley Jacob, associate professor of surgery at the University of Oregon Medical School. Jacob introduced DMSO as a potentially useful drug in 1962, nearly a century after it was first synthesized as a chemical. Jacob originally used DMSO to freeze kidneys safely in his laboratory. He soon saw other medical uses for it and began to experiment. To this day he has stood alone in continuing to push for its use, a crusade that has earned him the title "father of DMSO" — and many enemies.

Ken Niehans, then director of information at the medical school, was involved in the controversy almost as early as Jacob. "At first, we tried to keep it out of the press," says Niehans. "Then, a one-paragraph release from Crown Zellerbach (which makes the raw material for DMSO) caught the interest of a local medical writer. I got her the information she wanted and tried to get her to sit on the story. For a time, she did."

Then the contract between Crown Zellerbach and the Oregon State System of Higher Education to purchase the raw material was announced. "For the next three days," continues Niehans, "all the lines were busy with calls from London, Paris, *Life,* the *Saturday Evening Post. Life* would not give up. For six months I stalled them. 'It's just too early, we don't know.' Then a medical writer from *Life* called and said she'd be in Portland the next day. 'Either you cooperate or you don't. I'm going to do a story.' The next week the *Saturday Evening Post* said the same thing."

What Niehans finally did in desperation was to set up a series of interviews with people who believed in DMSO and with a group that thought that it was worth nothing. "When the *Life* story came out it was a reasonably accurate, slightly popularized account," he says. "A number of people went to the dean and thought I should be fired."

Jacob and Niehans decided to refer all outside calls to Niehans' office. The public-information people would then screen back the patient calls and deal with the press queries. "You should have seen the mail," he says.

Many doctors in the school identified Niehans as the reason for the controversy. "I took more abuses, I was blamed for it," he says, "even though there was nothing I did that the dean didn't know about. You couldn't have *Life* magazine sneaking around. The only thing to do was to show both sides of the controversy." At the same time he was fighting with doctors on the staff, Niehans was tussling with Crown Zellerbach, which would not respond to questions. "As a private company, they could do that," he says. "But we were supported by the taxpayers of Oregon."

The initial controversy subsided, although inquiries continued every year thereafter that Niehans was at the medical school. After the popular press dealt with the story, the medical journals came next, to be followed by the

National Enquirer for a sensational angle. In 1981, nearly twenty years after its first discovery and use, DMSO remains uncertified as a drug. The cult is still actively supporting it and so is Dr. Stanley Jacob, who remains an associate professor. A segment of *60 Minutes* on DMSO in 1980 rekindled the interest and the controversy all over again.

"It was a miserable time," concludes Niehans. "Time has shown who was right, how PR helped to handle the situation. Someday DMSO will have a place in medicine."

Analysis

Should Niehans have let *Life* magazine have its interviews? Should he have kept the lid on the story? DMSO is a subject that cannot be hidden forever. The best approach in such a situation is to tell everything you can as quickly as possible. The truth will never hurt anyone in the long run.

PR FOCUS: THE DIRTY PLASTIC MILK BOTTLE

Several years ago the public-information news bureau of Oregon State University issued a press release about a researcher's discovery that plastic milk bottles could not be totally cleaned when they were washed and readied for reuse. People had used them to hold oil, pesticides, even urine samples, and the remnants of whatever was inside would not go away after the bottles had been turned in for deposit and high-pressure cleaning. "When we did the release," recalls Dick Floyd, editor of the OSU Agricultural Experiment Station and the writer of the release, "we knew the dairy industry would not be happy."

Floyd was right. Leaders of the dairy industry, which had supported research at the university for years, were furious. They called the university president, influential state legislators, members of the press, and anyone else who would listen. "We were vilified for putting the story out," continues Floyd. After the furor had subsided, experiment-station officials and Floyd called a public meeting that was also attended by members of the dairy industry. "We had to defend why we were doing this."

To Floyd and university officials, however, there was little need to defend their action. "We had a responsibility to inform the public of a potential health problem," Floyd says.

Analysis

The plastic milk bottle incident exemplifies public information at its best: making the public aware of a problem, regardless of the consequences to the organization that is releasing the information. The incident also exemplifies the difference between public information and public relations: the ability of public information to tell the truth in an unvarnished way, regardless of the consequences. Public-relations people would not have been in a case like this. They would not have been able to be as forthcoming with the information initially, unless they had enlightened bosses. They certainly would not have issued a press release about the subject. Given the anger of the people on the other side, a public-relations person in an agency handling the account or working for the dairy industry would probably have been fired. In this case, the industry's support of dairy research at OSU continued uninterrupted.

PR FOCUS: THE AIR FORCE ACADEMY COVER-UP

In 1965, the United States Air Force Academy in Colorado Springs announced that it was conducting a formal investigation of a cheating scandal in which a group of cadets had violated its honor code. Within hours of the announcement, local and national reporters converged on the academy, which had always given good treatment to the press and which enjoyed a whole series of favorable articles about its programs and students and staff as a result.

Now, however, U.S. Air Force headquarters imposed an official silence on everyone but the director of information and one other officer. The other information officers were "not to answer questions, say anything, nor furnish any information."

"No Admittance" signs were placed on all doors in the information division except that of the small pressroom. As the number of reporters — and the pressure on them from news editors to get a story — increased, the silence continued. This led to speculation, half-truths, rumors, and hearsay. The academy information officer could not confirm or deny the stories, because of the official silence from headquarters. The reporters were even denied a daily press conference. All requests for interviews with the superintendent and with cadets were turned away as well.

After the Secretary of the Air Force sent a colonel to the academy to help in handling the by then bad public-relations problems, the reporters blew up. Their stories ridiculed the academy, its officials, and the honor code. Even after officials had released over the next three weeks the number of cadets who had resigned, the press was not mollified.

Obviously, a series of major blunders had taken place in the failure to anticipate the impact of the cheating incident, the closed-door policy toward the press, the need for Pentagon clearance for all releases, release of information on a piecemeal basis, the lack of proper press facilities, and failure to provide sufficient background material.

Later that year, after a new director of information arrived at the academy, procedures were developed to deal with future news events in a more open way. By the time of a second cheating scandal in 1967, the Air Force proved that it had learned its lesson. This time, the announcement of the scandal was made by the superintendent on February 27. By March 2 the number of cadets who had resigned was revealed officially. A nationwide furor ensued, and once again members of the press descended on the academy. This time, however, the whole thing was over in seven days, simply because officials made every effort to work with the press in getting out information. The public was thus generally sympathetic.

According to Major Richard F. Abel, former chief of public affairs at the academy, in an article in *Public Relations Journal,* the second scandal had better impact from a public-relations standpoint because of a carefully executed emergency plan.

When the cheating was discovered, the superintendent met with his staff to discuss the implications and to prepare a plan if a major scandal developed. He and the director of information then went to the Pentagon to brief high-level Air Force officials. Those officials agreed to let the academy release all information, with Washington furnishing support as needed.

After returning to the academy, the information director worked out a plan of action. The superintendent began the plan by meeting with four major publishers in the area and the owners of the two local radio-TV stations to ask their advice. Next, an interim reply was devised to any press query.

After the meeting with the owners, a press conference was called and the story released. This time, the members of the press got full cooperation when they arrived on the campus. Interviews with the superintendent, members of the honor committee, and cadet officers were easily arranged. Updated information was made available. No attempt was made to cover anything up.

Analysis

These two incidents reveal how even good institution-press relationships can fall apart in a time of crisis. If a negative situation is covered up officially, the members of the press will double their efforts to reveal all the details about it. The negative situation will thus become much worse and last longer than had a determined effort been made to reveal as much information as possible from the start. This case shows too that a bad situation can be repaired with a carefully planned and energetically executed program.

REVIEW QUESTIONS

1. What are the differences between public information and public relations? How do these differences affect you as a member of the audiences of both?

2.   In examining their different messages, are you more likely to believe and respond to what a nonprofit organization tells you than what a company says? Why? Why not?

3.   What are the probable publics for federal government agencies, universities and research organizations, and hospitals and medical centers? How do they differ? Why?

4.   How do the problems of public-information people differ from those of their counterparts in public relations? How are they the same?

5.   Is trying to cover up "bad" news by a nonprofit institution worse than if a company does so? Why? Why not?

ASSIGNMENTS

For Journalism Students

1.   You are an Air Force public-information officer and one of your aircraft has crashed in the Indian Ocean with an atomic bomb on board. How do you deal with the situation from a PR standpoint?

2.   You are a hospital public-information director and a major development in cancer research has just been made by one of your scientists. Only the *National Enquirer* knows about it, and it is demanding an exclusive story. Develop a plan to release the information.

3.   Develop a public-information plan for a university using the characteristics noted in this chapter.

4.   Develop a public-information plan for a local research laboratory or hospital using material in this chapter.

For Business Students

1.   You are president of the Business Roundtable, an elite group of corporate officials who comment on national and world affairs. You think that the group needs more public identification, and you want to hire a public-information director. What arguments will you use to the other members of the organization to get them to fund the new position?

2.   You are director of the New York Stock Exchange and a major stock swindle has just been uncovered involving two of your vice presidents. You turn to your information person for help. How would you direct him or her in developing a plan for dealing with the release of information about the scandal?

3.   Research business-related nonprofit organizations to see how they have dealt with the public, that is, foundations, the National Association of Manufacturers, the Industrial Conference Board, the various stock exchanges. Did they have a public-information plan? How does this plan seem to work? Compile your findings into a research paper.

CHAPTER 7

Planning a public-relations campaign

How will the various segments of public relations — agency, corporate, and public information — carry out their work?

A public-relations campaign begins with an idea in the mind of a PR person, or an agency client, or a company official. Something needs to be communicated to a public, either for the benefit of the client or company, or for the benefit of the public, or the benefit of both.

From those early meetings between PR person and client or company official, and the appearance of the final product in whatever form it takes, the idea will change greatly, expanded and contracted by those involved based on their backgrounds and experience and their own perceptions of what will succeed with the public, that vast assemblage of people about whom so little is known.

The public-relations campaign outlined in this chapter is a hypothetical one. Although it deals with the work of a mythical agency, RPL Associates, for a mythical company, National Oil Corporation, the plan is based on real campaigns conducted by real agencies. The steps to be followed would also apply equally well to the staff of an internal PR department. This campaign follows the DOING system of public relations already noted in Chapter 1.

DECIDING ON GOALS AND MAKING PLANS TO REACH THEM

National Oil Corporation, a medium-size oil company with all its sources of petroleum within the continental United States, has called in RPL Associates, a medium-size public-relations agency in its headquarters city, for help in solving a problem. National Oil exploration crews have discovered oil on an island tract of land in the state next to a private game refuge, and the company, forever short of crude oil, wants to begin pumping it out of the ground as soon as possible.

The game refuge presents a problem in this regard, however. It is a well-known preserve that was the subject of an award-winning documentary film

and a hit TV series about a biologist sponsored by the oil company several
years before. Its nature trails are a popular tourist attraction as well. The
company is afraid of ruining its public image by drilling for oil so near the
game refuge and then, because of the island location, taking it out by tanker.
Because the refuge is privately owned, however, its purchase by the oil company is among the strong possibilities available.

What should National Oil do? Its own PR staff does not have a solution
to the problem, so corporate officials contact the agency.

ORIGINATING PROGRAMS TO ACHIEVE THE GOALS

Agency officials agree to take the assignment and assign an account executive
to meet with the company president and the vice president for communications. The two officials outline the problem in an initial one-hour meeting.
The three of them then work out some objectives in a brainstorming session
that lasts another hour.

Establishing Objectives

After this meeting and a follow-up planning session back at his agency office,
the account executive develops the overall objectives of the forthcoming PR
campaign:

1.   to increase the awareness of citizens of the state about the oil supply
     situation and the need to find and pump out of the ground as much
     crude as possible;
2.   to detail the particular problems of National Oil in finding and refin-
     ing oil;
3.   to review the wildlife resources of the state and National's past interest
     in those resources;
4.   to show how the interests of the oil company, the public, and the wild-
     life can be served.

Presenting a Preliminary Budget

With the overall objectives worked out, the account executive returns to corporate officials with an outline of the objectives and a preliminary cost figure
and estimated budget items. The executives give him the approval to continue
his work.

Compiling Research Information

The account executive begins his work by gathering all the material he can on the public perception of the energy crisis and the oil situation. He asks the research department of the agency to compile the information he needs to develop his campaign. That department goes through the public library and the library of a local university to find pertinent newspaper and magazine information about the oil situation. Researchers also pick up useful facts and figures from official documents of the U.S. Department of Energy, the U.S. Congress, and in material supplied by the American Petroleum Institute. The research staff summarizes its findings for the account executive and attaches backup documentation from its sources. The conclusions indicate a continually worsening oil-supply shortage compounded by the volatile Middle East political situation and constantly increasing crude-oil prices.

The research department does not find out much about public attitudes toward the oil situation among state residents. So the account executive decides to go to an outside public-opinion polling firm for help. He contacts a friend in such a firm and commissions that organization to conduct a poll to find out how aware the public is of the oil situation.

As work on this poll is proceeding, the account executive goes back to his own research people for information on the state wildlife situation (how many species, what animals, where located), the history of the game preserve affected by the oil drilling, the record of the company in regard to wildlife. They get the necessary information from state government agencies, material from wildlife-preservation groups, company and game-refuge records, and interviews with people at both the company and the refuge. After getting their report, the account executive sends them back for more information. They have forgotten to include information on the fish and plant life in the waters around the island, waters that will have to be navigated by tankers taking out the oil. The agency researchers consult state agencies and the oceanography department of the state university to get this information. They compile these data and give them to the account executive.

As with public perception of the oil situation, the researchers find little about how the public views wildlife and ecology. So the account executive returns to the public-opinion polling firm and commissions another survey of public attitudes toward wildlife, fish, ecology, environment, the game refuge, and — most important of all — how these attitudes relate to the need for oil to solve energy shortages.

Developing an Approach

Armed with this background information, the account executive and others on the account team he put together at the agency (a copy writer, a graphic artist, and a researcher) meet for two days in brainstorming sessions to suggest and discuss ways to solve National Oil's problem.

After about 10 hours of such deliberations, the team arrives at the following preliminary suggestions:

1. National Oil will sponsor a series of institutional ads on wildlife in the state that stress a preservation theme; the ads will run on all television and radio stations and in every weekly and daily newspaper as well as in regional editions of the *Wall Street Journal, Sports Illustrated,* and the publication of the National Wildlife Federation.
2. The company will sponsor the showing of the Walt Disney True Life Adventure films on television stations in the two largest cities in the state; although a new film series would be preferable, time does not permit it.
3. The PR agency and the company will develop a series of booklets on wildlife of the state to be distributed free to all grade schools and high schools; the booklets will be lavishly illustrated and will include course outlines and lecture material; the documentary on the refuge will be made available as well.
4. After three months, the focus of the TV and print ads will change to one of detailing the energy situation, particularly that of oil.
5. In another month, the wildlife and oil themes will be combined into an ad series that stresses coexistence.
6. National Oil will also set up a foundation to finance the game refuge in the future; the company will not buy the refuge outright (that would look too self-serving) but will help pay administration costs and will pay for new visitor facilities and guides.
7. The company will also fund a university research study of ways both to detect oil spills early and to minimize their damage to fish, wildlife, and the environment and ecology in general.
8. The agency will arrange for a series of interviews on TV and radio talk shows and daily newspapers with the oil-company president to discuss refuge plans.
9. At the end of the year-long campaign, the company will pay for another public-opinion poll to measure results. Is the oil situation understood better? Do people think wildlife is being adequately protected by National Oil? How do they view National's new oil operation next to the refuge? Was it necessary for it to drill there, or is it only safeguarding its own narrow interests and well-being?

Presenting a Final Budget

With this specific outline of approach, the account executive returns to the president and vice president of National Oil to brief them on details and to give them a detailed budget and a final figure on the cost of the campaign.

With final approval gained from the top officials of National Oil, the account executive directs the team to prepare the material for the campaign.

Preparing the Print Ads

1. Select a theme for the ad series and delineate that theme in a specific number of individual ads.
2. Decide on the use of photographs or illustrations, layout and design, dominance of copy or art.
3. Write the copy to convey the theme, using the research information on wildlife and the public perception of it.
4. Make arrangements for placing the ads, and sign the contracts to run them in the publications concerned.

Preparing the Television Ads

1. Select a theme for the ad series that accompanies the print series and that augments its message nicely (for example, use of similar illustrations, type faces).
2. Decide on the use of film footage, still photographs, or animation.
3. Gather previously shot films of wildlife, commissioning a photographer to take film footage and still photographs at the game refuge, or hiring an animator to do work that will tell the story.
4. Write the copy to accompany the visuals to tell the story.
5. Get a musical score to play in the background from existing sources or from a composer.
6. Hire an actor or announcer to read the script.
7. Put the film, music, and soundtrack together in a commercial that runs the required amount of time.
8. Make arrangements for placing the commercial on the desired television stations, and sign contracts for it to be shown for a set period of time, paying careful attention to the kind of program to be sponsored (dignified but with high ratings).

Preparing the Radio Ads

1. Select a theme for the ad series that goes well with the print and TV ads (same voice, same music, same or similar message).
2. Decide on sound effects to be included with the narrator, and music to take the place of the visuals in the other two ad series, print and TV.

3. Write the copy to go with the music and sound effects.
4. Hire an actor or announcer, preferably the same one used in the TV ad series, to read the script.
5. Put the soundtrack, sound effects, and music together in a commercial that runs the required amount of time.
6. Make arrangements for placing the commercial on the desired radio stations, and sign contracts for it to be broadcast for a set period of time, paying careful attention to the kind of program sponsored (news programs during "drive time" to reach high-income, high-education people when they are going to and from work).

Organizing the Nature Film Program

1. Make arrangements with Walt Disney Productions to show the nature films on a one-time-only basis.
2. Make arrangements to show the films on TV stations in the two largest cities in the state.
3. Select and hire a host for the series to introduce and comment on each film before it is shown; a popular but dignified person associated with the outdoors should be used. The name of the company will appear only at the end.
4. Prepare a series of ads, one per film, that will publicize the showing of the films on television pages in newspapers and on radio stations.
5. Prepare a press kit of information about the films and the program to be sent to all television and outdoors writers in the state; the kit will include background on the films, background on the host, and the time and station of the viewing.

Preparing the Educational Package

1. Meet with state education-department curriculum experts and teacher organizations to get ideas on what to include in the wildlife booklets.
2. Gather material for the booklets by doing library research and interviewing wildlife experts at the state university.
3. Decide on the use of artwork and design of the booklets and assign photographers, artists, and a photo researcher (to find existing photographs) to work on the illustrations.
4. Write copy for the booklets.
5. Get copy, illustrations, and design for the booklet approved by officials at National Oil, the state education department, and the teacher organizations.

6. Contract with a printer to print the booklets, making sure to select one that handles color well.
7. Distribute the completed booklets to the schools of the state as well as to the press mailing list.
8. Write a news release to accompany those booklets sent to the newspapers, magazines, and television and radio stations in the state.

Preparing the Revised Advertisements

1. Prepare new print, television, and radio ads that combine the wildlife theme with one of energy conservation; the same music and "feel" will be used to give continuity.
2. Make arrangements for placing the ads on the desired TV and radio stations and in newspapers around the state.

Setting Up the Foundation

1. Prepare a prospectus for the foundation.
2. Work with lawyers to organize the foundation.
3. Reorganize the administration of the existing refuge, hire an architect and contractor to remodel the visitor center, supervise the hiring and training of guides.

Establishing a Liaison with the State University

1. Work out the procedures for giving a sizable grant to the state university to finance fisheries and wildlife research and early oil-spill detection.
2. Establish direct contact between technical people at National Oil and the head of the university research project.

Arranging Interviews for the Company President

1. Work out a schedule of interviews for the president of National Oil with editorial boards on every daily newspaper and important radio and television talk shows.
2. Prepare a briefing book for him of likely questions and his answers.
3. Train him in how to succeed in TV and radio interviews.

INFORMING THE PUBLICS OF THE MESSAGE

All the plans of the campaign are put into operation for the planned time period.

NOTING AND ANALYZING RESULTS

Conducting More Public-Opinion Polling

1. Hire the same polling firm to do surveys in the middle and at the end of the ad campaign to try to measure its effectiveness.

Doing Follow-Up Publicity

1. Write news releases for newspapers, radio, and TV that report progress on the construction and completion of visitor facilities at the game refuge and in the university research project.
2. Write an article in the National Oil external magazine a year after the oil wells are functioning to show how the refuge has been unharmed by them.

Compiling Press and Public Reaction

1. Keep careful track of press comment through clippings and copies of TV and radio scripts.
2. Keep a file of letters to the company and rank them pro and con.

Writing a Final Report

1. Review the original objectives and assess whether they have been reached in a final report one year after the start of the campaign.
    Total cost: $750,000 to $1 million
    Total value of oil pumped from the new field: $100 million

GOING AHEAD OR DEVELOPING NEW PROGRAMS

A similar campaign can be carried out for another company or a new one developed, depending on success.

SUMMARY

A public-relations campaign consists of a series of major steps — the DOING system of public relations — made one after the other in a careful way. The client, in the case of an agency, or the boss, in the case of internal PR staffs, needs to be consulted at every step. The campaign can come in many forms. The important thing is that the methods selected are appropriate in reaching the final goal and at a cost the client can afford.

REVIEW QUESTIONS

1. Why was a PR campaign the best way for National Oil to reach its goal?
2. Why was the preliminary public-opinion polling necessary?
3. Why was an institutional ad campaign the best way to proceed instead of a more product-oriented ad series?
4. Why did the oil company bother to set up the foundation? Couldn't it just buy the game refuge outright?
5. Why did the company decide to fund the university research on wildlife and oil spills?
6. Why were the press interviews with the oil-company president necessary?
7. Why was any follow-up needed? The oil was pumping so who cares what happens at the game refuge?

SECTION III

The DOING System

Part i:

Deciding on goals

CHAPTER **8**

Financial public relations

Potential investors. Current shareholders. Security analysts and the financial press.

These three groups are important for the success of any publicly owned company. The attention of potential investors must be attracted to infuse new money into the company. Current holders of shares of stock must be kept up to date on how the company is being managed and is using their invested money. The two groups that stand to one side as observers of the company and its affairs — security analysts and the financial press — must be given the information they need to do their jobs.

FINANCIAL PUBLIC RELATIONS DEFINED

Gathering the necessary material and disseminating it to these areas is the role of people in *financial public relations*. They prepare annual reports, quarterly reports, financial news releases, and other publications for this specific audience. The difference between financial PR and regular PR lies in the audiences addressed, the material presented to these audiences, and the official requirements for preparing the material. This segment of the profession, also called *investor relations* or *corporate relations,* has grown in importance in the past few years, especially since the Securities and Exchange Commission (SEC), the New York Stock Exchange, the American Stock Exchange, and the National Association of Securities Dealers (NASD) tightened their requirements for disclosing information for the companies under their jurisdictions. All these organizations require a company to disclose all corporate developments, favorable or unfavorable, that might affect the sale of its stock or influence the decisions of investors.

"Investor relations is a long-term effort," says J. Edmund Colloton, a veteran New York financial PR specialist. "The objective is a timely, meaningful disclosure of corporate information in good and bad times." You have to have the confidence of management to receive the information you need to do the job. And you do not earn the confidence of management overnight.

118

BACKGROUND

Two events have hastened the growth of financial public relations as a major segment of the profession.

Texas Gulf Sulphur Case

After its geologists discovered substantial deposits of copper and zinc in a test-hole core sample drilled in Canada in November 1963, the Texas Gulf Sulphur Company made no public announcement. Several officers and employees used this information as a reason to purchase company stock. When the company bought more land and resumed drilling the next spring, company employees bought more stock. The company, prompted by rumors in the press about the large size of the discovery, finally made its first statement on the drilling in a news release issued on April 12, 1964. The release played down the importance of the drilling results. Company officers and employees bought more stock the next week. On April 16, the company issued a more accurate news release that called the find "a major strike of zinc, copper, and silver" totaling more than 25 million tons of ore.

The SEC took the company to court and won a ruling that has had a major effect on corporate public relations and company disclosure policies. The courts decided in 1968 that the insiders purchased Texas Gulf Sulphur stock illegally based on material, nonpublic information about the ore deposits, and the company acted illegally when it issued its false and misleading news release of April 12 denigrating the drilling results. The courts said that both actions violated the SEC's rule 10b – 5, which prohibits misleading statements or omissions of "material" facts — facts that move the price of stock up or down and that are essential to the informed investor — that might defraud those who buy or sell the stock of a company.

The United States Court of Appeals, Second Circuit, found that insiders in the case "were not trading on an equal footing with the outside investors" because they alone were able to evaluate the major ore strike and invest in company stock with the expectation that it would go up in price. The Federal District Court in New York subsequently ruled that the April 12 news release violated the securities laws because it was misleading to investors and had not been prepared carefully. The United States Supreme Court refused to hear an appeal in the case by Texas Gulf Sulphur in 1971.

Since these rulings, companies have had to give careful thought to the developments they disclose; they have hired financial PR specialists to help them do it properly. The SEC, stock exchanges, and the NASD have always required the disclosure of material information. In the Texas Gulf Sulphur case, however, material facts were defined as "not only information disclosing the earnings and distributions of a company but also those facts which affect the probable future of a company and those which may affect the desire of investors to buy, sell or hold companies' securities."

Decline in Security Analysts

The other event affecting the growth in financial public relations is the reduction in the number of security analysts from the 1960s.

1. During 1976, the New York Stock Exchange reported that the number of individual stockholders in the United States dropped nearly 20 percent from about 31 million to about 25 million. In 1977, the number of New York Stock Exchange member firms had declined by 17 percent from late 1970 and by 39 percent from 1961.

2. In 1979 there were an estimated 900 major financial institutions in North America, nearly all of which manage $100 million or more in securities. They employ 4,500 to 5,000 portfolio managers or security analysts, still a large number to be dealt with by financial PR people. "When the market boom collapsed," says Craig Lewis, a New York public-relations agency president, "many security analysts went out of business." The work they were doing for stock brokerage firms of keeping up with developments in companies and entire industries for potential investors would now have to be carried out by others. The answer for many companies was to hire financial public-relations specialists to do similar tasks. Indeed, many former security analysts became financial PR people quickly.

THE JOB

A financial PR person does many of the same writing and editing chores as his or her counterpart in regular PR except that the tasks to be accomplished require more technical knowledge of procedures and terms, and the work done is subject to scrutiny by government agencies like the SEC in a way not necessary in regular PR.

Annual Reports

All companies that issue stock must prepare and publish an annual report and distribute it to stockholders. The SEC requires every company issuing such registered security to prepare the annual report on form 10 – K, a document that contains financial statements. Form 10 – K requires disclosure of balance sheets as of the close of the last two fiscal years, income statements for the last two fiscal years, and statements of the sources and applications of funds for the last two fiscal years. The form also requires disclosure of a detailed description of the business, revenues contributed by each major class of products, and a discussion of competitive conditions; a tabular summary of operations and an analysis by management of the summary; the location and general character of important physical properties such as mines, plants, and mineral reserves; an analysis of oil and gas reserves, where applicable; pending legal proceedings; a list of all parent and subsidiary companies; increases and decreases in outstanding securities and indebtedness; the number of stockholders; the identities and ages of executive officers; the identities, backgrounds, and remunerations of directors; arrangements for the indemnification of directors and officers; stock options granted to management; and the interest of management and others in certain transactions. Both the New York and the American stock exchanges require that a similarly specific list of financial information be included. As long as this material is included, a company can do what it wants to with its annual report in the way of design and other content.

The SEC and the stock exchanges also require that annual reports be released to the public and the press on a certain time schedule. The SEC even goes so far as to specify the type used in annual reports, noting that it must "be in roman type at least as large and legible as 10 point modern type . . . leaded at least two points." This requirement assures that information vital to investors will not be overlooked.

A similarly detailed list of requirements applies to quarterly reports issued by companies.

Corporate Disclosures

Along with the release of annual and quarterly reports, financial public-relations people must handle the prompt preparation and distribution of information about dividend and interest action — or failure to take action, the calling of stockholder meetings, stockholder subscription rights, stock splits, and stock dividends.

Public Stock Offerings

When a company is preparing to offer shares to the public for the first time, it must disclose certain material information as a guide to shareholders and the investing public. It must not, however, initiate publicity or disseminate information that is promotional or misleading. Because of the confusion over what is legal and appropriate, financial PR people are best advised to consult the company legal staff regularly during the registration period.

When a stock is offered publicly, the SEC requires the preparation of a registration statement, usually on its form S–1, which includes a preliminary prospectus outlining information on the nature, structure, and finances of the company. These prospectuses must be written in a readable and understandable way and include material facts, even adverse ones. The material on the cover page must be reduced to a few key items. Information that makes the stock high-risk or speculative must be summarized in **boldface** type, and charts must be used along with text to explain complicated information.

A company cannot sell stock unless it has filed a registration statement with the SEC. After the filing date and before the effective date of the registration statement, the company cannot use any written communication to sell stock except the preliminary prospectus. No sales may be made during this time. After the effective date, no sales of the registered stock issue may be made without delivery of a final prospectus to the buyer. The SEC is very wary of any form of publicity that might tend to project optimism about the company in the minds of the investing public. Any kind of special corporate publicity will thus be considered part of the selling effort, for example, an advertising or publicity campaign not normally carried on by the corporation.

The company can carry on its normal publicity, however, by continuing to advertise products and services; by sending out customary quarterly, annual, and other periodic stockholder reports; by publishing proxy statements; by sending out dividend notices; by continuing to make announcements, as long as the announcements do not estimate how the developments will affect earnings or sales; by continuing to respond to unsolicited telephone inquiries by stockholders, financial analysts, and the press for factual information; by observing an "open door" policy in responding to unsolicited inquiries about factual matters; and by continuing to hold stockholder meetings as scheduled and to answer the inquiries of stockholders about factual matters.

Proxy Solicitation

State corporate laws and stock-exchange rules require that matters affecting the rights of stockholders in a corporation must be submitted to the stockholders for approval. The customary procedure to get such approval is through the solicitation of proxies for use at the annual stockholder meeting or any special stockholder meetings. As with stock offerings, the SEC has established defined communications requirements for such proxy solicitation.

The proxy statement informs stockholders about the nature of the solicitation and identifies the group soliciting the proxies. In contested solicitation campaigns, where both management and rival stockholder groups are trying to win stockholder approval for their proposals, each side can prepare material, but this material must be accurate and dignified. A broad range of approaches can be used to sway votes — for example, reprints of letters, newspaper reports, magazine articles, radio or television scripts, and special advertisements — as long as they have prior SEC approval. Similar commission approval in advance is necessary for news releases or statements to be made at press conferences as well as for speeches to be given at special stockholder meetings. During a period of proxy solicitation, a company may still issue news releases or other kinds of printed material about its business.

Tender Offers

When one company or individual tries to take over another company by making a tender offer to buy large blocks of stock, certain rules apply. Information about the proposed stock acquisition must be submitted to the SEC at the time the tender offer is first published and distributed to the holders of the securities. Anyone or any group owning more than five percent of stock must disclose their identities, backgrounds, citizenship, employment information, criminal conviction, and source of funds used — or to be used — in making the purchase, and purpose of the transaction. If the purpose is to gain control of the business, the person or group must reveal plans to make any changes in the business or corporate structure. As with proxy fights, the bidder and "target" in a tender offer may use material to persuade shareholders to tender or not to tender their shares. This material may include letters, advertisements, and the distribution of reprinted newspaper and magazine articles. Any such material must be cleared with legal counsel before it is published and distributed; it must not contain false or misleading statements.

ONE FINANCIAL PR MAN

Ted Michel can easily dissect his job into its component parts. As director of investor relations for Levi Strauss & Company, Michel works the segments every day. "Thirty-five percent of my time is spent with security analysts — an average of two analysts a week visit the company — or in planning and conducting outside group meetings or in handling phone calls from investment managers," he says. "I spend another twenty-five percent writing the annual report, the quarterly report, occasional press releases, and financially oriented speeches; twenty percent goes to keeping up on what is happening in the company; and twenty percent is difficult to pin down, like preparing budgets and other miscellaneous activities."

Michel's program has three major categories: liaison with the financial community, shareholder communications like quarterly and annual reports, and financial-press relations.

The contact with the investment community is very important. "Every effort is made to increase the number of analysts who actively follow Levi Strauss & Company, to augment their understanding of the company, and to win their support on the personal as well as the business level," writes Michel in a long-range investor-relations plan for the company. Methods include written materials and telephone and personal contacts.

Beyond the personal contacts with individual analysts and groups of analysts, Michel considers the press an important adjunct to his program. He encourages coverage of appearances by company officials before analyst organizations. It increases the impact of what is said and reenforces the importance of the sessions with those who attended.

If a member of management speaks at society meetings, press coverage will increase exposure of the company, as will briefings for local financial editors. News releases on financial matters not required by SEC disclosure regulations — for example, capital spending plans — can be effective.

Michel spends much of his time working with security analysts because these analysts recommend the purchase of company stock, an activity vital to the health of any public company. In addition to arranging visits by analysts, which usually involve meetings with himself and appropriate company officials and tours of facilities, Michel arranges meetings with groups of analysts in other cities in the United States and Europe.

In preparing information for release, Michel has one major advantage over his counterparts in other companies. "Levi Strauss tends to be a relatively open company," he says. "We give out more information than the average company of this size." Michel is aided in his work by the fact that he reports directly to the chief financial officer with dotted line responsibility to the chief executive and chief operating officers.

Michel begins work on the annual report in August with a memo outlining contents for the report, which will be issued the following February. An outside design agency actually designs the report, but Michel writes it. The agency prepares the cover and three sample "spreads" or facing-page layouts, and Michel reviews them with company officers.

Beyond the SEC requirements for material to be included, Michel pays close attention to the writing. "The most important thing about business communication is clarity," he says. "Clear writing is better than lacing the report with a lot of metaphors. An ideal annual report is one which anyone with a working knowledge of business can read and understand the company in general and also have some perspective about what happened the previous year. We carry the same theme through each section. In writing the president's letter, I assume that the reader may not read anything else so I try to hit all significant issues concisely, the shorter the better."

In the occasional news releases he writes, Michel tries to be as clear as possible. "The *Wall Street Journal* does the best job," he says, "so I pattern my writing on theirs. What you have to avoid in a release is opacity. You must be very clear and watch for ambiguity."

Michel also prepares a company fact book for external distribution to supplement the annual report and form 10 – K as source material. The fact book will contain additional charts, a product-market list, a company history, and executive biographies. When a new analyst begins to follow the company, Michel prepares an information kit for him or her. It includes the last three annual reports, year-to-date quarterly reports, 10 – Ks, editorial reprints, and recent proxy material.

Michel enjoys his work in financial public relations. "You should not think of yourself as solely serving the corporation," he says. "You have a responsibility to those outside as well as those within. You also have to be able to talk to anybody. If you have to go into the president and say, 'the quarterly report is coming out, what should we say,' you're in big trouble. You shouldn't tell the president what to say, but you should be ready to suggest a general approach as well as interpret current financial community expectations. Integrity is your most important quality. You should be just as informative about the negatives as the positives. You also should treat all analysts equally, big and small."

SUMMARY

Financial public relations differs from regular public relations in the audiences addressed, the material presented to these audiences, and the official requirements for preparing the material. The audiences for financial public-relations work are potential investors, current holders of company stock, security analysts, and the financial press. Financial public relations has grown because of increased Securities and Exchange Commission and stock-exchange requirements for disclosing corporate development, particularly since the 1968 court rulings in the Texas Gulf Sulphur case and the decline in the number of security analysts due to the collapse of the stock-market boom of the 1960s. The work done by financial public-relations people, who are also called investor-relations or corporate-relations specialists, includes the preparation of annual reports and quarterly reports as well as material about corporate financial disclosures, public stock offerings, proxy solicitations, and tender offers.

PR FOCUS: SOME FINANCIAL AND BUSINESS TERMS

If you think a convertible debenture is some kind of new car, you may not belong in financial public relations. Because much of the job involves dealing with new and sometimes difficult-to-understand terms, some definitions are in order.

annual report — a printed report issued once a year in which a company or other organization reveals financial and other information about itself; required by federal regulation for all companies issuing stock.

assets — the things a company owns with positive dollar value.

bear market — when prices for securities are going down and there are few purchases of them.

blue-chip stock — common stock of old, established companies that are profitable and pay dividends regardless of economic conditions.

bond — a certificate of debt due to be paid by a government or corporation to an individual holder and usually bearing a fixed rate of interest.

boom — a time in the business cycle during which business activity is high.

bull market — when prices for securities are rising and purchase of them is at a high level.

business cycle — the phases of business activity over a long period of time including boom, decline, recession or depression, recovery.

common stock — a certificate signifying ownership of common stock in a corporation; the value of all shares is equal and stockholders have the same rights; common stockholders have voting rights and a right to the corporation's earnings.

debenture — a corporate bond unsecured by any mortgage, dependent on the credit of the issuer.

dividend — a sum of money paid to shareholders of a corporation out of its earnings.

finance — the management or transaction of money matters.

interest — a sum charged for borrowed money.

investors — those who put money in something offering profitable returns.

liabilities — the claims of outsiders against a company; what is owed by the company.

material information — important facts about a company, the public knowledge of which sends its stock up or down.

merger — the combination of two or more business enterprises into a single enterprise.

par value — the value printed on stock certificates.

portfolio — the group of securities owned by an individual or a company.

preferred stock — a certificate that shows ownership in a corporation but the holders of this stock usually cannot vote their shares as with common stock; stock that earns a fixed percentage paid before common stock payment is made.

prospectus — a summary of a company's stock registration statement filed with the SEC, including information about the company, its operations, its management, and the purpose of the proposed issuance of stock.

proxy — a person appointed to represent another person in voting, usually at a stockholders' meeting; the document assigning the transfer of that representation from one person to another.

quarterly report — the report of a company's earnings issued four times a year.

recession — a period in the business cycle when business activity is in decline.

recovery — a period in the business cycle after a recession, when business activity is expanding.

security — an evidence of debt or of property, as a bond or a certificate of stock.

security analyst — one who analyzes companies in order to recommend the purchase of their stock.

Securities and Exchange Commission (SEC) — the federal government agency that controls the operation of stock exchanges, stock brokerage firms, and corporations whose securities are publicly traded.

share — one of the equal parts into which the capital stock of a corporation is divided.

shareholders — holders or owners of shares, especially of a corporation (see stockholders).

stockholders — persons who own the common and/or preferred stock of a corporation (see shareholders).

stock market — the trading in securities, especially stocks, throughout a nation.

stock split — an action that gives a stockholder more shares but keeps his or her same proportional ownership in the corporation.

tender offer — an offer to buy a large number of shares of a company's stock to gain control; often the action is unwanted by the company whose shares are being purchased.

10 – K — a form required by the SEC to be used by a company as its annual report and containing financial information about the company.

REVIEW QUESTIONS

1. How does financial public relations differ from general public relations?
2. What was the Texas Gulf Sulphur case, and how did it affect the growth of financial public relations?
3. What is an annual report, and what part does a financial PR person play in its preparation?
4. What are some of the other requirements a financial PR person must fulfill in working on corporate disclosures, stock offerings, proxy solicitations, and tender offers?
5. How does Ted Michel's job at Levi Strauss differ from the regular public-relations jobs described earlier in this book?

ASSIGNMENTS

For Journalism Students

1. Analyze the financial news release of a company and compare it to a more general news release. How do the two differ? How are they the same?

2. Analyze an annual report of a large corporation in terms of its various parts, its writing style, the general information contained in it, and the financial information contained in it.

3. You are the financial PR person for a medium-size baby-food company that is about to be taken over by a large tobacco conglomerate owned by an unscrupulous and mysterious billionaire with reported underworld connections. Prepare a list of arguments for your boss to present to stockholders to stave off this tender offer.

4. Now become the financial PR person for the unscrupulous billionaire and prepare reasons the takeover would be beneficial to the baby-food company.

For Business Students

1. Analyze the annual report of a large corporation and make a list of the things you learned about the company by reading the report. How clearly is information presented?

2. Read the president's letter from two annual reports and determine if information about the companies is clearly and completely presented. Make a list of what you learned from both, and compare the two.

3. You are the president of a medium-size paint company about to be taken over by a large chemical corporation. Prepare a list of ways to avoid the takeover that you can give to your financial PR person, using the list of actions allowed by the SEC noted in this chapter.

CHAPTER **9**

Public relations and management

The relationship established between public-relations people and the members of management they must report to is a crucial one. Without the approval of corporate officials, neither company public-relations people nor PR-agency account personnel can do their jobs.

The process of getting the necessary approval and cooperation begins when a PR person accepts the corporate position or agency account, and it never really stops. This process requires constant attention not only to whatever PR problem the practitioner has been hired to solve, but to the company executive's understanding of the entire public-relations profession.

"The work you do in public relations is totally controlled by how the president and board chairman view the PR function," says Robert Neale, eastern public-relations director for Chrysler. "Make sure the decision makers in the company understand the constituents they are dealing with and the need to communicate," adds William Jones, manager of corporate communications at Standard Oil of California. "With particular constituents, the problems you run into sometimes come from the failure of management to think of the implications of their actions. You have to bring things to their attention. PR is not part of the normal mental process."

HOW TO WORK WITH MANAGEMENT

Although the situation varies with the backgrounds and philosophies of the people involved, it is possible to develop a list of rules that will help PR people and managers understand one another and work together. This list applies to both company PR people and agency PR practitioners. The agency people will probably have an easier time gaining access to executives because they are usually not taken for granted in the same way in-house PR people are.

Report as High as Possible

"If you report to the top, you can give advice and get answers fast," says Neale. "I have no hesitancy to call all the top officers at home. They know I wouldn't call if it wasn't necessary." As noted earlier in this book, access to the highest officials in the company also enhances the prestige of public relations elsewhere in the company and with the outside world.

Be Involved in Everything

Once a PR person has the desired entree to the higher realms of the company, he or she should make public relations a part of all aspects of corporate affairs. "Without being obnoxious or pushy, make sure you're involved in every facet," says Ted Weber, executive vice president of McGraw-Hill and its former PR director. "You need to get to know the financial and operations people. They'll be available to you if you need information."

Meet Regularly

After this high-level access is established, it is a good idea for PR people to meet regularly with members of management, both to gain information and to work out public-relations plans for normal company affairs or the occasional crisis. Standard Oil of California, for example, has a Public Affairs Committee that meets once a month.

Be Persistent, Not Pushy

"When management wants something done, the PR person has to understand the rationale behind it," continues Jones. "Don't take a 'no' if you can't do your job without knowing." Adds Weber: "You can't be afraid to speak up to executives. The best of them make mistakes and draw erroneous conclusions. The PR person has to be sure of himself enough to say, 'This is not the way to do it.'"

Prepare Carefully

The opportunity to meet regularly with company executives to gain information and to give advice should not be wasted. "You've got to do your homework," says James Lamb, manager of public relations at Xerox. "You don't

walk into an executive's office without knowing what you're talking about."
This means that a PR person is familiar not only with the subject to be discussed that day but knows all there is to know about the company's business.
It may mean, too, that a PR person finds out personal information about the
executive to prepare for the small talk that will start the conversation off on
a smooth basis — common interests in sports or hobbies, recent trips, family
information, for example.

Be Realistic

Public-relations people should never oversell their programs or promise results
that simply cannot be achieved. They will only do themselves — and the PR
profession as a whole — a disservice. "Being realistic about what can be accomplished is best," says Thomas Nunan, a vice president of Burson-Marsteller.
"You know how you did on past projects. You can really measure the results
of a PR effort and why some things work, some do not."

Be a PR Counsel, Not a "Flack"

The ideas a public-relations person presents to management should fit the company and the situation. If the company is somewhat flamboyant, the ideas
presented might be in the same vein. If the company is more conservative, the
plans and programs should mirror that philosophy, unless executives are trying
to alter that image. A PR counsel, by the very definition of that word, gives
well-reasoned, sound advice. To do otherwise is to be unprofessional.

Understand the Problems of Management

"Uneasy lies the head that wears a crown." William Shakespeare was right
in *Henry IV*. And the same statement applies to company officials. It is not
easy to manage a large corporation or a company of any size, for that matter.
Corporate officials have other problems to contend with than those of a public-
relations nature. Sales of the product, the relationship with government, the
relationships with the board of directors and stockholders — all these areas and
others might at times present problems more pressing than those involving
public relations. A PR person may have to wait in line to get answers and
approval for the things he or she wants to do. If that PR person is a true
counsel, however, he or she will be consulted about things other than those of
a strict PR nature.

Get Things in Writing

An earlier chapter dealt with the importance of preparing a PR plan. Such a plan forms the overall philosophical base for a solid relationship with management. On a more day-to-day level, however, it is a good idea for PR people to write regular reports about what they are doing and what has been decided in their meetings with management. The memos need not be long and detailed or another example of too much paperwork. They do provide good reference material, however.

Help Management to Understand the Press

A smooth relationship with the press helps a company's public relations more than any other factor. Whether members of management or the PR staff like to admit it or not, the press — both print and electronic — has the power to make a company and its officials look good or bad. The power may be wrongly placed with the press at times, but it is there and the sooner a PR person makes members of management realize this, the better off the company will be. "You must impress on management the value of dealing directly and forthrightly with the media," says R. E. Parr, manager of news services at Atlantic Richfield, "and in building faith in them in the media. You've got to get them not to look at the media as the perpetual enemy, out to do them in at every turn." One important way to lessen management suspicion or hostility toward the press is get the two sides together regularly, after carefully preparing the manager for the encounter. "You have to have the ability to deal with people on the management side and on the media side and overcome what might be deficiencies in their character."

A PR person must know both the reporter and the manager well to do so. Adds James Lamb of Xerox: "When the press asks to talk to your president or board chairman or executive vice president, find out what they want to talk about. They will give you subject areas. Then you can go in to the executives and prepare them. You can tell them what the reporter has written before and the proclivities of the reporter, that is, whether they love to zing you or have a dedication to accuracy. The nice thing about dealing with the press is that their track record is published. Also, it is important to remember, there are no command performances. You can say to a reporter, 'The executive declines to talk to you.'" When the process works, however, it can be helpful to both company and press. "Sometimes," concludes Parr of Atlantic Richfield, "the executives get to like to see their names in print."

HOW MANAGEMENT CAN WORK WITH PUBLIC RELATIONS

The interaction between members of a company's management staff and the public-relations department works both ways. These are suggestions that help managers deal effectively with PR people.

Know the Value of Public Relations

"Management has to realize that their public-relations department can be very, very helpful," says Walter Morris, a vice president of Standard Oil of California. "Management should use a PR department to establish the credibility and legitimacy of the business in communication and recognize that PR is a two-way street — what goes out will come back inside." The days are over when companies can adopt a "public be damned" attitude à la Commodore Vanderbilt. A successful interaction between the company and any number of its publics is crucial to its success in the marketplace.

Contact PR People Regularly, Not Just in a Crisis

"Don't lean on PR people to get you out of trouble," continues Morris. "In the worst case, you call in a PR man and say, 'Hey, Joe, we've got a problem. Get us out of it.' The day of glossing over and covering up doesn't exist any more. And you're not going to get around problems by hiring a PR staff when it is too late. You won't get anybody who is highly professional to stay very long. PR people can help you, but you have to be candid and honest and give them the full story."

Use PR People to Understand and Work with the Press

This means that executives should be accessible to their PR people at all times. "Executives must make a conscious effort to understand the role of the press," says Ted Weber of McGraw-Hill. "You have to avoid an adversary attitude. You can't refuse to cooperate and then complain that the press doesn't print the right story. Find out why the company has terrible press relations. There are probably unique circumstances, the product of a philosophy that does not value the role of the press in finding out about a company's business operation."

Standard Oil sends its executives to school to help them deal with reporters, particularly those from television. "TV is more difficult because there is that certain traumatic fear associated with it," continues Morris. Several years ago, the company hired the J. Walter Thompson advertising agency to train executives so that they would not fear their television appearances. Three hundred executives have attended a three-day course during which adversary press-executive situations are simulated. "We make it as tough as we can," says Morris. "The first thing we do is an interview on a hypothetical talk show. We teach them how to sit, how to cross their legs, how to answer questions, how to bridge one point to another. We teach them to be honest and give every bit of information they possibly can and make sure the reporter understands what they are trying to say." The same techniques apply to the printed press. With both the electronic and print media, Standard Oil teaches its executives that nothing is ever really "off the record."

Use PR People as Eyes and Ears

"There is no question that management is isolated," says Morris. "They read newspapers, but that's what they have PR people for, to help them keep up." This help applies to gaining information both inside and outside the company. A PR person can aid a high-level executive in knowing what is going on in a faraway plant as well as at the local press club. This process need not be a spy operation. It is only common sense to avoid the isolation that comes with being in management to the extent that it is possible to avoid it. "PR people can be the antenna to pick up what's going on 'out there' in matters of public opinion, the mood of the country," says Morris. "Let them pick up these signals and interpret them for you."

Know the Limitations of Public Relations

There is no substitute for sound public-relations advice in dealing with the various publics and problems a company encounters. A dedicated, enthusiastic, experienced, and reliable PR director who has common sense in handling problems is invaluable to an executive and a company. "They've got to be ingenious because you can't always turn to page 28 of a textbook for the answers," says Morris. But the value of public relations cannot be overrated. A major mistake will not go away like magic even with the best PR person working to ease its effects. Black will not become white by the wave of a PR wand. In solving a seemingly insurmountable company problem, good public relations may help, but it is no panacea. Other factors must come into play as well. Rabbits come out of hats only for magicians. PR people are far from being magicians.

SUMMARY

Public-relations people cannot function without a smooth relationship with the members of management for whom they work. The process of gaining the approval and acceptance needed to function begins when the PR person accepts the job or agency account, and it never really stops. The process requires constant attention not only to whatever PR problem the practitioner has been hired to solve, but also to the company executive's understanding of the entire PR profession. Other rules that help a PR person work successfully with members of management involve reporting to people as high as possible in the company, being involved in everything, meeting regularly, being persistent, preparing carefully, being realistic, being a PR counsel, understanding the problems of management, getting things in writing, and helping management understand the press. For their part, members of management can work well with public-relations people if they know the value of public relations, contact PR people regularly and not only in a crisis, use PR people to understand the press, use PR people as their eyes and ears, and know the limitations of PR.

PR FOCUS: WHAT TO TELL THE BOSS ABOUT JOURNALISM

Winning the support of a somewhat conservative corporate executive for open and frequent contacts with reporters is a difficult task. Lectures on the merits of a free press and the First Amendment will be lost on someone who thinks that the press hounded Richard Nixon from office, or who was burned in his or her last interview with a reporter.

The interchange between executive and reporter might be helped, however, if the executive understands a few basic things about the press as noted in some common journalistic terms. Although a PR person cannot actually "lecture" an executive about journalism, it might be helpful to explain the basic workings of the profession from time to time.

advertising — paid printed and broadcast messages that try to sell products by stressing their advantages.
assignment — the instructions a reporter gets on what to cover.
attribution — the source of a story, usually noted in the first paragraph.
background — information that helps a reporter write a story but that might not appear in the story.
beat — the part of the publication's service area covered by a reporter on a regular basis, for example, business.
by-line — the name of the reporter who wrote the story, usually noted at the beginning under the headline.
civil libel — printed and published defamation of a person, written maliciously

and falsely, that results in those responsible paying damages; executives
have a tendency to threaten to sue reporters for civil libel when they write
distasteful things about them, an action that should be discouraged by
PR people.

copy — the stories written for publication.

copy editor — an editor who edits reporters' stories and writes the headlines
for them.

criminal libel — libel that results in a breach of the peace.

deadline — the time when the final version of a story is due; the time you as
a PR person cannot ignore if you want your news releases to appear.

editorializing — inserting opinion into a news story or a feature story as opposed to a clearly labeled editorial; something to keep executives from
doing as they rewrite news releases in rough-draft form.

exclusive — a story that only one reporter knows; something to avoid granting
very often lest all other reporters covering the company get angry.

features — stories about people, places, or things that are less tied to the day's
news.

First Amendment — the amendment to the United States Constitution that ensures freedom of the press; very important to reporters and editors.

follow-up — a story that appears the day after a news event to provide new
information.

handout — a news release or other printed material given by PR people to
the press for direct use or background.

hard news — news that is current, happening today, as opposed to *soft news*.

headline — large, bold type appearing over stories to catch attention; headlines
are not written by reporters but by copy editors.

interview — the discussion between a reporter and a source that results in information for a story.

lead — the first paragraph of a story.

mug shot — a photograph of a person's head and shoulders that usually appears in a small size.

news peg — the reason to publish a story; the element an executive must have
in mind in suggesting that a PR person call in a reporter or write a news
release.

news release — a story, written by the company, to give its view of an event,
that the PR people of the company hope the publication will publish; it
will not be used unless it has real substance; also called *press release*.

news source — the people who give reporters their story ideas and stories.

not for attribution — information whose source cannot be revealed in the story
but whose substance can be included; not to be confused with *off the
record*.

off the record — material from interviews that serves only as background and
that cannot be used in print; not to be confused with *not for attribution*.

photojournalism — using photographs to tell a story.

press — printed publications, like newspapers and magazines, considered as a whole.

press release — the "release" of information to the press; also called *news release*.

public relations — promoting goodwill toward a company by printed or other means; known also as *PR;* that which the executive is paying you to do; not to be considered "free advertising."

quotes — the words of an interview subject set off by quotation marks (") when used in a story.

reporter — a person who gathers material by interviews and other research, and who writes news and feature stories; not an enemy to all corporate executives.

rewriting — editing stories to improve them; that which will be done to news releases and the speeches of corporate executives before they appear in print.

soft news — stories that are not always timely but that are interesting and informative nevertheless; features are usually considered "soft" news, while news stories are "hard" news.

style — the way publications want their stories to be written in terms of abbreviation, spelling, capitalization, etc.

PR FOCUS: WHAT PR PEOPLE SHOULD KNOW ABOUT MANAGEMENT

A *manager* is a person who works through other people, called *subordinates,* who perform operative tasks. A manager brings their efforts together to accomplish goals.

Management is the process of managing, a collection of managers, or an area of study. Management is necessary in an organization that seeks to accomplish objectives. Without it, an organization becomes a collection of individuals, each going in his or her own direction with no unifying guidance toward organizational goals.

Managerial work is decision making. Everything a company does is the result of decisions made by managers.

These basic ideas on management come from John A. Reinecke and William F. Schoell in *Introduction to Business* (Boston: Allyn and Bacon, 1980, chapter 5). They are important to any basic understanding of business and management by public-relations people.

PR people will find three levels of management with which they will work: top management (board of directors, chairmen, president, executive vice presidents, vice presidents); middle management (department heads, plant managers, plant superintendent); lower management (foremen and supervisors). They will probably work most often with the first two levels.

Managerial work includes planning (preparing for the future and setting objectives over different time periods and deciding on methods to achieve them); organizing (relating people, tasks, and resources to each other so the organization can meet its objectives); staffing (recruiting, selecting, training, and promoting people to fill both managerial and operating positions in a company); directing (encouraging subordinates to work toward achieving company objectives by proper communication with them and through leadership of them); and controlling (monitoring operations to see if goals are being reached).

A public-relations person can interact with members of management in all these areas and help them accomplish each task. The skills of managers and PR people mesh well if given the opportunity to do so.

"Businesses are living things that seek to accomplish objectives," write Reinecke and Schoell (p. 176). Proper management, which the authors call "partly an art and a science," helps reach these objectives.

REVIEW QUESTIONS

1. Can a PR person function without the cooperation of management?
2. Is it realistic to expect a corporate official to understand public relations and how it functions?
3. Can any of the rules for successfully working with management be skipped? Why? Why not?
4. Can any of the rules for management to use in working well with PR people be avoided?
5. How important is public relations to the successful management of a company?

ASSIGNMENTS

For Journalism Students

1. You are a PR person and you have just been called to a meeting with the new president of your company. He says that he knows the company's past public-relations policy has been terrible, and he wants you to bring along some suggestions to improve them. Prepare a short presentation for him.
2. Using the information in this chapter, prepare a series of guidelines for managers in the successful use of public relations.
3. Write an essay on the topic, "I Am a PR Counsel, Not a Flack." Make sure to give examples that indicate the difference between the two.

For Business Students

1. Write an essay on the topic, "Managers Need PR People in Order to Manage."
2. Write an essay on the topic, "Managers Do Not Need PR People in Order to Manage."
3. Write an essay that either (1) challenges the validity of, or (2) accepts the truth of, the list of rules in this chapter for working successfully with PR people.

Working with agency clients

Regis McKenna forgets that he is a public-relations person when he is dealing with the officials of the companies who are the clients of his agency. "In the industrial and electronics industry," says the agency president, "it is unlikely that the public-relations manager moves up to marketing manager or any other directing management spot in a company. Why? Because he or she is not specifically educated or trained, and second, because the position is generally considered a 'dissected' corporate activity."

It is not that in-house PR people are not skilled professionals. In some cases, they are as good as the agency people who are brought in from the outside. It is just that many company executives seem to think that their own PR staffs are best given the easy tasks, like writing news releases and planting stories in trade publications. They call on agency people for help in setting policy and strategy. Understandably, this causes resentment among the in-house people.

AIMING FOR THE TOP

The best way to succeed as an agency public-relations counsel is to deal with the client on as high a management level as possible. The same is true for in-house PR people, although they do not always have the same success at high-level access. "You've got to report as high as you can," says George Hobgood, a senior vice president of Hill and Knowlton. "The lower you report in, the more problems you'll have. If you deal with a client on a high level, that shows everyone else that high management participated in and endorsed your project. You can also get decisions made in a hurry by a chief executive officer while it takes longer on lower levels. Less and less justification is needed."

It is also best to report to as few people in the client company as possible. This speeds decisions and simplifies the working relationship. Cooperation by important officials does not mean that they understand the work of public rela-

146

tions, however. "I don't think they like anyone messing around in their business," says Hobgood.

Once agency public-relations people have the attention and cooperation of high-level officials in their client corporations, they should not abuse the privilege. They need to be prepared to deal with these officials and not waste their time. "If you're dealing with a marketing vice president," says Thomas Nunan, a vice president of Burson-Marsteller, "you've got to try to be an effective part of the marketing team. It's a question of doing your homework so you know the markets the company is in. Top management expects good ideas that are well executed and a measure of results when possible."

But the going is not always that easy. "If you can relate results to money spent, you're lucky," says Jeff Clausen of Marx, Knoll & Mangels. "Unfortunately, you can't always measure it. How much value does a client get out of a full-page article in a trade publication? How do you tell? You have to convince management there's a need for doing such things, however."

John Pihas tries to understand the decision-making process in the companies his agency deals with. "There are some chief executive officers who really don't care what the public might think or what their employees might think," says the president of Pihas, Schmidt, Westerdahl Company in Portland. "Others are in tune."

It is extremely important for the public-relations agency account executive to know the difference between these two extremes of thought. "You've got to know or be 180 degrees away," Pihas continues. "You've got to try to be one-to-one with the chief executive. You take him to lunch and talk confidentially, at least once a month. Being a communications vent is not enough." To Pihas, this means having an understanding of what those executives want to do. It also means talking their language. "If you can't talk about things like net earnings after taxes, the executive is soon going to ask, 'Why did I pay $35,000 for that communication?' So many PR people are too glib. You've got to cut the show biz. You're in business."

OVERCOMING AN INFERIORITY COMPLEX THROUGH KNOWLEDGE

Once an agency public-relations person has got the attention and confidence of management, he or she must overcome a tendency to feel inferior to all the managers and engineers who have to be dealt with. The task is not always easy. "Few industrial companies see public relations as an integral part of the corporate strategy or the marketing plan," continues Regis McKenna. "Few see public relations as the positioning of the company or a product line, the setting out of strategies for announcing products or developing a company's recognition in new markets."

Because many corporate officials have this view of public relations, agency people who work with them must take the initiative and not be relegated to any lesser status. An in-house public-relations person might have to take such treatment, but an agency person does not. An agency is brought in to provide extra help, and if the advice of its experts is not taken, it might as well resign the account.

The way to avoid such castigation is knowledge — of the corporation, its products, its problems, its goals, and the personalities and backgrounds of the officials being dealt with. "You've got to be knowledgeable about the business your clients are in," says McKenna. That way, a public-relations person can sit at the same table as other department heads and talk about the business intelligently and be viewed as making a genuine contribution.

The process involves becoming an expert not only in communications but in the business, markets, products, and the place in the industry of the company concerned. "You have to rise above the daily tasks of getting out the next release or article and immerse yourself in a long-term, self-imposed education program," says McKenna. "Public-relations people should act if they were editors within the company. Find out what's going on. Ask marketing and product marketing to include you in strategy-making and review sessions. Take a marketing manager to lunch once a week and ask him to educate you. Always write a communications plan before implementing a program. Include a review of the market situation, the competition, the strategy, and objectives."

As their work becomes acceptable to corporate officials, agency public-relations people must be careful not to alienate the internal PR staff. In-house people are naturally going to resent it when company officials bring in an "outsider" to do what they think they should be doing. The best approach is to make friends with the people and establish a feeling of mutual trust and a "we're all in this together" attitude. If this fails, agency people should ignore the in-house PR people and *never* fight openly with them.

TEN WAYS TO KEEP ON TOP OF THINGS

McKenna uses ten ways to keep up with the affairs of businesses he is serving.

1. Keep a daily notebook or log in which you write everything down that deals with the account.
2. Develop a list of ten or twenty key editors and industry contacts, and maintain frequent contact with them.
3. Read a limited number of journals, primarily ones that are business and marketing oriented.
4. Use a clipping service to keep up with the great number of publications that might use the material prepared by you about your client.
5. Keep your management informed by passing along to them relevant and helpful items, documents, articles, and reports.

6. Get access to financial and industry reports, such as those from financial analysts and research firms like A. D. Little, and the annual reports of competing companies.
7. Ask for copies of internal documents like marketing plans, status reports, and annual and quarterly reports.
8. Use the telephone to talk to an editor a day, to customers, and as a way to expand your contact list.
9. Travel to other cities to meet with members of the press with or without officials of your client company; editors and reporters of some publications will never visit the company so the next best thing is taking the information to them.
10. Keep communication files including financial and industry reports; clippings and articles; information on markets, products, the industry, the competition, and corporate background history. Such files provide background for editors and help you prepare strategies and plans.

Having done all these things to become informed about a client, a public-relations person is in a better position to help that client solve its PR problems. "You must really give the client tangible evidence in its terms about why good communication is important," says McKenna.

THE ROLE OF THE PR COUNSEL

After the public-relations agency person has gained the confidence of officials in the client company on as high a level as possible, and learned as much as possible about the company and its products, the next step is to begin giving advice to help solve public-relations problems or to avoid them. In this, the PR person is acting in much the same way a lawyer does.

Even if things develop well in the agency-client relationship, problems can develop. "Unfortunately, the very people who hire public-relations people have a distorted view," continues McKenna. "As a result, the public-relations people find they spend much of their time discussing what their role is or should be within the company." He thinks people often bring in PR people merely to deal with the media: to receive but not necessarily to respond to editorial inquiries, to write and place technical articles, to influence the media to write good things about the company and its products, and to issue press releases, "the content of which is generally prescribed by marketing, engineering, or management," he says.

While media relations are important, they form only one aspect of public-relations activities. The role of a good public-relations counsel consists of a number of important criteria.

Understanding Expectations

This understanding comes from constant questioning of management and marketing people inside the company, and people like editors from the outside, according to McKenna. The answers to these questions will establish an understanding of what the people both inside and outside the company expect PR to accomplish. Although PR people cannot meet every expectation, it helps them work better to know what they are.

Representing Editors

"To the editorial community you represent your company," continues McKenna, "but to your management you must represent the press. In this role you must act as an inquisitor," finding out everything about the company. PR people must also tell members of management how the press will view the company, the new product, or the company action. "They must be aware of the task PR has to accomplish," he says. "If you perform this role well, you can only gain respect from both management and the press."

Being Honest

To McKenna, PR people must be honest with themselves, with management in respect to the viewpoint of the press, and with the press. "If you don't know something, say so," McKenna continues. "If you need to do more homework, say so. Your company's product may be the best in performance, but the press may see it as an 'also-ran.' Your management must understand that a PR person can never, never mislead the press. This does not mean 'telling all.' It does mean that a communication strategy must take into account facing up to difficult situations, having confidence in a long-range partnership with the press, and knowing when to be silent."

Homework — Yours and Others'

Although it is not possible — or expected — that a PR person have all the answers, he or she must try to keep up with developments within the company. This information will provide the basis for developing a written communications plan that includes strategy, objectives, a timetable, and a budget to accomplish the task. Helping others do their homework is more difficult, according to McKenna. The press wants to hear directly from management, but most managers do not know how to deal with the press. PR people can prepare managers to meet the press by getting them to think before they speak, and by giving them as much written material as possible to help them get ready and to have an idea of what reporters want.

Planning

McKenna thinks that this is one of the most difficult tasks PR people have to perform because, he says, "they often lack visibility within the scheme of things. Most companies have a business plan and may even go so far as to make a yearly marketing plan. Without the guidance of those two plans, public relations loses its meaning." In return for this information, PR people must insert themselves into the affairs of the business and insist that all marketing plans contain a communications strategy and plan.

SUMMARY

The best way to succeed as an agency public-relations counsel — or in any PR position, for that matter — is to deal with the client or as high a management level as possible. In this way, PR people can get decisions made more quickly with less justification necessary. Once PR people have the attention of top officials, however, they should not abuse the privilege by being unprepared. They should go into such meetings with a thorough understanding of the company, its products, its officials, its competition, and the industry. This knowledge provides a better framework upon which to build a workable PR program.

In encounters with officials from specialized and technical areas of the company, PR people should not feel intimidated or inferior. They must be prepared to justify the worth of their proposal, and insist on its inclusion in the overall management philosophy of the company. The best way to succeed in such an effort is to develop ways of getting information to help the client. There is a definite role for a PR person to plan in a company and it is, at its best, the role of counsel offering sound advice to solve problems in much the same way a lawyer does.

PR FOCUS: FINDING A CORPORATE IDENTITY THROUGH SYMBOLS

One of Hill and Knowlton's services to clients is its corporate identity program. Companies, organizations, and institutions increasingly seek to establish and maintain a clear identity. Corporations, often complex in structure and diversified in operations, find it particularly important that their identity be communicated to the investment community, the news media, government, the public, and their own shareholders and employees in a clear and convincing way.

A corporate identity program includes the development of a logo, or visual identifier, and the implementation of its use. The program begins with internal and external research to determine how the company is viewed by employees and outsiders. This research is then analyzed to find out what it means and in what direction it seems to be pointing for solution. Recommendations and the formulation of objectives come next, followed by the working out of design criteria. In the next phase, Hill and Knowlton experts conduct a visual audit of the client's graphic materials to determine if they are consistent with the proposed new image. It also determines if there are any inconsistencies in the organizational structure. A number of designs are then prepared and presented to the client for review, and a final design is selected. The new design is then placed on all company stationery, checks, forms, signs, literature, and every other appropriate form. Company employees are also given printed guidelines to aid in the continuation of the program.

In one case, Hill and Knowlton experts helped the Dennison Manufacturing Company change its image from that of an old-line stationery firm to one that reflects its new acquisitions using physics, optics, chemistry, and electronics in a broad range of systems and products. No one understood the changes in the company or the marketing organization that had been developed. Hill and Knowlton defined five key market groups for Dennison and developed an overall corporate identifier in a contemporary framework. A graphic system was then worked out using that identifier in order to communicate the new market-oriented approach of the corporation.

For the Lutheran Mutual Life Insurance Company, Hill and Knowlton recommended a new corporate symbol that helped it change its identity from a small fraternal society founded 100 years before to a rapidly growing national organization that is among the top ten percent of life insurance companies in size. The new symbol reflects the company's desire to make clear its rural heritage and commitment to service.

The Kuwait-based Alghanim Industries, Inc. is one of the largest privately held corporations in the Middle East, primarily a trading company. Its owners wanted a new name and new identity that recognized the company's change into a westernized international marketing and manufacturing organization while keeping an orientation to its Middle East origins. Hill and Knowlton experts suggested a new name that they felt incorporated the essence of industrialization and modern technology yet kept the equity of the original name. The corporate identifier was designed to incorporate the new name, indicate the company's new global scope, but reflect the Middle East origins.

Analysis

There is more than one way for an agency to serve its clients. Corporate identity help is an "extra" of the kind that smaller agencies cannot provide. In an era where instant recognition of symbols or logos can make or break a product, such assistance is useful. It is also intangible and difficult to measure. How can anyone say for certain that the sales of a product went up or down because customers or potential customers liked or did not like the corporate symbol as it appeared on the sales literature or the product package?

REVIEW QUESTIONS

1. Is there more to public relations than getting the client's name in print? What are the main purposes of public relations?
2. What is the best way to prepare for meetings with high officials of your client company? How can you gather the information you need to get ready?
3. How can a public-relations person assert himself or herself in meetings with technical people of a client company and not feel inferior to them?
4. Are there any other ways to keep up with the affairs of a client company than those listed in this chapter?
5. Is it realistic for a public-relations person to think of himself or herself as a counsel — in the same way a lawyer is viewed?
6. Is the advice of a PR person as important as that given by a lawyer? Why? Why not?
7. How would you justify the work of a PR person serving the clients of an agency?

ASSIGNMENTS

For Journalism Students

1. You are a PR-agency account executive getting ready to have your first meeting with a new client, the president of a large corporation who has hired you to carry on general public-relations activities. Compile an agenda of what you want to discuss with this important client.
2. Prepare a short position paper that justifies the role of public relations agencies and why they are important to companies.
3. Select a major corporation and carry out as many of the "10 ways to keep on top of things" as possible on that company. Present your findings to the class.
4. Imagine that you are the agency account executive for a company whose major product is glass for tall buildings. You have planned a PR campaign around the opening of a new building, but the glass has begun to "pop out" and fall on pedestrians below. Organize the arguments you

will present to management to improve the resultant bad public image of the company.

5. You are the **PR** account executive for a manufacturing company client and your major new idea — building a youth center in a ghetto — has just backfired. The youths have burned down the new building even before it opened. Prepare a written justification of the original idea, and ways to offset the negative publicity resulting from the fire.

For Business Students

1. You are the president of a large corporation about to meet the **PR**-agency account executive you have just hired to do general public-relations activities. Compile an agenda of what you want this **PR** person to do.

2. Do you need public-relations help? Put yourself behind the desk of a company president and prepare a short position paper arguing for, or against, the need for public relations.

3. Take the role of "devil's advocate" and argue against each of the criteria listed in this chapter.

4. Take the same list and insert the role of the corporate executive in each area as a help to the public-relations person.

CHAPTER 11

Public relations and government

Government touches many lives in this country, not the least of which are those of people in the public-relations departments of companies that must deal with government agencies.

Few large corporations are without government contracts of one kind or another, although the scope of the individual contracts is much less than in the height of the missile race in the late 1950s and early 1960s or the space program of the 1960s. In order to get these contracts, companies have to agree to abide by certain rules on releasing information to the press, and they have to furnish certain information to the government as well. The system is a complex one fraught with complications and frustrations.

Companies also employ lobbyists both to help them get such contracts in the first place and to keep up with the day-to-day activities of governments at all levels. Any consideration of public relations and government must begin with a look at lobbying.

HOW A LOBBYIST WORKS

To lobby is to try to influence the voting of legislators.

The word *lobby* first appeared in the English language in the middle of the sixteenth century. It comes from the Latin *lobium*, which means a covered walk or cloistered area in a monastery. As the parliamentary system developed in England, the word came to mean the corridors and halls outside the House of Commons in London.

The American humorist H. L. Mencken traces lobby-agents in this country to as early as 1829 in Albany, New York. In that year, forerunners of today's lobbyists hung around the lobby of the New York Legislature trying to influence the votes of members as they walked in and out of the chamber. The name stuck and so did the practice.

Large-scale lobbying in the United States accompanied the Industrial

Revolution. The rapid rise of business and industry in the nineteenth century brought great fortunes to a small group of people. These people decided that they needed protection from institutions like government that might take their fortunes away through legislation. As a result, the main characteristic of lobbying at that time was the protection of private property.

By the 1850s, the total annual value of manufactured goods reached $1 billion, thus exceeding the value of farm products for the first time. The nation's economy was thus based more on industry than agriculture, and it was the task of the lobbyist to see that things remained that way.

The Civil War further enhanced big companies. From its end until 1885, lobbyists were in their heyday, spending lavishly to influence already corrupt legislators in Washington and in a number of states. Lobbyists were involved in the scandals of the Grant administration, for example. In 1875, a Massachusetts congressman put through the first attempt to regulate lobbyists. The resolution, which lasted one session, required lobbyists to register. It would be over seventy years before another such attempt was made.

The basis for the lack of control was the apparently widespread feeling that whatever big companies did was all right. This belief limited the regulation of businesses and their lobbyists in Washington until after World War II.

Congress first regulated lobbying in 1946 in the La Follette-Monroney Legislative Reorganization Act. Its Title II, the Regulation of Lobbying Act, requires that any person "who shall engage himself for pay or for any consideration for the purpose of attempting to influence the passage or defeat of any legislation by the Congress of the United States shall, before doing anything in furtherance of such object, register with the Clerk of the House of Representatives and the Secretary of the Senate." This act governs the activities of lobbyists today. The registration statement requires the lobbyist to state under oath "his name and business address, the name and address of the person by whom he is employed, and in whose interest he appears or works, the duration of such employment, how much he is paid and is to receive, by whom he is paid or is to be paid, how much he is paid for expenses, and what expenses are to be included."

As long as a person continues as a lobbyist, he or she is required to file what is called a "detailed report" every three months, stating under oath how much has been received and spent on lobbying during that quarter, to whom money was paid and for what purpose, the proposed legislation he or she is supporting or opposing, and the name of any newspapers or magazines in which the lobbyist "caused to be published any articles or editorials."

This requirement has not dimmed the attraction of lobbying as a career or the use of lobbyists by major segments of American life. Thousands of corporations, railroads, airlines, trade associations, consumer groups, labor unions, public utilities, medical interests, educational groups, far groups, even foreign governments spend millions of dollars pleading the cause of their special interests on the national, state, and even the local levels. They exert their pressure through information programs, publicity, promotional campaigns, threats of political reprisal, or promises of support. In the United States, lobbying has become an accepted part of the political system, supplementing geographical representation. These companies and other organizations keep large staffs in Washington and in many state capitals to do this work.

PUBLIC RELATIONS AND LOBBYING

The link between lobbying and public relations is a direct one, primarily because both use communication with various publics as their major means of operating. This common ground is often obscured, however, by a fear on the part of many companies to admit that they do such nefarious things as try to influence the way a member of a governmental body votes. Another factor that blurs the line between PR and lobbying is the use of "public affairs" as a title to describe both activities. Some companies call their lobbying unit public affairs while others use that term to describe their public-relations department, or at least that part of the operation that deals with government.

Although the two activities have similar goals, PR people do not have to register in the same way lobbyists do. Their efforts are much more subdued than those of lobbyists. A PR person will try to get to know the government officials and members of Congress who deal most directly with the area of interest to his or her company. This means getting to know people informally by entertaining them, and officially by meeting them in their offices or in hearing rooms. His or her job is to become familiar with the officials and how they work. If in the process the two become friends, all the better. Every detail of this contact is reported back to officials of the corporation or nonprofit organization for which the PR person works.

PR people involved in public-affairs work spend a very large amount of their time keeping up with the activities and actions of the government organizations they are assigned to. They read official documents, drafts of legislation, and final versions of laws; and they attend regular meetings, hearings, and sessions of those organizations. All of what they find out is relayed to their superiors in the corporation.

Standard Oil of California is a typical example of a company using public affairs to help its fortunes. One person in corporate headquarters keeps track of political activity, and this encompasses everything from assessing major issues emerging in legislation to deciding what political financial contributions the corporation will make. Public affairs also includes a planning and research group that tries to look ahead in such fields as energy and to develop company positions on alternative sources of supply like shale oil.

Another company may have an entirely different aim in its public-affairs activities. Xerox might be interested in legislation that changes the copyright law and limits the copying of books and articles. IBM might be concerned about a new law that restricts the use of computers to store information.

When members of management of the corporation or other organization receive the information their public-affairs people have got from personal contacts with government officials and from observation of their legislative and regulatory actions, they use this information to benefit the cause of that corporation or other organization. Everyone accepts this course of action as proper. The information may be used only as background for these corporations or organization officials as they manage their affairs. It may, on the other hand, form the basis for a more traditional public-relations campaign that attempts to influence publics beyond those aimed at by the lobbyist. If so, public-relations people will use the information supplied by the lobbyist or public-affairs person to write news releases; to prepare "filmed" releases for television and public-service announcements for TV and radio; to produce brochures or other publications; to plan press conferences, speeches by executives, or appearances on television talk shows; or to do any number of other PR activities.

Another way for PR people to keep up with government is to make contacts with their public-information counterparts in the agencies themselves. The activities of this group of people has been described in Chapter 6. Added to these agency public-information people, however, should be the press secretaries and PR people employed by members of Congress. While the hiring of press secretaries was rare until recent years, nearly all senators and representatives now employ them. Congress spends a great deal of money on its staff, and its resources make it a formidable opponent in any confrontation with a company.

Usually, the press secretary is like a one-person public-relations agency doing all the things required to give the boss as much publicity as possible: arranging press conferences and interviews with reporters, especially those from home-state newspapers, magazines, and television and radio stations; writing speeches; preparing background material on legislation proposed by the senator or representative; publishing newsletters.

Beyond these rather mechanical things, a press secretary has a greater value to a company wanting information about, and influence in, Washington: background information on what the senator or representative thinks and plans to do in the way of introducing legislation on a given subject. This information is as useful to a company or agency PR person as it is to reporters covering Congress. Of course, a press secretary might be more interested in providing it to a reporter because of the publicity value to the boss than to a PR person. It is worthwhile to cultivate the friendship of these press secretaries, no matter how difficult this is to do.

The press secretary might also serve as the conduit for getting a senator or representative to listen to the views of a company executive on a subject of interest to both the legislator and the company. A PR person could approach a congressional press secretary and, because they presumably speak the same language due to similarity of jobs, get some action.

HOW PUBLIC RELATIONS WORKS WITH GOVERNMENT

But all contact between government and public relations is not associated with lobbying or public-affairs work. As noted earlier, the connection often involved the fulfilling of contractual requirements, most often to supply documentation and to get copy cleared.

Getting Copy Cleared

Most contracts between federal government agencies and companies include provisions controlling the release of information about the product being produced. The requirement began as a necessity to protect classified information developed in work on the product. As such, it was legitimate and necessary.

The problem is a serious one for public-relations people, who are caught between the contract signed by officials of their companies restricting the information that can be revealed, and the need to communicate with the press and other publics to carry out their PR programs.

The most common battleground for these skirmishes is the clearance of copy for news releases and other printed or filmed material issued by the company. As noted in most contracts, the clearance procedure is lengthy and labyrinthian. The process usually begins with the sending of whatever copy is involved to an employee of the government agency. This person then looks the copy over for violations of national security and government policy, and for instances of inaccuracy. The last aspect of the clearance process is often beneficial because errors are caught by the technical people who look at the material.

Most often, however, the system results in long delays. During the time the government clearance is being sought, nothing can be released. Plans for news releases, press conferences, brochures, public appearances by company officials — nothing can go forward. Even when the material is returned reasonably quickly, changes might have been made that render it less newsworthy and usable than in its original form.

There are few options for a PR person in such a situation. He or she can put pressure on their government liaison for faster action — or get a member of the press or influential government official to do the same. Sometimes, a reporter can get faster action by dealing directly with the government agency than can the PR person involved.

Meeting Contractual Requirements

If they work at it, PR people can use the great resources of the federal government — and some state governments — to obtain information. They can also use the requirements for reports and other documentation as a means to organize their client companies and marshal their resources to get the job done. For example, in order to get a government contract, a company might have to work out a PR plan or determine a chain of command for the first time.

In the preparation of materials for a government agency, PR people should strive constantly for clear, concise writing; well-designed, graphically pleasing publications; and electronic productions that are contemporary looking.

SUMMARY

Public-relations people have to work with government agencies on several levels, some by design, others by contractual requirement. Many corporations and other large organizations employ lobbyists or public-affairs people to keep track of the activities of law-making bodies and governmental agencies, and to influence voting on legislation. The information gained by these specialists helps the companies and other organizations determine how to deal with the government on a regular basis and get new business. Once the company has got a contract from a government agency, problems arise for PR people, primarily in getting information about the project cleared for release to the press and public.

PR FOCUS: HIGH-LEVEL LOBBYING

Countries, like corporations, often need help to conduct their affairs. Take Israel, for example. That nation has had the services of experienced public-relations people and lobbyists from time to time. Over the years, the Jewish organizations in the United States have zealously guarded the welfare of the struggling country by lobbying successfully for military and other aid, and by the selling of bonds to finance development.

In 1979, Israel turned its attention to its image. Worried that his country was considered too warlike and intransigent, Prime Minister Menachem Begin called in New York media consultant David Garth for advice. Although the substance of their talks was not revealed, the expert no doubt schooled the prime minister in the vagaries of American public opinion. Israel could no longer count on its previous perception as the underdog in Middle East politics. Its refusal to give up territory on the West Bank and insistence on establishing settlements there seriously hurt it in American public opinion. Egyptian president Anwar Sadat's peace initiative and colorful personality endeared him to the American public in a way that the dour Begin never could, no matter how much expert public-relations advice was called into play.

But Israel is not the only nation whose government calls on American public-relations agencies for help. Over fifty foreign regimes a year hire PR agencies to help them.

The military junta in Chile retained Marvin Liebman, a New York public relations man to improve its bad image in the United States, according to an article in *Politics Today* ("Hired Guns," May/June 1979, pp. 48–52) Liebman proposed a $100,000-a-year budget to promote the Chilean cause in this country through the hiring of a Washington lobbyist, the preparation of "friendly" articles ready for publication, the funneling of information to cooperative journalists, and the financing of trips to the country for congressmen and members of the press. The aim of the campaign was to have been to generate congressional and journalistic pressure on the White House and State Department for a more positive posture toward Chile and an end to the cutoff of U.S. arms sales in retaliation for that country's violations of human rights. The process did not work because the Justice Department stopped the PR campaign for various reasons.

Tongsun Park was no public-relations man, but he was a trained lobbyist who used bribery with large sums of money to keep many members of Congress friendly to South Korea in the areas of military aid and of rice contracts.

Norman Wolfson, another Madison Avenue publicist, helped former Nicaraguan president Anastasio Somoza maintain a good U.S. image. He acted as the president's personal spokesman and made him available for interviews. Wolfson said his role was to kill rumors and get Somoza to reach the media. According to the *Politics Today* article already cited, Wolfson conjured up the image of "a kindly figure whose only concern is the well-being of his people" (p. 51), not the man who sent out his National Guard soldiers to kill teenage guerillas.

Aerospatiale, the British-French firm producing the Concorde supersonic jetliner, hired three PR firms in its campaign from 1975 to 1977 to secure landing rights in the United States. Local opposition in Washington and New York was strong, but the PR agencies (and seven law firms) went to work to convince the regulating bodies to approve the landing rights. After many months of pressure — and $1.3 million in fees — the PR firms helped win the prize and their underfunded opponents were overwhelmed.

Costs of such public-relations and lobbying effort are very high. For example, Argentina reportedly paid Burson-Marsteller $848,000 in 1978 to build confidence in that country as a place to invest. It cost South Africa $650,000 for one year's services of Sydney S. Baron & Co., and the Philippines paid $460,000 to get Doremus & Co. to work for it.

The only official constraint on such activities is the Foreign Agents Registrations Act, which was enacted in 1938 to control propaganda aimed at keeping the United States out of the war (Germany) and trying to persuade it to come in (Britain). This law requires that agents register, disclose the services they carried out and the fees they received, and identify foreign sponsorship on all printed matter. In 1966 this law was broadened to include more commercial activities and rewritten to exempt lawyers conducting normal business.

Analysis

Is it ethical for U.S. public-relations firms to accept assignments from foreign governments if the aim of their work is the manipulation of American public opinion? A client is a client, and few PR firms are wealthy enough to turn someone away merely because he comes from another country. Such assignments can be challenging and stimulating and can include exotic travel. The ethics come with the purposes of the PR campaign. If the foreign government wants to do something that is in any way detrimental to the welfare of this country, the PR person should resign the account immediately no matter how high the fee.

REVIEW QUESTIONS

1. How does a lobbyist work?
2. Are lobbyists too powerful? Shouldn't congressmen, senators and other government officials be left alone to vote as their consciences dictate?
3. Why does the government require that the companies working for it submit copy for news releases and other publications to it for review?
4. What are the principal duties of the presidential press secretary? How have the men holding that job in recent years conducted themselves?
5. Why do foreign governments want to influence American public opinion as badly as their willingness to hire PR firms indicates?

ASSIGNMENTS

For Journalism Students

1. Prepare a research paper on a recent instance in which a company appears to have influenced a federal government action using a lobbyist or PR person.
2. Prepare a research paper for a foreign government's use of lobbying the U.S. government.
3. You are a PR person contacted by a Middle East country for help in getting the federal ban on its major product — dates — lifted. The foreign government, left-leaning and anti-American, needs the U.S. market to survive. It offers you a flat $1 million. Do you take the account? If not, why not? If so, how will you proceed?
4. A South American dictator wants a better image in the United States and hires you as the PR person to do it. You accept the account because of

the high fee and because you think he has been misunderstood in the United States. What approach will you take?

For Business Students

1.   You are a company president and you badly need to establish your new plant in a certain African country because of the abundant natural resources and cheap labor there. The country, however, is run by a president who is dictatorial and guilty of human-rights violations toward his enemies. You call in a big New York PR firm to talk about your image if you do build the plant and the African president's image. What do you want him to do?
2.   Write an essay on the subject, "American Business Needs Lobbyists."
3.   Research a recent instance where a major corporation hired a lobbyist. What approach was used? What was the result? Your research can be conducted in a library or firsthand in a state legislature or city council.

SECTION IV

The DOING System

Part ii:

Originating programs

CHAPTER **12**

Writing news releases

Sophisticated public-relations techniques come and go, but the news release remains the single most important way to reach the public.

WHY A RELEASE

Through a release, a PR person can convey the client's side of the story to the press directly without the "filtering" process that happens when reporters attend press conferences and take notes about what goes on, or when they interview company sources individually. In such instances, the reporters will have their own interpretations of what went on, using the words they themselves heard to write their stories.

Reporters are only human, so errors occasionally creep into what they write. The news release avoids such problems because it presents the client's point of view with all names spelled correctly and financial figures given accurately. Releases will be rewritten before going into print, and they should be. Reporters will still ask questions as well. Errors can result from both activities. But the release gets the official version on paper as a point from which to begin.

News releases should not become a crutch to the exclusion of other PR techniques. They can be a fast, efficient, and inexpensive way to do a good job for the boss or the client, however.

PITFALLS AND HORRORS

The reporters and editors who will read — and, hopefully, use — the release in print or on a television or radio station must be uppermost in the minds of the PR person as he or she prepares it. "When I sit down to write a news release, I put myself in the position of a reporter," says Jeff Clausen, director of public relations at Marx, Knoll & Mangels. "I make sure everything I give is newsworthy. I have a good reputation in town. Once you damage your reputation as a reliable source of information, you might as well leave town."

Adds one of the editors whose publications PR men like Clausen are trying to get into, Robert Henkel, a senior editor of *Business Week:* "You write to get somebody's attention just like newspaper headlines and magazine layout. You try to attract the eye of the editor. Despite their experience, many PR people fail to realize that that is their only reason for existence. A great many releases are done for vanity. They are written for internal consumption. This is especially true in agencies that do what looks good to the management of client companies. They put the chairman's name so he'll see it, never saying what the news is."

Attracting the attention of an editor is very important, according to Victor E. Pesqueira, manager of public-relations projects at Xerox. "I really believe there are very few PR people who know how to write a good press release," he says. "Most say, 'Write it the way they'll print it.' That doesn't make sense because the toughest markets for releases — they're usually the best ones too — will rewrite any press release they use. As much as a PR man likes to see his work in print, most of us suspect that an editor who runs a release verbatim isn't doing his job. So, you don't try to appeal to the thought processes of a publication's readers. What you should be doing is appealing to the thought processes of an editor. If he doesn't understand your release, that's as far as it will go. You must answer questions he has. The challenge is to craft a piece that reads smoothly and gets your point of view over quickly and clearly, without being overbearing. That's a hard writing job."

Such an approach takes experience, both in the press and in public relations. Even with a good background, however, the quest to get releases to be printed or broadcast, or even used as sources for stories, is an arduous one — especially on the national level, usually the publications PR people in companies and agencies are trying to attract.

Business Week, for example, gets 10,000 news releases a week in its New York editorial offices. Henkel, the editor in charge of the magazine's Industrial Edition, gets 400 a week personally addressed to him.

A 1979 survey by Palo Alto, California public-relations man Regis McKenna revealed similarly high numbers of news releases going to general publications like the *New York Times* and the *Wall Street Journal* and trade magazines like *Electronics* (400 a week), *Electronic News* (500 a week), and *Machine Design* (500 a week). The same thing is true for most other general and specialized national publications. Although the numbers are smaller on their medium- and small-size counterparts in cities around the country, the scale of inundation is equally great.

Given this flood of paper, the editors and reporters who have found themselves on the mailing lists of the companies for whom the releases are prepared can deal with the situation only in the fastest way possible. A *Wall Street Journal* editor estimated to McKenna that he typically spends less than half a second deciding whether a release is worth more time. ("Almost none are," he added.)

Such a chilling revelation must be taken as an indictment of current news-release writing practices and form the basis for change, or a big part of a public-relations person's job is rendered irrelevant before it begins. A PR person need only spend an hour standing next to any editor's desk as he goes through the mail to be humbled and to realize the difficulty of getting news releases even read, let alone used.

The envelope from the company or agency, if it is opened at all, is ripped apart hurriedly and the release yanked out. With a swift sweep of the eye, the editor scans the headline and lead and decides whether to throw the release away right then in the large wastebasket at his or her feet or put it in a small pile of other releases that deserve further consideration.

If a PR person is lucky, releases will be dealt with in this way the day they arrive in the editorial office. Publications offices are hectic places, however, and editors do not always get through the mail each day. If a release is not opened that first day, it will be buried by the next day's avalanche of more of the same, and its timeliness may be gone by the time the editor reads it.

The releases that make this first "cut" to the pile on the desk can still be thrown away when the editor has time to read them again. Usually, however, the editor will write the name of a reporter on the top and give it to that person for rewriting, expansion into a slightly longer story or as the basis for an article that uses the idea but not the actual content of the release. In this case, the PR person will probably be called for help in providing the information or in getting the reporter together with people in the company who can do so.

This ideal situation does not happen as frequently as PR people would like. More often than not, their hard work becomes scrap paper.

Avoiding this "waste basket fate" is not impossible, however. Care and attention to the writing of releases will enhance their use and effectiveness. The process of preparing a news release for distribution involves a number of steps that begin before any words touch paper.

PREWRITING

Decide Carefully That a Release Needs to Be Written

The world is too full of news releases already to need another one without good reason. "Don't put out a news release unless you have some news to release," says Craig Lewis, president of Earl Newsom & Company, a New York PR firm. Adds R. E. Parr, manager of news services at Atlantic Richfield (ARCO) in Los Angeles: "I try to write as few news releases as I can, only truly newsworthy ones. I try to guard against the company insisting on push-ing out copy. Stories that aren't very significant are not likely to get attention from a news desk. Editors get accustomed to this policy so when they receive a story from ARCO, they know it's worth looking at." Sometimes, it may not be easy to fashion such a policy and stick with it. Many company executives will push constantly to have releases written that mention their names along with those of the company and its products. They should be resisted, when-ever possible. If nothing else works to discourage them, perhaps the statistics noted earlier in this chapter will help.

Good reasons exist for issuing releases, however. Major company or or-ganizational developments involving management, financing, research, or prod-ucts are legitimate to write about. In nonprofit organizations, major grants and research results always make solid release material. But releases on every minor personnel change soon benumbs editors into thinking that every release records something equally minor, and all releases from that source will all wind up in the trash can. Setting minimum standards for events to write releases about is essential. The Xerox philosophy of issuing releases is a good, practical approach to the problem. "We always start with ones you have to issue," ex-plains James Lamb, manager of public relations. "The Securities and Exchange Commission requires broad, simultaneous distribution of 'material' informa-tion — that information that will move the stock up or down like earnings reports, price information on copiers, external developments like the opening and closing of government investigations and lawsuits, the acquisition of pub-lic companies, and executive changes. If we're doing a material announcement, we tell the stock exchange and people there judge whether to close down trad-ing of the stock.

"The next category includes customary news releases announcing some level of personnel change — a vice president or head of a major operating unit — new product announcements, price changes and acquisitions that may not be material, 'victory' statements after contested litigation, investigations, or other accomplishments. The last category is discretionary, releases we have a choice not to do like year-end roundups, feature releases, interesting uses of products, and good works of the company."

"Customized" releases fall into this last category. These are stories sug-gested to, and prepared for, specific editors on specific publications. Such re-leases are usually too limited — either by geography or subject matter — to warrant being sent out as a general release. Numbers are not great, even for a large company like Xerox. For the first ten months of 1979, Xerox issued thirty-seven releases.

Conduct Research

After deciding that a release can legitimately be written and distributed, a public-relations person must begin by gathering material about the subject. If it is a person, information about him or her can be obtained from personnel files. If the person is more eminent, the company library or public library can be consulted for the appropriate entry in *Who's Who* or other biographical dictionaries as well as anything he or she may have written in journals or books. If a technical subject is involved, the current literature on it should be read at the company library or a local university or public library. This research will fill the PR person in on the background of the subject to be written about and enable the preparation of detailed questions for the people to be interviewed in the company or organization. These questions can be written out formally or only kept in mind as the PR person makes the appointment with, and then interviews, the technical expert who knows about the subject to be covered in the release. "Major errors occur when PR people don't research and know their subject," says a former trade editor now in PR.

Interview the Expert

Selection of the source within the company is important. It should be someone who knows the subject and who is able to convey that knowledge in an understandable way. If the PR person does not understand what the expert has said, he or she will not be able to convey it to the readers of the release. "You've got to take time to cultivate contacts within your organization so that when you're reporting a story, they will be available to help you," continues the former trade editor. "These contacts should be at all levels, from nonsupervisors to those as close to the top as possible." Most internal sources will be at ease when the PR person comes around to gather information. The two work for the same organization, and the source will have the opportunity to read the copy — preferably for technical accuracy only — before it is distributed as a release. This is different from the situation in which an outside reporter comes in, interviews the expert, and usually refuses to show copy later. After the interview, PR people should transcribe their notes quickly before they get "cold" and the handwriting illegible.

Consider Several Versions of the Release

Two versions of a release can sometimes result in more widespread use. If a subject is primarily financial but involves product aspects as well, for example, a release can be written that emphasizes finance for the financial press and the product for the technical press. This could mean that the releases will get into print — in their varying forms — while a more general approach would have met the wastebasket fate noted before. "We did two versions of a recent release on Mazda cars," recalls George Hobgood, a vice president of Hill and Knowlton in Los Angeles, "one for financial editors and then the same release and two more pages to automobile editors."

WRITING

Construct the Lead Carefully

"When you have some news to release, state it in the lead," says Craig Lewis. "Try to organize the story after that in a way that presents the subject clearly without trying to mention everyone in management involved in the program. Too many releases bury the substance in four golden paragraphs on the third page. Too many releases are written like magazine pieces, with a slow lead that backs into the story. If you are competing for attention in an age where space is scarce, you can't make editors work to get the point of journalistic relevance. It is the antithesis of good communication. Why obscure something that can be made clear?" Adds Hobgood of Hill and Knowlton: "Put your message up front. If they chop, they'll do it from the bottom."

Use a Good Transition to Get into the Body of the Release

One device is simply to pick a word or phrase from the lead paragraph and use it to begin the second paragraph. Similar words and phrases can be employed to get from one paragraph to another for the remainder of the release. Often, it becomes a matter of logic: telling the story, fact upon fact, in a way that makes sense. Beyond this, a PR person must not forget to mention the company high in the story, but not too obviously. A good way to do this is in the attribution for the lead, either in noting a person's title or in the line, "Such-and-Such company announced today." "You ought to get the name of the company or product on the first page," says Victor Pesqueira of Xerox, "if not in the lead. If the story details how a product is being used, stick the name of the company somewhere else. Sneak it in, bury it if you have to, but get it in."

Watch Language

"To write very simply — lean, sparse, unaffected, to make it seem easy to read as though the writer didn't expend much effort although you know he did — that's the ideal," continues the former trade editor now in PR. "There's a practical reason for this. You've got to capture the attention of editors and reporters. They are busy people. As a reporter, I didn't want to be impressed. I wanted a quick understanding." For this former editor, the quick understanding comes in the writing of sentences. "A great many releases use the passive structure," he continues. "This comes from proposals in government, an academic without reference to personal pronouns. The problem is that it creates ambiguity and wordiness, and people get confused. There's no rhythm.

There are too many strings of prepositions and nouns. This is because the infinitive 'to be' appears in a great deal of PR writing. When you use 'is' in a sentence, you have to use nouns to carry the weight of the meaning. 'It is the purpose of this blah, blah.' The emphasis of a release should be on clarity and organization. And, by the way, be sure to get all parallels straight." As with any kind of writing, it is important to rewrite releases. In PR, there is always time to do so.

Another tendency in public-relations writing is the use of superlatives. Such words lead to exaggeration and further discredit the PR person in the eyes of the editors and reporters receiving the releases. "Releases are full of value judgments like 'tremendous,' 'exciting,' 'first,' 'only,'" says Dianne Sichel, news editor of a weekly newspaper in a suburb of Portland, Oregon. She always edits out such words if she uses the release in the newspaper at all. They signify a less-than-professional attitude and ability by the PR person who wrote the release. She also finds too much of what she calls "folksiness" in releases crossing her desk, that is, the use of the first names of people mentioned in the release. "This comes from companies, not just publicity women in big hats," she says. It goes without saying that a PR person should never lie or cover up "bad" news in a release. It is better not to mention the matter in a release at all than to risk a loss of credibility by being caught later in a lie.

Consider Length Carefully

Few editors have the space to run a five- to ten-page release. If the subject is that important, they will assign their own reporter to cover it. Hughes Aircraft Company used only a page and a half to explain the first unmanned vehicle to reach Saturn, and two and a half pages to discuss the first manned expedition to Pluto. "If you want to include backup data, put it in a fact sheet," says the former trade editor. "If you write well, you'll come out with your fair share of copy space." One page to a page and a half is the best length for the average release. Any longer and the PR person will risk boring the editor sitting there over the ever present wastebasket. (The style for a TV and radio release differs and will be discussed in a later chapter.)

Pay Attention to Format

All releases should be typed on a good typewriter using a modern typeface that is easy to read. They should be prepared on $8\frac{1}{2} \times 11$-inch paper and doublespaced throughout. The use of a preprinted letterhead is up to the PR person. A nonprofit organization wanting the image of simplicity should avoid an elaborate letterhead. A conventional company can use a letterhead, often one that is part of an overall graphic design for all publications. In any letterhead, simplicity and understandability are key factors. If the design is unclear or the color too dark, the identification will be obscured. Also, if the company PR people have misused the privilege of contacting editors with too many unnecessary releases, the appearance of a logo on a release or envelope will trigger a negative reaction in the mind of the editor, and the release may be thrown away unread.

Beyond these decisions, the rest of the format varies and is an individual choice. Craig Lewis has some definite ideas: "My pet peeve is a release written like a news story that says, 'So and so was announced today.' Let the editor write who announced it. Also, I don't like headlines on releases. I sometimes slug them with a few short identifying words. The name of the company, the phone number, and the PR contact should be at the top. You don't need a dateline. You should put a date on so readers know it is fresh. You can put 'For immediate release' at the top so they know they can use it and there is no embargo on what the date is." Some PR people avoid a "For immediate release" designation, however, feeling that if it is mailed out, a release is obviously ready to appear unless an embargo date appears indicating otherwise.

POSTWRITING

Compile Mailing Lists Carefully

Nothing defeats the purpose of a news release more than sending one out to people who have no reason to receive it. "I'm a little surprised at the lack of professionalism of people in PR about really knowing what the media is," continues Dianne Sichel. "They don't understand what a newspaper is. They don't know I'm running a story not because it helps them but because it's of interest to readers. They don't study the market and look at our newspaper to see the type of stories we run." Who are the readers of the publications on the mailing list? What kinds of stories does the publication run? What jobs do the people hold who are getting the releases? Are they in a position to influence the stories that get into publication? If not, they will do little good for the PR person. These are the questions a PR person must ask in compiling a list of names to be reached with releases. Quality, not quantity, is the most important thing in developing such a list. "A list shouldn't be too big," says George Hobgood of Hill and Knowlton. "Sending releases to 100 people one year, then the next year to 500 people is not going to give you five times as much coverage."

Purge Mailing Lists Frequently

Not only do the wrong people frequently get news releases, people who are no longer with the news organization — indeed, people who might even have died — regularly get news releases addressed to them or, rather, their former

Chevron U.S.A. Inc.
Public Affairs (415) 894-4246, 894-0538, 894-4358, 894-0776
555 Market Street, San Francisco, CA 94105

News

Chevron

<u>For Immediate Release</u>

SAN FRANCISCO, CA., Dec. 6, 1979-- Chevron U.S.A. has
announced that it will begin a trial market of gasohol in the State
of Washington to customers in selected service stations in the Bellevue
area, near Seattle, during January 1980. The product, to be known as
Chevron Unleaded Gasohol, will be a blend of 90 percent unleaded
motor gasoline and 10 percent ethyl-alcohol (ethanol).

About 30 Chevron dealers are expected to participate in
Chevron's trial gasohol marketing program in the Northwest.

"Gasohol is receiving a great deal of attention as a supple-
mental fuel because of the worldwide shortage of crude oil," said
Chevron's Marketing Vice President D. L. Mulit in San Francisco,
"but we don't see gasohol as the answer to all motorists' gasoline
needs."

Mulit pointed out that the trial program will give Chevron
a chance to evaluate consumer acceptance and product performance, as
well as increase our research knowledge of the product. "We recognize there are many areas of uncertainty regarding gasohol and this
leads to our interest in the conduct of such a trial. We don't know
at this point whether this alternate fuel will be in demand in greater
quantities during the next five years," Mulit continued. "It may
serve regional needs well, but fall short of nationwide requirements."

- 2 -

The ethanol to be used in Chevron's gasohol is anhydrous
alcohol produced in a fermentation process from renewable resources.
It is thought to offer better performance qualities than methanol,
an alcohol made from materials such as coal, or waste materials.

CS:jh

12/6/79

\# \# \#

Figure 12.1
*This news release for Chevron USA follows a typical format. Unlike the one for
the OSU Agricultural Experiment Station reproduced in the PR Focus segment
of this chapter, this release has color in the heading. The word "news" and
the company logo are at the top in order to attract attention. Chevron is glad to
pay the extra cost, a thing the nonprofit experiment station cannot do lest it create
the impression that it is spending too much money on costly "frills."*
    *At the top of the release is the preprinted address and telephone number of
the public-affairs department. Often, the name of a specific person in that department is included so that the inquiring reporter has someone to ask for. Most news
releases include the phrase "For immediate release" at the top to signify that the
information in the release can be used as soon as the reporter or editor receives it.
Some PR people and reporters think this practice unnecessary. The purpose of
any news release is to get information out, they say, so any such phrase is
redundant. Other PR people think that designation is needed to signify the
difference from the occasional release that cannot be used until a certain day.
In such a case, the words, "For release at noon, Friday, May 1" would appear
at the top just before the lead.*
    *This release does not use a headline or identifying "slug" but goes right to
its subject after a dateline and the place of release. This release is slightly over
one page in length. It is double-spaced and easy to read. (Reprinted with
permission, Standard Oil Company of California.)*

news organization gets the releases. And even if the information is of interest to the publication, the release will probably be tossed because it seems as outdated as the name on its envelope. This lack of care will undermine a company's image with the news organization. For this reason and those noted on page 177, PR people must purge their mailing lists at least every six weeks.

As in the Soviet Union under Stalin, a "purge" means that the names — in this case, not the people — are eliminated from the list. This action can be made in several ways: by a postcard sent to every name on the mailing list requesting a return for those wanting to continue getting the releases, or through a telephone call to the news organization asking for the person on the list to find out if he or she is still with that organization and, if so, still wants to get the news releases. The cost of this survey is compensated for in the savings on postage for the wasted releases, not to mention the image problems thus eliminated. Those not heard from can be dropped from the list.

"News" vs. "Press" Releases

Should they be called "news" releases — because of what their PR sponsors think they contain — or "press" releases — because of the people on the list to receive them? The argument is an old one. Although they admit that "news" is often a misnomer when it is applied to releases, most public-relations people seem to prefer it.

"PLANTED" ARTICLES

Beyond news releases that are prepared and distributed to the editors and reporters on a mailing list are articles that are written for, and "planted" in, specific publications.

The publications in question are usually trade publications, and the articles are of a technical nature. A company or agency public-relations person will build up good relationships with editors at trade magazines and newspapers covering the field served by the company the PR person represents.

The PR person will make periodic visits to the editors to suggest that the publication run a specific article on a research development or a product or a trend at the company. The PR person then returns to the company or agency and researches and writes the article specifically for the trade magazine or newspaper, following the normal stylistic approach of that publication. The article is then sent to the publication and it runs, often without any indication that it came from a PR person. True, it is usually rewritten. But the major thrust of the article has come from public relations, a thing readers of the publication never know.

Staffs of many trade publications are too small to cover their fields adequately. This assistance from PR people helps them. This approach does not work on general magazines, many of which are staff written and of the opinion that such "planting" is unethical. As long as the information presented is factual, accurate, useful, and interesting, it is a legitimate way for a PR person to serve his or her company or client.

SUMMARY

The news release is the single most important way for public-relations people to convey information about their company or client to the general public. In this way, the PR people tell the company's side of the story directly, without the misunderstandings that sometimes occur when a reporter covers an event or conducts an interview. True, the editors of a publication will usually rewrite a release before putting it into print. But the essence of the original release will usually be retained. But the news release as a public-relations tool is not without its drawbacks. Too many of them are sent out to editors and reporters on publications, who are benumbed by the sheer number of them they receive each day. Many of them are a waste of time to read, and they make it hard for those that contain something of substance ever to be seen. At times, in desperation, a beleaguered editor will throw the whole stack of daily releases in the trash can just to make way for the next day's deluge.

There are ways to write usable news releases, however. PR people need to be careful in deciding that a release has to be written in the first place. They need to conduct research to get ready for interviews with the people in their organizations who will provide them with material for the releases. They might consider two versions of a release if more than one kind of publication is desirable. In writing a release, PR people should construct the lead carefully, use a good transition to the body of the release, and watch their language, especially in avoiding superlatives and other words of exaggeration. They should never lie. They should not write a release longer than two pages because it may not be read. A double-spaced, typed release with a dignified letterhead and the name of a PR contact and telephone number at the top is preferable. Mailing lists of those to receive releases should be prepared carefully so that only editors and publications in a position to run the releases get them. Such lists should be "purged" every six months so that people who have left the publication are no longer getting releases.

PR FOCUS: THE ANATOMY OF A NEWS RELEASE

The process is invariably the same.

Richard Floyd, editor of the Oregon State University Agricultural Experiment Station, calls up one of the many scientists in that far-flung organization either to see if anything newsworthy is going on or to verify a report he

From Oregon State University   WILD HORSES GET
Department of Information   7/28/77   SPECIAL STUDY
Telephone 754-4611   IN OSU RESEARCH

(Note to News Directors: For an audio cut of this story, call 754-3615 at
OSU between 9 a.m. and 12 noon, M-F. Cut runs 93 sec.)

Wild horses can't keep two Oregon State University scientists from their research
project.

In fact, without the wild horses of the Bureau of Land Management's Vale District,
Martin Vavra, animal scientist, and Forrest Sneva, range scientist of the Agricultural
Research Service of the U.S. Department of Agriculture, would not be peering down from
helicopters, walking through desert streams and climbing over cliff rocks.

The wild horses of the federal BLM Vale district (malheur, part of Harney County
and a bit of Idaho) have kicked up conflicting thoughts about their future. Idaho,
Montana, Wyoming, Utah, Arizona, California and other parts of Oregon have similar
wild horse problems of dwindling space, food and water.

More than 1,150 Oregon horses have been adopted from holding corrals near
Burns in the last 3½ years. Horses will be available through the Adopt-A-Horse program
this summer in California, Oregon, Nevada and Wyoming.

"We don't really have much technical information about the wild horses' food, water,
cover or living space," said Jerry Wilcox, Vale District wild horse specialist who works
with the OSU scientists.

"Most of the captured ones have been in fairly good condition. Their seasonal use
patterns and space requirements are not well understood."

The district has 12 herds. The biggest has about 2,000 horses; the smallest, 16
animals.

"We now are reaching the point where forage and water are not adequate to
sustain the herds which we estimate increase from 17 to 22 per cent annually," said
Wilcox.

"Based on our current information, we estimate that we need to reduce horse numbers
from about 2,800 to 1,200. The new data from the OSU study will provide information to
assist us in developing a horse management plan and determining the proper number of
horses so they will be in balance with other resources."

Vavra and Sneva, from OSU's Eastern Oregon Agricultural Research Center's stations
at Union and Burns, hope to answer some of the questions about the wild horses.

They started in September to gather fecal samples, only a few hours old, from wild
horses, cattle and deer.

(more)

WILD HORSES 2-2-2-2

The fresh samples are frozen and taken to the Union Experiment Station for analysis.

"Each individual plant species has its own epidermal cell characteristics which do not change," said Vavra. "Basically, what we study is the undigested portion of the plant material in the fecal samples."

After analysis, the samples are sent to a USDA soil scientist at Kimberly, Idaho, for further analysis to determine the amount of soil ingested by the animals.

Said Sneva:

"We want to determine the botanical diet composition and selectivity of the animals through the grazing season with one year of collecting.

"We also will compare diets of the animals, particularly horses and cattle, grazing different parts of the region. Then we want to see which plants are being selected by the animals at the end of the grazing season compared to the beginning."

Results of the study, funded by the Agricultural Experiment Station and BLM, will not be known until this fall.

"But we think there will be a strong parallel to results from a fecal collection study finished early this year near Burns," said Sneva.

The two-year study near Burns of diet competition among wild horses, cattle and dear showed that, year-round, horses consume almost 100 per cent grass. Cattle liked the same grass diet, except in the spring and early summer when their diet contained up to 20 per cent sagebrush.

Sheep preferred a diet of about 80 per cent grasses in the spring and 20 per cent shrubs. The rest of the time, their diet was similar to that of cattle.

In the spring, antelope ate 60 per cent broad-leaf plants including weeds. Dear consumed equal parts of shrubs, grass and broad-leaf plants in the spring and preferred shrubs the rest of the year although not to the extent the antelope did.

The study showed that there was a severe dietary overlap among cattle, sheep and wild horses.

                                    # # # #

Figure 12.2
A news release from the Oregon State University Agricultural Experiment Station about wild horses. (Reprinted with permission, OSU Agricultural Experiment Station.)

had heard elsewhere, that interesting work is being pursued. In either case, he asks the scientist to send him written material.

"There may or may not be a story," he says. "I read the material to see if there is a story. I make my decision based on my experience. I ask myself why we would want a story and, if so, what to do with it — a print release or film or both."

The written material also helps him develop the questions for his interview with the scientist. He next conducts the interview and writes the story. "I send back the story for the source to read," he continues. "They often have a fear of being misquoted and ridiculed. They approve the story and send it back. I may not approve of their changes but you lose a few, win a few."

Floyd followed his normal approach in the release reproduced here, on an Oregon State University wild-horse research project of several years ago. "This was an interesting story in several ways," he recalls. "I first found that the animal scientist was interested in doing research by talking to him at a meeting. Then, the wild-horse interest broke into a canter nationally. The idea for a research story then became more concrete when a copy of the grant from the Bureau of Land Management to the Experiment Station came across my desk. I checked with Martin Vavra, the animal scientist, several times by phone to see how things were going."

When the project got underway, Floyd set up a time when he and Forrest Sneva, a range scientist for the U.S. Department of Agriculture based in Burns, Oregon, could meet. On the appropriate day, Floyd and Dave King, his assistant editor, drove to the Vale area of Oregon to meet their sources. "We took pictures of them, talked with them about some of their problems, and made arrangements to consult with them about results," he says. "Then we went to the Vale Bureau of Land Management office and met with several BLM officials who worked on the wild-horse program."

While Floyd continued interviewing BLM people about the horse program, his compatriot King went up in a small plane with a 16mm camera to try to film wild horses in the nearby desert hills. After they returned, Floyd wrote the story and King produced a radio cut and a TV story, showing the wild horses at home on the desert and using the Vavra-Sneva information with some film of them.

In writing the release, Floyd used a derivation of an old saying, "Wild horses couldn't keep me away from etc., etc." "The key words to the whole story are wild horses," he says. "By using an obvious literary link, it's a flag for attention. Most of our stories are very timely and I use a straight news lead. Because this one was not, I tried to titillate the readers a bit, to jangle their memory with a key word or phrase. But you've still got to be accurate enough that you don't mislead. A lead is a magnet. If you do not get someone to read your story, all of this is a waste of time."

Beyond the lead, Floyd presented the information in what he calls "encyclopedic" fashion — the facts and figures of the wild-horse program, its promise and problems. "I used direct quotes to present most of this information, which ran a little longer than most of our news releases," he continues. "Releases can't be too long — two or three pages. They have to be thought out and written so lay people can understand technical terms. You must incorporate all details into the story. You can't oversell. You've got to deliver all you've promised, tie up all the loose ends, explain everything that's unfamiliar."

He checked the copy with Vavra, who then checked it with Sneva. The story came back with only a few changes. It was disseminated, along with photographs of wild horses and their colts, by the OSU Department of Information to most Oregon dailies and all TV stations and most radio stations.

"Usage was high," he says. "The public was hungry for more information about wild horses because of national publicity, so acceptance was not a problem. From our viewpoint, the story was different because it made heavy use of our own scientists and experts from another agency. It was made more interesting for both Dave and me because we went far afield to run down the information and pictures. We had a great deal of information. Selectivity was our chore."

REVIEW QUESTIONS

1. Why are news releases so important as a public-relations tool?
2. Why do some members of the press ignore the news releases they receive?
3. How do the better publications use news releases most effectively?
4. How can a PR person avoid the problems associated with news releases in the minds of the editors and reporters who receive them?
5. What kind of writing style is best for a news release?
6. What is the best format for a news release?
7. Why is it important to prepare and update mailing lists carefully?

ASSIGNMENTS

For Journalism and Business Students

1. Study a news release from a company or nonprofit organization. Analyze it in terms of format, content, writing style, and organization. Is it effective? Why? Why not? Report your findings to the class.
2. Interview an editor on a local newspaper and ask him or her what he or she thinks of news releases. How many of them does he or she use in an average week? What, for he or she, is the ideal news release? Report your findings to the class.
3. Interview a local public-relations person to find out his or her philosophy of news-release writing. When does the company or nonprofit organization

issue a release? What style and content does an average release have? How effective are the releases in terms of telling the organization's story? Report your findings to the class.

4. Ask a local editor to give you a day's news releases. Look them over and decide which ones you would save for use in a daily newspaper (to run as stories or as a source for a reporter's story) and which ones you would discard. Ask the editor to do the same. Compare the final decisions (your own and those of the editor) and report your findings to the class.

5. Interview a local business person about a subject of mutual interest and write a one-page news release with the material you obtain.

6. Select a story from a newspaper business page or the *Wall Street Journal* dealing with "bad" news (a decline in earnings, a scandal, a high-level firing, a product failure, etc.) and rewrite it as a news release from the company.

7. Go through your daily newspaper for one week and select the stories you think were originally news releases. Why did you make the selections you did? What percentage of the "news hole" in the newspaper do they represent? Verify your selections with the city editor. Report your findings to the class.

CHAPTER 13

Preparing brochures and press kits

In some agencies they are called *collaterals,* extras that are produced for clients beyond the standard commission. In some companies they are considered nuisances that get in the way of real PR work like writing news releases.

Brochures, booklets, and press kits are more than either of these designations, however. Very often, their preparation will solve a problem for a client or company in a way not possible otherwise. Too many public-relations people think that a news release is the answer to every problem. They never think to go beyond it to something more imaginative like a brochure, a booklet, or a press kit.

WHAT IS A BROCHURE?

A *brochure* is a multipanel publication that conveys information, usually on a single subject, to those who read it. Small and compact, the brochure usually tells its story as the reader unfolds the panels, one after the other. A brochure, also called a *pamphlet,* a *flyer,* or a *folder,* can be handed out to its audience or mailed, either in an envelope or by leaving a space on one of the panels for an address label, in which case it becomes a *self-mailer.* A *booklet* has much the same purpose as a brochure except that it has so many pages that it must be stapled together rather than folded. It can also be handed out or mailed, either in an envelope or as a self-mailer.

Companies and other organizations need brochures and booklets for a variety of reasons: to explain a new program, process, or product; to describe a new building, plant, or laboratory; to ask for contributions; to sell a product by describing its virtues. These publications are reasonably inexpensive, relatively fast to produce, and can create a good impression for their readers if prepared carefully.

190

BROCHURE DESIGN AND PREPARATION

The principles of designing a brochure are not different from those used to prepare a magazine spread or a newspaper page, except in the size variations and in the fact that brochure design is interrupted by folds. The principles of design are the same for all publications whether they be brochures, booklets, annual reports, or company magazines: balance, proportion, sequence, unity, and contrast. These principles of design are explained in the PR Focus sidebar at the end of Chapter 15; printing techniques and type classifications are described later in this chapter.

Although most PR people will have the services of an in-house or outside freelance graphic designer, it is important for them to know how to design a brochure or booklet so that they can guide the artist. Once in a while, they might even have to prepare such a publication themselves. "The function of the piece will dictate form," says Marilyn Holsinger, assistant professor of art at the University of Missouri. "That's a truism one can't escape. A flyer that is to announce a temporary kind of event that is a one-time thing is not going to be attended to with the same amount of care and attention as a brochure or booklet describing in detail some product or program or promotion of some type that is more complicated. It goes back to what it is you want to say. That is the hardest part: deciding what you really want to say in the printed piece. This sounds so simple but it isn't. If you can answer that question, half of your job is done."

Brainstorming

Holsinger's search for the answer to what a publication will say begins with an analysis of what problem the piece is being designed to solve. Copy, budget, and illustration decisions all come from that point. "You need to get as much information as you can in a who, what, when, where, and why journalistic way," Holsinger says. "Are you going to be visualizing it or is it complicated enough to hire a technical or scientific illustrator? Who will write the copy and gather the information for the copy?"

After the basic decision on what the brochure will say has been made, the next step is to *brainstorm,* a process in which the writer, artist, and anyone else connected with the project meet and talk about ways to do the job. "Sometimes you say the craziest things possible in these meetings, just to get across ideas," Holsinger continues. "That's what your job is, to get across ideas. You meet like this so minds can spin off, act as foils for the development of ideas. There may be a dozen ideas floating around and you go off chasing them and they may not go anywhere. But there may be a connection. Just remember, there are no new ideas in the world, only old ideas newly connected."

Thumbnails

This quest for solutions leads next to the preparation of a series of *thumbnails,* or thumbnail sketches, rough design possibilities done with a soft pencil one-fourth to one-half the size of the original. Thumbnails are almost doodling in that the elements of the design — copy, headlines, and illustrations — are all done quickly. Lines are usually drawn to denote copy, headlines are X'd in, and an illustration is shown as a solid mass. In as little as fifteen minutes, however, a good designer can come up with ten or twelve design suggestions for a single printed publication. The small size allows the speed. Doing larger layouts would take much longer. And, if he or she squints, the viewer can get a good idea of how a final printed version would look because of the ease of visualizing copy, headlines, and illustrations from the way they are rendered on the thumbnails. Does the illustration dominate? Is the headline too small or placed wrong? Is there too much copy? A thumbnail will answer such questions.

Layout Preparation

Once the PR person and the graphic designer have agreed on a design, the next step is for that designer to prepare sample layouts for the entire printed piece. Two stages are possible. A *rough layout* is almost a large-size thumbnail, that is, it has all the elements of the pages in place and indicated in a rough form lines for the copy (now done with a straightedge and not freehand as in the thumbnail), Xs for the heads (although a technique called "Russianing" or "Greeking" can also be used; by including these letters resembling the script forms used in writing Russian and Greek, a designer can show that a headline will be there, but it cannot be read), and sketches for the illustrations. A *comprehensive layout,* also called a *comp,* is usually prepared when a client or member of management who needs to approve the project cannot visualize how a publication will look by seeing the rough layout. A comprehensive looks like a printed piece, so perfect is it in every detail: type is set or hand-lettered to look as though it has been set, illustrations are prepared, color and good paper used. "If a job is super classy," says Holsinger, "I do a comprehensive."

Writing Copy

The copy, or text, is the most important part of the brochure or booklet, its reason for existence. It will probably be the last thing seen, however, because design so dominates small publications. The reader is more concerned with getting the brochure open than in reading what it says.

Once the reader gets to the copy, however, a number of considerations are important. The writer must establish a theme for the publication as soon as its main purpose has been decided upon. Again, the small size of the piece makes this crucial. A reader will be finished with the brochure so quickly that the writing must not be disjointed and lacking unity. Thus, it is best to cover only one subject per brochure.

An opening statement should set the tone of the piece or explain the theme. From here, a good way to proceed is through a series of headlined sections that divide the material into understandable segments, one or two per brochure panel, that are not carried over from panel to panel, again for reasons of reader comprehension. The text should end with some finality. Appropriate quotes from famous people are a good way both to open and to close a brochure or booklet. If the piece is designed to sell something or get the reader to do something, the last paragraph should include an appropriate call to action, with a return blank when needed.

The style of writing should fit the overall aim and character of the piece — dignified or humorous, technical or simple. The copy writer must keep in mind the space limitations of a brochure and, to a certain extent, a booklet. It is impossible to get a great many words onto six panels or even sixteen $8\frac{1}{2} \times 11$-inch pages. This means that writing must be brief and to the point, every word must count, and every section and illustration must have a reason for being included. Writers will have to remind the officials in the company who approve copy of this fact. Invariably, they will want to add information here and there until the publication has grown considerably, well beyond its original brochure size.

Designing for the Space

Whether the space to fill is a narrow brochure panel or a full-size magazine page, the problem is the same: How can the elements be arranged most effectively and pleasantly? A *grid* solves the problem. This system divides design space by a series of vertical and horizontal lines so the designer knows the limits he or she has to work with in terms of margins, the outer edges of pages, and columns of varying widths. Designers can buy standard preprinted forms using various grid configurations, or they can prepare their own to suit their needs better.

A grid helps divide the space easily and uniformly, and also assures that the elements of a page will be properly aligned, headlines above copy and illustrations on line with headlines and copy, or out of line in an orderly way if that is desired. "The grid is a modern, geometrical division of space that allows you to determine that the information is put into type economically over a certain number of pages determined in advance and where the photos and illustrations will go," says Holsinger. "The judicious use of your space will affect cost." Sometimes the designer will include more *white space* than the client thinks is economical. That is, the designer will use empty space as part of the design so the headlines, copy, and illustrations are more predominant and effective. An uninformed client might find this white space wasteful, thinking it can be filled in with copy to cut down on the number of pages and reduce cost. Such shortsightedness should be resisted because it will ruin the design. (For more about design principles, see the PR Focus in Chapter 15.)

Paper Selection

After design, paper selection is the next important technical element in the preparation of any printed publication. Not only does paper affect the look of the publication, it enhances the design of the panels or pages and determines whether the photographs are clear and, indeed, whether the words are read at all. But paper also represents from thirty to fifty percent of the final cost of the printing job. Paper that is too thick will not fold well and will increase costs of mailing. Paper that is too thin will look limp as a brochure, and will tear easily if it is mailed without an envelope.

PR people and designers should discuss paper with printers' and manufacturers' representatives before making selections. The big paper companies prepare sample books that show all kinds of paper — smooth, coated, those with a finish or a texture, how photos will look printed on them, and papers of various weights from cover to inside varieties.

Paper characteristics include four elements important to remember. *Grain* shows how the fibers used to make the paper are placed (usually their length is parallel to the manufacturing machine). Designers should always do their work with the direction of the grain because paper can crack or get rough if folded crossgrain. Paper is more stable in the grain direction and expands or contracts more in the cross direction when moisture changes, and thus is strengthened by these fluctuations. *Basis weight* is the weight in pounds of a ream (500 sheets) cut to the basic size of that particular grade of paper. When looking at a paper sample book, for example, a designer will see "basis 60" or "60 lb." or other designations printed on the various sheets. This means that 500 sheets of the basic size of paper (for example, the basic size for text, a paper grade commonly used for brochures, is 25" × 38") will weigh 60 pounds. As noted earlier, weight of paper is important for cost and durability. *Strength* of paper is determined by the nature of its fiber and usually comes with weight in terms of deciding whether a paper is durable enough to suit the intended purpose of the piece. *Stretch,* the amount of distortion a paper undergoes, is usually of concern only to printers.

Paper also affects design in terms of cost and the use of standard paper grades. A printer will be able to determine final cost of a job by knowing how many pieces are to be printed, in what size, and on what kind of paper. If the designer chooses an unusual size, the printer will not be able to get as many pieces from the standard-size sheet of that particular paper grade. This will increase costs because paper will be wasted in that only so many pieces can be cut from a single basic-size sheet. If the designer — or more likely, the client — does not care about this added cost and waste, the project can go forward. Perhaps part of the wasted paper can be turned into memo pads. The size of a publication is a consideration that cannot be overlooked. Whenever possible, however, it is best to stick to standard sizes.

Color of paper and ink are important decisions that affect the final look of a publication and its cost. Four-color (or full-color) photographs or illustrations in a publication add greatly to costs because of the elaborate printing procedures that must be followed. The primary colors red, yellow, and blue, plus black, must be printed separately to produce the effect of full color, with presses cleaned and ink changed for each press run. Three-color or two-color printing are also possible, eliminating a color and some of the cost each time.

The decision on color is an important one. Sometimes color is overused, adding to cost unnecessarily and creating a publication that is too lavish for its purpose. A single color will serve nicely for most small brochures and booklets. The single color need not be black ink nor does a brochure have to be printed on white paper. There is only a small extra charge for a different color ink on a colored stock, because only one press run is necessary. In this case, however, the designer must be careful to choose paper and ink combinations that are complementary. A dark color of ink on a dark-colored paper can be illegible. Other colors can clash or look drab. Good paper and ink color combinations include black ink on yellow paper; green, red, blue, or black ink on white paper; and white ink on blue (an effect that can be achieved by overprinting blue ink with the white paper showing through for letters).

Type Selection

Picking the type for the headlines and body (or text) copy of a publication is important to its success. As the wide variety of classifications noted later in this chapter indicates, type can enhance the look of a printed page or detract from it. Type can express a mood or aid readability. Types are masculine and feminine, delicate and sturdy, formal and informal. Proper selection of type is just as important as good design and good writing. Many printed pieces have failed to get across their messages because of type that is inappropriate or hard to read.

"I consider type an art in itself," says Marilyn Holsinger. "It is greatly underrated. It is a mood setter along with the illustrations, the paper, the photos, the size, the color, the whole impact of the piece. They all create a mood, but type is central to what kind of impression the publication will make, to how the reader responds."

Type selection begins with a consideration of how the various typefaces available from the printer relate to the theme of the publication. After the designer has picked a typeface or typefaces (it is best not to use more than two per publication — one for body copy, for example, and another for headlines), he or she must decide on type size, which should be large enough to be readable but not so big that it dominates the page. Type size is measured in points (approximately 72 points to an inch). It is best not to go below 8-point type for body copy, or above 11 points.

Other factors relating to type include a decision about its boldness (generally, boldface type should be reserved for headlines and emphasis because it is hard to read) and whether to italicize it (italic type, that which leans slightly forward, should also be used sparingly, as for emphasis or captions, also because it is hard to read). All capital letters in anything but a short headline should be avoided as much as boldface and italic, again because capitals are hard to read.

Should the columns of type be justified, that is, each line uniform on the right, or unjustified or ragged on the right? Studies differ on which style is more readable. After years where justified type dominated, unjustified columns are on the rise, especially in smaller publications. Ragged columns do offer variety, a contemporary look, and cost savings.

The last decision relating to type involves vertical and horizontal space. The width of the columns at which the copy is to be set is the first consideration in this regard. The line length of type is measured in picas (approximately 6 picas to an inch). A column that is too wide is hard to read, as is one that is too narrow. Readability studies have shown that a line width of 14 to 25 picas is easiest to read. Another part of space measurement is leading, the space between lines of type. A designer can have body copy set with no space between lines ("set solid") or anywhere from one to two points of leading, or space, between lines. For most publications, the absence of leading makes the copy hard to read so "set solid" should be avoided. On the other hand, 2 points of leading is a good compromise.

Putting It All Together

The process has begun with a decision on the need for a brochure. The theme has been arrived at in a brainstorming session. The design has been worked out through thumbnail, rough layout, and comprehensive layout stages. The copy has been written. The theme, layout, and copy have been checked with higher authority. Paper, ink, and type have been selected with purpose, theme, design, and illustrations in mind. What happens next?

The designer marks the type specifications (called "specking the type") and other instructions to the printer, like column width and leading on the typewritten copy. After the type has been set and corrected, the columns are cut to fit onto a premeasured, lined sheet and glued or waxed into place. Headlines are also positioned that way. The designer is following a *dummy*, or plan of each panel or page. This time, however, he or she must be careful that the headlines and columns of type are straight and correctly aligned according to the design. A T-square or triangle is best for this purpose. If line art illustrations are to be used, they can also be pasted up. If a photograph is called for, a space should be left for it. It will need to be "screened" by the printer, that is, put through a process in which a tiny dot structure is imposed upon it that retains ink during printing. During the pasteup, designers should be sure that the columns of type are clean and not smudged or covered with rubber cement or wax, which will show up on the final product. After this process is complete, what emerges is a *mechanical,* the entire publication ready for printing. Before taking it to the printer, the designer or PR person should read everything one last time to catch any errors.

Most printers will run a press proof on their printing jobs. This proof, also called a Van Dyke or a blueline, gives the designer one last chance to catch errors, although changes should be avoided at all costs at this stage because of the high costs of correcting them. Indeed, a designer or PR person should *never* show a press proof to anyone in higher authority at the company because these people will invariably begin to edit copy and suggest design changes. Such things should have been done long before in the more preliminary stages of the product.

The publication will then be printed and delivered to the PR person. Careful thought needs to be given to who is to get a publication long before it is ready. Mailing lists should be prepared and updated. Copies should be delivered to other company locations together with instructions on how to distribute them.

Working with Printers

The selection of a good printer is as important as any step in the process just outlined. The quality of that printer's publications and his rates need to be determined in advance. It is a good idea to "shop around" in advance of making a final selection and get at least three bids, especially for major jobs. "Look at their work and look at their shops," says Marilyn Holsinger. "Be wary because of all the hip-pocket printers around now. The ease of offset printing has attracted people who have seen they can make money but have no background or ability."

There are two categories of printers: commercial and in-house. A commercial printer is in business to make a profit and must be competitive in price and quality to do so. An in-house printer is one employed by the large organization for which the PR person works, and who does all printing for that organization, including that needed by the PR office. There is thus no profit motive for the printer, and the PR person must compete for attention with other parts of the organization.

Usually, a PR person working for an organization with its own printer will have to use that printer no matter what the cost and quality; the organization pays the printer's salary and wants such services used. Such an arrangement is rare in a company but is more common in public institutions like universities or hospitals. Even in this kind of arrangement, however, a PR person can often go outside for special jobs to commercial printers.

In selecting a commercial printer, it is best to get estimates from at least three printers for one job. Look at samples of past printing work, find out how long the printers have been in business, and if possible, inspect the plants and equipment. If a PR person has a large number of jobs a year of varying kinds, it is advisable to use several printers, for example, a high-quality, expensive one for jobs of that kind and a more economical one for less demanding jobs. No matter what type, however, it is important for PR people, designers, or anyone working with a printer to know as much as possible about the printing business. They should know the terms so that they do not measure specifications in inches rather than picas. They need to know when a job has turned out badly because of printer error and demand that it be redone with the printer paying the added costs.

For any printer, commercial or in-house, it is important to write a list of clear and concise instructions for every job — size, shape, number of folds, paper, typefaces, number of copies, ink. It is also imperative that the PR person give the printer information about changes during the progress of the job, for example, on number of copies or paper weight.

A deadline should be established right from the start with the printer and adhered to by both sides. It is also a good idea to establish at the outset who pays for mistakes. Usually, a printer pays for mistakes made in setting type; the customer must pay for errors in marking copy or changes not on the original.

A BROCHURE OR A BOOKLET?

The decision to design a publication as a brochure or a booklet is usually made for one of three reasons: it will look better as one or the other, a brochure will cost less and the budget is small, or there is too much material to fit into a brochure so a booklet will have to be used.

Folds

If a brochure is the style selected, a number of overall size and fold configurations can be used: four-panel, six-panel, eight-panel, twelve-panel, sixteen-panel. In deciding on the number of folds, a designer should remember that ease of reader comprehension is important. In other words, a designer should make the brochure "foolproof" so that it can be easily opened and the copy read, from one panel to the next. A designer need only observe a reader try to cope with a badly organized brochure to see the importance of this point. If people tear the paper as they open it, or have to keep turning it over to read panels, it is badly designed.

Binding

The main difference between a brochure and a booklet is that the latter has to be bound and has pages like a book. A brochure, on the other hand, is folded and needs no binding. There are a number of binding methods. Most booklets are *saddle-stitched,* that is, they are stapled at two points in the center and lie open easily. If a booklet has too many pages for this kind of binding, it can be *side-stitched,* that is, held together with thicker staples; the cover is sometimes glued on. This kind of publication will not remain open on its own and will constantly snap shut. Other kinds of binding are used in manufacturing books and are not needed to put together brochures and booklets: *edition binding,* with pages held together by special sewing thread, glue, or cloth; *perfect binding,* with pages held together by glue only; and *mechanical binding,* with pages held together by wire or plastic coils.

ORGANIZING A PRESS KIT

A *press kit* combines the news releases and brochures explained in this chapter and the previous one with other pertinent information about the company and organization into a neat package that can be given to members of the press before a press conference or a tour of a plant or laboratory. The information in the kit gives members of the press the background they need to cover the story at hand or simply to understand the organization as a whole.

A press kit begins with the outer folder, best preprinted with the name of the company or organization on the cover and with pockets inside on the right or left in which to insert the items to be placed in the press kit.

The right side of a press kit usually has the news release about the event for which the press conference is being held, followed by a background sheet on the event, biographies of the people involved, and sometimes even glossy photos. The left side of the kit usually holds less timely information: a background sheet or brochure on the company and the last annual report.

Even though the reporters receiving the press kit will still have questions, the information contained in the kit will give them a head start on doing their stories.

A typical press kit is the one shown in Exhibit 13.1, prepared by Burson-Marsteller for Systems Consultants, a San Diego computer science and technology company. The cover is imprinted with the name of the product to be introduced at the press conference, PLMX, in large type, with the "X" and

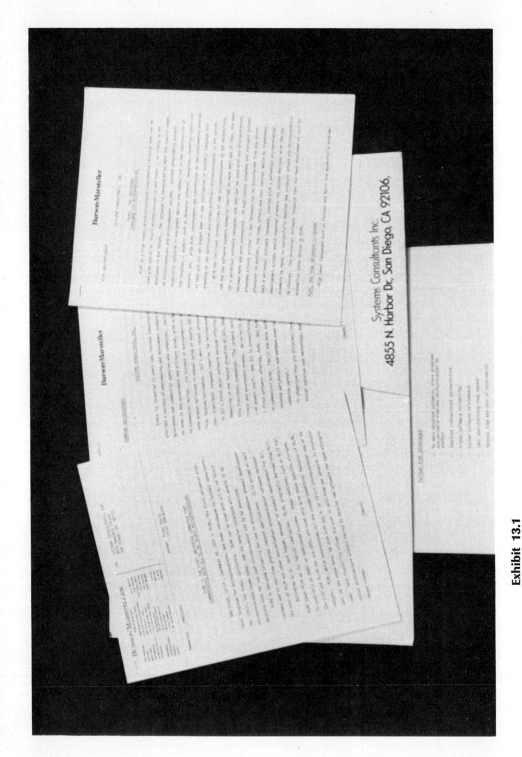

Exhibit 13.1
A typical press kit. (Reprinted with permission, Burson-Marsteller.)

the subhead, "The first universal language for microprocessors," printed in red for emphasis. The right flap, with the name and address of the company printed on it in red and black ink, contains the main news release describing PLMX, a six-page "backgrounder" on the company, and a ten-page backgrounder on PLMX. The left pocket of the kit contains only typed reports that list brief facts about the company and the product and its significance in brief, easily understood form.

Even though press conferences have declined in use, press kits are still a popular PR technique. Indeed, many companies and agencies keep empty, preprinted folders ready to put together for all visitors or anyone writing for information about a company. In this case, the kit can be put together in the publications storeroom, putting in assorted releases, brochures, background sheets, annual reports, the latest copy of the company magazine, company histories, and even copies of articles from publications about the company and the industry of which it is a part.

SUMMARY

Brochures, booklets, and other publications solve special problems for companies and organizations that a news release cannot handle. A brochure is a multipanel publication that conveys information on a single subject to those who read it: to explain a new program, process, or product; to describe a new building, plant, or laboratory; to ask for contributions; to sell a product. A brochure becomes a booklet when more space is needed or a different format is desired. It is stapled rather than folded. Brochures and booklets are prepared — by a designer or, in instances of a small budget, by the PR person — in a series of steps that begins with the decision to produce a publication and continues to include the selection of a theme; the design of the panels or pages; the writing of copy; the selection of type, paper, and a printer; the setting of type, correcting of proof, and pasting up of pages; the distribution of the brochure or booklet. A press kit is another effective public-relations tool. It combines news releases with brochures, booklets, and other publications in a tool that provides background to an outsider on the company or organization, its products or research discoveries, and the people involved.

PR FOCUS: THE ANATOMY OF A BOOKLET

Like any business, the Oregon State University Department of Journalism thrives on new customers, in this case students who want to major in technical journalism. But the department long ago discovered that it could not sit back and wait for students to enroll in its program automatically. It would have to advertise its wares through use of a brochure.

Because of my experience in preparing such publications and in teaching a course about production, I was asked by the department chairman in 1973 to do the first brochure. It was a reasonably cheap eight-panel publication on yellow paper that emphasized the various technical minors required by the department. Some of the various minors were depicted in a series of unusual photographs: home economics by a woman student putting a typewriter in an oven, forestry by a male student typing while sitting on a log, oceanography by a wet-suited figure (another woman student, actually) typing underwater (Exhibit 13.2).

This early brochure was distributed to new and prospective students by mail and sent to all newspaper editors in the state for information purposes. It was generally used in a low-key way as befitted the OSU journalism program at the time. It was updated once to add some new minors and a photograph of the department's new video display terminal.

By 1979, however, it was time for a change, and the chairman once again asked me to design a department brochure. We had again added minors, more video display terminals and other computer editing equipment, and more photographic equipment, and we had just been accredited by the American Council on Education in Journalism (ACEJ), an event we had reason to publicize. Although he didn't say so, I could tell by his tone that he wanted this brochure to be a bit more splashy than the first one.

I "brainstormed" with myself for a week or so and decided that I wanted to emphasize the strong orientation of the department toward practical experience. Although some journalism educators, including many of the officers of ACEJ, frown on too much project and internship work, I think that a student who goes out into the world with only a list of courses and no work samples or experience will have trouble getting a job.

I decided to explain the department's emphasis on getting experience by asking a group of recent graduates to write me statements about what their journalism education at OSU had meant to them in terms of their preparation for the job market. The tried-and-true personal testimonial had worked for years in commercial advertising. I decided to see if it would work in a brochure.

The selection of the graduates presented a few problems. First, as always, were the political considerations. I knew the other instructors in the department would be miffed if I chose only my advisees. Then too was the fact that I could not possibly include testimonials from people representing all thirty-two minors. I pondered the problem for a few minutes and decided that my former advisees had done as well as anybody else's and represented a good cross section of departmental minors. Most important of all, I knew my advisees well enough to know that they would express themselves well on the subject. These factors were more important than the bruised egos of my colleagues, some of whom would criticize me no matter what I did. I picked seven graduates, making sure that three of them were women, another political consideration.

The next problems were logistical. How to get the material from the people and good candid photos of them on the job? I wrote letters to the seven graduates, asking them to be a part of the project. Six of them readily agreed, and I sent each of them five questions dealing with what their OSU journalism education had meant to them. Three of my sources were local so I arranged for the university photographer to take photos of them. Two of the other three worked on jobs that regularly brought them in contact with photographers. The sixth graduate was a photographer. I gave them each a deadline, a month away.

With that phase of the project launched, I began to gather together the material I would need for the rest of the copy: facts and figures on the department, its history, its courses, its equipment. I also began to work on the part of the copy that would "sell" the department and its program to readers.

I have always liked to use quotations to set the mood of a printed piece. With my experience theme in mind, I turned to my copy of *Bartlett's Familiar Quotations* to search for an appropriate quote. I soon found a great one from the poet Tennyson, who was no journalist, of course, and that was a slight problem. My first brochure for the department had used something from Walter Lippmann, but neither Lippmann nor any other journalist in *Bartlett's* had apparently talked about what I wanted them to talk about. I finally decided that the mood the quote would create was more important than who the source was.

With the quote in front of me, I sat down to write the opening copy block. I would state my case forthrightly and play off the quote. "Experience." A one-word paragraph. "It counts for a lot in life. It helps you get to where you want to be, like in the right niche in journalism." I had got a good start.

Right here, I had gone against a rule I usually make in my writing of never addressing the reader directly through use of "you." (Of course I am breaking an even more firm rule in this PR Focus of never going to the first person or bringing myself into my writing; I could not tell this story without it, however.) Once this "you" approach begins, it must be consistently followed to the end. In this case, I decided the "you" would involve the reader in the subject more quickly and more directly than the more impersonal "students."

I finished the rough draft of the copy, checked it with my chairman for his opinion (he liked it), and began to edit the answers to my letters to graduates, which were by now beginning to come in. Most were just right. A few had to be shortened so they would be the same length (politics again). I had been correct in my choice of people. All of them found that the practical experience gained in the department was valuable to them in their professional work, and said so in their replies. I tied the end of the copy with the beginning — a good technique in any writing — and added another quote about experience, this one from John Locke, another nonjournalist.

I now had a good idea of length so I went to see the director of publications at Oregon State, Tom Sanders. Because the brochure would be paid for with state funds, it had to go through the publications office. It would be designed there and printed at the OSU printing department.

BUT WE HAVE THINGS

to offer in our program that you will not find elsewhere—with the big schools and departments of journalism.

• specialized training • a flexible program.

these are the key elements in our four year major in technical and scientific journalism which leads to a Bachelor of Arts or Bachelor of Science degree.

Specialized training

The program began with the idea that graduates can best be placed in jobs if they can offer some kind of training in specialized areas. That is, we believe it is no longer enough for you to know how to take notes, write complete sentences, and type on one side of the paper.

You still will have to do all of that, of course, but as journalism has become increasingly specialized, it has become more important for the reporter, both in a beginning status and beyond, to know how to deal with more complicated subjects in the interview, writing and typing stages. What the reporter knows how to deal with—no matter how technical—may be crucial in the future to getting a job.

It is with this in mind that we have constructed our journalism major, which consists of a course of study in basic journalism:

Survey of American Journalism (J-110X), Newswriting (J-111), Newswriting and Reporting (J-212), Copy Editing (J-214), and Special Feature Articles (J-317)

followed by upper division courses concerning more specialized aspects of technical and scientific journalism:

Technical Reporting (J-319), Industrial-Business Publications (J-333), and Contemporary Technical Journalism (J-393).

Along the way, we can also give you a number of courses that will show you how to be a more versatile journalist:

Editorial Writing (J-223), Public Information Methods (J-331), Photojournalism (J-334), Mechanics of Publishing (J-335), and Industrial Advertising (J-350)

and a more well-informed one:

Seminars in Critical Reviewing, Law, and the History of Journalism (J-407), and a course in Media and Society (J-450).

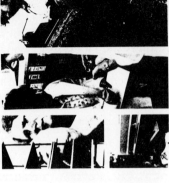

To keep up with changing technology, the department now has video display terminals and special electric typewriters to instruct you about how to prepare copy for optical character readers. As a student, you will use this equipment in a seminar in computer editing and a publications production laboratory where you will set copy for several student magazines and newspapers.

The big difference in journalism at Oregon State University, however, comes in the series of technical minors you take along with your major in journalism. Our theory is that you should have specialized training in the field you will write about. To this end, we offer 31 minors in eleven areas.

Agriculture—minors in agricultural economics, agricultural education, agricultural engineering, agronomic crop science, animal science, extension methods, fisheries and wildlife, food science and technology, horticulture, poultry science, rangeland resources, or soils.

Business—a general minor including courses in business administration, finance, law, marketing, management, and accounting.

Engineering—a minor in civil engineering technology.

Forestry—minors in forest engineering, forest management, natural resource conservation, or wood industry management.

Health and Physical Education—a minor in applied safety studies or a minor in health science with an option in community or environmental health.

Home Economics—a minor in foods and nutrition or courses from four departments: clothing, textiles and related arts; family life; foods and nutrition; or home management.

Oceanography—a general minor including courses in biological, physical, geological, and chemical oceanography.

Pharmacy—a general minor including courses from five departments: pharmaceutical science, pharmaceutical chemistry, pharmacology, pharmacognosy, and pharmacy administration.

Reserve Officers Training Corps (ROTC)—minors in aerospace studies, military science, and naval science.

Science—minors in atmospheric sciences, computer science, and earth sciences.

Veterinary Medicine—a general minor.

You may also take journalism as an area of concentration in the professional home economics communications program of the School of Home Economics, as a minor in general agriculture in the agricultural and agricultural technology curriculum of the School of Agriculture, or as a sports communication minor in the School of Health and Physical Education.

A basic minor in journalism is offered by the department through the School of Education for those interested in teaching journalism in secondary schools.

A flexible program

The department places special emphasis on student projects and here is where the flexibility comes in. In these, you can work on a one-to-one basis with a faculty member on a publication, research paper, or article that will, in many cases, be published and later serve as a sample of your work. You also get credit and sometimes pay for your efforts. You also get a flexibility to try your hand at things you'd never get the chance to try if you were always restricted to the classroom.

In the past, these projects have included work on publications for the Schools of Agriculture, Engineering, Forestry, Pharmacy, Education, Home Economics, Business, the Department of Journalism, and the OSU Alumni Association; planning and carrying out public information and writing assignments for the Sea Grant program, the OSU Extension Service, the OSU Department of Information,

In the Department of Journalism at Oregon State University, we put truth in the first place.

Department of Journalism
Oregon State University
Corvallis, Oregon 97331

Oregon State University

Non-Profit Org.
U.S. Postage
PAID
Permit No. 200
Corvallis, OR 97331

Because we do, we must candidly admit from the start of this brochure that we are not the biggest or the greatest or the most wealthy of journalism schools or departments in the nation.

OSU Summer Term, the Heart Association and the Oregon Lung Association, designing and producing brochures and pamphlets for organizations like the Corvallis Chamber of Commerce, the OSU student government, OSU student services, the Corvallis school district, and the OSU Outdoor Program; researching and writing articles for newspapers around the state; and conducting studies relating to technical journalism.

You also have the chance to work for student publications: the *Barometer*, the daily newspaper; *Beaver*, the yearbook; and *Prism*, a magazine of student work published three times a year.

The same project approach applies to photojournalism as well as to writing. After you've taken the basic course, you can choose from a number of special aspects of photography taught on an independent study basis—color, wildlife, portraiture, underwater, and technical-industrial photojournalism.

You can also get credit and sometimes pay for taking photographs for brochures, pamphlets, or other public information activities for the same organizations already listed.

It is also possible for you to participate in internships through the journalism department. One, at the *Corvallis Gazette-Times*, includes summer work and a scholarship. Another, for students interested in medical writing, offers a term or a summer of work in the public information department of a hospital. The Kate L. Bartholomew Scholarship of $500 is also given annually to a junior in the department. The E. R. Jackman Scholarship goes each year to a journalism student with a minor in agriculture.

Your raw material

The location of the Department of Journalism at Oregon State University offers you the chance to gather material for articles and perfect your ability as a technical journalist firsthand. As a primary science center, OSU employs a number of scientists and technical specialists who work on or near the campus in a variety of specialized agencies.

The presence of so many scientists and technical people will give you your raw material—without leaving campus.

A recent department link with the OSU Extension Service will also provide you the opportunity to work around the State of Oregon.

What's in it for you?

This all sounds well and good, you might think, but how will it help me get a job when I am through?

When you graduate, you are prepared for editorial positions on business, trade, scientific, medical, technical, industrial, and other specialized publications; specialized editorial jobs on general interest newspapers and magazines; more general writing and reporting assignments on newspapers, magazines, or radio and television stations, and work in special kinds of public relations and government information posts.

That's not to say we can guarantee you a place at the top right from the start of your career. But, recent graduates have found the kind of specialized reporting and information jobs they desired. Much depends on individual abilities and the employment situation at the time you graduate.

But with this, a different kind of program under your belt and in your head, you have a better chance than many of your compatriots with more general training.

Journalism is changing and we believe we have designed a program to meet many of those changes. If you'd like to join us, we'd like to have you.

That is the truth—in both the first and second places.

for more information write:
Chairman,
Department of Journalism
Oregon State University
Corvallis, Oregon 97331

Published by the Oregon State Board of Higher Education

Exhibit 13.2

The old Oregon State University Department of Journalism brochure. (Reprinted with permission, OSU Department of Journalism.)

Sanders and I talked about the purpose of the brochure and the approach. We also discussed length, cost, and timetable. I was able to give him an idea of the length of various copy blocks because of the first draft I had now finished. He made a copy of it.

He agreed to design the publication and have a rough layout for me in several weeks. I told him I hoped to have a square publication, probably 8 × 8. We both decided that because of the amount of copy, the publication could not be a brochure, that is, a multipanel, folded piece; it would have to be a booklet, that is, a multipage stapled piece. I left to refine the copy and press my sources for the photographs.

When we got together in several weeks, Sanders presented me with a rough that was 8½ × 11, not the square publication I had asked. I resisted at first, sticking to my original concept of the square format. He argued that the larger size would handle the copy better, was more journalistic in that he wanted to make it look like a magazine with the word "journalism" at the top like a masthead. He also explained to me that he was trying to establish a certain "look" for all OSU school and department brochures and a standard size for them. The more I thought about his reasons, the less I resisted. He was right, and I really liked his concept and rough layout.

From this point, the process was fairly simple. Sanders specked the type and sent it to printing, deciding in the process to use Palatino, my favorite type, elegant and easy to read. A problem was that the OSU Department of Printing did not have Palatino. But Sanders got special permission to go to another typehouse in the nearby town of Eugene to have the copy set. For variation he later used Revue for the main journalism heading and name of the department on the cover of the booklet.

The photos arrived in varying degrees of quality. Far too many of them showed our graduates at typewriters, but how else do you depict journalism other than talking on the telephone, which is even more of a cliché? The university photographer took shots of the department's photo and computer equipment and the student publications.

There then arose the need to show a minority student in a photo. This need causes a problem for all editors and designers: Show that minority people are accepted and already a part of your organization without being too obvious about it. The picture that resulted looked staged (which it was) and the people looked awkward (which they probably felt). I was embarrassed to ask the black student to pose as a "token" representative of his race and our liberalism. Fortunately, the photographer took shots around the office of the student newspaper and got the black student in some of them.

But Sanders decided to use that photo on the cover, a choice I felt put the wrong emphasis on our program. Besides, due to the "staged" look that emerged, the photo was not a good one. I told him I wanted another photo. Time was running short. My chairman had decided that he wanted to distribute the booklet at the May awards banquet. and we would all have to hurry to have it ready.

The photographer came to one of my classes and got the cover photo we used: a shot of two students working at typewriters (typewriters again!) processed in high contrast to give a stark look and with film frame holes visible as well. The other photo was used inside.

I did not like another thing when the first proofs came back: Tennyson's name was set in type as large as that of the quote. I did not want to emphasize this nonjournalist that much. Also, Sanders had mistakenly thought the first line and paragraph of my copy, "Experience," was a headline. Even though it was large enough to be a headline, I explained it was a line of copy. This matter was rectified by the addition of a period after the word, which meant a further protrusion of type into the photo.

The last decision involved the use of color on the cover. Sanders felt that the extra cost was worth it for the emphasis it would give. It would appear only on the little slash area on the cover that said, "Department of Journalism, Oregon State University." I checked the cost problem with my chairman and he immediately agreed.

What color should it be? I was tired of orange, the university's traditional color. It was gaudy and overused. My favorite color is yellow, but I always hesitate to pawn that off onto other people. I would let Sanders decide. After all, he is the graphic designer. And besides that, I am colorblind.

We made the final decision on the telephone.

"What color do you think, Tom?"

"Well, you know a brochure has to stand out. It's often put in racks at high schools with other brochures. Kids should be able to see it clearly."

"That's true. What would you recommend, Tom?"

"How about yellow? It's a nice bright color."

"Good idea, Tom. That sounds fine to me."

The brochure came out on time and has been a reasonable success, the cracks about "yellow journalism" notwithstanding.

PR FOCUS: TYPESETTING AND PRINTING

When working with a printer, the PR person will encounter three basic printing processes.

Letterpress

This technique uses the oldest form of printing with its raised surface (the type) pressed against a flat surface (the paper). It was developed from the art of woodcutting, in which craftsmen gouged out the surface areas of blocks of wood not meant to print, leaving the letter to be printed raised in relief. At

Journalism

These on-campus projects are strengthened by the closeness to all of the technical expertise at Oregon State. OSU is a major center of scientific research and the work of the many scientists and engineers provides the raw material for journalism students.

Recent projects include the preparation of newsletters, brochures and articles for various academic departments like the OSU Sea Grant College Program, the School of Home Economics, the School of Education, the School of Oceanography, the School of Agriculture, the College of Liberal Arts, the Office of Student Services, the Office of University Publications, the Office of Information, the Transportation Research Institute, and the Gerontology Program. Off-campus organizations like the Jackman Institute, the Girl Scouts, the Oregon Heart Association, the Corvallis Chamber of

Commerce and United Way have been helped too. If you are a photographer, photo projects for these and other organizations also can be arranged.

Internships have been carried out by students at the Oregon Museum of Science and Industry, the Oregon State Public Interest Research Group, and several Portland hospitals, and can also be worked out with various daily and weekly newspapers in Oregon.

The Robert Ingalls Internship is available every year and includes a summer job at the *Corvallis Gazette-Times* and a scholarship. Other scholarships include the E. B Aldrich Journalism Scholarship ($600), the Kate L. Bartholomew Journalism Scholarship ($500), the Jackman Institute Scholarship ($750), and the W. Verne McKinney Scholarship ($600).

BUT there is more to journalism training than courses and books. This is where the projects (J-406) and internships (J-410) come in. They give you the opportunity to work in professional situations right on campus.

"*T*HE MOST important thing about the OSU journalism department is the many opportunities students have to get something—anything!—published prior to commencement day. In the newspaper business, city editors aren't interested in the A-you got in basic newswriting. They want to know if you can write. My three years of experience on the *Daily Barometer*, the last one as editor, were instrumental in landing a job on a daily newspaper after graduation. I barely noticed the transition from student reporter and editor to professional reporter. I believe being from OSU helped my chances in a tight job market."
— Bob Goldstein, county government and political reporter, *Walla Walla (Washington) Union Bulletin*, winner of the 1977 national feature writing award from The Society of Professional Journalists, Sigma Delta Chi; a 1977 OSU journalism graduate with a minor in earth sciences.

"*I* WOULD recommend the OSU journalism department because I think the program is diverse enough so you aren't locked into one part of journalism. You can bend it to fit your interest because you get a wide enough background in various areas. I gained an understanding of all the various parts of publications through the projects I did, how they fit together and how to get them ready for printing from beginning to end. I also did a variety of writing and learned to adopt my writing and change from one style to another when required. For example, although some of my training at OSU was on the newspaper, I wound up writing for an engineering company."
— Karen Kerrsick, technical editor, CH2M-Hill, Corvallis, Oregon; a 1978 OSU journalism graduate with a minor in agriculture.

"*O*NLY SO much can be learned from a textbook. A real education and appreciation of journalism requires varied publications experiences. The OSU journalism department offers that, and more: a small enrollment, personalized instruction, a wide range of projects, not just work on the daily newspaper or yearbook. At a larger, impersonal university, your experience can be limited. My experience at OSU made me more marketable as a graduate, more confident in my job responsibilities. My career began at OSU."
— Gary Chesnutis, advertising and sales promotion specialist, Hewlett-Packard Computer Systems Group, Cupertino, California, winner of first and third place, The Society of Technical Communication 1978 Awards competition for manuals; a 1977 OSU journalism graduate with a minor in fisheries and wildlife.

Exhibit 13.3
The new Oregon State University Department of Journalism brochure. (Reprinted with permission, OSU Department of Journalism.)

Journalism with a minor

The department received permission from the Oregon State Board of Higher Education to award a bachelor of arts or bachelor of science degree in journalism with the stipulation that students complete a technical minor. The theory behind this approach is the feeling that journalists are better equipped to work if they have a body of knowledge in a field they might write about. The small number of minors available that first year has increased to 32. These minors range from aerospace studies to wood industry management and are explained in a supplement to this booklet.

In 1978, the department's technical journalism degree program was accredited by the American Council on Education in Journalism. Chapters of The Society of Professional Journalists, Sigma Delta Chi; Kappa Tau Alpha, the national journalism honor society; Women in Communications; the National Press Photographers Association; and Agricultural Communicators of Tomorrow have been organized in the department.

"My JOURNALISM education at OSU enabled me to combine a nursing background with writing to develop a career that is interesting, challenging, and different from nursing per se, without really giving up my 15 years in the health care field. The classroom experience was invaluable for learning writing techniques that help me every day. The internship experience at the University of Oregon Medical School gave me insight into health care organization and communication. My education helps me on the job in other ways. For example, my relationships with the press are secure and based on trust I learned through the emphasis OSU faculty place on ethics. I do not have to hide touchy issues and can present information with credibility. The OSU program is valuable for the informality of the classes. The groups were small and there was time for interaction with the faculty which gave us a more comprehensive view of the realities of journalism as a career."

— Jeanne Moore, director of public relations, Women & Infants Hospital, Providence, Rhode Island; a 1974 OSU journalism graduate with a minor in health science.

When you graduate, you are prepared for editorial positions on business, trade, scientific, medical, technical, industrial, and other specialized publications; specialized editorial jobs on general interest newspapers, magazines, or radio and television stations; and work in special kinds of public relations and in advertising.

Although the department has only been authorized to grant degrees since 1969, journalism has been taught at OSU since early in this century. Noted alumni from those early years include Frank Bartholomew, retired board chairman of United Press International; Ed Dooley, former editor of the San Francisco *Examiner*; Charles Buxton, editor of the Denver *Post*; Lou Seibert Pappas, formerly with *Sunset* magazine and now food editor of the *Palo Alto* (California) *Times*; the late Hope Chamberlin, author and lecturer; and Mercedes Bates, a vice president of General Mills and its "Betty Crocker" and a graduate of the home economics/communication program at OSU.

YOU ALSO have the chance to work for the *Daily Barometer*, the student newspaper; the *Beaver*, the yearbook; and *Prism*, the student magazine. All of these publications are housed in the new Student Communications Center. Several laboratory newspapers are also published each year by students in several classes. As is the case with projects and internships, time spent on such publications will give you good experience and valuable work samples.

Basic classroom instruction

"If I hadn't attended OSU and become involved in the department, I sincerely doubt I would have received awards or even had a career in journalism. When I entered OSU as a freshman, I had no intention of majoring in journalism. After two indecisive years with no particular major, I took an introductory journalism class. The class was small and I received much individual attention. Because of the smallness of the department and the healthy interaction between students and professors, I was quickly absorbed into a program that was ideal for my needs. The student publications I worked on an excellent steppingstone. The J students at OSU come first in the professors' eyes. The professors sincerely care about each student's welfare."

—Chris Johns, photographer, Topeka (Kansas) Capital-Journal, 1978 National Press Photographer of the Year; a 1974 OSU journalism graduate with a minor in agriculture.

Some are in basic journalism: Survey of American Journalism (J-110), Newswriting (J-111), Newswriting and Reporting (J-212), Copyediting (J-214), Editorial Writing (J-223), Special Feature Articles (J-317), and Public Information Methods (J-318).

These are followed by classes in more specialized aspects of technical, scientific, and business journalism: Technical Reporting (J-319), Industrial-Business Publications (J-333), Contemporary Technical Journalism (J-393), and a Seminar in Technical Editing (J-407).

Along the way, you take other courses that teach you how to be a more versatile journalist: Photojournalism (J-334), Technical Photojournalism I and II (J-434 and J-435), Photography for Industrial Publications (J-384X), Environmental/Wildlife Photography (J-385X), Mechanics of Publishing (J-335), Industrial Advertising (J-350), Broadcast Journalism (J-431), and Television News Reporting (J-407) . . . and a more well-informed one: Media and Society (J-450), Law and Regulation in Mass Media (J-465), and Seminars in Critical Reviewing, History of Journalism, and Science and Medical Writing (J-407).

storage unit, a tape reader, and a tape punch and a high-speed printer. The system makes it possible to set reproduction proofs which can be pasted up and readied for printing. The computer editing laboratory was made possible by a grant from the Gannett Foundation, the Jackson Foundation, and an anonymous donor.

The photojournalism labs have all of the necessary facilities to develop and print photographs. Students in advanced photo courses use special color and black and white darkrooms.

Basic classroom instruction is supplemented by specialized equipment.

In the computer editing laboratory, you can set and correct course assignments and copy for special project publications on six video display terminals (VDT). The lab also has a disc

Are you convinced?

"Experience is an excellent teacher. Working on the Barometer and several special projects — newsletters, brochures, and booklets — gave me the experience I needed to get my first newspaper job. Long hours editing copy and adjusting layouts taught me to budget space and time, recognize priorities, and write concisely. The time was well spent and my job now is much easier because of it. That is why I recommend the OSU journalism program. Few others offer such a variety of learning experiences."

— Jill Carroll, agriculture/forestry reporter, Oregon Statesman, Salem, Oregon; a 1977 OSU journalism graduate with a minor in resource recreation management.

Graduating, with a list of courses and nothing else may not be enough to get a job in these days of heightened competition. As some recent graduates in these pages tell you, it helps to show that you've worked a bit in some part of journalism and have the samples to prove it.

In other words, it will help if you have some experience. It counts for a lot.

"No man's knowledge can go beyond his experience."

–John Locke

For enrollment information write:
  Fred C. Zwahlen, Jr.
  Chairman, Dept. of Journalism
  Oregon State University
  Corvallis, Oregon 97331

Exhibit 13.3 continued

211

the same time that the Chinese were using such a system in about 800 A.D., monks in European monasteries were still copying books by hand. Johann Gutenberg, a German, invented movable type in about 1448, a significant development that changed the way things had been done for centuries. His letters looked like those done by the monks, but they could be used again and again.

Printers arranged the type on a flatbed, or tray, inked it, laid paper on it, and tightened the platen, a wooden plate that pressed the paper against the type, creating the image. But it took time to unscrew the platen after each impression, so inventors added steam as a power source in 1822. Later, for more speed, printers substituted a cylinder for the platen. The cylinder picked up the paper and carried it over a moving type bed. Two cylinders were used in a few years to allow printing on both sides of the paper. By the middle of the nineteenth century, a revolving press was perfected on which type could be rotated instead of being held in one place. This development led to stereotyping and modern rotary presses.

Type is set (see below) and lines of type collected in galley trays, which are corrected and then put together as pages with headlines and engraved illustrations added.

In stereotyping, these pages of type are formed into metal facsimiles for placement on the press. A page-size papier-mâché sheet is laid over the flatbed of type and is sent through a stereotyping machine that rolls it under great pressure. A mat comes out of this machine, a perfect duplicate of the type. After being dried and curved into a half-cylinder shape, the mat is placed in an autoplate machine and is filled with hot lead. The page emerges as a cylindrical metal plate, a duplicate of the original flatbed of type. After cooling, this plate is placed on the press.

For years, type for letterpress printing was set in the same way as in Gutenberg's time: by hand. This method was slow and expensive so a group of New York newspaper publishers financed Ottmar Mergenthaler, a German watchmaker, in the search for a substitute. The Linotype was ready in 1886 and it revolutionized printing. In the machine, hot metal is injected into brass letter molds. Operators put the molds in place and set the copy by hitting a keyboard. Within seconds, the Linotype turns molten metal from a heated container on the back into a line of type evenly spaced and cool enough to touch. No longer would type have to be set by hand; the lines of type could also be melted and reformed into lead bars for reuse in the machine.

Offset

This technique differs from letterpress because it prints from a flat surface rather than a raised one, involves a chemical process rather than a mechanical one, and makes an indirect impression rather than a direct one. Copy for offset is prepared for printing by photographic means, so material is not confined to that cast from hot metal as it is in letterpress.

Offset was discovered by accident in 1796 when Aloys Sevefelder, a Bavarian actor and playwright, developed a way to print from the flat surface of a stone. He could not afford to have his plays printed, so he was trying to reproduce them by writing backwards on the stone. He used a flat stone rather than engraver's copper because the stone could be used again. At one point, he wrote something on the stone with a greasy substance and discovered later that water would not wash it away. Quite by accident, he had discovered the basic principle of offset printing: Greasy surfaces accept only ink and reject water.

Early in the twentieth century, an American printer took the development one step further when he noticed that a precise image would sometimes show up on the back of a sheet as he fed paper into his press. When a sheet did not go in correctly, the image went onto the impression cylinder and appeared on the back of the next sheet. He incorporated this idea into a new press in which a rubber-covered cylinder received the image from the plate and "offset" it onto the paper.

Type for offset is set by any number of means, from a typewriter to a sophisticated, computer-driven typesetting machine. Many of these typesetting systems use video display terminals (VDT), a kind of electronic typewriter with a keyboard for typing, and a video screen to display what has been typed; an electronic "cursor" makes changes. In all of these new typesetting systems, reproduction proofs emerge for correction. These proofs correspond to the galleys of letterpress days.

The proofs are dried and cut to fit a page dummy to which headlines and illustrations are added. All these elements are attached with wax or rubber cement to page dummy sheets. When these dummys have been read and corrected, they are taken to the camera room and photographed. The negative that results is developed and dried. The negatives are placed over thin flat metal plates that have already been made light sensitive. The plate is then "burned" — exposed to light through the negative. The plate is developed like a photograph by chemicals rubbed on it to harden the emulsion in the exposed areas, causing the image to emerge.

After the image has been developed, the plate is gummed to prevent oxidation, bent to fit the press, and locked onto the press, where its surface is moistened with water and an additive. The water sticks to the nonimage area and ink, when it is added, adheres to the image area. The offset aspect comes when the press is revolving: the plate does not touch the paper but leaves an inked image on a rubber-blanket cylinder. The rubber blanket transfers the image to the paper from the plate.

Gravure

This technique transfers images to paper from ink-filled depressions in a surface instead of the raised type of letterpress or the flat surface of offset. A typical use of gravure is in business cards or formal invitations. The material to be printed is cut into a plate, which is then coated with ink and wiped clean. The ink remains in the depressed areas, and paper picks it out when pressed against it. When the image emerges, it is raised on the paper. A more complicated use of this principle occurs for reproducing color posters and photographs in good quantity. *Rotogravure* works in the same way: wells are filled with ink, the excess ink is scraped from the surface, and paper is applied to the plate under pressure. The acid-edged copper cylinder goes around, presses through ink, and is scraped clean by a steel knife. Ink remains only in the wells of the image area. When the paper touches the plate, the ink is sucked onto its surface.

The choice of printing process is generally governed by the kind of equipment a printer has. Letterpress is more slow and more expensive than offset, but quality is usually higher. Offset allows more flexibility in use of illustrations and typefaces. A mix of printers, each with a different printing capability, might be a good solution: offset for fast, cheap, and small jobs like mailers and internal announcements; letterpress for external publications like annual reports, books, and expensive brochures where quality is important; and gravure for longer runs of high-quality posters or photographs.

PR FOCUS: TYPE CLASSIFICATIONS

There are six type classification groups in existence, and hundreds of typefaces within those larger groups. The different faces are manufactured in sizes from 6-point to 12-point with a *font* — or complete assortment of any one size and style containing all characters — available for each one. Such variations as light, bold and extra bold, italic, and expanded or condensed are also manufactured. Body type ranges from 6-point to 14-point, and headline or display type from 14-point to 72-point. Type can also be set in various ways: by hand, by machine, or with the power transfer or press-on type, where letters can be rubbed onto paper from plastic sheets. Type is measured from the top of an ascending letter (called the *ascender* as in a "d") to the bottom of a descending letter (called the *descender* as in a "p"). As a result, the face of any letter is not its full point size. So letters in the same size type but different type classifications might have different heights. The measurement is made not of the letter itself but of the entire surface of the piece of type slightly above the ascender and below the descender and including the *X-height,* or *body,* the main part of the letter.

The main groups of type are as follows.

1.   *Text* resembles the type of Gutenberg's time and was used for centuries in German schoolbooks and newspapers. William Caxton, the first English

printer, took the German faces and fashioned them into Old English. Typefaces in this classification group should be used sparingly because they are hard to read. Now they appear mostly in formal invitations.

𝕰𝖓𝖌𝖗𝖆𝖛𝖊𝖗𝖘 𝕺𝖑𝖉 𝕰𝖓𝖌𝖑𝖎𝖘𝖍

2. *Roman* was gradually developed from text by Italian scribes, who wrote more gracefully and more lightly than the Germans. Another influence were the alphabets carved on ancient Roman buildings. This group has three variations.

   a. *Old style* was derived from the classic Roman with wedge-shaped *serifs* (the finishing strokes at the ends of a main letter). The contrast between thick and thin strokes is not great, making letters open, wide, round, and easy to read. Example: Caslon

Caslon

   b. *Modern* has a greater contrast between thick and thin strokes and has delicate hairlines and serifs. Example: Bodoni

BODONI

   c. *Transitional* has characteristics of both old style and modern but is more refined than old style and less mechanical than modern. Example: Baskerville

Baskerville

3. *Sans Serif* typefaces (also called Gothic) were introduced in the early nineteenth century as a protest against Roman type. They were inspired by the Industrial Revolution, derived from ancient Greek letters, and had strokes of uniform width. There are no serif endings in these types, which rival Roman styles in their frequency of use. Example: Futura

Futura

4. *Square Serif* is essentially a sans serif face with serifs added. Its letters have uniform strokes and square or blocked serifs. Example: Clarendon

Clarendon

5. *Scripts and Cursives* bring back the hand-lettered look that printers were at first trying to avoid. They have limited use and are hard to read. Script letters are connected, cursives are not. Example: Commerical Script

Commercial Script

6. *Novelty and Decorative* types are the most fun to work with and the easiest to use creatively to give a publication a mood or distinctive look. They are also tricky to use because they can be overpowering and hard to read. Essentially, the group contains everything that does not fit elsewhere. Examples: Broadway, Fat Face, Gold Rush, Madame, Pinocchio, Stop

Broadway   MADAME

Fat Face   **PINOCCHIO**

GOLD RUSH   STOP

Decisions on type should be made with suitability and readability in mind. Studies differ about which type groups are easier to read, Roman or Sans Serif. Popular typefaces are available in both, and the choice is the designer's, who should keep in mind the overall design of the publication and how the type contributes to it. Roman and Sans Serif faces should be concentrated on, with Square Serif and Novelty types used occasionally for headlines. Text and Scripts and Cursives should be avoided because they are too hard to read.

"Learn as much about how type is set to know the difference between good typography and bad," says Allen Wong, an Oregon State University art professor and former New York graphic artist. "You must go beyond the prime consideration of legibility and readability. The choice of type depends on your publication. The type for a company newspaper should not be as elegant as for an annual report."

Wong suggests that designers or PR people who do designs become familiar with how certain types look in print. "You need to know that there are different degrees of quality of type. Sans serif is used more and more as the public gets used to it. Serif Roman is more familiar to us. You can mix the two if you are careful. The same is true for novelty and decorative faces. Like seasoning, use them sparingly, as an attention-getting device. As a rule of thumb, don't use more than three different type faces in one printed piece."

REVIEW QUESTIONS

1. Why should PR people go beyond news releases and use brochures, booklets, and other publications?
2. What is the difference between a brochure and a booklet?
3. What does "brainstorming" mean, and what is its value?
4. What are the various stages of laying out a publication?
5. What is the process of writing copy for a brochure?
6. What are the important points to remember in paper selection?
7. What are the important points to remember in type selection?
8. What is the best way to work with printers?
9. What is a press kit, and what does one usually contain?
10. What is the value of a press kit?

ASSIGNMENTS

For Journalism and Business Students

1. Join another class member in conducting a one-hour "brainstorming" session in which you come up with themes and approaches for a new brochure for the journalism department or the business school.
2. Do six thumbnail designs for the brochure.
3. Do a rough layout from one of these designs.
4. Write the copy for the brochure.
5. Clip samples of each kind of major type classification from magazines, mount them on pieces of paper, and label them correctly.
6. Go to a rack of brochures in the Student Union or a travel bureau. Select five of various sizes and paper qualities. Analyze them in terms of their effectiveness, sticking strictly to the question of size and paper stock and how those factors relate to the overall effectiveness of the brochures.
7. Do a rough layout for a design that emphasizes each major design principle: balance, proportion, sequence, unity, contrast. Your subject is volcanoes.
8. Obtain a press kit from a local company PR department and analyze its contents.
9. Now write a story using information from the press kit.

CHAPTER 14

Preparing annual reports

Once a year, publicly held companies are required to prepare a report of the year's events for their stockholders. The requirements dictate that certain financial information be included, and it always is, near the back. For the past fifteen to twenty years, however, many large corporations have used the annual report as a chance to discuss company philosophy and products, and have sent it to a large external audience — indeed, to anyone who asks for a copy.

TRENDS: BROAD AUDIENCES AND LAVISHNESS

"People try to make annual reports all things to all people — every shareholder, every analyst, for company recruiters and salesmen," says Ted Michel, director of investor relations for Levi Strauss & Company and in charge of its annual report. "For the first time next year, we'll have a general capabilities brochure to do some of that."

Adds George Hobgood, a senior vice president of Hill and Knowlton, who writes annual reports for a number of that agency's clients: "It's used for too many purposes. I'd like to see different versions of the annual report — one for shareholders and one for employees, which would be a cross between a regular annual report and a company magazine, and which would simplify finances and be written in everyday English."

Beyond this misuse and dispersal of the annual report has come a lavishness in production that observers like Hobgood think is out of control. "I think annual reports are overdone," he says. "They're much too expensive and have gotten out of hand. The annual report has become the source of ego gratification for some chief executive officers. They send them to each other with greetings attached written on beautifully engraved notepaper. But they do not read it. They thumb through it. The graphics are overdone, too often a substitute for thin content. These are designed by people who know nothing about finance."

Many corporate officials have decided, however, that the annual report is the right vehicle to display their companies' uniqueness and brag about their accomplishments. However, they are preparing reports that are less flamboyant than they have been in recent years. McCormick & Company's 1979 annual report smelled like a vanilla milkshake, as befitted a spice manufacturer. Gulf & Western had its sixty-three-page 1978 annual report printed in *Time* magazine for $3 million. CBS once bound its annual report in leather. The list of such unusual bids for attention will no doubt continue.

A few companies are following Hobgood's advice and are issuing separate reports for employees. In 1980, General Motors published a separate report on its public-interest activities.

PROBLEMS

Costs of these elaborate reports are increasing yearly. Large corporations spend between $50,000 and $100,000 on annual reports, some as much as $250,000. The 45,000 copies of the Levi Strauss 1979 report cost $100,000, for example.

The approval cycle for the material included in the annual report has become more complicated. Not only do a large number of company officials have to approve copy; since 1974, when the Securities and Exchange Commission increased its requirements for the financial information to be included, external bureaucrats must be pleased as well. Now companies have to publish certified financial statements for the previous two years, a five-year summary of operations, a general description of the business, and a management analysis. They must also identify all executive officers and directors and offer a free copy of form 10 – K, the legal annual report filed with SEC, discussed in greater detail in Chapter 8.

The great bulk of material has led to a greater amount of time needed to do the annual report — in some companies as long as a year — and an increasing number of pages. Some experts think that the 100-page annual report is not far away.

These same experts decry the fact that the time spent, length of report, and expense of production have not increased the average shareholder's understanding of the company. The only people gaining are those in accounting firms, law firms, printing companies, and paper companies.

BACKGROUND

The New York Stock Exchange first required that its members make annual financial reports in 1869. Very few companies complied because of a penchant for not letting the public or their competitors know what they were doing. The Securities Exchange Act of 1934 expanded the New York Stock Exchange requirement to every issuer of a registered security in the United States. The format to be used was the infamous form 10 – K. Companies began slowly to comply with this federal law, but the early annual reports were quite modest. IBM, for example, published a simple twenty-page document in the same plain format for forty years. In 1955, the corporation hired graphic designer Paul Rand to do its annual report, however. Rand produced a lavish report that looked like a magazine: good paper, modern type, photographs by noted photojournalists. The report began a new era in annual report production. Most large companies began to pay more attention to — and more money for — their annual reports.

A TYPICAL CORPORATE ANNUAL REPORT

The 1979 annual report of Levi Strauss & Company is a typical example of a lavish, expensive and effective corporate annual report (Exhibit 14.1). Investor relations director Ted Michel began the planning for the report, issued in February 1980, the previous August with a memo outlining possible contents. He circulated the document to company officers for their comments.

With the preliminary plans approved, Michel turned his ideas over to an outside design consultant, Robert Miles Runyan & Associates. That firm then prepared three spreads and the cover for approval by the chairman, the president and chief executive officer, and the chief operating and chief financial officers.

A natural theme for that year was the company's involvement in clothing the U.S. Olympic team. The warm-up suit on the front and back cover was developed for team members and had served as a prototype for similar apparel marketed by the Activewear Division. Michel would later have to tone down the Olympic tie-in with an explanatory note on the first page after President Carter announced a possible boycott of the Summer Games in Moscow. "If this should happen," read the note, written in January 1980, before the final decision on the boycott had been made, "Levi Strauss & Co. is prepared to modify its marketing plans and promotional strategy. It is our intention to provide continuing support to the Olympics consistent with our Government's position, and to maintain planned advertising investment and promotional support through our sports promotion program."

The inside cover shows the emblems of all divisions of the corporation with a list of their products. Page 1, before its Olympic explanation, lists financial highlights and contents in clean, easy-to-read type, nicely arranged. That page also talks about the cover and explains that the photos inside "show the diversity of the company's products in settings which depict them as wardrobes assembled prior to packing."

The next three pages contain the letter to the shareholders from the three top corporate executives. This section, written by Ted Michel, reviews the important events of the year within the company. "An ideal annual report is one that anyone with a working knowledge of the business is able to read and then understand the company in general and also have some perspective

Exhibit 14.1
Cover of the Levi Strauss & Company annual report. (Reprinted with permission, Levi Strauss & Company.)

about what happened the previous year," he says. "I try to hit all significant issues concisely in the shareholders' letter, the shorter the better. You assume that the reader will read this letter and nothing else." Page 5 in this particular report pays tribute to two retired officials who had died during the year.

The operations review section begins on page 7, with the first of the lavish color photos of products ready for packing — this one on western wear — on the facing page. Small graphs are used at the top of each right-hand page as well. "You go for a different level of detail in this section," continues Michel. "You say a little about every operational unit." In such sections, writers and designers must be careful to give amounts of space proportional to each division's size for political reasons and to avoid hurt feelings. To this end, Levi Strauss USA is covered in greater detail than Levi Strauss International. This section goes on to discuss the company's work in social responsibility (it has organized more than 100 "community involvement teams" to assist the communities where company plants are located), equal employment opportunity (increasing the number of women and minorities it employs), legal developments (like its efforts to prevent misuse of its trademarks and the sale of counterfeit Levi's jeans), and a note on the groundbreaking for a new corporate headquarters. Each spread of this section contains another four-color photo on the left-hand page.

On page 16 the report leaves the photos behind to begin the lengthy and complicated financial-review section. The section runs to the end of the thirty-two-page report to cover a great deal of financial information: sales; gross profit; marketing, general, and administrative expenses; interest expense and income; income taxes; net income; inventories; receivables; debt and equity; and the effect of currency fluctuations.

Charts give quarterly results compared to the past two years, sales by geographical area, a ten-year financial summary, consolidated balance sheets, a consolidated statement of income, a consolidated statement of stockholders' equity, a consolidated statement of changes in financial position, accounting policies, and notes about such aspects of the business as acquisition, income taxes, short-term borrowing, long-term debt, common stock, stock options, leases, and commitments. This section ends with the accountant's certifying statement. The last page and inside cover list officers, directors, the location of the corporate headquarters, the time and place of the annual meeting, the name of the stock transfer agent, the stock listing, and where to write for the more detailed form 10 – K.

PLANNING

1. Begin the planning process by working backward from the date of the annual meeting. The New York Stock Exchange requires that each listed company publish an annual report and submit it to shareholders at least fifteen days in advance of the annual meeting, but not more than three months after

the close of the fiscal year. The American Stock Exchange requires that annual reports be submitted to shareholders at least ten days before the annual meeting, but not more than four months after the close of the fiscal year. The Securities and Exchange Commission requires that form 10 – K be filed with it within 90 days after the close of the fiscal year, except for certain schedules that may be filed up to 120 days after year's end. When the date is set, work out a reasonable schedule with a printer so that copies of the annual report will be available at least two weeks before they are needed. (Do not tell the printer, by the way, that the reports are not needed on the date set, to build in a small cushion of time.)

2. Meet with the company official responsible for the annual report and annual meeting. Usually this person is the corporate secretary. It is best to deal with other members of management through this person, as long as he or she is able to make decisions. If this person is a "yes man" who will run to others for advice on every aspect of the material to be approved and thus delay the process, set up a line of approval that includes a wider circle of officials.

3. Go into the first meeting with the secretary or other members of management with a proposal for the annual report listing any theme suggestions, possible contents of the letter to shareholders, and the main segments of the company to be covered in the review-of-the-year section. List suggestions for photographs and other illustrations in the proposal. Present a preliminary budget.

4. Once members of management have approved the concept, meet with the in-house artist or outside designer to review the proposal. Give the designer clear goals for the report. Decide right then whether the graphics of the report will be elaborate or subdued. After several years of flamboyant design, annual reports are becoming more calm. "Graphics are good when you get something that needs a graphic treatment," says George Hobgood of Hill and Knowlton. "Too often graphics are put in for the sake of graphics. Elaborate graphics are good if they help an investor understand, but not good if they complicate the message."

RESEARCH AND WRITING

5. Gather the material for the report by interviewing division or department heads. What have their units done this year? How has that affected the company? What are future plans?

6. Get the financial people to compile the financial information needed for the half of the report dealing with finances. This is what investors, stock brokers, the SEC, and the stock exchanges are interested in. The first half is only window dressing. The financial people know that the two major stock exchanges require balance sheets, income and retained earnings statements, sources and applications of funds statements for the two most recent fiscal years on a comparative basis. But are they aware of the need for the address of the

principal company office; names and addresses of trustees, transfer agents, and registrars; number of employees; number of stockholders; and number of shares under option, changes in number during the year, and the number of shares available for the granting of options according to the company's listing agreement if the company is listed on the New York Stock Exchange? In addition, the SEC requires that information be included from form 10 – K, which has presumably already been filled out: a brief description of the company's business; a summary of the company's operations for the last five fiscal years and a management analysis of them; a business-segment breakdown for the most recent five years of intersegment transfers, including operating profit revenues and identifiable assets attributable to each segment; the identities and backgrounds of directors and officers; material differences, reflected in financial statements, from established accounting principles or practices; the principal market where each voting security is traded; price ranges for voting securities quarterly for the two most recent fiscal years. The company must also be prepared to issue a copy of form 10 – K free of charge to any shareholder who asks.

7. Write the copy for the annual report with the average reader in mind. "What you send to the little old lady from Pasadena who owns some shares is different from what you send to Chase Manhattan Bank," continues Hobgood. Nevertheless, both kinds of people must be served. Usually, the average shareholder or would-be shareholder looks at the president's letter, the financial highlights, and the review of the year. The banks, brokers, and stock-exchange officials can get what they need in the financial section and form 10 – K. "In the president's letter, I write about what happened," says Hobgood. "I write to answer an investor's questions. Do I keep my stock or do I buy more? What does this tell me about the future? By the time the annual report is out the facts of the earnings are history." To do a good job, the writer of an annual report needs to know how well the company did, and why; new products; capital investments; the economic and social trends affecting business; and the outlook for the year ahead.

8. Get the president or chairman to write, or at least contribute to, the letter to shareholders that bears his or her name. "Too many times I have seen an annual report that is never shown to the chief executive officer until it is written," says Hobgood. "He makes minor adjustments and that's all — and then is not quite satisfied. Why? Because it was written by a committee and has no point of view. What's in management's head about goals, how to make money? That should be in there. I always spend a great deal of time with the CEO to find out his views before I start writing."

9. Keep political factors in mind when assigning space to the various parts of the company. Be careful not to leave any area out, even if it has not done much during the year. The safest way to allocate space is to make all major divisions equal in number of lines and illustrations. The only exception would be when a new unit or product of special promise was founded or developed during the year. In this case, it could be featured as such.

10. When having copy reviewed, establish firm deadlines with the re-

viewers, even if they are high company officials. Do not be afraid to remind them that their changes are late. Usually it will help to mention "printer's deadlines" and the fact that missing them will add to cost. Be firm about having them look for factual errors, and avoid grammatical nitpicking.

11. Be careful in getting sample designs approved by too many people. Invariably, one person will not like some aspect of the design. Yet, it is risky to avoid showing the report to officials until after it is finished and in print. A balky company president might decide to scrap the whole enterprise a week before the annual meeting, regardless of the SEC and stock exchanges. It is best for the PR person to establish himself or herself as the expert and fend off all but the best suggestions. Also, show the designs to officials only once. Get releases signed so that someone does not say later that he or she did not approve the copy or layout or whatever.

DESIGN

12. Impress upon the designer from the start the high-quality nature of the annual report. "The annual report is the company's best foot forward," says Allen Wong, OSU art professor and former New York designer. "It should have the best quality printing, use the best quality paper. The company should spend time and money to get solid photos, good graphs and charts. An annual report reflects a company. A shoddy annual report will create a bad image. If people are interested in buying stock they will ask for the annual report, and it will be their first introduction to the company."

13. Get the designer to establish a consistent format: a full-page photograph on each left-hand page, for example, as in the Levi Strauss annual report, and two 18-pica-wide columns on the right-hand page with a smaller photo in the remaining white space.

14. Remember the importance of type to establish mood, carry out the theme, and aid readability. Body type should be 9 point or 10 point. The SEC, however, specifies that footnotes must "be in roman type at least as large and as legible as 10 point modern type . . . leaded at least two points," to avoid a company hiding an important fact. Tables cannot be set in type smaller than 8 point.

15. Establishing the size of the annual report is important. Most reports are 8½ × 11 inches. Although variations are possible and sometimes make for good design, designers need to be careful. Most security analysts file annual reports on shelves or in filing cabinets, and an outsized report may not fit or a small report might get lost. "You want them to keep it," continues George Hobgood. "If it won't fit, it will be thrown away. Some reports are so big they look like the collected works of Ernest Hemingway."

16. Make the format flexible, to allow for changes by company officials and the SEC. New accounting footnotes are being added late in the annual-report process, and some of them are long. The SEC may make changes up

until the last minute, as so might company officials. To gain flexibility, two techniques are recommended by the S. D. Warren Company, the manufacturer of paper used in many annual reports. Arrange to run text copy in the front of the report so that it carries over from spread to spread or page to page within a section. In this way, the writer is not forced to cut or add copy to fit a specific page at the last minute. Leave "swing" pages within the report, pages for which no type or illustrations are planned. They can be used later for copy, if necessary, or filled with a photograph if copy runs short.

17. Choose paper with high postage rates in mind, but be careful not to give the annual report a flimsy feeling. Warren recommends coated text paper of rough or smooth textures. Coated papers or embossed coated papers reproduce photographs better, however, so they might be used in the front review half, with text papers in the all-text financial half.

18. If photographs are used in an annual report, they should be in color, despite the increase in cost. The only time black-and-white photos might do is where a particularly stark and dramatic look is desired — or where the cost of four-color printing is impossible for a company to bear. Color and black-and-white photos can be mixed, but not on the same page or spread.

19. Select the photographer carefully and, for the sake of consistency, use only one to do the annual report. Instruct the photographer carefully on the approach to be used in the annual report: theme, number of sections, possible areas to be photographed, "must" areas of the company to be photographed. Make all the arrangements and get all the necessary clearances so that the photographer can work unimpeded at a plant or out-of-town location or in the executive suite. Most photographers charge a daily rate of from $200 to $1,000 plus expenses.

20. Do not neglect artwork to illustrate a report, however, especially on charts or graphs, which can be dull if they contain statistics alone. Sometimes, artwork alone will be used to illustrate an annual report. The 1967 report of Litton Industries, for example, reproduced thirty of the world's most exquisite stained-glass windows, all of them dealing with business subjects. Most of the time, however, photographs are deemed more realistic and better able to convey the company's strengths than "artsy" illustrations.

21. Do not forget that the cover of the annual report is just as important as that of a magazine. The photo or illustration on it should dominate and entice the reader to open up the publication. Sometimes, a provocative headline in large type on a dark background will have the same effect, as will the company name, unusually displayed. Whatever the approach, the company name and year and the fact that it is an annual report must be visible.

BUDGETING

22. Remember that only a preliminary budget was presented along with the first proposal to management. A final budget can be drawn up once the format

has been established and number of pages decided, quantity determined, paper selected, typesetting and printing costs estimated, photography and art decisions made, and mailing and distribution agreed to.

SCHEDULING

23. Keep the project within the budget by keeping everything on schedule. The Warren Company says that cost overruns come mainly when things are done after a deadline. Changes in the text after it has been set into type instead of in the typewritten copy can double or triple typesetting costs; changes in the mechanicals after they have been pasted up or after the job has been sent to the printer can also add greatly to costs; changes to photographs, like retouching, might cost $50 in an early stage, about $650 after color separations have been made, and sometimes $2,000 just before printing.

DISTRIBUTION

24. Select the envelopes for mailing the report carefully so that they are durable but as inexpensive as possible.

25. Give the mailing company or the company mailroom supervisor a dummy of the report and envelope to make sure that they can be used on equipment, and doublecheck the postal information preprinted on the envelope (a permit number avoids the need to stamp each envelope) to make sure that it is correct.

26. Consider sending the reports third-class bulk mail if there is time. It is a lot less expensive.

SUMMARY

Publicly held corporations are required to publish an annual report of their successes and failures in a given year. Most large companies use this occasion to make a bold and often lavish statement about themselves. Annual reports have become a costly endeavor for companies, which use them for purposes not originally intended, like general brochures, sales tools, or personnel recruiting. The steps required to produce a successful annual report include planning, research and writing, design, budgeting, scheduling, and distribution. The process is not easy. Delays and last-minute changes can result from meddling corporate executives, worried accountants, and balky bureaucrats from the Securities and Exchange Commission.

REVIEW QUESTIONS

1. Why is an annual report so important to a company?
2. What problems exist for annual reports?
3. What are the steps to go through to prepare an annual report?
4. How important is planning? Why?
5. How does one do research and write an annual report?
6. What considerations are important in design, paper, and type selection?
7. How can delays and cost overruns be avoided?
8. How should the annual report be distributed?
9. How does one establish the deadline system for an annual report?

ASSIGNMENTS

For Journalism and Business Students

1. Select an annual report from a major U.S. corporation, and analyze it in terms of writing, design, and overall effectiveness. Report your findings to the class.
2. Take two annual reports from different companies and compare and contrast them in terms of writing, design, and overall effectiveness. If you were a prospective stockholder, whose stock would you choose and why? Report your findings to the class.
3. Gather the material for, and write, the year-in-review section of an annual report. The company can be a local one where you can do research first-hand, or a national one with facts gained in a library.
4. Produce a company annual report and take it to the rough layout stage ready for typesetting. Write the copy, design the pages, select and mark up type and paper specifications.

CHAPTER **15**

Preparing company magazines and newspapers

The magazine looks like those around it on the coffee table. It has a color cover and good graphics and easy-to-read type. The articles are interesting and informative. At first glance, it is impossible to notice any difference between this magazine and the copies of *Newsweek* and *Popular Photography* sitting next to it.

The magazine in this case could be any one of thousands of company magazines (and newspapers) in existence today to serve employees, their families, and people in the outside world. The International Association of Business Communicators, the professional organization for writers, editors, audiovisual specialists, and others who work on such publications, has over 5,000 members, who reach an estimated audience of 460 million. But not all company magazine editors belong to the IABC. There may be as many as 10,000 such publications in existence.

WHAT IS A COMPANY MAGAZINE?

They come in as many shapes, sizes, and degrees of quality as the companies they chronicle. They are read and discarded with as much regularity as trade publications, general magazines, or newspapers. With company publications, however, there is one difference: they have only one editorial line and major purpose, and they do not try to hide it. They are unabashedly in favor of the company and its well-being. They are used to inform employees and the public about the organization, its people, and its products. No one hints at any other purpose.

The quality depends on the willingness of management to provide the budget for an adequate staff to gather material, write articles, and take photographs, and to pay for good paper and good quality typesetting and printing. A good magazine also results when editors are allowed to produce their publications without frequent and embarrassing proclamations of company virtue. The more objective and journalistic the content, the better the magazine.

234

Although formats differ depending on management philosophy and available funds, the company magazine falls into one of three categories:

Internal — where the company is reaching only its employees with information of interest exclusively to them (what the new pay policy is, who won the company bowling tournament, etc.); the quality of internal company publications varies greatly.

External — where the company is aiming at an audience outside its doors to create a good image, convey information, and create good will, usually in a lavish way.

Internal-external — where the company uses the same publication to reach both the public and employees.

Whatever the specific format approach, the idea has definitely been accepted by management in companies with an average of 15,000 employees or more, although many IABC members work in organizations with less than 1,000 employees. Company magazines and newspapers are the only really effective way to reach an audience inside and outside the company with facts about it.

A company can hold a press conference to announce a new product or a major change in management. Reporters covering the press conference will write stories about it. But what they write will be their own interpretation of what is being done, and why. There has to be a place for the company to put forth its own point of view.

A company can announce a new employee policy over a public-address system or by handing out photocopies to workers in the lunch line. But why not wrap up such information in a more attractive package and send it to the employee's home so that his or her family can read about the new policy along with lists of who is getting twenty-five-year pins and having babies?

The way this is done can enhance the process or detract from it, and that seems to be where many company publications run aground today. Some company magazines are unprofessionally done. The writing is bad, the layout is chaotic and hard to follow. The typeface looks like something used in Lincoln's time. The photographs are too dark, and out of focus at that.

Such publications are not fulfilling their goal or living up to their promise. They have captured the attention of employees and the outside world, but they are abusing it. One thing a company magazine editor must remember above all else is the competition, the other magazines and newspapers the employee subscribes to that are sitting there on the mythical coffee table mentioned at the start of this chapter. If the company magazine does not measure up to them, it will not make it to the coffee table. It will be glanced at and quickly discarded. Readers are exposed to too many sophisticated publications and slick television advertising, each with good graphics and type and clearly written copy, to respond well to a shabby publication, even if it is from their own company.

The same thing holds true for external publications, but here a slipshod magazine works against the overall image of excellence the company wants to create with the press, shareholders, and other influential members of the public. It is bad enough to have employees ridiculing the company magazine, but it is far worse if the arrival of that magazine in a newsroom invites the derisive comment, "Here's another issue of that terrible magazine."

A company magazine can fulfill its goal as an instrument of management without forgetting the need to attract the attention of readers in an interesting, informative, and contemporary way.

HISTORY

Company magazines are not a new form of communication. They can be traced as far back as ancient China. Most historians, however, credit the first effort to the House of Fugger, a sixteenth-century German business firm. The term that company magazine editors dislike using to describe their work, "house organ," began with this early publication. Next came *Lloyd's News*, published in 1696 by a London coffee dealer.

In the United States, the first company publication was the *Lowell Offering*, a magazine published by a cotton mill in Massachusetts from 1840 to 1847. The publication was renamed the *New England Offering* in 1847 and was taken over by the women millhands as a means to publish their literary work. The company had nothing to do with the magazine, which did not contain news. Rather, it published the poems and essays of the women, many of them former schoolteachers who had gone into the mill for higher pay. It sold for 6¼ cents a copy and went out of business in 1850.

The first distinctly recognizable company publication published in the United States was *The Mechanic* (1847), aimed at dealers and consumers of the H. B. Smith Company, a woodworking machinery company. The Singer Sewing Machine Company put out *The Gazette* for dealers and customers from 1850 to 1862. The Travelers Insurance Company started *The Travelers Record* in 1865 as a monthly general-interest external magazine. It has continued in existence since then as a publication for agents.

The Locomotive, started in 1867 by the Hartford Steam Boiler Inspection and Insurance Company, was the first technical company publication. Its editorial policy, "accident prevention to boilers and machinery," has remained constant since that time. The first internal company publication was *NCR Factory News,* founded by the National Cash Register Company in 1887 for employees. It has been published continuously since that date.

Developments in printing helped speed the expansion of company publications after 1870. First wood and steel engravings, then photoengravings about 1880 and the Linotype in 1886 all contributed to the growth of this kind of magazine. By 1910, about fifty company publications existed. They continued to grow because of the increase in the size of companies and the added complexities of business. The old personal relationships of the past had either changed drastically or vanished entirely. It was no longer possible for an owner or a manager to know every employee personally and discuss new policies as they passed out pay envelopes in the lunch line on Fridays.

When personal contact became impossible and bulletin boards failed to meet the communications needs of companies, internal publications were the answer. The idea was growing in use as the twentieth century began. But many of these publications had been started too quickly. As business declined slightly in the early 1920s, a number of internal publications were stopped. A 1922 study conducted by the trade publication *Printers' Ink* showed that 30 percent of company magazines begun in 1920 were out of business within two years. Apparently, too many of these publications had been introduced without a clearly defined editorial program.

By 1925 the National Industrial Conference Board noted that 539 internal publications existed. Of 490 analyzed by the board, 252 were published by manufacturers, 82 by commercial concerns (like department stores), 36 by railroads, 90 by utilities, 22 by financial concerns (17 of these by banks), and 5 by mining companies. Over 400 of these publications appeared monthly. In this period, external publications were all sales oriented. The image-building external magazine would come much later.

After the 1929 stock-market crash, the number of company publications began to decline again as companies started to feel the effects of the Depression. Of the 575 company publications in existence in 1928, only 280 had survived by the end of 1930. By 1936, that figure had climbed to 700.

World War II resulted in the rapid growth of internal company magazines as corporations recognized the importance of publicizing their efforts on behalf of the war effort. The figures grew steadily during the war: 1,000 company publications in 1941, 3,000 in 1943, 5,000 in 1945. By 1951, 76 percent of all companies with operating revenues of over $5 million had employee publications. Today, virtually all medium and large companies and nonprofit organizations — and many small ones — publish internal, external, and combination internal-external magazines, including specific ones for specific audiences.

THREE COMPANY PUBLICATIONS

TWA Skyliner

Really not a magazine at all, the *TWA Skyliner* is a newspaper published biweekly for 35,000 employees of Trans World Airlines (Exhibit 15.1). "The principal purpose of any employee publication is to create a management

Exhibit 15.1

TWA Skyliner, a typical internal company publication. (Reprinted with permission, Trans World Airlines.)

Box 605

Misinformed

Q Soon I retired last year. I have been asked to submit an item, a check for any pass that my mother uses. If I were married and had 85 children, a service charge-free pass would be issued to me for each of my family members. Since I am single I must pay a charge for each pass that my mother uses. The charge is the same as travel. So please issue a term pass to my mother that she can use at will, the same as my married retired friends have.

— Charles T. Craven
Upper Darby, Pa

A From Helen Gardner, supervisor — central pass bureau: You apparently have been misinformed about your mother's retired pass.

According to our records you hold a Class 7 term pass. If your mother is your dependent and travels on your pass, she is allowed a total of two Class 7 trip passes each year. As these passes are service charge exempt, you are not required to submit a check for service charges. However, her club class 7 term and trip passes are subject to first class surcharges.

quently, you would be required to pay a surcharge if you or your mother wished to travel first class. These surcharges can be purchased through the central pass bureau in advance of travel, or at the ATO at time of travel.

In regard to your request for a term pass for your mother, under longstanding policy TWA does not issue term passes to parents of either active or retired employees. All travel by parents must be accomplished on trip passes. After the employee retires the maximum number of trip passes allowed dependent parents is two legs per year. However, they are allowed unlimited 50% and 75% reduced rate transportation over TWA's systemwide routes.

Editor's Notes

History buffs and TWA veterans of World War II organizations take note. There is — will be interested in a new book "The Sole Survivor," by Captain Guy Squadron, a retired Captain George Gay. Captain Gay was the sole survivor of Torpedo Squadron 8 in the Battle of Midway. *Sole Survivor* contains his recollections of that turning point in the war, as well as a portrait-view of airplanes used in combat.

Sole Survivor may be obtained by sending check or money order for $14 directly to Captain George Gay, P.O. Box 8088, Naples, Florida 33941.

Incidentally, he'll be pleased to autograph copies on request, as well as answer any special questions you wish to add.

Cincinnati mechanic Bob Armitez and his wife, Beverly, are foster parents. They have just written a book for foster children. Called *Sharing a Fun.* The book helps children at foster care and in the foster home adjust to their new situations," says Beverly.

Profits from sales of *Sharing a Fun* will go to the Foster Parents Association of Northern Kentucky. For a copy, send $2.50 to Process Resources, Box 259-A, Route 1, Union, Kentucky 41091. Foster parent grandmothers or any good proceeds can buy the books for $150 per hundred ($1.50 each) and resell them for a profit. They will be shipped C.O.D.

Over the coming months, thousands of people will suffer eye injuries when they try to revive their frozen cars. The danger, according to the Better Vision Institute and the Foundation of Blindness, is that a battery can explode.

To jump-start, remember:

spraying battery fragments and corrosive acid in all directions.

Dick Holmes, TWA safety director, representing the society's warning against five "good ops:"
1) Use of a match or cigarette lighter for light.
2) Incorrect connection of cables.
3) Sparks from careless use of tools near batteries.
4) Smoking near the battery.
5) Incorrect connection of a battery charger.

Also on the subject of automobile safety, Dick warns against allowing children too close to the luggage area at hatch-back vehicles.

"It looks like fun, but it can be deadly," he says, explaining that tailgate and hatch-back latches may be in sloppy cases accompanied in the check-in counter.

Jim continued: "The ticket agents all had their own problems, but one gracefully took the time to get me checked in and to the gate, and the flight attendants on Flight 289 in Kansas City, made everything to make my mother comfortable."

"It made me proud to be, for 29 years, a part of a company that went out of its way to help an employee, and I just feel some day I'll believe you," said Jim.

A TWA employee helped 76-year-old Iona Briggs when she ticketed by Capt. Wat 82nd and Orbise in Fort Myers, Florida. Mrs. Briggs would like to personally thank the TWA people, but unfortunately she didn't get his name. She appealed to the *Skyliner* for help. Would that good Samaritan please call Mrs. Briggs collect at 813-

The Museum of Transportation in Boston is preparing a new display of commercial aviation since 1945, and would like memorabilia. TWA has provided a variety of airplane parts and other obsolete items. Individuals who have anything they believe would be suitable for display, and would like to contribute to the museum, may contact Dave Vetre, area director of public affairs, at 605.

Since the discussion in the October 29 issue of the economic squeeze in which the many mail-carry freight and other year-to-date financial results. Like those cited previously, they aren't good.

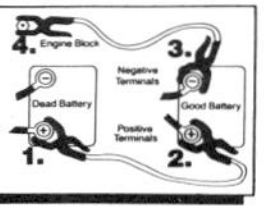

F/As Serve as Volunteers

"We do it all for you" is the sentiment this group of TWA flight attendants means to convey to parents who may stay at the Ronald McDonald House in New York while their children receive cancer care. They acted as hosts at the opening of the center this month. Pictured (from left) are Dee Schiavelli, Beverly Frazier; Suzanne Jeffers, chairman of the Children's Oncology Society; Kathy Powers, who organized TWA's participation; Toni Russo, president of the society; and Barbara Brigham, Vickie Leisey and John Burks.

A group of TWA flight attendants served as volunteer receptionists for the opening in New York City this month of a Ronald McDonald House. The house, funded in part through the efforts of McDonald's restaurants, will service as an inexpensive residence for families of children receiving cancer treatment in New York medical centers.

The transformed double brownstone at 418 E. 86th Street was formerly the convent of St. Joseph and was purchased from the New York archdiocese. It has sleeping accommodations for up to 35 persons. It has a communal kitchen, library, playground and other facilities.

The house is owned and operated by the Children's Oncology Society of New York, a nonprofit organization which provides supportive services to parents of children with cancer.

"A flight attendant (I failed to get her name) on Flight 451 from Hartford to New York personally got us a limousine and accompanied us to the check-in counter," Jim continued.

London TWA's Maurice Potter would like to hear from anyone who was interested in entering teams in the 1980 junior soccer tournament at London. The date is to be determined. Write to Maurice Potter, TWA district service agent, Heathrow Airport, London.

While attending a convention in Hartford, the 85-year-old mother of Kansas City TWA'er James Finley became ill and was hospitalized. "We received word two days later that she could return home," Jim said. "My first reaction was dismay," said Jim. Chaney had secured emergency passes and made arrangements for Jim to fly to Hartford to accompany his mother home the next day.

In the News

'21' Comes Aboard

The merger of Century 21 Real Estate Corporation into a newly formed wholly-owned subsidiary of Trans World Corporation has been reflected in last fall increases. Indeed, some transcontinental regular fares now exceed transatlantic economy fares, despite the much longer distances associated with the latter.

"We are delighted to welcome Century 21 to the family of Trans World service companies," said TWC chairman and chief executive officer of Century 21, said "As the nation's largest real estate brokerage organization, Century 21's achievements have been extraordinary and we confidently expect their future strengths to be reflected in their future performance."

Arthur E. Bartlett, chairman and chief executive officer of Century 21, said: "We are proud to become a significant part of one of America's leading service companies. Our decision to join Trans World Corporation was based upon the mutual belief that our resources and service by each other will be enhanced by the combination. We believe the business opportunities and growth prospects for Century 21 are greatly improved as a result of joining Trans World."

October Traffic

TWA's system traffic in October rose 0.5% over last year to 2.41 billion rpms. Domestic traffic was down 3.7%, reflecting the combined effect of planned capacity restraint, discount coupon programs of major competitors, and industry-wide softening of traffic growth. International traffic rose 7.7%.

For the first 10 months of 1979, system passenger traffic rose 17.8%, to 27.24 billion rpms — up 20.6% domestically and 12.6% internationally.

	Oct. '79	YTD '79
RPMs		
Domestic	+1.7%	+6.7%
Int'l	+2.7%	+20.6%
System	+0.5%	+17.8%
Available Seat Miles		
Domestic	+3.9%	+14.6%
Int'l	+4.6%	+14.0%
System	+2.3%	+17.5%
Load Factor		
Domestic	-1.2 pts (61.6%)	-3.2 pts (65.9%)
Int'l	-2.5 pts (58.7%)	+1.0 pts (65.4%)
System	-2.0 pts (59.6%)	-1.9 pts (60.2%)

Seek Fare Increase

TWA has asked for an across-the-board increase of 7% on all transatlantic fares, effective December 15. The airline cited continuing steep increases in the price of jet fuel for requesting the increase.

"From June 30 to September 30, the average contract price of jet fuel used on TWA's international flights has soared 22% to 80.7 cents per gallon, 35% more than anticipated," said John Heilner, vice president-pricing.

In announcing its fare increase actions in recent months to reduce expenses and increase efficiency, denial of the fare increase would result in continuing loss of $30 million next year in North Atlantic operations," he warned.

Clements formerly was a manager-passenger sales in Boston. From 1976 to 1978 he was an instructor at the Breech Training Academy.

United Airlines lost $21.5 million in the third quarter for the nine months, the carrier lost $80 million, compared with a profit of $271.5 million a year earlier. Of course, in addition to higher fuel prices, the carrier is recovering from a 58-day strike and the DC-10 grounding. As a result, United plans furloughing more than 100 more employees, mostly in general services, and inflight services.

Pan Am's third quarter earnings dropped to $40.9 million, from $41.1 million a year ago. Blaming fuel costs and low fares, the airline announced it is abandoning several routes, deferring expansion plans and selling Intercontinental Hotels, Pan Am is the world's largest charter operator.

Among services being suspended is Pan Am's morning flight from New York to London.

Delta's earnings in the third quarter were $12.8 million down from $17.5 million a year ago. National lost $6.1 million, compared with year-ago earnings of $2.3 million. Southeast World Airlines, the cargo carrier, lost $3.7 million, compared to a profit of $3.7 million a year ago.

Clipped Wings

(from page one)

the HGF as its charity 10 years ago, the TWA, alumnae have donated nearly $270,000 to the foundation. Nearly 50 former attendants who worked in those two decades came to Denver for the event

Travel Agents Preview Florida Services

by Vic Page

A preview of Florida attractions prior to TWA's startup of service between 10 major cities in the Northeast and Midwest and six Florida cities was organized recently for 180 of TWA's top travel agents from 14 cities.

"Because the CAB has not granted normal economy-fare increases," Heilner observed that "it is, ironically, the discount-fare users who have borne the burden of increased fuel and other rising costs." He added: "If normal economy fares increases had been permitted all along, we would not need to raise fares again this year."

... and emerges to pose with some of the 180 international region travel agents he accompanied to Florida for a briefing on TWA's new services to the Sunshine State.

dent sales and services, TWA's "Board of Ten" were invited to view some of the major attractions of the Sunshine State, including Disney World, Circus World and Cypress Gardens.

And it was at CircusWorld that Steve Long, marketing director for Century 21, delighted his guests by entering into the spirit of the circus by appearing in clown makeup.

Appointments

Peter Williams has been named manager-domestic passenger pricing, succeeding Jessica Morris, whose appointment in the new position of manager-discount planning & control was announced previously. He will report to Andy Price, director-domestic passenger pricing.

Mo Williams will be responsible for the evaluation and development of new domestic fare actions.

Paul G. Clements has been named manager-passenger sales for New Jersey, regional manager Jeffrey L. Warner announced.

Deaths

George R. Carroll, supervises materials handling, receiving/shipping and control at MCI, died on his sleep October 3 of a heart

attack. Mr. Carroll had been with TWA 34 years. Starting at Newark, he served in purchasing positions including LaGuardia, New Castle, Delaware (the wartime I. C. D. operation), KCK and, later, MCI. He is survived by his wife, Margaret, who works at KCAC and son Ronald.

Orlando Cruz, 54, international region veteran, died October 17 in Jeddah, Saudi Arabia, where he had been working with Saudia since entering from TWA in 1975. During 29 years with TWA, he served in the finance and sales & service departments in Lisbon, Tokyo and Hong Kong. He is survived by his wife Bernadette.

Captain Earle T. Hall died Sept. 18. He had flown with TWA for 34 years, officially retiring April 1 of this year although he had been on leave of absence the past five years because of a heart condition. Capt. Hall and his wife, Pauline, who survives, had attended the Flyers' Retirement party in Phoenix in September.

Sherwood H. Loomis, 72, retired New York fleet service helper, died August 29. Mr. Loomis had worked for TWA from Aug. 31, 1944 until July 31, 1972.

Worth. Highlights of this year's Clipped Wings convention was a reunion (right) of flight attendants from the 1930s and 40s. Denver, Colorado was the host city for the get-together.

Newly elected officers of Clipped Wings convention include (from left): secretary Edie Sauoe, fourth v.p.; Jonai Storer, third v.p. Barbara Diver, president Mary Ann Sparkman, first v.p. Gwen Mahler, second v.p. Ann Pirotto and treasurer Sunny

TWA SKYLINER

Published for Employees by the
Corporate Communications Department
605 Third Avenue, New York 10016
Printed in U.S.A.

Dan Kennitz, Editor
Anne Saunders, Associate Editor

November 12, 1979

November 12, 1979   2

3   November 12, 1979

239

Exhibit 15.1 continued.

Cruising English Waterways: Dream Vacation Comes True

by George Prager

George Prager, director-administration flying, retired in 1978 after...

TWAers Roll Up Their Sleeves

Chicagoan Marks 29 Years

English "narrow boat" is aptly named — it's less than seven feet wide.

Roy Davis: Out of the Ordinary

by James Warren

Reprinted by permission of Chicago Sun-Day Sun-Times.

Roy Davis (left), director-technical services, ORD, talked flying recently with old friend, actor George Kennedy who portrayed Davis (alias Joe Patroni) in the film "Airport." A gold model of a '27 cockpit by TWA's area manager of public affairs at Chicago, Steve Forsyth.

JFK G.M.'s Flying Hold Reunion

TWAers at JFK and LaGuardia donated over 500 pints of blood during the Greater New York Blood Program's drive at those stations in late October. Joe Albano, JFK A&P mechanic, gets ready to make his contribution.

November 12, 1979

Book Review: Aviation History

by Ken Fletcher

Plan Seniors Meetings

November 12, 1979   5

Travel Tips
by Harry Mickle

Mrs. Wilson Baumgren of Sebastopol, California writes to advise that her experience with the Melia Hotel in Madrid was anything but. The tour group she was with here recently. "Four of us just returned from a great trip to Spain and Portugal and we did it the Melia Way. It was worth every penny undiendly, and the manager did not acknowledge a 50% discount or any other travel agency consideration for TWA employees. Anyway, the rooms start at $80 per night. We did, however, have a beautiful room and then found service at the Princess Plaza. Just thought I ought to tell you," she said. Incidentally, Mrs. Baumgren highly recommends, as do we, the government-operated paradors in Spain and pousadas in Portugal. They are, as Mrs. Baumgren discovered, very beautiful and clean, and average about $32 per night, with bath.

Pousadas, government-owned inns throughout Portugal, are a best deal for travelers. Most are heavily booked. To contact the Portuguese National Tourist Office at 548 Fifth Ave., New York 10036 for a brochure, program and reservations.

For car rentals in Portugal, I recommend European Express at $19.50 per day with unlimited mileage (5-day minimum). Write to Europcar, 21 E. 40th St., New York 10016; phone (800) 223-5555.

Gift certificates are available for interline vacation travel from Carsal Hotels. They may be purchased in any amount, with a $50 minimum, and there is no expiration date.

For details on how to give a gift of travel to Europe, write: Carsal Hotels Interline Vacations Dept., 7730 Forsyth Blvd., St. Louis, Missouri 63105 or phone (314) 727-1503.

London. Shakespeare country and Stonehenge come together in a 7-day package from Carsal Hotels.

For those who want to combine a $50 supplement can be eligible at a $59 supplement. Departures on a special Victoria Station. The rate is $1 a day, for which you are provided mileage, insurance, a map, and a helmet. You have to leave a deposit, but it can be used for it either.

Eastern Airlines: Effective immediately, EAL will deny boarding to passengers or crew members who do not comply with its dress codes, do not present proper ID, do not comply with carry-on baggage restrictions. Be sure to check the departure gate when processing would delay flight departure.

Specifically ... Men must wear a

Bass-o Profundo!

Who's the best bass fisherman in the world? Jerry Dyer, that's who! The Boston mechanic won the honors at the **Bass Angler's Sportsmen's Society Amateur Tournament at Lake of the Woods, Ontario.** Jerry pulled in a catch of 14 bass weighing 33 lbs., 11 ozs. in 27 hours of fishing, using lures he makes himself. He said he plans to go after a 17-foot bass boat and trailer.

jacket and tie, except for intra-Caribbean travel; women must wear a dress, skirt and blouse; suit or pantsuit. For children under 16, clothing equivalent to the honors at the *Identification* — Present TWA ID along with pass or ticket when checking in at the gate. Family members must have acceptable proof of identity. *Carry-on Baggage* — Carry-on articles which will not fit under the seat in front of you must be checked. *Check-in* — Space available travelers must check in at least 20 minutes before flight departure time.

Eleven Reservations is featuring a special $11 dinner offer to TWA employees through January, 1980. The rate is offered at all of the group's six oceanfront hotels in the Daytona Beach resort area, including the Beachcomber Inn, Mayan Inn, Treasure Island Inn, Acapulco Inn, Sheraton Inn and the Whitehall Inn. Reservations and additional information call (305) 858-9600.

Lights...Camera...Action...

A star is born. LaGene's mechanic Walter Silvosky awaits direction for his next scene in "321 Contact," a new series being produced by the Children's Television Workshop. The part of the crew who work in noisy environments and how they protect themselves.

Anniversaries

November
40 Years
John P. Cooper, MCT
James M. McKenzie, MCT
James H. Singleton, LGA

35 Years
Betty M. Bauer, MKC
Hamm H. Baum, MKC
Charles E. Bauer, SFO
Robert D. Blee, MCI
Andrew Pesckus, SFO
Alfred L. Egbert, MCI
Carl W. Gordon, JFK
Harry S. Hooven, JFK
Jerome Kingsley, LAX
Dale C. Amos, DEN
Bernice F. Kirkendall, JFK
Leonard O. Moore, MCI
David L. Phillips, JFK
Ruth E. Wessel, CVG
Joseph F. Willis & MCI

30 Years
Joseph B. Cisneros, LAX
Jay R. Diedon, SFO
Lee E. Horne, ORD

25 Years
James W. Ashmann, MKC
Bruce J. Carlson, SFO
Edward A. Charlotta, LGA
Lawrence L. Greenwell, PHX
Samuel J. Head, OMA
George S. Hunt, IND
Harvey H. Larson, LAX
Mary Ann Leahy, STL
Thomas W. Long, LGA
Robert J. MacKenzie, LON
Edmund M. McKee, LAX
Warren J. Myers, ORD
Eileen M. McKay, LAX
William F. McNamara, NYC
Emigue Mesta, MAD
Glenn P. Morris, ORD
David E. Reavson, LAX
Dennis L. Schuerr, DEN
George A. Sherman Jr, YMO
Philip Solar, LAX
Robert J. Watkins, BNA
Bernard J. Yackey, MCI
William J. Young, IND

20 Years
Paul J. Acardson, MCI
Vincent L. Daviau, ORD
Ralph H. Brandon, DEN
Carmen Carczza, JFK
Albert E. Cmar, PNL
Daniel C. Cooper, MKC
Milford D. Dernelson, MKC

How to Survive Hotel Fire:
A Firefighter's Crusade
by R. H. Kauffman

Mr. Kauffman is a captain with the Los Angeles County Fire department. He has been a firefighter for 14 years. The following is an edited version of "Warning: Hotels Could Be Hazardous to Your Health" reprinted with permission.

Have you ever been in a hotel during a fire? It's a frightening experience. There have been hundreds of hotel fires with thousands of deaths over the years. In many of those people would not have died if they had known what to do.

Hotels have no excuse for being ill-prepared, but you cannot depend on the staff in case of a fire. Believe it or not, most hotels will not call the fire department until they verify whether or not there really is a fire and try to put it out themselves. Hotels are very reluctant to disturb their guests, and fire engines in the street are embarrassing and tend to draw crowds.

[... additional text ...]

Winners in PHX Open Tennis Tourney

Mixed doubles winners and Darlene Kreuz, CHI; and Arman Abadji, JFK (first).

The First TWA/Phoenix Open Tennis Tournament was played at the Arizona Biltmore Hotel Oct. 5-7 in Phoenix. Open will be held June 5-8 reports Joyce Capece, Chicago sales account rep and tournament program director. Details will follow.

November 12, 1979

Exhibit 15.1 continued.

241

presence in the consciousness of employees," says William Brown, director of creative services and in overall charge of this and several other company publications. "It is a parallel channel of communication that augments the regular chain of command. It communicates accurately and quickly the reason for a policy change and the background to it. It also fosters pride and successful achievement."

The November 12, 1979 issue provides a good example of the latter. One of the front-page stories in that issue details the success of TWA in handling the U.S. visit of Pope John Paul II. The story lists unabashed praise for the company, all from church officials and reporters covering the trip. With employees the only audience, however, such back-patting is permitted, especially if it is designed to make employees feel good about themselves. This issue does not feature any direct messages from management on policy changes, although a long article on productivity points out that improving the company's productivity was "the key ingredient in the plan to increase TWA's profitability, making it better able to resist negative economic forces — from the outside and from within."

The remainder of the issue contains a series of news and feature stories about company business (a new system to save fuel on the TWA fleet of 727 aircraft) and people (one about the TWA director of technical services at Chicago's O'Hare Airport, who was the model for a character in the novel and film *Airport*). There is an article on an employee's vacation spent cruising English waterways written by him and with a byline, a book review about a new history of airlines in the United States, and a piece written by a Los Angeles County fire department captain on how to survive a hotel fire.

Scattered among these longer pieces are news stories and photos that mention as many employee names as possible. Retirements, sports, blood drives, reunions, awards are all commemorated in photos. The only real sign of management presence in this issue is a small photo of the company president on the back page as he testified before a congressional committee.

Standard Oiler

A slick magazine published eight times a year, the *Standard Oiler,* reaches 39,000 employees and 11,200 retirees of Standard Oil Company of California and is sent to external people as well. "We have a diverse audience, scattered all over," says Charles Michals, editor. "We're speaking to Ph.D.s in the esoteric sciences and to laborers. How do you speak to that broad range in a magazine that is thirty-two pages long? We try to include in each issue something for everybody."

The September – October 1979 issue reflects this diverse audience and the editorial policy established to serve it. The cover story, "Telling Our Story," explores how the company deals with the press. The short commentary on the

Exhibit 15.2
Standard Oiler, *a typical internal-external company magazine. (Reprinted with permission, Standard Oil Company of California.)*

inside cover next to the contents discusses oil glut as a thing of the past. A sidebar story tells employees how they can answer oil-industry critics.

An article on the hoarding and handling of gasoline is particularly timely, for shortages have caused people to store more gasoline in their homes, a dangerous practice as the story shows in photos and interviews with fire-department officials. "Games Creative People Play" is a series of puzzles in keeping with the company's centennial theme of creativity. They had been submitted by employees.

Another piece deals with energy conservation and the various ways to accomplish it from setting thermostats low to insulating the attic. "Bob's Blubbery Friends" is about an employee who spends time as a volunteer at a marine mammal center. "Chow Time at Chevron" talks about the work of the various company chefs aboard drilling ships and at refineries.

The last part of the magazine gets into more familiar territory for internal company publications: a spread of photographs of employees doing various things, a page of opinion from inside and outside the company, a page of cartoons contributed by employees, a spread of service awards and retirements, a page of management changes and employee deaths, a page listing the staff and including an editor's note. The back cover is an in-house ad dealing with an oil-industry problem and Standard's answer to critics.

"Stories originate in a number of ways," continues Michals. "We get an idea or sense a need, employees call us with ideas, and we constantly invite readers to talk to us by letter or telephone." Most stories are written by members of the corporate communications staff, although Michals uses an occasional freelancer. "Our executives sometimes are reluctant to talk to freelancers but they will open up to staff editors," he says. "I don't think freelancers can get as much material on sensitive stories. It's also hard to use freelancers on technical subjects because they don't know the jargon. Typically, they are good on nontechnical subjects requiring creative treatment."

The *Standard Oiler* is cleared by corporate executives prior to publication. "But this is not much of a problem," says Michals, "as can be seen from the fact that the magazine is presented for clearance in color dummy form. We avoid clearance problems by going to the top for our original marching orders when we decide to do a story, and we avoid like the plague the 'nervous Nellie' types who are afraid to see the time of day in print. We clear the technical stuff with the technical people, we clear policy matters with appropriate officers of the company, and, when dealing with lawyers, we ask them to look at the copy for legal problems and to tell us how to fix them if they find some."

Michals puts out the *Oiler* with the help of an associate editor, an art director, a production coordinator, and several writers from the corporate communications staff. It costs eighty-five cents a copy to produce. The magazine contains thirty-two pages plus covers with sixteen pages in four colors.

Concludes Michals: "In communicating, I believe that employees deserve the most, the best, and the first. Our industry presently is under siege," he says. "Right now we are being classed with used-car salesmen and I believe employees have a role to play in setting the record straight with their families, friends, and the public at large."

Exxon USA

A slick, four-color external magazine, *Exxon USA* is published quarterly by Exxon Company, U.S.A., the large petroleum corporation. It is designed to leave its readers with a favorable opinion of the company, which, like the entire oil industry, has been criticized over the past decade. "In recent years especially, we have been under heavy criticism from the government and public," says Otto W. Glade, coordinator of publications and film services. "Management recognizes the need to involve the public with the facts about our business."

One attempt to achieve this public involvement is this magazine, which conveys its message in a sophisticated combination of popular articles and well-researched pieces on energy exploration, the energy crisis, and doing business as an oil company. Unlike some company publications, which cannot seem to resist the urge to sell their products by referring to them rather blatantly on nearly every page, *Exxon USA* follows a more restrained approach.

Editor Downs Matthews calls the magazine an "external advocacy journal." "As editor, I am responsible for giving readers useful information, attractively and accurately presented, in a high-quality package," he says. "My primary job is that of communicating to some 200,000 thought leaders — and ultimately to the general public — through *Exxon USA* on behalf of Exxon's management." Matthews says that his secondary audience is 45,000 company employees and shareholders.

Press runs for the magazine average 262,000 copies per issue at forty-four cents each. Each issue is read by 3.2 persons per copy, so the per-reader cost is fourteen cents. The magazine, paid for by the Public Affairs Department of Exxon, consists of thirty-two 9 × 12-inch pages in full color. "*Exxon USA*'s objectives are necessarily those of the Public Affairs Department," continues Matthews. "The magazine serves as an Exxon advocate, speaking on matters of controversy. It seeks also to make friends where Exxon needs friends. Its job is to whittle away at mistaken perceptions about Exxon and the energy industry and to replace these with positive and favorable points of view. I define every story in terms of specific objectives that management states to be of real and current concern."

Matthews says that the current topics fall into two categories. "In one we

Exhibit 15.3
Exxon USA, *a typical external company publication. (Reprinted with permission,*
Exxon USA.)

have those recurring themes that never quite go away as public issues — such matters as the environment, regulation, credibility, hostility toward size, the corporation's social responsibility, and the private-enterprise system," he says. "In the other basket, we have several specific problems that we must deal with today in the expectation of moving on to other things tomorrow. For example, *Exxon USA* will play an important role in helping the public to understand the need for a synthetic-fuels industry. We have also been active in working problems generated by the wilderness issue, particularly in Alaska."

A great percentage of articles deal with energy in general and oil in particular, but readers gain facts, not hyperbole. Of course, the magazine cannot be expected to denounce the oil industry or advocate total government regulation. Anything other than its subdued approach would be an insult to its "informed-public" readers and counter to the overall goals of the magazine.

The Fourth Quarter 1979 issue is typical of *Exxon USA*. An arresting sketch depicting chairs set up for an outdoor concert is on the cover. The story that goes with the cover inside, "Supporting the Performing Arts," discusses how big corporations like Exxon are aiding the arts: subsidizing concerts from New York's Central Park to a hall in Sitka, Alaska; training young conductors; paying for festivals to help people participate in the arts.

"That Fuelish Feeling" uses tips from a driving expert to show how people can get more miles per gallon from the gasoline they use in their cars. "Getting Out of the Ghetto" outlines an innovative program that helps disadvantaged children stay in school. Buried deep within the story is the fact that the program is being sponsored by a grant from the Exxon USA Foundation.

The greatest amount of space in the issue (seven pages) is reserved for "Protecting Prudhoe Bay," an analysis of how oil companies like Exxon are protecting the environment as they drill for oil on Alaska's North Slope. Illustrated with striking color photographs, the article reviews programs designed to preserve terrain, animals, and plants in Alaska (doing most of their work in winter when the ground is frozen, banning hunting, monitorig effects on wildlife, even cleaning up litter). The message is subtle, but clear: 40 percent of America's undiscovered petroleum reserves lie in Alaska but oil companies are not damaging nature to get the oil out. The remainder of the issue covers a boys' camp sponsored by the company and how public buildings, hospitals, and museums can halt energy loss, an article that is illustrated with an easy-to-read chart explaining heat loss.

Matthews follows a systematic approach in planning each issue. "The initial step begins with me," he says. "Bearing in mind the public-affairs objectives, I review the company's activities for opportunities to develop stories that will enable me to address the appropriate issues. When I find something that looks promising, I usually check it verbally with knowledgeable people to determine if, indeed, there is a story there that can be told."

If a story looks promising, Matthews prepares a synopsis that states what the story will say and why the magazine needs to say it. He submits an abstract of the story to several people in the hierarchy of the Public Affairs Department who will later review the completed story. If these people like the proposal, he puts it on a list of story possibilities that the same people approve.

"With their blessing I can then begin to spend money and get the story underway," he says. "This usually means the hiring of a freelance writer or undertaking the job myself. I work approximately a year in advance and will have around two dozen articles at various stages of development. For one reason or another, some stories may take as long as two or three years to complete. Others can be done in perhaps a month."

Matthews drafts a tentative table of contents for a given issue six months before publication date. He sends a copy of the table of contents and a brief description of the proposed stories to his superiors in the Public Affairs Department. If they agree with his selections he proposes a formal table of contents three months before publication date. This goes to his public-affairs superiors and a member of top management, who usually approves. "Occasionally, he may ask a question or comment on an article while approving it," says Matthews. "Once in a great while, he may ask that an article be dropped or postponed. To my recollection, this has only happened twice. Normally, no one on the forty-second floor (where corporate executives have their offices) sees the magazine before it is published."

When Matthews gets a finished article from an author, he has it reviewed for accuracy by appropriate people inside and outside the company. He also routinely runs a copy of each story through the law department.

After everyone has reviewed and signed off on the six stories selected for a given issue, Matthews submits the package to the head of Public Affairs for final approval, usually about two months before press date. Later, he shows this official the photographs and illustrations for each story and the layouts designed for them. "Following these approvals, we create what is called a silver-print, a photographic proof, and the last one anyone sees before we print the magazine," he says. The public-affairs officials look it over one last time and the magazine goes to press.

Does the magazine, when printed, reach its goals? Matthews thinks it does. "Our surveys give us these facts: ninety percent of our readers say they react favorably to the company's reasons for sending them the magazine," he continues, "ninety-three percent say the magazine is of help to them in learning about the subjects covered; twenty percent say *Exxon USA* contributed to their taking specific action or to changing their opinion on matters of public concern, and to shift from disagreement to agreement with the company's position."

The benefits go beyond this. "Data such as these tell us that *Exxon USA* is probably the most effective medium available to management for the purpose of changing minds and influencing attitudes," concludes Matthews. "We have patiently cultivated a nationwide audience of friends for Exxon. No other oil company has such a spokesman" (Figures 15.1 – 15.3).

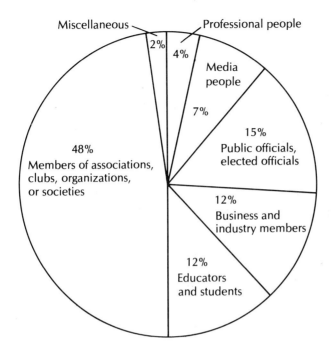

Figure 15.1
Breakdown of regular external audience by category for Exxon USA. (*Reprinted with permission,* Exxon USA.)

Figure 15.2
Outline of criteria for selecting material for publication in Exxon USA.
(*Reprinted with permission,* Exxon USA.)

Material selected for publication in *Exxon USA* has its origins in the official objectives of the Public Affairs Department, and in the emphasis areas annually determined by the department in concordance with top management. For 1980, the department seeks to:

1. Emphasize the way in which the company is helping to manage the country's energy transition.
2. Develop a working image of cooperation rather than antagonism with federal and state governments, public interest groups, and consumers.
3. Publicly evaluate business strategies in the context of expectations regarding corporate social responsibility.
4. Actively participate in defining the corporate role in a changing U.S. society.

These objectives address problems that are regarded as having the potential for significantly and materially affecting the company's welfare, and the management's ability to achieve business goals. Nothing is published in *Exxon USA* that cannot be justified in terms of these objectives. Each story helps the company in resolving problems, answering reasonable questions, or advancing the company's best interests.

Exxon USA, then, is a public advocate for Exxon Company, U.S.A. It seeks to make friends for Exxon where Exxon needs friends, to muster support for the company in the realization of its legitimate goals, and to contribute to public understanding and acceptance of the realities of energy supply and demand. Ideally, *Exxon USA* is a proactive voice in favor of rational solutions and realistic answers to the country's energy-related problems and needs as expressed within the context of the private enterprise system.

In choosing material to publish in *Exxon USA*, the editor reviews the company's objectives and considers its policies, practices, and operations that fall within the parameters of these objectives. The company's work and its effect on the American public provide ample opportunity for creating stories that speak to management's concerns, and which also are suitable for publication in a quarterly magazine in a feature article format.

Exxon USA story opportunities are to be found in:

1. Technical papers and documents reporting on research and engineering programs and projects.
2. Public statements by executives on current issues.
3. Reports, studies, surveys, and forecasts, such as the Energy Outlook.
4. The company's policies and practices.
5. Actions, events, achievements, and plans of the company's departments, subsidiaries, and affiliates.
6. Activities originating outside the company in which the company is involved as a partner or participant.
7. Activities of organizations to which Exxon has given grants, or to which Exxon belongs and supports.
8. Review and analysis of subjects in which Exxon has a specific concern.
9. Review and analysis of events, proposals, and opinions which could materially affect Exxon.
10. Examination of subjects or topics of interest and concern to groups or organizations with which Exxon hopes to make friends, and whose support Exxon needs.

The decision as to which opportunity to develop for publication depends on (1) how effectively it can be made to serve as a medium for articulating the company's objectives, (2) how high it ranks in the hierarchy of priorities, and (3) how appealing it might be to readers in its visual and literary impact.

Downs Matthews

Figure 15.3
Proposed target audience, typical issue, Exxon USA.

Preserving Wyoming's Past	
Wyoming list	150
American History teachers	5,290
Historical societies	3,116
Museum directors	5,752
Parks & Landmarks — national	284
Coal mining company executives	5,000
	19,592
Reassessing Our Environmental Imperative	
Environmental editors	155
Conservation publications	253
Medical publications	803
Public health officials	7,680
Hospital administrators	7,920
Medical associations	914
Environmental health officials & executives	6,066
	23,791
You and Your Driving	
Women's page editors newspapers	975
Automotive editors	451
Safety directors	7,117
NAWHSL list	
Marketing list	400
Women's club officers (selected)	14,090
	23,033
Overregulation: Can We Afford It	
Center for Study of American Business	2,000
Chamber of Commerce officials	6,566
Business editors	565
Business writers	121
Fortune 500 list (presidents & chief executives)	1,500
Professors of government	2,404
	13,156
Who Says Economics Can't Be Fun	
School superintendents (city)	12,129
Junior Achievement	200
Professors of economics	11,300
Junior Chamber of Commerce	3,079
	26,708
Where Are the Trees in That Forest	
Utility executives (gas, light & power companies)	4,222
Economists	14,774
Professors of business economics (department heads)	3,064
American gas association (list)	
	22,060
TOTAL	128,340

PLANNING

1. Develop the concept that best serves the company. The decision about the format and frequency of the publication depends on the audience, goals, and budget available. An editor hired to develop a company magazine begins the task by meeting with appropriate members of management to find out whom they want to reach. Do they want to create a new image for the company with the press and other influential publics? Do they want to inform employees of new policies and company news? The frequency and format follow accordingly.

2. Work out a format to fulfill management's goal. As in the other publication preparations noted in earlier chapters, company-magazine development begins with a bit of brainstorming. Using the round figures available from management, come up with several approaches to the problem: a slick, four-color quarterly for a totally external audience with a monthly variation using black-and-white photos and an occasional two-color process; a monthly magazine or a weekly newspaper for an internal audience. Get production estimates for both in terms of typesetting copy, preparing articles and illustrations, printing issues for publications of varying sizes — sixteen, thirty-two, and forty pages for magazines; eight, twelve, and sixteen pages for newspapers. Magazines are usually $8\frac{1}{2} \times 11$ inches, and newspapers are in a tabloid or other small format.

3. Outline your ideas to management in a formal presentation, ideally to include some page dummies to give them a feel for what the final publication will look like. Several magazine covers and nameplates should be developed.

4. Conduct a survey to determine the need for the proposed publication. Do employees or an outside audience really want to know about the company? Or do they know so little that a publication would be helpful to inform them? This survey can be done with the help of an outside polling firm or by distributing a simple questionnaire within the company.

ORGANIZING

5. Once management has agreed to the publication concept, organize the staff needed to do the job. Usually, the more frequent the number of issues, the greater the need for staff. A weekly newspaper will require more material than a quarterly magazine. In this case, however, the regular staff of two or three editors and an artist can be augmented by "correspondents" in outlying plants who send in stories or story ideas. A quarterly magazine that runs longer articles can be put out by an editor, an artist, and a generous budget to hire competent freelance writers. This is less expensive to the company in the long run because freelancers do not have to be paid benefits. Often, work by "name" writers can be procured for $1,000 to $2,000 an article.

6. Work out a deadline with the printer and set up a production schedule that works backward from that; the schedule should include due dates for copy editing and management clearance, illustrations, rough and final layouts, typesetting and proofreading, delivery of final mechanical to printer, printing, binding, final delivery, and mailing.

PUBLISHING

7. Develop ideas for several issues ahead, in addition to the one being worked on at the time. The company and its people and products present a vast array of possibilities. Tie-ins with national news events are natural stories, for example, TWA's handling of the pope's visit. Tie-ins can also be with subjects bearing on the welfare of the company, like Standard Oil's way of handling the press so that it understands the energy crisis. Editors need to look ahead to upcoming events and keep a future items book or a master calendar in the same way a city editor keeps track of the city council or county planning commission.

8. Try to keep blatant references to the company to a minimum. The credibility of an external magazine will be enhanced if the company is played down. Its name is in the staff box or on the cover. That is enough mention. If every story mentions the company and its products, the external audience will lose interest. In an internal magazine or newspaper, this is a bit different. Employees are often proud of their company, and the publication can be a bit more chauvinistic about it, although even loyal workers will become bored if the emphasis on the company is overdone. ("Our Company" did this or "Your Management" did that.)

9. Get on every mailing list for company memos and develop friendships with people at all levels of the company in order to keep up with what is going on. Story ideas do not come from sitting in an ivory tower. A company magazine editor needs to be as attentive to sources of information as the reporter or editor for a regular publication. In the case of an internal publication, the network of correspondents around the company will serve as eyes and ears.

10. Travel as widely as possible and become the personification of the publication in the eyes of the company and its employees.

11. Develop a stable of freelance writers who also take photographs if the publication is an external one. Give them clear direction about what is needed to fulfill the assignment in terms of word length, writing style, kinds of photographs, deadlines. Pay freelancers promptly. Most of them are used to being paid late for their work and will become loyal in a hurry to a company-magazine editor who pays them early.

12. Work out a "look" for the publication that befits its character and that of the company. Keep the page design and type selection within that ap-

proach, and try not to surprise readers with a different design or new type every issue. Readers like consistency.

13. Strive, with the help of an artist or graphic designer, for a clean, easy-to-read format that uses type and illustrations well and where copy is simple and unadorned.

14. Remember the importance of the cover. Magazines always consider the "cover story" the most important. Its selection should be made with the reader in mind. What will cause a reader to open the issue and not throw it away unread? Even though the magazine is not vying for attention on a newsstand with other publications, it is vying for attention among a pile of mail at home.

15. Prepare a chart of various things to be completed for each issue together with their deadlines, and cross each one off when it is finished.

16. Organize a copy and issue clearance process involving as few company executives as possible, stressing to them the importance of speed to meet printer's deadlines.

DISTRIBUTING

17. Select the quickest and most economical means possible to get the magazine or newspaper into the hands of readers. A weekly internal tabloid newspaper might best be given out in the office or plant. A point to consider here, however, is that employees have more time to read at home, where their families can also be reached. A monthly or quarterly magazine is best sent in an envelope or as a self-mailer to names on the mailing list. Third class is best for this because it is the cheapest. Material in the magazine is usually not so timely that a delay really matters.

18. Update such lists constantly by "purging" those who have left the company or address from the list. It does a company's image no good to have a magazine arrive twelve times a year addressed to someone who has been dead five years.

19. Survey readers at least once a year through a questionnaire in the magazine or a separate mailing. How do they like the magazine? What do they like and dislike about it? What would they like to see in future issues? Editors can use answers to make needed changes and to gain increased budgets from management.

"Company magazines create a stable, consistent image that is important for a corporation," says Peter Britton, a New York freelance writer and photographer who used to edit *Pepsi Cola World*. "They are much better if the approach is soft, with only a tenuous link to the company and its products."

Adds Craig Lewis, president of Earl Newsom and Company: "Company magazines are overused, but they can be effective. It's easy for a PR person to recommend that one be published and see the bosses' eyes light up. But management people don't always understand what a magazine should be doing. If an editor pays attention to the audience, they can be useful. Too many people don't do this, however."

Not all public-relations departments or agencies need the services of a full-time photographer for help in illustrating articles in company magazines and annual reports, or for taking photos to accompany news releases. When the time arrives for such photography help, there are certain ways to make sure that good photos result. At other times, especially for company magazines, a PR person may want to go to a freelance writer to do articles.

PHOTOGRAPHERS AND PR PHOTOGRAPHY

Photographers help public-relations people in two ways: by doing simple and routine photos of people and events to send out with news releases; and by doing more elaborate photographs for annual reports, company magazines, special events, promotions, press kits, and breaking news stories.

Far too many public-relations people treat photography as a necessary evil. They include a glossy print with every news release without really giving any thought to the photo's composition beforehand, or trying to include elements of interest to entice editors to run it.

The photograph of a person, commonly called a "mug shot," is routinely included with every news release announcing a promotion. Unless the newspaper or magazine has a "people in business" column, however, the black-and-white photo will wind up in the wastebasket, often with the release. A somewhat provocative shot of the person doing something interesting, or even taken from an unusual angle, might lead the business page that day. The same need for uniqueness exists for photographs of events, manufacturing operations, and products. The challenge is to present editors with photographs that are so eye-appealing that they will not be able to bear to throw them away.

The photographs for annual reports and company magazines are somewhat different from those for news releases. Because they are usually in color, these photos need to be more "pretty" to begin with. Color shots glorify everything, so the subject matter should merit such attention.

In an annual report, for example, the obligatory but boring shots of corporate executives can be interesting if they are photographed in unusual settings or while doing something different. Inside shots of products or locations can be equally absorbing if they are handled right.

Company-magazine articles need a slightly different approach. More successful photographs will contain people and some kind of action. Although they cannot all be news oriented, they should at least try to convey the essence of the story in an artful, pleasing way. An increasing number of company magazines use photos only to tell a story (Exhibit 15.4).

When it comes to thinking up unique ways to photograph products for public-relations agency clients, no one in the business equals John A. DeMilia, vice president and director of pictorial news at Carl Byoir & Associates. As the series of photos reproduced here indicates, DeMilia has a knack for directing the photographers who work for him to capture the unusual elements of often very mundane-looking items. Captions have much to do with selling the photo too. DeMilia thinks they have to be as eye catching in their own way as the photos they explain.

"The object," says DeMilia, "is to create the feeling of action in a still picture. I have often been asked, 'Just what is so different about a Byoir picture?' The answer can almost be found in the question. The Byoir picture is so different, so unlike the average publicity still, that over the years it has gained exceptional editorial acceptance and has become almost a benchmark of our work. When we speak of a Byoir picture we are thinking of a feature photograph with caption, designed to stand on its own merits as a one-shot news feature. It is seldom intended to be a how-to-do it picture. In the context we are discussing, it is not a spot news picture. Our pictures are intended to accomplish two objectives: to explain our client's capabilities in the industrial environment being covered and to enhance pictorially the page on which the editor uses it. These two objectives are closely interrelated, interdependent, for if the editor is not likely to use it, we are wasting the client's money; and, if it is not purposeful to the client, we should not even consider making it."

Byoir photos almost always include people. "A man or woman performing an interesting task supplies the dynamics a good picture demands and guarantees against the static flatness of so many ordinary publicity pictures," explains DeMilia. Because most assignments take place out of town, the Byoir director-photographer team uses client employees instead of professional models. "This lends realism and convincing dimension to our pictures," he continues. "Careful planning and precise execution are essential to many areas of photography, and public-relations work is certainly no exception to this rule. As you might gather, we believe photography that serves the client is good photography — and good photography is no accident."

Exhibit 15.4
A gallery of public-relations photos. (Reprinted with permission, Carl Byoir & Associates and Eastman Kodak.)

Mummy-like wrappings contain laminations of steel that are the cores, or basic components, of transformers being built by the Picker Corporation in Highland Heights, Ohio. The units, when completed, will be used to power the company's new Vector X-ray system which offers more thorough anatomy coverage of a patient's gastrointestinal tract, skeletal system, and other vital organs. In action above, Rodman Starkey is installing a primary coil on a core. Picker says the Vector system has the capability of cutting examination time and hospital costs, while reducing a patient's apprehension usually encountered with lengthy X-ray exams.

DeMilia: *"On more than one occasion when I've stopped to observe a worker, the client contact has often seen fit to advise me 'that's not a picture, it's something we do every day.' That's my point, the person making the statement has no eye or judgment about what makes a picture because he sees it as a job that is being done day after day."*

Stretching technology to the upper limits of fun, Howard Bollinger, vice president of preliminary design at Cincinnati-based Kenner Toys, demonstrates the *pullability* of *Stretch X-Ray*, one of the 60 to 100 new toys the company produces each year. Bollinger, who developed the corn syrup-filled latex doll with his twenty-five-man creative department, says "a good toy implements fantasy, stimulates thought, evokes emotion and causes kids to expand their vision."

DeMilia: "*What does a man who creates toys on a year-round basis look like? Is he tall, short, fat, thin, a fun guy? Our assignment called for a photo to accompany a story that would be given to the press during a pre-Christmas tour by toy designer Howard Bollinger. Since action is the missing ingredient in too many stills, the decision was made to photograph Bollinger in his working environment at the Kenner Toys offices. It paid off. In this shot, the man's personality is dominant and certainly is more interesting than a portrait of him or a photo of him at a desk, doodling or whatever.*"

Anvil chorus — Even in this era of high technology, skilled blacksmiths are relied upon for special custom-made tools and equipment for technical applications at Eastman Kodak Company in Rochester, N.Y. Kodak blacksmiths have performed an essential function in company operations for more than fifty years.

DeMilia: *"The majority of good pictures we make are those of actual situations. Of course, one must be selective. While knowing what to shoot is important, it's even more important knowing what not to shoot. In my opinion, if you can't shoot to a client's advantage, don't shoot at all. Why document failure?"*

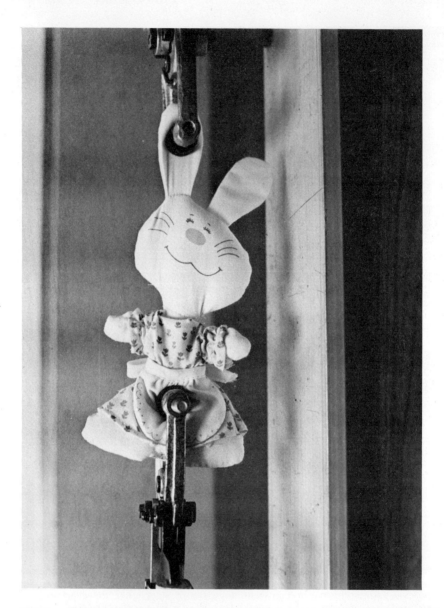

Rabbit wrencher — Bunny doll keeps smiling while locked in the grip of an ear-pulling, body-stretching testing machine at the Hallmark Cards plant in Kansas City. Its part of the company's consumer product safety program.

DeMilia: *"The integrity of a product is a major concern of all responsible corporations. Depending on the product, some safety testing procedures and equipment are more elaborate than others. Tensile testing pictures, for the most part, are purely functional and not exactly photogenic. What made the 'Rabbit wrencher' different? The smile on the bunny doll's face."*

Snake charmer — This snake-like outer covering of a flexible metal hose is rounded up by Sheryl Fitch (minus a flute) at UOP's Flexonics Division plant in Bartlett, Ill. The flexing braid, sheathing a bellows-type carrier for liquids and gasses, not only protects the bellows convolution but increases the pressure-carrying capacity by restricting elongation. The chemical and energy industries are major users of these hose assemblies because of their pressure, temperature, and corrosion resistance. They're made of stainless steel, bronze, and other high-grade alloys.

DeMilia: *"Many interesting photos can be made daily in almost any manufacturing facility, large or small. In most situations all that needs to be done is a little house cleaning. The photos are there, believe me."*

Putting on the dog — Steeplejacks George Luft (left) and Barry LaPoint check this four-ton, twenty-five-and-a-half-foot-tall reproduction of Nipper, the famous trademark of a little fox terrier listening to "his master's voice" on an RCA phonograph. Their effort preceded RCA's announcement today (October 31) in New York that it was bringing Nipper back as part of a major corporate marketing program. The king-size trademark symbol has been a landmark and tourist attraction in Albany, N.Y., since 1954 when it was erected atop the RCA (cq) Corporation building. Nipper's right ear supports a flashing beacon to warn low-flying planes.

DeMilia: *"This picture is a classic example of a large corporation wanting to revive a dormant trademark — a little fox terrier listening to 'his master's voice.' The dog's name was Nipper and a four-ton, twenty-five-foot reproduction of the fox terrier has been an Albany landmark and tourist attraction since 1954. Since we were looking for unusual visuals to help RCA in a major corporate marketing program, we decided to concentrate on the 'world's largest Nipper.' Shooting pictures of the dog alone lacked an important ingredient — human interest. So we suggested that steeplejacks check Nipper for structural defects, if any, and that some effort be made by them to either clean or repaint the fox terrier. The result speaks for itself."*

Whatever the type of photo, the photography is helped greatly if public-relations people know what they want and convey those desires to the photographers they hire. Photographers work best if they know what their photos are supposed to accomplish and how they will be used in print.

John DeMilia works that way. "What do you want to say? What are the objectives of the client? We have to know what it is that a client wants," he says. DeMilia has the experience of twenty-five years in public-relations photography to validate his approach. As vice president for pictorial news at Carl Byoir & Associates in New York, DeMilia is responsible for fulfilling the photo needs of 100 or more PR clients a year. When things go well for a Byoir-made photo, one picture placement a month for one year for a client can mean 60 million viewers.

DeMilia and his staff of visual directors at Byoir do not take photographs themselves. They direct either the full-time agency photographers or freelancers hired from the outside. They develop both long-term picture programs and individual picture ideas. Depending on the type of photo desired, they begin by gaining a thorough understanding of the client's objectives. "When we know the story, we try to tell it in a picture," continues DeMilia. This approach means careful advance planning and a walk around the plant or site to be photographed.

Often, these days, the subject matter may deal with breaking news. An assignment several years ago from a film maker exemplifies the Byoir photo style. The film was first shown in Washington, after which a reception took place for government and art-world figures. Among the guests was Chief Justice Warren Burger, a man with a well-known aversion to the press in general and photographers in particular. Before the reception, a Byoir visual director gave the producer a small strip of film and instructed his photographer to try to get the chief justice and the client in a shot examining the frames of film. At one point, the producer held up the film strip and Burger could not resist looking at it. The Byoir photographer — and a number of others standing around — snapped their cameras, and unique photos resulted, all widely used in various publications.

"The object is to create the feeling of action in a still picture," says DeMilia of that photo and his philosophy in general. "Editors hate talking heads, two people with a gap between. We never leave a blank space; we put someone doing something."

After the photographs have been selected and printed, DeMilia and his placement specialists offer them to the two wire services or national picture syndicates for their editorial consideration. One "hit" on the wire service makes up for a 5,000-piece mailing to names on a list, the conventional approach to distributing PR photos. "It is not sufficient to take a good picture," says DeMilia. "You can lose it if the caption is too long and not cogently written. You have to write tight or you lose the reader's interest. We put as much emphasis on good writing as we do in creating pictures."

FREELANCE WRITERS

Most public-relations people can write, even if they have to go outside and hire skilled professionals for other items like photography. Full-time public-relations people write news releases, longer articles, stories for company news-papers, copy for brochures and booklets, scripts for slide-tape presentations, and, on occasion, films. If a company has a slick quarterly magazine, however, the editor may turn to outside freelance writers for help from time to time.

The hiring of outside writers has several advantages. It gives variety to the magazine. It allows an outsider to look at a subject without the bias of the company point of view. It can be cheaper than hiring an equal number of in-house staff writers, who must be paid benefits as well as salaries.

Most external company magazines use freelance writers to do articles. The better editors give specific assignments to the writers, making clear from the start the objectives of the article and the aim of the magazine. If a com-pany editor uses freelance writers for every issue, he or she soon builds up a stable of them, each specializing in certain subjects.

The preparation of a list of guidelines for writers is helpful. This one-page sheet should note overall magazine objectives and expected approach. Is the company name to be mentioned often, occasionally, or never? Are any subjects or words taboo? What is the word length and deadline? What rights will the magazine hold? Can the writer sell the article elsewhere to a non-competing publication? Who will take the photographs, or will the article be illustrated with artwork? All these questions need to be answered and the answers explained clearly at the start of any working relationship with a writer.

One such company magazine freelance writer is Peter Britton. He has worked successfully in that field in New York for ten years. "I work with several company magazines as a freelance writer and photographer of articles on energy, oceanography, technology, and other subjects," he says. "The trick is to make them appeal to the mythical 'Aunt Millie,' the stockholder and aver-age person who doesn't care much about company business. She just likes to read something interesting about her company's business and know that the company is 'solid' and 'on top of things.' The good company editors know exactly what their audience is and what it wants in a story. These editors can tell you precisely what they need."

Britton gets an average of $3,000 to $3,500, plus expenses and extra money for research on the articles he does. The assignments give him a chance to travel and write about what he wants to write about. In doing so, of course, he must pay attention to the needs of the magazines and the whims of editors, learning which ones want blatant company "plugs" in the text and which ones allow a more journalistic style of writing.

SUMMARY

The company magazine or newspaper is an important way to reach employees and people outside the company with information about people and products, or as a means to create a good image. Such publications are internal, external, or a combination of the two, and come out weekly, monthly, quarterly, or eight times a year in formats ranging from simple, unadorned tabloid newspapers to slick, four-color magazines. The choice depends on management goals for the publication and its willingness to fund it. There are as many as 10,000 such publications in existence. Company publications began in the United States as early as 1840. The appearance of a company magazine is a careful combination of planning, organizing, publishing, and distributing. Outside professionals are often hired to help produce a company magazine. Two of the most important are photographers and freelance writers. Photographs are important in all segments of the PR product, used often to accompany news releases and in brochures.

PR FOCUS: A BRIEF GUIDE TO WRITING AND EDITING

Writing

1. Use simple, straightforward sentences, each with a subject and verb, uncluttered with unnecessary adjectives, adverbs, or subordinate clauses.
2. Keep one or, at the most, two ideas to a sentence.
3. Use the present tense whenever possible to keep the sentences moving.
4. Group like subjects into the same paragraph, unless that makes the paragraph too long. If it does, divide the paragraph arbitrarily into two.
5. Use the active voice whenever possible, avoiding the passive voice because it slows down a sentence.
6. Let the story tell itself, allowing sources to speak to readers through direct quotes or a paraphrase of those quotes.
7. Strive for an interesting lead paragraph that captures attention without putting off readers by its cuteness; a summary or news lead should be avoided, except on stories containing real news, because it will bore readers.
8. Use precise words that quickly tell the story, and explain all necessary complicated and technical terms in parentheses or in an accompanying glossary.

9. Keep yourself out of the story completely, avoiding personal pronouns at all costs.
10. Know when to let the story go and turn it in; prolonged and belabored changes usually weaken writing that has been gone over once or twice.

Editing Your Own Work and That of Others

1. Keep a dictionary and standard style manual available at all times, and consult them whenever in doubt on spelling and style.
2. Leave a piece of writing for a time after finishing it to let it settle; going back the next day will enable you to see it with fresh eyes.
3. Consider the lead paragraph first. Does it interest you and if not, why not? Are the important elements there or hinted at in such a way to interest readers?
4. Does the story get from the lead to the body in an understandable way? The transitional sentence should be like a bridge over a stream in the way it carries the reader along.
5. Does a theme emerge in the writing, and is it carried through to the end? Is there a smooth end that ties with the beginning? Or is the ending abrupt?
6. Simplify writing by removing as many subordinate clauses and prepositional phrases as possible.
7. Remove all uses of the passive voice.
8. Explain all technical terms and foreign phrases without complicating reader understanding.
9. Make sure that subjects and verbs agree, quotes are attributed, and vague references like "it" and "this" are explained.
10. Be careful to avoid sexist references, but when you do, do not commit a grammatical error by making "he or she" a "they" on second reference.

PR FOCUS: WHO ARE THE COMPANY MAGAZINE EDITORS?

According to a 1979 survey of members by the International Association of Business Communicators (2,742 responses), the typical company magazine or newspaper editor is a woman between thirty-two and thirty-five years old with a bachelor's degree in journalism and two years of experience or less. She reports to a public-relations manager in a manufacturing firm with about 1,000 to 3,000 employees, and that manager, in turn, reports directly to the chief executive of the company. The woman earns about $17,000 a year. (Men in similar jobs earn slightly more.)

Of IABC members surveyed, 35.1 percent publish magazines, 26 percent newsletters, 18.5 percent newspapers. Over 25 percent of respondents work in public-relations departments, 20 percent in communications, and 12 percent in employee communications. More than eight out of ten respondents said that they had direct access to the top person in their organizations. The editors who responded worked primarily for corporations and financial institutions (64.1 percent), and for associations, educational institutions, hospitals, and government units (21.7 percent).

As far as major challenges faced by company-magazine editors are concerned, the respondents choose "addressing workers'/members' needs, interests, and goals" (49 percent); "the need to educate top management on the importance of communication" (46 percent); "striving for more candor within the organization" (40 percent); "keeping abreast of industry/organizational trends and issues" (33.3 percent); "effecting major change through communications program" (32.9 percent); "responding to higher audience expectations" (25.8 percent); and "keeping up with technological advances" (12.1 percent).

Audiences for the company publications surveyed included: management (83.3 percent); salaried workers (80.2 percent); hourly workers (62.9 percent); union workers (38.5 percent); customers and dealers (25.2 percent); community residents (19.8 percent); members (17.6 percent); stockholders and financial analysts (16.9 percent); national and local opinion (15.5 percent).

As noted earlier, magazines are the most popular format for company publications. In 1979, monthly frequency of publications was down slightly, with the number of quarterlies remaining constant and weeklies and biweeklies increasing.

The survey showed that 30.9 percent of those responding comprise a one-person staff, with 29.6 percent having two people. Only 13.7 percent of publications have three staffers, and 5 percent had four. Two out of three publications (66 percent) cater to an internal audience, while 11.7 percent go to external readers. The other 20.4 percent are sent to a combination internal-external readership.

The company publications surveyed pay most attention to covering organizational news and operations (44.6 percent), then organizational trends and issues (24.9 percent). Human-interest material and employee or member news got 18 percent each. Beyond these major emphasis areas, editors write most about human-interest features (44.6 percent); personnel changes and retirement news (43.5 percent); benefits information (38.9 percent). News about organizational issues, trends, and operations totaled 37.3 percent. One out of five editors print regular messages from management, and one in four include economic information.

Of editors responding, 55 percent wanted more reader feedback, with 38 percent desiring more candor. They said that their publications were candid and honest "most of the time" (54.8 percent); "always" (23.8 percent); "sometimes" (16.3 percent); "seldom" (4.5 percent); "never" (0.6 percent).

Only 43.6 percent of editors responding have a written publications policy. Seven of ten respondents devote 50 percent or less of their time to producing their publications, of which 32 percent cost fifty cents or more per copy to produce and distribute; 14 percent reach 20,000 or more, while 57 percent have a total circulation of less than 5,000.

Based on the 1979 IABC survey, the typical company publication is a monthly, black-and-white magazine of fourteen pages. It costs between twenty-five and thirty cents a copy to produce and distribute to its primary audience, which is internal. Two or three people work on its staff, and it is printed externally.

PR FOCUS: THE PRINCIPLES OF DESIGN

The design of any printed page should be carried out through use of the five principles of design: balance, proportion, sequence, unity, and contrast (Exhibit 15.5).

Balance brings order to a page in that all elements on either side of an imaginary line are equally weighted. Usually, they are centered or symmetrical. Sometimes, to avoid the monotony of this kind of design, one element is moved to give an asymmetrical look to the page — and some excitement.

Proportion involves the way that space is divided into unequal divisions instead of equal ones that are too predictable, like a checkerboard. A design following this principle is asymmetrical with spaces separating elements divided in a more unusual way than in a balanced approach.

Sequence takes advantage of the eye movement of readers — usually from left to right and then down the page. But that does not mean that all designs have to start in the top left corner with main headlines. The attention of a reader can be attracted to anywhere on the page if the elements used are large enough. The important thing is to take readers from one element to the other in an orderly and understandable way that will not confuse them.

Unity dictates that everything goes together on a page — headlines, copy, illustrations, type styles. "If things are working right," says OSU art professor Allen Wong, "there is no orphan. If you put in an element, make sure that it belongs." Under this principle, designers must pay attention to details.

Contrast goes along with the search for an asymmetrical look. One element on a page should stand out from the other elements. If not, two elements will fight for attention, ruin the design, and confuse readers.

"Because most company magazines are produced in great volume," continues Wong, "they are not produced with quite as much care as an annual report. But a company magazine has to have a more lively appearance to attract an audience and hold it, with well-written stories and articles and good

Exhibit 15.5
The principles of design: balance, proportion, sequence, unity, contrast.

graphics. There are so many magazines in business today catering to special interests, people are more sophisticated. They see good design on TV too. This means that company magazines have to be better designed than in the past. They can't go overboard but must find the right approach to attract attention, hold attention, and get readers to react in the desired way — by buying a product or thinking well of the company."

REVIEW QUESTIONS

1. What role does a company magazine or newspaper play in the life of a company?
2. What are three kinds of company magazines, and how do they differ from one another?
3. What are some of the historical highlights of company magazines? How have these magazines changed over the years?
4. What are the steps required to publish a company magazine?
5. What editorial approach is best for the usual company magazines?
6. What should be included in a photograph to be sent out with a news release?
7. Why are so many PR photos thrown away?
8. How can mundane subjects be photographed in an interesting way?
9. How important are captions, and how should they be written?
10. What is the best way to work with freelance writers?

ASSIGNMENTS

For Journalism and Business Students

1. Select a company magazine from a major corporation and analyze it in writing in terms of format; content; quality of layout, type, and illustrations; overall success.
2. Interview a company-magazine editor to find out how he or she does the job: steps in production, problems, views on a career as a company-magazine editor. Report your findings to the class.
3. Develop a presentation to management for a new publication in which you select a format, a frequency, an audience, a series of suggested articles and features. You should get printer's estimates and decide on staffing requirements.
4. Design a sixteen-page company external magazine in an $8\frac{1}{2} \times 11$-inch format that takes it to the rough layout state. Make a list of the articles to be included and where they will come from.

5. Design an eight-page tabloid newspaper for an internal audience that takes it to the rough layout state. Make a list of stories to be included.

6. Go through the Sunday issue of your local newspaper and clip out all the photographs that seem to come from public-relations sources. Why did you make the selections you made? Call that newspaper's photo editor to check your selections, and report your findings to the class.

7. You are a PR person explaining to a photographer how you want some photos of a new laser pencil sharpener taken. Give the photographer five suggestions for unusual photos.

8. Select a PR photo from a newspaper or call a PR person and ask for one to be sent to you. Analyze the photo in terms of content and effectiveness.

9. Now write a caption for the photo used in assignment 8.

10. Make a list of photographs you want a freelancer to take at the annual July 4 company picnic. The subject is mundane, but you must have a color spread in the next issue of the external magazine on the picnic because it is a favorite activity of the president's wife.

11. Prepare a list of guidelines for freelance writers you will be hiring to work for your external quarterly magazine.

CHAPTER 16

Using television, radio, film, and slide-tape presentations

In any public-relations department or agency, print is the primary means of communication. News releases, brochures, booklets, annual reports, and magazines, if they are well prepared and carefully distributed to press and public, can do a great deal to help further the communications goals of a company or nonprofit organization. These printed pieces are tangible evidence that a PR person is doing something to promote the cause of the organization. Each of them can be held in the hands of the intended audience, and can be referred to again and again.

But such printed means are only one segment of the vast array of techniques at the disposal of a PR person. Visual and electronic means are available as well. Words are a part of this approach, but they are heard and not seen on a printed page. Television, radio, film, and slide-tape presentations augment greatly the tools to accomplish the public-relations job.

Far too many people get all their news from television, for example, to ignore that medium. Far too many people drive great distances and listen to their car radios to forget that long-established outlet. People belong to a great many clubs and organizations, and these clubs and organizations need programs. A good film or slide-tape presentation, shown at a club meeting or even a convention, brings in yet another audience for the message of the company or nonprofit organization. If the film is good enough, a showing on public television or a local commercial station might also be arranged.

Many public-relations people, particularly if they come from print journalism, concentrate on the more established print techniques already noted. They are indeed preferable most of the time. But in the last few years, electronic and visual approaches have become increasingly important as PR media.

TELEVISION

Two devices predominate in the use of television as a public-relations tool.

The Filmed News Release

This news release resembles a print news release except that the words for the filmed version are fewer, and a film clip is sent along with the script to television stations on the PR department's mailing list. As with print, the PR person has no control over whether a station will use the filmed release. If it is well done, chances are that it will be used because the amount of airtime to fill is vast, and few local stations have the resources to turn down good film footage.

The Television Public-Service Announcement

Really a short program (thirty to sixty seconds), the television public-service announcement presents a message through film and narration for a company or nonprofit organization. The PSA is then sent to the same list of television stations that get the filmed releases in the hope that they will play it. The chances are that these stations will use it, although the time of the broadcast is unpredictable. The reason for this certainty of use lies in the fact that all broadcasting stations, both television and radio, are licensed by the Federal Communications Commission. Every three years these stations must file for renewal of their licenses to stay in business. One of the factors that bears on the FCC decision to renew the license is the kind of programming presented during the three-year period. If a station includes the use of PSAs at times of low viewing — like late at night or on Sunday morning — chances for license renewal are enhanced, and the announcement will be seen by thousands of people. Sometimes the stations will drop a PSA into a prime-time slot after a network show. For a public-service announcement of national interest, such national exposure, although rare, is worth the wait.

But problems abound for commercial companies when their PR people try to get television stations to broadcast either filmed news releases or television PSAs. If the message is too strident, too sales oriented, or too much like a paid commercial for the company, the stations will not use it. The best approach is a low-key approach in which the company presents information of an educational nature and mentions its name only incidentally. A good example of this technique is the series of "Bicentennial Minutes" prepared by Shell Oil Company at the time of the U.S. Bicentennial in 1975 and 1976. Another way to proceed is to discuss a research development made in a company laboratory and only vaguely mention the name of the company. A nonprofit organization like a hospital or university has an easier time placing filmed news releases and PSAs because of the absence of any direct commercial gain. Future funding may rely on good research results, widely disseminated to the public and legislators, but the process is much more indirect and subtle, and thus more palatable to TV-station program directors.

The process of preparing a filmed news release for dissemination to a mailing list of television station news directors and program directors begins with a decision on what development at the company or nonprofit organization will lend itself to television treatment. Because of the need to concentrate on visual images, this means that the subject must be colorful and must contain some action. A dull meeting or panel discussion or laboratory discovery had best be left to treatment in a print release. The wild-horse story noted in the PR Focus in this chapter is a good example of a natural story for treatment in a filmed news release.

The PR person then directs a film photographer to the proper location to shoot the footage. Given the recent switch of almost all television stations to color, the film must be in color and preferably 35 mm. The PR person should go along with the photographer to gather material for the script that will be sent along with the film clip to the stations. Large PR departments may have their own TV specialists who can shoot film footage, gather material from sources, and write the final copy.

After the film footage has been shot and the material for the script gathered, the PR person and photographer work together to develop the one- or two-minute release to distribute. As with any kind of writing, the script for a filmed news release should make its point quickly in the lead sentence and move along with the rest of the story in as few words as possible. A long TV release that meanders aimlessly for five minutes without clearly stating its point will not be used. Even stations in need of material cannot afford to devote that much time to a story.

TV writing uses many active verbs and few adjectives, and is in the present tense. The script must also be timed and coordinated with the film footage so that the reading pace of the usual TV announcer will result in the script and the footage ending at the same time. If the release includes both a narrative script and an "actuality," that is, a point when someone in the TV news release will himself or herself talk, that fact must be noted carefully on the material sent to the station, together with the words uttered by the person in case the sound fails or the announcer decides to paraphrase the words of the speaker.

The television PSA is both similar and different when compared to the filmed news release. The material for the script is gathered in the same way as is the film footage. The difference comes in the way those two elements are assembled. The PSA is doing more than just presenting news and information. It is conveying a message and a point of view in a dramatic fashion to get the audience to do something, whether that be to save whales or appreciate history or curb cancer with a checkup and a check. The TV PSA thus relies on dramatic writing and music in addition to its film and facts. It is also shorter: usually thirty to sixty seconds.

The narrative in a PSA begins with the presentation of a theme that is authenticated through the use of facts. The narrative ends best by tying it into the beginning and restating the theme for reenforcement. There should always be a *tagline* in which the name and address of the sponsoring organization are imposed on the screen so that viewers can write for more information.

Beyond time and treatment, the PSA differs from the filmed release in another major way: it must be in a complete package with the words of the announcement already recorded on a soundtrack that goes along with the film. The television station gets the film cassette ready to play, and the news announcer there never sees the script.

Costs for filmed news releases or television PSAs vary from one part of the country to another because of film-processing charges. While $1,000 a minute is standard in Oregon, for example, the amount can go as high as $3,000 a minute in New York. A professional announcer or actor must also be hired to read the script. An unprofessional-sounding voice can ruin an otherwise well-prepared TV PSA.

Television coverage is a good way to gain exposure for more newsworthy and timely events than can be included in a filmed news release or television PSA prepared over a period of two weeks. Television news directors will send reporters, camera people, and sound people to press conferences and other planned events, especially if something visual has been set up for them. Talking heads are boring, but an interesting laboratory demonstration will get used. TV stations might also show color slides of people, products, or events if they are sent along with a standard news release. An interview on a local or national talk show with a company official is also good exposure.

As with print outlets, television stations can be a great help to PR people if these people use care and ingenuity in developing programs.

Filmed releases that are blatantly commercial or just plain uninteresting will not be used by television stations. Editors are looking for material for programs other than news shows, like fillers after sporting events, or on local feature programs or local talk shows. News programs are sometimes interested in film footage as background for late-breaking stories in fields like medicine, energy, science, women's rights, electronics, transportation, even travel. If a company or nonprofit organization has filmed some of its important operations and sends the footage to stations, the footage might be used at a later date. It must be well produced and ready to go on the air. It should also be accompanied by a script that explains what is going on, even if the script itself is not read on the air; it will still furnish good background.

RADIO

Radio can be much the same great ally of the public-relations person as television. It is also cheaper — for example, a set of four radio PSAs will cost $250 while a single TV PSA can run over $1,000.

As with television, there are two primary ways to use radio.

The Radio News Release

This news release is a story, sent to a mailing list of radio stations, that presents information about the company or nonprofit organization from the point of view of that company or organization. A radio news release should be written in radio style so that it can be read by an announcer without much editing. Although better radio newspeople will rewrite the releases they get, many of the employees at smaller stations will not do so, so the release should arrive in a format and style suitable for immediate reading over the air (see the PR Focus at the end of this chapter).

The Radio Public-Service Announcement

The radio PSA is also like its television counterpart except for the absence of film footage. Instead, good radio PSAs make use of sound effects and the voices of the people interviewed in the gathering of material for the PSA. A good approach to take is one with a dramatic beginning that states the theme in an attention-getting way, uses an actuality to convey more information, and ends with a return to the theme stated in the original opening. Along the way, music and sound effects can enhance the words of the narration. Music is especially good if the PSA is one of a series; the music lends continuity in the same way that a logo identifies printed material in a series. As in TV, the choice of a narrator is important. Although such people must be paid, their voices lend professionalism to the PSA, which may not be played on the air if it sounds otherwise. The use of somebody's wife or a friend will not work if the voice quality is bad and the person does not know how to read copy understandably. Listeners and TV viewers are used to hearing and seeing the best, and they will "tune out" — either literally or figuratively — if they encounter a PSA that is otherwise than professional in quality.

FILM

The preparation of a film by a company or nonprofit organization is infinitely more complicated and expensive than putting together filmed and broadcast news releases and public-service announcements for TV and radio. Because of their great cost and complexity, films should be produced only after careful consideration.

"Any kind of highly technical communications technique like a film needs to be approached with some degree of caution," says Gwil Evans, chairman of communications for the Oregon State University Extension Service. "A film or a multiprojector slide show or a display using video — all these have elements of technical sophistication that a communications generalist may not be able to deal with. It isn't enough to say, 'We ought to produce a movie.' It is important to look first at the message and the audience. Then it is best to acknowledge that you as a **PR** person with a background in print need some help."

Evans, who produced a film for the university's Sea Grant program several years ago, says any person contemplating the production of a film needs next to talk to people who have done films for their companies and organizations, and ask them how things worked out. He also advises people to read widely about film making. *Photomethods,* a monthly magazine published on the subject by the Eastman Kodak Company, is a good place to start, as are two books from that company, *Images, Images, Images* and *Designing for Projection.* (An Index to Kodak Information can be obtained by writing to the company in Rochester, New York 14650.)

Joan Dolph is a former print PR person who taught herself film techniques and who used them as director of publicity and public relations at West Point Pepperell and in freelance assignments for Pepsi Cola. "You really can't have company films and expect the press to be interested in them," she says. "Films have got to be entertaining and have some news value. You make your point about the company or the product in a subtle way and hope that the point is not so subtle that it is missed by the audience." Her chance came in a film she made about the Lady Pepperell House. There had been a real Lady Pepperell, who had lived in a house in Kittery Point, Maine before the Revolutionary War.

The house was now a museum run by a group of local ladies. Her ladyship's ancestors had long ago sold the original furnishings. When the company offered to refurnish and decorate the house in its original style in return for its use as the focal point for future product promotion, the ladies agreed, and Dolph went to work. "Lady Pepperell looked like someone in a painting by Copley," she continues. "She had left a diary so I was able to find out how she felt, and to work her impressions into my script. We had descendants of Lady Pepperell come back and look at the house, marveling at how beautiful it was."

The final film was shown on television women's programs because of its historical interest. Dolph prepared standard news releases about the house as well, and included still photographs of the restoration. Decorator magazines and textile trade publications sent reporters to do stories on the house too. The company advertising department also used the refurbished rooms as the setting for ads. The company thus got more than its share of use out of both the film and the house it had paid to redecorate.

Public-relations people who propose a film should have a good reason for doing so because of the costs involved. A film should be produced only when other, more conventional communications techniques have failed or have been considered and abandoned for good reason. Where is the film going to be shown, and why is a film necessary?

A film needs a story line of some kind as it conveys its message or its informational content. As with TV and radio presentations, work on a film begins with research and fact-gathering, followed quickly by the filming itself. Unless they are experienced, PR people should not do the filming but should hire an experienced photographer, unless the film is done in animation, in which case an animated film company would be contacted. A film in which real people and objects are photographed is called a *live action* film. Even if PR people can write, they might be better served if they hire a skilled scriptwriter as well, with the PR person becoming overall producer to make sure that the company's needs are being met and that costs are kept under control.

Those costs include rental or purchase of cameras and lights, the talents of actors and a narrator, transportation, film and processing, cutting and printing. A simple 10-minute film can cost as much as $2,000, but that amount can go easily to $5,000 or even $10,000 if expenses are not watched.

But such costs are worth it if the film conveys its special message well and gets good audience reaction when shown at meetings, conventions, schools, and trade shows, or on public or local TV stations. The winner of the 1970 Academy Award for best animated feature, "Is It Always Right to Be Right?" began life as a film on how employees should work together paid for by the Ohio Bell Telephone Company. That corporation hired Stephen Bosustow Productions of Santa Monica, California to do the film, which was cleverly illustrated and which had a narration read by Orson Welles.

Such diverse topics as personal motivation, creativity, history, worthy causes, famous people, technical processes, new company programs, world problems, and many other subjects can be handled in films.

A good film can reap benefits beyond the dreams of its PR originators and photography and scriptwriter creators. Having a one-line company credit on a well-done motion picture is worth more than all the institutional advertising that money can buy. But such accolades cannot be anticipated in advance. The quality of the final product itself will bring praise, and that quality will be established and maintained if company PR people who decide to make films do not make the commitment without good reason and adequate budget.

SLIDE-TAPE PRESENTATIONS

One step down from a film in complexity and cost, a slide-tape presentation is still a technique that requires careful thought and advance planning. Like a film, there should be good reasons to do a slide-tape presentation instead of a more conventional and less costly approach.

The primary use of slide-tape shows comes in meetings to explain a program, product, or way to do something, or in courses as a teaching device. Such a presentation consists of a series of slide photographs and a taped soundtrack, with the two carefully synchronized so that the slide shown on the screen matches what is being said by the voice on the tape.

Slide-tape presentations are best if they are totally automatic, that is, if the slides move through the projector automatically (preferably two projectors with a "dissolve" unit so that one slide appears as the other vanishes on the screen) as the taped soundtrack plays. If the presentation is going to be sent on its own or into areas without sophisticated equipment, however, it will need to be designed accordingly. An operator will advance the projector having heard a slight "beep" on the tape.

As with TV and radio and film productions, a slide-tape presentation begins with careful thought about purpose, goals, and costs. What is the subject? Where and how will it be used? Why is a slide-tape show the best approach?

Once these questions have been answered satisfactorily, work on the slide-tape presentation can begin with the establishment of a theme or story line, which should be outlined; next comes the taking of the slides to illustrate the script. A photographer can begin shooting from the outline but really needs a rough script to make sure that all necessary things have been photographed. If clearances and permissions are needed for the photographer to work in company locations, the PR person should take care of getting them.

The PR person can probably write the script, although special nuances are needed in its style: timing, cadence of language, and some dramatic effect. Research and interviews come before the actual writing, and the people contacted inside or outside the company or nonprofit organization should be selected in the same way that interview subjects for any story are picked: for their knowledge of the subject.

As the writing progresses, the photographer is continuing to take the photographs. It is best to have the photographer shoot three or four times the number needed in the final presentation so that only the finest shots are included. After the film has been processed, a good photographer will gladly pick these shots, although the person putting together the final presentation should ask for the rejected slides because the pile might contain a good shot that fits the script better than those selected by the photographer.

After the first "cut" of slides and a rough script are finished, the writer should go through the slides and begin to organize them to go along with what is being said in the script. With a large number of good photographs, there is a tendency to include too many of them. This predilection should be avoided because an audience will want to linger over a good shot for a moment and will be disappointed if it rushes by too fast in the presentation.

After making final slide choices and organizing the slides in a tray, the writer should run the slides through one by one and write the number of the tray slot at the point in the script where the slide should be changed. As in a film or TV presentation, a slide-tape show should move quickly, capturing the attention of the audience with a smooth combination of picture and story. Slides should not be used unless they add to the telling of the story: that is, they should not be included just because they are excellent photographically.

Music will add to the quality of any slide-tape presentation as background, quiet in the middle, more loud and stirring at the beginning and end. Since songs are copyrighted, the best course of action on music is to select something at the sound company that records the narration. Such companies have available many different kinds of appropriate music with the right to use it included in the recording fee. A good sound company can also recommend and arrange for a professional announcer to read the script for recording. A skilled "voice" can usually do the whole narration in an hour without retakes, and even in a number of versions (British, Texas, "foreign" sound, young, old) — all of this worth the several-hundred-dollar fee. As with the radio and TV PSAs or a film, the use of a nonprofessional — the PR person or a family member or friend — on a slide-tape show will sound like "amateur night" and will reduce the quality and credibility of the whole production.

When the slide-tape presentation is finished, it should be packaged in an easily transported case containing the slide tray (preferably a circular one), the cartridge of tape, instructions on how to start the slides and the tape synchronously, and a copy of the script with slide numbers marked, in case the tape fails and the words of narration have to be read.

A slide-tape presentation should be evaluated regularly by the PR person involved in its production. That person should show it to groups once in a while. If the audience seems bored and inattentive, the length might be shortened. If it does not understand the content, the script might be rewritten. Short questionnaires passed out after a showing can yield useful suggestions. A slide-tape show should not be used for more than six months. There should be enough sets available so that desired audiences get to see it quickly.

After a slide-tape presentation has been withdrawn, its worth should be carefully evaluated before a replacement is produced. Is a slide-tape presentation the best way to convey the information to the desired audiences? If so, a new one should be prepared. If not, other techniques should be used.

SUMMARY

Although print is the primary means of communication in public relations, several visual techniques expand the choices available to reach desired publics. Filmed news releases for television, radio news releases, television and radio public-service announcements, films, and slide-tape presentations are all acceptable methods to put across the message of a company or nonprofit organization. Each of these approaches must be considered carefully before it is used. Is a TV PSA or a film or any of the other possibilities a good way to communicate? Is it worth the extra cost? Does the subject lend itself to a visual treatment? If these questions can be answered affirmatively, the PR person can proceed with research and scriptwriting and supervision of the still, TV, or motion-picture photographer hired for the project.

Unless a PR person is a good photographer, it is best to pay for an outside freelancer. The same holds true for scriptwriting, especially of a film. An amateur production will reflect badly on the company or nonprofit organization. "Amateur night" has no place in a world competing for the attention of listeners and viewers who have become quite sophisticated from years of watching slick television and motion-picture productions. All these visual and electronic approaches to PR need a story line that is clearly communicated to an audience. Distribution must also be careful and, because of cost, effectiveness of the film, PSA, or slide-tape show must be evaluated frequently.

PR FOCUS: COMPARING A FILM AND A PRINT RELEASE

As noted in Chapter 12, "The Anatomy of a News Release," the material for Dave King's television filmed release on Oregon wild horses was gathered at the same time his boss, Dick Floyd, was researching the conventional news release for print publications. King, an assistant editor at the OSU Agricultural Experiment Station, went up in a small plane to take aerial views of wild horses and also got footage of them on the ground. He got the film processed, cut it to the proper time length, and had prints made to mail to the television news departments around Oregon.

King also needed to send along a script that the TV anchorperson could read as the film footage was shown (usually with the credit "OSU film" superimposed on the screen) (Figure 16.1). A radio release would follow a format identical to the TV script.

The TV script, which is a page and a half shorter than the print release (see Figure 16.2), begins with a notation on where to start the film. The lead is a bit abstract and designed to attract viewer attention in much the same way the print release did, for example, in the use of "kicked up conflicts" as a play on the horse subject matter. The second sentence of the lead gets to the point more quickly than the print version does. It has to do so because of the short time available.

The body of the TV release makes its points more directly and in shorter, more simply written sentences than does the print release. The one direct quote has no direct attribution. The sentence before it begins with "Vavra said," so that the connection when Vavra begins to speak is obvious. The one-page release runs ninety-three seconds when used with the film footage.

PR FOCUS: HOW TO WRITE FOR TELEVISION AND RADIO

Writing for television and for radio are almost identical, except that television involves film footage whose images must be taken into consideration during

WILD HORSES GET
SPECIAL STUDY
IN OSU RESEARCH

<u>TV COPY</u>

START FILM
HERE --------Wild horses have kicked up conflicting thoughts about their future
in the high desert of Oregon and other western states. One problem is competition
with range cattle for dwindling space and food on the range.

Two Oregon State University scientists and Bureau of Land Management personnel
are studying habits of the horses to see how severe the competition is with cattle.

In the BLM's 4.6 million acre Vale District in Eastern Oregon, there are 12
herds of wild horses. The biggest has about 2,000 horses and the smallest has 16
animals. Martin Vavra (vaa-vra) and Forrest Sneva (snee-va) from OSU's Eastern
Oregon Agricultural Research Center have been collecting fecal samples of wild
horses, cattle, antelope and deer. The scientists search for herds from helicopters
or on the ground with four-wheel drive vehicles to collect fresh samples. The
samples are then frozen and taken to the Experiment Station in Union for analysis.

According to Vavra, each individual plant has its own epidermal cell characteristic that is inchanged by digestion. The undigested portion of the plant can be
identified under a 100 power microscope. After analysis, the samples are sent to
a USDA soil scientist in Kimberly, Idaho for further scrutiny.

Preliminary results show that wild horses eat almost 100 per cent grasses.
Cattle diet seems to be very similar except in the spring when they may eat up to
20 per cent sagebrush. Sheep eat 80 per cent grasses and 20 per cent shrubs. The
scientists said this indicates a severe dietary overlap.

Vavra said that in terms of species of plant consumed, the competition is
very severe between horses and cattle because they do eat the same species of grass.
"The important thing is the stocking rate of both cattle and wild horses on the
range. When either animal gets over populated, then we do have a problem."

Sneva is on appointment to OSU from the USDA Agricultural Research Service.

# # # #

Figure 16.1

*The script for a filmed news release. (Reprinted with permission, Oregon State
University Agricultural Experiment Station.)*

284

```
From Oregon State University                    WILD HORSES GET
Department of Information      7/28/77          SPECIAL STUDY
Telephone 754-4611                              IN OSU RESEARCH
```

(Note to News Directors: For an audio cut of this story, call 754-3615 at OSU between 9 a.m. and 12 noon, M-F. Cut runs 93 sec.)

Wild horses can't keep two Oregon State University scientists from their research project.

In fact, without the wild horses of the Bureau of Land Management's Vale District, Martin Vavra, animal scientist, and Forrest Sneva, range scientist of the Agricultural Research Service of the U.S. Department of Agriculture, would not be peering down from helicopters, walking through desert streams and climbing over cliff rocks.

The wild horses of the federal BLM Vale district (malheur, part of Harney County and a bit of Idaho) have kicked up conflicting thoughts about their future. Idaho, Montana, Wyoming, Utah, Arizona, California and other parts of Oregon have similar wild horse problems of dwindling space, food and water.

More than 1,150 Oregon horses have been adopted from holding corrals near Burns in the last 3½ years. Horses will be available through the Adopt-A-Horse program this summer in California, Oregon, Nevada and Wyoming.

"We don't really have much technical information about the wild horses' food, water, cover or living space," said Jerry Wilcox, Vale District wild horse specialist who works with the OSU scientists.

"Most of the captured ones have been in fairly good condition. Their seasonal use patterns and space requirements are not well understood."

The district has 12 herds. The biggest has about 2,000 horses; the smallest, 16 animals.

"We now are reaching the point where forage and water are not adequate to sustain the herds which we estimate increase from 17 to 22 per cent annually," said Wilcox.

"Based on our current information, we estimate that we need to reduce horse numbers from about 2,800 to 1,200. The new data from the OSU study will provide information to assist us in developing a horse management plan and determining the proper number of horses so they will be in balance with other resources."

Vavra and Sneva, from OSU's Eastern Oregon Agricultural Research Center's stations at Union and Burns, hope to answer some of the questions about the wild horses.

They started in September to gather fecal samples, only a few hours old, from wild horses, cattle and deer.

(more)

Figure 16.2
The script for a print release on the same subject. (Reprinted with permission, Oregon State University Agricultural Experiment Station.)

The fresh samples are frozen and taken to the Union Experiment Station for analysis.

"Each individual plant species has its own epidermal cell characteristics which do not change," said Vavra. "Basically, what we study is the undigested portion of the plant material in the fecal samples."

After analysis, the samples are sent to a USDA soil scientist at Kimberly, Idaho, for further analysis to determine the amount of soil ingested by the animals.

Said Sneva:

"We want to determine the botanical diet composition and selectivity of the animals through the grazing season with one year of collecting.

"We also will compare diets of the animals, particularly horses and cattle, grazing different parts of the region. Then we want to see which plants are being selected by the animals at the end of the grazing season compared to the beginning."

Results of the study, funded by the Agricultural Experiment Station and BLM, will not be known until this fall.

"But we think there will be a strong parallel to results from a fecal collection study finished early this year near Burns," said Sneva.

The two-year study near Burns of diet competition among wild horses, cattle and dear showed that, year-round, horses consume almost 100 per cent grass. Cattle liked the same grass diet, except in the spring and early summer when their diet contained up to 20 per cent sagebrush.

Sheep preferred a diet of about 80 per cent grasses in the spring and 20 per cent shrubs. The rest of the time, their diet was similar to that of cattle.

In the spring, antelope ate 60 per cent broad-leaf plants including weeds. Dear consumed equal parts of shrubs, grass and broad-leaf plants in the spring and preferred shrubs the rest of the year although not to the extent the antelope did.

The study showed that there was a severe dietary overlap among cattle, sheep and wild horses.

# # # #

Figure 16.2 continued.

script preparation. Both television and radio differ greatly from print, however, and a few basic rules must be followed or the result will be less than satisfactory.

1. Keep all stories short and simple, remembering that the viewer and listener have only one chance to understand what is being said and cannot go back to reread a word or sentence.
2. Stick to a straightforward sentence structure at all times, avoiding long subordinate clauses.
3. Get to the point of the story quickly unless the writing is deliberately obscured for dramatic effect or reasons of reader interest.
4. Give attribution more directly in radio and TV copy than in print. For example: "Five Oregon State University scientists think" rather than ". . . according to two OSU scientists."
5. Avoid using words that need to be read to be understood, for example, "fete" as a word for entertain.
6. Hold down detail to a necessary minimum and disperse it among several sentences rather than one sentence in which the many elements are separated by commas. For example, in the OSU release, the sentence "The two-year study near Burns of diet competition among wild horses, cattle and deer showed that, year-round, horses consume almost 100 percent grass" (Figure 12.2) became, in the TV release, "Preliminary results showed that wild horses eat almost 100 percent grasses."
7. Emphasize present action by using the present tense as often as possible; it makes the story move more quickly.
8. Simplify identification. For example, "Martin Vavra . . . from OSU's Eastern Oregon Agricultural Research Center," not, "Martin Vavra, animal scientist, Oregon State University . . ."
9. Avoid abbreviations; they might confuse the announcer, who may not get the chance to read the story before going on the air.
10. Avoid use of the indefinite article "a" or any word or phrase that could be ambiguous when it is heard and not seen. For example, "a hundred" might sound like "eight hundred."
11. Simplify and write out large numbers. For example, change "$525,204,061" to "over 525 million dollars."
12. Spell names or other difficult words phonetically in parentheses after the regular spelling to aid pronunciation. For example, "Vavra (vaa-vra) and . . . Sneva (snee-va) . . ."
13. Avoid awkward phraseology when using direct quotes. Instead of "quote" or "unquote," write "what he says" before the paraphrase of the quote. For example, "Vavra is working on what he calls the most significant study ever made of wild horses."
14. Avoid hyphenating words at the end of a line because it is too easy to lose the sense of the sentence from one line to the next.

15. Do not carry over a sentence from one page to another.
16. Emphasize negatives by capitalizing or italicizing them (*"not"*); this avoids the accidental dropping of them and the reversal of the meaning of the entire sentence.
17. Time all copy to make sure that it is not too long to be usable; if a broadcaster has to rewrite a news release, he or she may not use it. Using premarked copy paper or a certain typewriter margin and line count per page (equal to *x* number of minutes) will speed this process; so will experience.

REVIEW QUESTIONS

1. What means of communication other than print can be used in public relations?
2. Why are visual and electronic PR methods growing in importance and popularity?
3. What is a filmed news release, and how does it differ from its print counterpart?
4. What is a PSA, and how does it differ from a news release?
5. What are the important elements to consider when deciding to produce a company film?
6. How does a slide-tape presentation differ from a film? a PSA?

ASSIGNMENTS

For Journalism and Business Students

1. Watch a local TV evening news program for a week, and count the number of filmed news releases used. List their subject and sponsoring organization, and rate their quality.
2. Contact the sponsoring organization and find out the details of production. When was the release done, how much did it cost, how was it put together? Report your findings to the class.
3. Listen to a local radio station for a week and count the number of PSAs used. List their subjects and sponsoring organizations and rate their quality.
4. Select one radio or TV PSA and contact the sponsoring organization to find out how the PSA was put together from idea through writing, production, and final mailing to the station. Report your findings to the class.
5. Contact several large companies in your area and ask to see their films.

Analyze the content and production quality of two of them and compare them.

6. Do the same for two slide-tape presentations.
7. Pick a subject and gather the material for, and write, a radio PSA.
8. Write a radio news release.
9. Write the script for a television filmed release after taking some suitable film footage.
10. Write a proposal for a company film or slide-tape presentation, justifying production, listing steps, and estimating costs.

CHAPTER 17

Setting up external events

The planning had begun almost a year before, but Homer Schoen was taking no chances. He was personally checking a number of last-minute details himself. "What you don't see, you don't have," says the public-relations man at Xerox in charge of the company annual meeting. "Don't live on promises. I have a rule. I say, 'That's fine. Show me.' "

The 1980 event was especially important because for it the company was returning to its founding city, Rochester, New York, where many of its original stockholders live. That meeting was also especially difficult. Along with the great number of loyal shareholders was the lack of a large enough hotel to accommodate the expected crowd. Instead, the company was pitching a tent in the parking lot of its manufacturing plant for the third time in its history. This added to the problems for Schoen but might create a festive atmosphere for the meeting.

If it was not the tent, it would be a hundred other things. The planning of an annual meeting, although it lasts only about two hours, is one of the most important activities of a public-relations department — and one with the most potential for problems because of all the details that need to be taken care of.

ANNUAL MEETINGS

Both the New York Stock Exchange and the American Stock Exchange require that companies call an annual meeting of stockholders when an election of directors is to be held or when it is necessary to vote on other matters requiring stockholder approval. At most annual meetings, the company board chairman and president review the year and discuss future plans, thus communicating with stockholders and the world at large because reporters usually attend.

There is also a period for questions from those stockholders who are present or people representing groups of stockholders. In recent years, the question period has been a fractious one at annual meetings because of the attendance of two or three "professional" stockholders who do little more than ask management embarrassing questions. Because they hold at least one share of stock, they are eligible to attend the meeting, but normally have no purpose in mind than to confuse and divide management and other shareholders. They usually fail.

Annual meetings during the 1960s were also the scene of takeover attempts by large conglomerates of smaller companies. The "swallower" most often arrived at the meeting with the voting power of enough proxies from absent stockholders to try to force out the management of the "swallowee" and assume control. Such tactics are less frequent now, but annual meetings are still an important company event, the chance to brag about successes, make excuses for errors, look at the future, and generally create a good impression about the company.

The experience of Homer Schoen of Xerox typifies that of PR people in other companies in charge of annual meetings. Schoen's problems and solutions to those problems serve as a useful guide for anyone with the assignment. "Each year is different," he says. "The first decision is location. At first it was always Rochester but we later decided to move the meeting from city to city to reach more stockholders. We've held it in New York, Chicago, Dallas, San Francisco and are looking now at Washington and Boston. There have to be enough stockholders in a city to justify a meeting."

After that choice has been made, usually by management, Schoen prepares what he calls a "working document" that informs everyone to be involved in the annual meeting of his or her responsibilities. He heads an internal committee that works on such aspects of the meeting as calendar, location, procedures, catering, and sound system. He recruits about 100 people from the company's field organization to help at the time of the meeting with controlling traffic, escorting stockholders to their seats, acting as floor attendants. Schoen puts together a group of other people in the company to help him as he goes along.

"I build a small team of my own people whom I identify and make sure they are aware of the meeting so they don't discover later they have no free time," he continues. "I don't recruit them directly; I go to their bosses." Schoen's main contact point with management is the corporate secretary, whom he keeps informed of progress throughout the long months of planning.

After the city has been chosen, Schoen settles next on a hotel. "The size of the meeting is usually about 1,000 people," he says. "Since we need a hotel ballroom, we recognize that there will very likely be an eighteen-month to two-year reservation cycle." Schoen travels to the city and looks at the hotel, taking careful notes as he walks through the facilities to be used for the meeting. He also sets up a good working relationship with the hotel staff. "We tip generously, not wildly," he says. Closer to the actual meeting, Schoen sets up an office in the hotel complete with a telephone system and telecopiers. "There is a whole page in the plan for telephone arrangements and a page and a half about office equipment," he says.

Everyone who attends the annual meeting gets a kit that includes an annual report, admission tickets, and badges. All these items as well as parking-lot direction signs, proxy election booths, and other printed materials contain the same graphic design to achieve a coordinated look.

Some of Xerox's annual meetings include a display of products, others do not. "We have a product exhibit if we have new products," says Schoen. "It can be costly and the available space is not always ideal."

Security arrangements must be made, usually with a guard service or local police. No one is admitted to the meeting without proper tickets, and no one gets tickets without proper credentials. There is always a luncheon after the meeting that requires arrangements like menu selection and flowers.

What are Schoen's rules for successful annual meetings?

"Be successful," he says. "That is the first rule and it saves time in future planning because people in the company trust you.

"Communicate your decisions to people without flooding them with paperwork. If you make sure decisions are communicated to people, you get it on the record.

"Have a strong nervous system.

"Work your plan item by item. There is no way but to manage detail.

"Be prepared to work around the clock. What you haven't done, isn't done.

"Have a standby location in case something happens to your arrangements with the hotel.

"Try to get mileage out of your investment by having a family day or an employee day to see the displays or to hear a similar presentation.

"Discourage employees from attending the annual meeting itself to make sure seats are available to shareholders."

Be prepared for high costs. "It's hard to see the meeting cost less than $100,000," says Schoen. A meeting several years ago at the Waldorf-Astoria in New York cost $42,000 for just the meeting facilities.

In all the annual meetings Schoen has set up, he has had few major problems. "The first glitch happened to me in San Francisco," he recalls. "We had a good hotel and good liaison. On the final day, the directors were going to the Palo Alto research facility and a separate group made the arrangements for the bus. There was to be coffee on board for which I was responsible. I had not checked back, however. I got to the bus and found there was no coffee. I immediately got a nervous stomach. I also got the coffee. I ran inside the hotel and spotted a hotel employee who knew me. I talked him into getting me some, from where I still don't know."

Schoen's nervous stomach comes back as the day for the event approaches. "As you get closer and closer to the time, you have very few options but to do it," he says.

The meeting in the tent went well, with the tent rating a phrase in the *Wall Street Journal* story describing what went on. The crowd had apparently got into the festive spirit of the event. "Held in an enormous tent adjacent to Xerox's biggest manufacturing complex in this Rochester suburb, the meeting was attended largely by diehard Xerox loyalists, some of them elderly investors who grew rich on the stock," read the story. "The company's officers and directors were being vigorously applauded even before the meeting was called to order. . . ." (1979)

That kind of atmosphere suits Schoen just fine. "The days of clamorous advocacy are going by," he says. "The last meeting was a great success. It was extremely dull."

PRESS CONFERENCES

"Good morning, ladies and gentlemen. On behalf of Consolidated Industries, I'm happy to welcome you to this press conference. This is a big day for us at Consolidated. We are proud to unveil our newest product line and our new research laboratory. After some introductory remarks here in the auditorium, we want to have you tour our facilities to see what we're talking about. To start things off, I'd like to introduce Joe Jones, our president, who has his own words of welcome. Joe."

To a smattering of applause, the dapper-looking public-relations man turns the microphone over to an expensively dressed executive, and another press conference has begun.

This scene was quite common a few years ago. Both company and agency public-relations people called press conferences on a regular basis. Even though the subjects to be discussed were often somewhat flimsy, the PR people could usually be assured of attracting a respectable number of print and electronic reporters. One reason was that the press conference was usually tied to a social event — a breakfast, luncheon, dinner, or cocktail party; held at an exotic location — a resort, public building, or on board a ship or railroad car; or included the distribution of free gifts — everything from pen sets to liquor.

Often at such press conferences, the topic under consideration was the last reason for reporters to go. If they had some time to kill or wanted a free meal or free drinks, they would sit through the presentation. Even if there was not a story in it for them, they might at least make some contacts for future reference.

Now, all that has changed. "Press conferences have gone down the tube," says Barbara Lamb, bureau chief for McGraw-Hill World News in Los Angeles. "Companies used to have two, three, four, five a day. Now, nobody goes to them. Everything you'd get there you can get in a press kit. There are no more big luncheons. PR people still try, particularly in agencies. It's good for their client relationships to be able to get the press out. But anytime they want you there, it's probably not important for you to go. It's been when they don't want you there that you should see about going."

Several factors have caused a decline in press conferences. PR people abused the technique by calling too many such events when they had little news value to offer. Journalists generally are too busy to waste their time. A heightened concern for journalistic ethics since Watergate also has caused more and more reporters and editors to reject anything of value, including drinks, dinners, and gifts.

The clash between the representatives of the print press and those from the electronic media added to the decline. Anyone who has tried to observe the speaker around a TV camera and camera person, or see at all under the glare of hot lights, would just as soon avoid the experience. TV people in big cities usually arrive at press conferences late, going through the distracting process of setting up lights and taking light readings and testing the sound levels, only to leave early after repeating the same process in reverse. TV reporters also usually reveal a lack of preparation by poor questions, and this angers their print colleagues. "The electronic media ruined the press conference," continues Lamb. "The print press just doesn't go."

The alternative to this situation has been the establishment of the media tour. "Rather than have a press conference that takes half a day for reporters and editors with no time to spare, we have found it better to have people from our clients sit across the desk from editors and talk about a story," says Thomas Nunan, a vice president of Burson-Marsteller. Nunan takes the company source to the publications where they can go into a subject in detail. A number of stories usually result from such meetings because the two sides are better prepared than in the old "scattergun" approach of the press conference, where either reporters did not know what to ask or, if they did, hesitated to divulge exclusive information to the other reporters present. For the cost of a trip for the technical source and the PR person to New York or wherever the targeted publications are located, the company can get a great deal of coverage. Another advantage of this idea is that it gives the reporter or editor a technical source to be called in the future for background help. The reporter will be grateful to the PR person, and the company will probably always be identified in print.

Despite their drawbacks and increasing disuse, however, press conferences do have a place in public relations. If an event is important enough, reporters will attend a press conference. If the press conference is well organized, the experience need not be a frustrating and empty one.

A few rules help avoid problems with press conferences.

1. *Do not call a press conference without good reason.* "The fewer the better — that's the best rule," says a former trade-magazine editor now in public relations. "The ultimate test is, will the press come? You'd better have something truly important to say, defend, or explain."

2. *Be prepared with good background material.* A complete press kit must be organized and handed out to all reporters at the press conference. If

possible, the kit should be mailed or hand-carried to the reporter's office several days in advance, so that that reporter can prepare questions for the conference and begin to plan stories. A good press kit might also be kept in the files of a reporter or editor for future use.

3. *Hold the press conference in a place convenient for reporters, unless there is a good reason to do otherwise.* A meeting room in a downtown hotel is preferable to a stuffy conference room in the suburbs. If the company location plays a part in the event — as the site of a new assembly line or as the place to be toured — the press conference should be held there. Reporters should have a reason to drive the extra half hour.

4. *Make arrangements carefully.* "The simpler you keep it, the better off you are," says Craig Lewis of Earl Newsom & Company. "If the electronic media are involved, you have to arrange for power outlets. Otherwise they might blow out all the lights in the hotel." If reporters are coming to a company location, parking needs to be arranged. If some kind of major announcement is involved, especially a matter of interest to the wire services, Lewis suggests the installation of an extra bank of telephones to augment those already in the hotel. If some of the reporters attending the press conference are from out of town, it is a good idea to make typewriters available in a separate room and even to hire several people as messengers for the exclusive use of reporters in running copy across town to an office or to a Western Union facility. Stories are rarely telegraphed these days, however, except from remote areas or in cases of excessive length. Usually, reporters telephone them into a stenographer or recording machine. If projectors and screens are to be used, they need to be arranged.

5. *Consider holding separate press conferences for print and electronic reporters.* The old wounds will not be reopened as readily if reporters from newspaper and their counterparts from television and radio stations attend different meetings. "This gives both sides a better opportunity to get the story," says Ken Niehans, who used to be director of public affairs at the University of Oregon Medical School. "They both have different needs." Sometimes, this was impossible because of the unavailability of the doctors to appear at the conference. But when he could, Niehans held them a half-hour apart, making sure to leave a space for cameras in the front of the room. Separate press conferences saved Niehans trouble. "You don't make the newspaper reporters who have done their homework resent providing questions for the television reporters who haven't."

6. *Pick official participants in press conferences carefully.* "Make sure you know your people," continues Niehans. "Some of them don't come across well. You've got to get a subject willing to talk who won't answer 'yes' and 'no' to everything."

7. *Schedule press conferences to give everyone an even break.* In a city with a number of newspapers and television and radio stations, a PR person should alternate the time of press conferences so that a reporter who misses a deadline and thus a news break with one afternoon press conference will hit it

with the next one. "If you are in a situation where a reporter initiates a story and then you decide to call a press conference about that subject, let that reporter get the details early, then let them break it at the time you hold the press conference," says Niehans.

8. *Control the press conference from start to finish.* The PR person should open the meeting with reporters by introducing himself or herself, lay out any ground rules for the subject matter (secrecy, legalities, etc.) and then introduce the person who will be answering the questions as quickly as possible. After that, the PR person should stand to one side or sit in the front row, on call but not in the center of the action. An inexperienced official will need help and reassurance from time to time. It is best, however, for the PR person not to intercede unless absolutely necessary. The press corps did not come to hear from the PR person and will resent intrusions except when necessary to clarify or simplify what the official is saying. Once in a while, a PR person might have to rescue an unwary official who has been backed into a corner by a reporter's question. A PR person should be prepared to cut off questions after a reasonable amount of time, a half hour to an hour, with the statement, "We have time for two more questions."

EXHIBITS

Organizing the exhibit to be shown in a company-sponsored booth at a convention or trade show presents another way for public-relations people to communicate with external publics. The job is often shared with the sales department in that new products are often the principal thing on display. Occasionally, however, a company will decide to fund an exhibit at a convention or trade show or museum for educational purposes only. The often blatant commercialism of a heavily sales-oriented approach is forgotten in the quest to educate and inform the people who stop to look at the exhibit.

The Standard Oil of California creativity exhibit set up to commemorate the centennial of the company in museums around the country is a good example of this type. The large corporate pavilions at recent world's fairs and expositions are of a similar nature. They are costly and time consuming, and usually they are developed by firms that make a business out of organizing exhibits.

The more common exhibit involving a PR person is one set up in a booth at a convention or trade show. A convention is usually more oriented toward substantive discussion than a trade show, so many companies will decide not to pay for an exhibit. A trade show is different. An industrial trade show gives a company the chance to present its products and services to potential buyers. Because of the sales orientation of most shows, the role of PR is largely a supportive one, furnishing brochures, booklets, and other publications; preparing a slide-tape presentation to be shown continuously at the booth; making arrangements with the organizers of the convention or trade show; and working out a budget for the exhibit.

The major elements of such a budget are the cost of the space for the exhibit, the cost of constructing the exhibit and the shipping container, the cost of labor to set up and tear down the exhibit and transport it to the site, the cost of utilities and clean-up, and the cost of the slide-tape presentation and printed materials.

Once constructed, booths and at least the exhibit framework can be kept and stored for use at another trade show or convention. An exhibit should not be used for more than one year, or at the same trade show or convention more than once. Not only will some of the attendees have seen it, but it will probably get a bit beat up in the setting-up and tearing-down and transportation stages of its existence and look a bit seedy by the end of the first few months.

In addition to helping the sales staff in the ways already noted, public-relations people can help the company in another major way at a convention or trade show. By attending the event and spending part of every day at the exhibit, they will be able to meet reporters and editors from trade and technical publications and talk to them about company developments, arranging interviews and discussing story ideas and future coverage.

MISCELLANEOUS EVENTS

Beyond annual meetings, press conferences, and exhibits, there are several miscellaneous events that public-relations people might organize from time to time to meet special needs of their companies or nonprofit organizations.

Appearances by Famous People

Sometimes a person associated with a company or nonprofit organization is famous for other activities. Actress Joan Crawford, for example, was a member of the board of Pepsi Cola in the 1960s and spent a great deal of her time publicizing that company and its products. Rosemary Stroer was the person from the Pepsi public-relations department assigned to travel with the actress as she talked about her career in films and as a businesswoman in the United States and abroad. Stroer set up interviews and kept track of the publicity that Crawford and the company got as a result. On a typical tour, the wives of Pepsi bottlers and businessmen in important communities would host Joan Crawford at fashion shows held in department stores. Crawford always appeared at the annual bottlers' convention as well.

Although Rosemary Stroer enjoyed the glamor and interest of working with the aging actress, life on the road with Crawford could be hectic. "She had her moments," says Stroer, "more of exhaustion than anything else, when she'd do her star routine and make excessive demands, like ice-cold champagne at midnight. She'd renege on things and refuse to appear some place we had scheduled her, although this didn't happen very often. She was very meticulous and on schedule. Things had to be planned minute by minute. She would make up a list and all the things on it had to be done before she'd set foot outside New York. It was a pain in the neck but it avoided difficulties later. She always had excessive amounts of luggage, always an assistant, and always traveled first class." Other noted people at times become associated with companies, and the link can be a PR asset depending on how it is handled and who the people are.

Association with Other Events

At one point in the 1960s, West Point Pepperell sponsored "the flying grandmother," one of the entrants in the Powder Puff Derby airplane competition for women. "She came into the office," recalls Joan Dolph, then director of publicity and public relations at Pepperell, "and the more we talked, the more I realized that with her strong personality, she'd be good on TV and radio. We decided to make a whole campaign out of it." At this time, Pepperell sheets were being made for the first time of permanent-press material and in vivid colors, so Dolph had clothing for the pilot designed from the sheets as well as curtains for her plane. "Every editor was sent a live parakeet in the colors of the sheets and invited to a press party at the designer's boutique in New York," she says. As the flying grandmother flew across the country, Dolph arranged press coverage for her in a number of cities. Similar sponsorships by companies of sporting events or scientific expeditions can be capitalized on in similarly low-key, dignified ways.

Organization of Company Events

Sometimes a company or nonprofit organization will pay for the organization of an event itself. Unlike the previous instance where the air race was already set up, a company will decide to create its own activity. At Pepsi, it was a series of art exhibits set up in a 5,000-square-foot space on the main floor of its New York headquarters. "All countries with a stake in Pepsi were asked to exhibit their best graphic art," says Rosemary Stroer, the Pepsi PR person who arranged the exhibit. "It was a subtle form of public relations." The series lasted nine years at the rate of ten to twelve exhibits a year of both foreign and domestic graphic artists. Some of the exhibits were sent to other museums under the auspices of the Smithsonian Museum. The entire project cost about $75,000. For each show Stroer wrote a press release and planned a reception for artists, government representatives, and the press. If the budget allowed, she also had an elaborate brochure designed. She kept track of press coverage and recalls that it was invariably favorable to the company and its image. Other similar events are the Standard Oil creativity exhibit detailed in Chapter 20 or the setting up of a company pavilion at a world's fair.

SUMMARY

External events vary greatly in cost, complexity, and worth to the companies and nonprofit organizations sponsoring them. Annual meetings are required of all publicly held companies. They can be useful if they are organized in such a way that they present information quickly and clearly. Planning for annual meetings should begin six months to a year in advance, and one person in the PR department must keep track of all details carefully. Although press conferences are not held as often as in the past, they still offer a good opportunity to brief reporters and editors on important subjects. The press conference should be held at a time and place convenient to reporters, the person doing the briefing should be skilled, and separate conferences should be considered for the print and electronic media. Trade-show exhibits and company sponsorship of appearances by famous people and special events constitute legitimate external events to be planned and publicized.

REVIEW QUESTIONS

1. Why are annual meetings held?
2. Why have press conferences fallen into disuse?
3. How should a press conference be organized?
4. Why is it valuable to organize an exhibit?
5. What are several other kinds of external events that can be organized?

ASSIGNMENTS

For Journalism and Business Students

1. Attend a company annual meeting and analyze it. How was it organized, what took place, how did it turn out?
2. Attend a press conference and analyze it. How was it organized, what took place, how did it turn out?
3. Write a memo listing your plans for a press conference to announce a major new company product. What steps must you take?
4. Plan an exhibit for a trade show, listing the things you must do to put it together.
5. Select five companies of varying types and make a list of unusual external events that could be organized to publicize them in a tasteful and ethical way.

CHAPTER 18

Public relations and advertising

The two have similar characteristics and goals. They sometimes share audiences and media outlets. But, in total, public relations and advertising are very different professions.

DIFFERENCES: PUBLIC RELATIONS AND ADVERTISING

Communication

In public relations, communication goes directly to an editor or reporter through news releases and other means used. The editor or reporter accepts or rejects the information, changes it in some way, and then passes it along to the audience. In advertising, the communication of the message is more direct: the advertisements are prepared, space and time are purchased for their presentation, and they are communicated directly to the audience of the publication or the radio or television station from which the time has been purchased. The output of PR appears with uncontrolled frequency. Advertisements, on the other hand, appear with controlled frequency whenever the publication or radio or TV station has scheduled to run them.

Content

The subject matter of public-relations materials is generally expressed in a reasonably free way. No client will allow a release to contain negative information unless it cannot be avoided, but the information has to be expressed in an objective way for it to be accepted by the intended audience, usually the editors and reporters. The PR people stress this to the client and the client agrees, sometimes grudgingly. In advertising, however, content is controlled by the client company, which, after all, is paying for the space and time to do with what it wants. The consequence, however, is that most advertisements are perceived as being biased and not as credible as the output of public-relations people.

In the specifics of content, the news releases and other materials produced in PR are print oriented, except for filmed news releases or public-service announcements. Advertisements, on the other hand, are visually oriented. As a result, the focus of the writing is entirely different. PR people have some space to tell whatever story is being told. Ad people have almost no space or time to do their jobs, a factor that can result in exaggeration and distortion as they strive for simplification.

Effect

The effect of PR materials is difficult to measure. They work or do not work, and the PR person who originally prepared them never really knows why — or whether. A news release is written and makes its way through the labyrinth of a publication's editorial hierarchy and eventually out to the reading public. Only later, through a clipping service or other informal means, does the PR person know even if the news release was used. Then through a painstaking comparison of the release and the stories, the PR person can see how the wording or focus of the story was changed. The effect of a brochure or annual report might never be known.

With advertisements, the effect can be more easily assessed. Did the ad draw inquiries from potential customers? Did sales of a product go up in the areas in which the ad ran? Research can answer such questions for an ad person. The work of public-relations people usually concentrates on long-term image building. Advertising, on the other hand, usually concentrates on short-term image building.

People

The people involved in public relations are most often former journalists or people with a formal education in journalism. As a result, they work well with the editors and reporters with whom they most frequently deal. The people working in advertising, on the other hand, are from more varied and less journalistic backgrounds. They deal with the sales staffs and publishers of the publications, and station managers for radio and television, in which they are placing their ads. They rarely have contact with editorial staffs.

PUBLIC-RELATIONS ADVERTISING

These differences aside, public relations and advertising can work together to create the total communications concept that most client companies or organizations want. This amalgamation begins when public-relations people and advertising people realize that they are part of the same team insofar as the client company is concerned. Sometimes, this means that a PR agency with its own ad department will have to work with employees of another ad agency. At other times, the advertising people to be worked with will be from a division of the PR agency.

From whatever situation, the two entities will get along best if they forget their historic and fundamental differences and combine for the good of the client. As they learn to unite, however, the representatives must not forget to stand up for their own ideas and overall approaches to getting the job done.

Public-relations people usually turn to the field of advertising because their more traditional means of communications have failed to achieve the desired intent of themselves and management, and a more quick, direct, and widely disseminated form of communication is needed. The results of their combined efforts are called *public-relations advertisements* (Exhibit 18.1).

A good example of such PR ads is Hill and Knowlton's work for Pacific Southwest Airlines in a 1978 proxy fight. A financier had been buying PSA stock over a time and suddenly made a move to win control of the company by soliciting shareholder votes. Hill and Knowlton was brought in a month before the election to try to stave off the takeover attempt. "You go in there and find out the dirt about the other side," says George Hobgood, the agency senior vice president who handled the account. "He [the financier] had done this before and had a raider's reputation. It was not that difficult to track down information. But you can't say anything you can't substantiate."

Hobgood got what he needed from Securities and Exchange Commission (SEC) documents and library research and compiled the information into a series of five letters to PSA shareholders. These letters were then prepared as a series of four advertisements placed in the *Wall Street Journal* and the major newspapers in San Diego, Los Angeles, San Francisco, and New York, the cities where a computer analysis had revealed the majority of PSA shareholders lived. Running the letters as advertisements reenforced their message to shareholders and also attracted the attention of the press and general public outside the company.

When examined closely, the letters reveal a skillful use of the facts to the advantage of PSA. The first one began by heading off an obvious negative factor that could be used against the company: the mid-air collision — and crash — of a PSA airliner and a small private plane the previous month. While deploring the loss, the letter moved quickly to offset the damage to the company and its management.

Later letters and ads moved to the specifics of the proxy fight and advised that shareholders vote against the takeover attempt. They also revealed adverse information about the man leading the attempt.

The short time period made things more difficult, as did the requirement that the SEC had to approve the language of the letters and the advertisements. Hobgood stayed in San Diego, the headquarters city for PSA, and worked with company officers and lawyers there. The company retained an attorney in Washington to take the material to the SEC for approval. Once approved, the letters were prepared and mailed, and the newspaper ads were flown to printers for swift preparation.

"In a proxy fight situation like this, you have to work under tremendous pressure," says Hobgood. "You can't postpone anything." The chief operating officer of PSA also called large shareholders to ask for their votes. In the end, the company won the vote handily and thanked its shareholders for their support in the final letter (and ad), along with yearly earnings and its hopes for the future.

A similar direct — and effective — approach to a corporate crisis was McGraw-Hill's reaction to the early 1979 takeover attempt by American Express. McGraw-Hill board chairman Harold McGraw explained the management position against the acquisition move in a series of ads in the *Wall Street Journal* and *New York Times*. The ad campaign accompanied the more traditional public-relations approach of issuing corporate news releases, holding press conferences, and making corporate officers available for interviews. "We never lied, but in a situation like this you cannot be responsive to every query since you might be tipping your hand on strategy and tactics," says Ted Weber, executive vice president of McGraw-Hill. In the end this public-relations approach helped the corporation win its fight, and American Express withdrew.

The most well-known instance in which a company uses advertising to convey a public-relations message is Mobil Oil Company and the ads it has run since 1973 on the Op Ed page of the *New York Times* and at other times in other newspapers, magazines, and on television and radio. The ad campaign is directed by the public-affairs department of the company. These ads resulted from Mobil's failure to get the television networks to accept its so-called "idea" commercials on energy. The company had prepared the commercials as an alternative to its old product advertising, and because it felt that television news was not properly covering the oil embargo then underway and its adverse effect on the nation's oil supply.

The networks found the ads too editorial, so the company ran a newspaper ad that described its problems of getting a less controversial commercial — on offshore drilling — accepted by the networks. This ad got good response from readers and led the company to begin the series that has continued since.

Such public-relations-based advertisements are different from regular advertising in that they consist primarily of copy with little or no graphics. They also contain more detailed information than the average ad. They need the copy and the detailed information to explain their points. A short, catchy slogan or lavish four-color photo will not do.

Another difference between PR ads and regular product ads is that the PR advertisements are usually controlled by the PR agency or department. The advertising agency gets involved on matters of design and placement, but at a point much later than it would in the case of a regular product ad.

No. 1 in a series.

Exxon's profits and what is being done with them.

C.C. Garvin, Jr.
Chairman, Exxon Corporation

Exxon's third-quarter profits announcement disturbed many people. Some have questioned the size of our profits at a time when supplies of energy are tight. Many people think that the profits are going only to a privileged few and they feel that the profits are much greater than they need be.

We are very concerned about the criticism expressed by elected officials and the public at large. We feel it is important to do a more thorough job of explaining why we think such profits are necessary and how they are being put to work as new investments to provide future energy.

Simply stated, the oil business is risky and it is big. Large sums of money are required to make the investments called for to develop new and expanded sources of energy. A good deal of that money has to be generated through profits. Because we think it is important for you to know more about our profits and what is being done with them, we will be publishing a brief series of advertisements with facts which may help you make better judgments about the size of Exxon's profits—and the size of our investments.

C.C. Garvin Jr.

Exhibit 18.1

A series of typical public-relations advertisements that Exxon ran in newspapers in 141 cities in the United States after it had high third-quarter profits. The ads attempt to explain why the high profits are necessary: for use in developing new and expanded sources of energy. (Reprinted with permission, Exxon Company, USA.)

No. 2 in a series.

Exxon makes 5¢ on a dollar of sales and most of that goes back into the business.

Many people are angry about oil company profits because they think that more than half of what they pay for petroleum products ends up as profits.

In fact, Exxon's worldwide profit from all phases of its operations averages about 5¢ on a dollar of sales. This is far less than many people would guess.

It is also less than the total of 6¢ which goes back into the business (3¢ from retained profits and 3¢ from depreciation).

2¢ is paid to Exxon shareholders as dividends.

5¢ Net profit

3¢ from profit is reinvested in the business.

3¢ Depreciation—reinvested in the business.

2¢ 3¢

3¢

48¢ Crude oil & products purchased from governments and non-Exxon companies.

48¢

28¢

28¢ Income, excise & other taxes—United States and foreign governments.

THE EXXON SALES DOLLAR

16¢

16¢ Operating expenses

Exxon had sales of $59 billion during the first nine months of 1979. Our net profit from all sources on those sales amounted to $2.9 billion.

That is 5¢ on the dollar.

Exhibit 18.1 continued.

Exhibit 18.1 continued.

No. 4 in a series.

Exxon's profits should be judged by the need to generate capital for large investments.

Exxon's profits are large but so are its investments in energy. When Exxon's profits are put on a comparable basis with the profits of other U.S. manufacturing companies, we do only a little better than average.

In 1978, for example, only two companies reported higher profits than Exxon. But 545 companies were *more profitable than Exxon* according to the *Fortune* magazine list of the largest 1,000 U.S. manufacturing companies.

The difference between "profit" and "profitability" is important. "Profit" is like a worker's take-home pay. It tells you little about how many hours were worked to get it. Take-home pay might be large simply because of a lot of overtime. So, "profit" could be large, even though "profitability" (dollars earned per hour) is not.

Shareholders invest dollars instead of time, so to have real meaning, profits must be related to the amount of money which is invested. A common measure of earning performance is "return on shareholder investment."

During the past decade, Exxon's return on shareholder investment has ranged from a low of 12.4% in 1970 to a high of 20.6% in 1974. So far in 1979, our return has been at an annualized rate of 18.5%.

We don't know how long this current rate of return will last, but we do know that finding and developing energy is getting increasingly more expensive. Oil companies need to be at least as profitable as other companies if they are to continue to be able to attract the funds necessary for the high risk, big investments vital to the delivery of energy in the future.

EARNINGS AS A PERCENT OF SHAREHOLDER INVESTMENT

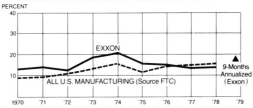

Exxon's return on shareholder investment has generally been somewhat above that of all U.S. manufacturing companies. In 1977 and 1978, however, it was below the average.

Exhibit 18.1 continued.

Exhibit 18.1 continued.

INSTITUTIONAL ADVERTISING

The ultimate in combining public relations and advertising comes in *institutional advertisements,* in which image and reputation are what is being sold rather than specific products or services. Here too the public-relations agency or department probably directs the advertising agency more than in straight product advertising. The ads are produced with a more subtle message and with an intent that is part of the overall public-relations aim of the client company. More help is needed from the advertising people in developing the design of the ad and its wording, which must be simple, direct and "classy."

There is a thin line between the PR ads discussed earlier in this chapter and institutional ads. The biggest difference is that PR ads are aimed at provoking action, so they are specific and hard hitting in their messages, as in the Mobil Oil campaign. PR ads may also be run for a shorter duration to accomplish a specific purpose, as in the PSA and McGraw-Hill series. Institutional ads, on the other hand, are part of a greater overall corporate strategy that aims to build cumulatively, over time, a good public impression of the company.

A corporation decides to use institutional advertising for many reasons: to create goodwill, to counteract adverse press comment, to make known its public position on an important issue, to inform the public about its product and employees, to educate the public about an industry or an issue. Usually, the action desired is less immediate and concrete than in the straight PR advertisements explained earlier.

A unique example of an institutional advertising campaign is Standard Oil of California's decision to celebrate its centennial as a company with an exhibit on creativity. "We looked at the traditional things but decided that the public mood of criticizing oil companies prevented a 'bands and balloons' approach," says William H. Jones, manager of corporate communications. "We knew we'd have to play it cool."

The company turned to J. Walter Thompson, the biggest advertising agency, for help, and the agency recommended the 4,000-square-foot exhibit on creativity to be installed at the California Academy of Sciences in San Francisco at a cost of $3.5 million. The exhibit features examples of human creativity over the years. "We are trying to establish the reputation of the company but we're doing it in an oblique fashion. We're trying to rebuild our credibility in a low-key way." The exhibit has received good press attention and might lead to a series on public television.

Other well-known examples of institutional advertising campaigns include the "Great Ideas of Western Man" series done over the years for Container Corporation of America, Gulf Oil Corporation's promotion for the National Geographic specials it underwrites on public television, most of IBM's corporate ads, and, because of the useful information presented to motorists, Shell Oil Company's "Answer Man."

In devising a public-relations-oriented institutional advertising campaign, an agency PR person needs to work closely with the management of the client company to find out what this group wants to achieve in the ads. It is not enough to have the board chairman's wife like an ad she saw on television and have that be the reason for the development of a similar series for the company. Not every corporation and its products and problems lend themselves to the institutional advertising approach.

Before an effective institutional ad campaign can be devised, corporate objectives and specific policies must be determined and worked into the ads at least indirectly. What are the problems of the company, and how will the ads help solve them? Research to support the company's position will also solidify the reasons behind the ads.

Such ads must also be part of the corporation's total communications program, and must fit well with the other parts. If, for example, a company relies heavily on direct sales to consumers, product advertising and brochures for the sales staff should not be canceled so that the company can spend all of its advertising budget to underwrite a prestigious program on public television. One might kill the other. If, on the other hand, a company can afford to do both advertising activities — and they are justified in the total communications plan — the situation is entirely different.

After an institutional campaign is going, its effectiveness must be evaluated periodically. Such campaigns are expensive, and even a wealthy company cannot afford to waste its resources.

Public-relations people control the concept, theme, budget, and media selection for institutional advertising. According to *Public Relations Journal,* the primary objective of institutional advertising for the companies responding to a survey is improving stockholder-financial relations. Improving consumer relations was next, followed by better government relations. Increasing product sales came next in importance, followed by enhanced relations with suppliers and industry. Last as an objective was a miscellaneous category aimed at employees, community, image, public acceptance, and communicating an energy program.

THE ADVERTISING COUNCIL

The Advertising Council, a nonprofit organization funded by the advertising industry to develop and conduct public-service advertising campaigns, began during World War II. It was then called the War Advertising Council and was started because of public criticism of the advertising business.

Media donated the space and time for the ads, which were prepared by agencies that contributed the time of their creative people; advertisers loaned members of their managements. The council carried out successful campaigns encouraging military recruitment, the planting of home "victory" gardens, the salvaging of scrap metal, the purchasing of war bonds, and care against careless and damaging talk among workers in defense plants. The latter had as one of its slogans, "Loose lips sink ships."

The council worked so well that it was reorganized and renamed after the war. Since then, the Advertising Council has been responsible for millions of dollars in print and broadcast advertising, many advertisements among the best prepared by the industry: the prevention of forest fires through "Smokey the Bear," the support of the United Negro College Fund, and other series condemning energy waste and pollution. As with the War Advertising Council, everything is donated.

SUMMARY

Although they are different in their method of communication, content, and effect, and in the backgrounds of the people working within their ranks, public relations and advertising often have to work together. The amalgamation occurs when PR people decide that their traditional forms of communication (news releases, brochures, etc.) have not reached the goals of the client company, and that more quick, direct, and widely disseminated means are needed. The results of their combined efforts are called public-relations ads and institutional advertisement. Both kinds of ads are similar. PR ads put across a corporate message in a hard-hitting way, like an editorial, for a short period of time while institutional ads are more subtle and graphically pleasing, and might be run in publications and on television over a longer period. Both PR ads and institutional ads differ from regular advertising in that they are not selling products, only ideas and information to gain a changed image.

REVIEW QUESTIONS

1. What are the major differences between public relations and advertising?
2. When should a public-relations person turn to the advertising business for help?
3. What is the difference between public-relations ads and institutional ads?
4. How do the ads produced by the Advertising Council differ from the institutional-ad campaign of a major corporation? In what ways are the two similar?

ASSIGNMENTS

For Journalism Students

1. Go through the latest issue of a national magazine and pick out two public-relations ads. Write a research paper in which you analyze each

ad as to aim, content, and effectiveness. Tell why you picked these ads, and how you were able to identify them as PR ads.

2. Go through the same magazine and pick one institutional ad. Prepare the same analysis as in assignment 1, but add the differences between this ad and the two PR ads you used in assignment 1.

3. You are a PR-agency account executive and one of your clients, a textile mill, has had a year of strikes with violence and a loss of sales. The strike has been settled and your client wants you to prepare a series of PR ads to repair the damage to employee relations, sales, and overall company image. Prepare that program for class.

4. You are a PR-agency account executive, and one of your clients, the biggest cigar company in the world, wants you to suggest the approach to take for a new series of image-building institutional advertisements on the theme, "Productivity has made America great." Prepare your suggestions for class.

For Business Students

1. Conduct the research for and write a paper that answers the question, "Why Does My Company Need a Public-Relations Advertising Campaign?"

2. Research a good PR campaign of the past five years and analyze in writing why it was good in terms of form, content, and reaction gained from the people who read the ads.

3. You are a company president and your company, which makes chemicals, has just been fined $500,000 by the Environmental Protection Agency for polluting a major river in the Midwest. You have paid the fine, but think that the EPA and the press have been unfair to the company. You have called in the account executive of the PR agency that handles your account. You want a series of hard-hitting PR ads prepared. Put your ideas for their series in writing.

4. Now prepare a list of your ideas for a more subtle, understated series of image-building institutional ads that extol the virtues of the chemical industry.

SECTION V

The DOING System

Part iii:

Informing the publics

CHAPTER **19**

Public relations and the press

Publics may come and publics may go, but the relationship that exists between public-relations people and the press is the single most important factor in their success as PR people. Many of the programs they devise to reach all publics rely on the press as the means of distribution, for example, news releases, filmed news releases, public-service announcements, press conferences, and speeches by corporate executives. A hostile press standing between their company and their publics can make their job difficult, if not impossible, to do. Although a PR person should not overly concentrate on the press, he or she will ignore it at no small amount of peril.

"Media people are always in the driver's seat as far as PR people are concerned," says Jeff Clausen of Marx, Knoll & Mangels, Inc. "When you go into a newspaper office with a news release, for example, you'd better have a good reason. Even then, the reporter you're going to see will say sarcastically, 'You've got a hot item for me, haven't you?'"

PRESS VS. PUBLIC RELATIONS

That kind of remark reflects the hostility that some reporters and editors have for public-relations people, whom many call "flacks." The origins of this derision vary. Some reporters probably resent the high salaries that PR people get paid. Others think that they have "sold out" because they must put out a company point of view even if it varies with their own. Some think that PR people stretch the facts or overly shade them. Still others fear a future when they will become PR people, making high salaries and hewing to a company line that compromises their journalistic ethics.

There is another aspect to the situation, however. Reporters need PR people to help them get information out of a company, to arrange interviews for them, and to set up tours of facilities. Although reporters can get what they need on their own without help from PR people, it is infinitely more easy to do it with their help. "When you have a quick deadline and need to get to someone in top management in a hurry, the right person to speak on a subject, you call PR," says Barbara Lamb of McGraw-Hill World News in Los Angeles. "Whether they realize it — or like to admit it — members of the press need PR. The realization will come to them sooner or later. Perhaps they won't appreciate a good PR person until they've dealt with a bad one."

Members of the press have their own side to the story.

"There are several classes of PR people," says Robert Henkel, senior editor of *Business Week*. "Number one is the worst kind. They want to go out to lunch so they can tell their management they know people in *Business Week*. It looks good on their expense report. Class number two is a guy who wants to help you all he can but he doesn't know his company. Whatever his title, he's a flunky, a 'go for,' whom the president calls in and says, 'Jones, come in here. We've hired So-and-so to be chairman, put out a release.' Or, 'We've just had an explosion in our New Jersey plant. Go out there and keep the story out of the papers.'

"Class number three, management listens to him, he gives advice and participates in decision making, just like a lawyer. Smart companies use PR that way. Class number three I'll answer the phone to talk to, even on a busy day. He continually keeps in touch in good times and bad. He knows his company. He treats it like a beat and develops sources. He goes into division managers and says, 'I'm really here to help you. I'm your communications counsel, working in the same way as a legal counsel. If you have a communications problem, call me up.' "

Kemp Anderson, a vice president of McGraw-Hill Publications Company and former chief editor of *Electronics,* is more benign in his view of public relations. "I think PR people are invaluable to the technical press in many ways," he says. "For instance, you may want to talk to an expert in a specific discipline or field, but unless you know a company well, you'll have trouble reaching the right person. A PR person who has done his homework and knows his company can bridge this gap and put you in touch with the right source with a quick phone call. It works to the benefit of both. I am of the school that thinks when you're after information, you do the interview yourself. You don't want to interview the PR person, but you want to get directly to the source. I've found that the most effective PR programs are found in a company that believes in PR to the point of encouraging executives to participate in interviews."

Sometimes, however, PR people try to prevent the release of information. "My biggest problem with PR people comes from finding out about information they are not ready to release," continues Anderson. " 'Hey, if you won't use it,' they say, 'I'll give it to you when it breaks.' I've been burned. Many times, stories get out from under the PR person. Sometimes when I have agreed to a delay, I've regretted it. I've lost stories. Other times have turned out OK. From both the journalist's and PR person's viewpoint, this is a touchy situation. My usual preference is to run the story if we can verify the facts."

HOW TO WORK WITH THE PRESS

This is not to say that all PR-press contacts are negative and pugnacious. The situation varies with the individuals involved. Press relations is one of the most difficult parts of PR. It is also one of the most important. Bad press relations can wreck the career of a PR person if done badly. As hard as press relations is, thousands of people work well with reporters and editors every day. A few general rules will help in most situations.

Responsiveness

"If you tell reporters you'll get back to them with a piece of information they desire, get back to them," says Victor Pesqueira, manager of public-relations projects at Xerox. "Many PR people never call back. Reporters hate them for it. Call them back even if you can't give them the information they want." If one of the main elements of a PR person's job is to respond to requests from the press, quick and complete response to press requests is important, whether the reporter concerned wants a financial figure quickly for a story or interviews arranged with ten company officials to get material for a cover article.

"If nothing else, PR people should be good door openers," says James Roscow, a freelance financial journalist in New York. This responsiveness should be constant, at all hours. "Too often, PR people are not dedicated enough to their companies to make themselves and other executives available after normal business hours on the same day they have issued important news," says William Cushing, a freelance business journalist in Seattle. "Morning newspaper deadlines often mean that reporters won't call until late in the day, and sometimes the PR office has closed up tight."

Honesty

If a PR person cannot deliver the information or honor the request, he or she should say so immediately. "Remember, you're not working for reporters, you're working for the company," continues Pesqueira. "You sometimes have to tell a reporter 'no' without giving a reason. It is much better to tell reporters 'I don't know' or 'I can't tell you' than to lead them into thinking they will get the information from you later."

Knowledge of How the Press Works

"It's common courtesy not to call a guy in the middle of a deadline," says George Hobgood, a senior vice president of Hill and Knowlton. "You learn what the deadlines are. If you do it once by mistake, don't do it again." Such an action by a PR person causes Henkel of *Business Week* to relegate the caller to the dust bin of history. He instructs his assistant not to put such calls through to him, but still they come in, as many as thirty to forty a day. "A PR person should never, ever call into a national publication," he says.

An appreciation of workload, deadlines, and other journalistic procedures comes with experience and the PR person's own background as a reporter or editor. Many PR people come into the profession from journalism, so they have the advantage of knowing the likes and dislikes of reporters and editors. If they cross the invisible line into PR, they should not forget their own ways of operating in journalism.

It is also extremely important to know the story needs of particular publications and to suggest ideas relating to those needs. "It is annoying to have a PR person contact you about something that in no way is a story for your publication," says Sandra Atchison, manager of the *Business Week* Denver bureau. "He ought to be familiar enough with my publication to know we don't cover plaque unveilings, and he should suggest that there is a greater story in the reason for the company award for environmental innovation or whatever."

Knowing Members of the Press Personally

It helps to be friends with reporters, as long as the two sides — press and PR — remember their own goals. Most reporters will not treat PR people as though they have just landed on earth from another planet. They are cultivating PR people as future sources in the same way that the PR people are cultivating them as conveyors of the corporate message.

"PR people get wrapped up in corporate activity, doing any number of things, and neglect the press," says a former Los Angeles trade editor now in public relations. "They should join the local press club and get to know editors. They should have lunch with reporters twice a week. It is difficult to get close to some reporters. But you can offer them a great deal, like backgrounding them on a particular subject. You've got to do more than sell them stories." What will often emerge is a friendship that will help both PR and press later. "You build up personal contacts, people that trust you, so if you need something badly and a PR person trusts you, they'll help you," continues Barbara Lamb.

Explaining the Problems of PR to the Press

An understanding reporter or editor will listen when a PR person discusses the reasons for a company action or an inability to reveal information. "On occasion, you can depend on a PR man to give you off-the-record background that makes it easier to understand a situation," continues Sandra Atchison. "I recall one instance when I was trying to find out why a company had announced an unusual policy, then quickly changed its mind. The PR man confided that the founder was senile, and his secretary, who usually blocked his orders, was sick. Another time they may tell you what companies are doing poorly in an industry or that a company president is sensitive about his age, which was why he was annoyed about your question about retirement."

Organizing the PR Department to Help the Press

The chain of command of the company or other organization should be established so that press inquiries are handled in a systematic way. All inquiries should go to one or two people trained to know what to do. If the request is of a routine nature, the PR person should handle it in the same way for every reporter from publications large and small. If the request is more specific and unique, the PR person should find out from management whether or not the reporter's wish can be granted, then make the arrangements or decline the request. The press will appreciate it. "It is much easier to go through a single individual than wallow around in the company trying to figure out whom to talk to," says Sandra Atchison.

Preparing News Releases with the Needs of the Press in Mind

Few publications will print a news release verbatim. Fancy leads and belabored approaches are a waste of time. Many good reporters use releases as a source of ideas, however, so the salient facts should be there, written in a straightforward manner. "What a release should do is tell about a development in a company, using the facts like stepping stones for the reporters to write their own stories," says the former Los Angeles trade editor now in PR. "It should tell them enough to bring up the knowledge level to write a story but not attempt to write the full story. The only goal a corporation should have in a release is to get them started, then make the jump to their own story. The goal is not to provide them words. That's for lazy reporters."

Kemp Anderson of McGraw-Hill says that most trade magazines use news releases as background information, especially in the new-product area. These magazines have problems in doing so, however. "It's surprising how often you find errors in new-product information — especially carelessness in handling technical information — and this can affect your creditability. I'd suggest care in writing news releases."

Nothing sours reporters and editors more on a company than to print a news release or information contained in a news release, then to have it proved erroneous later. Adds William Cushing, a Seattle business journalist: "Reporters need carefully thought-out story ideas tailored for individual publications backed by a readiness to cooperate — not cutely written, self-serving news releases that the reporter knows have gone out to countless others also on mailing list code B." (News releases are discussed at greater length in Chapter 12.)

Staying in the Background

A public-relations person is the conduit for getting information from the company to the reporter and into print. As such, he or she is the vital link in the chain. This value, however, must be largely anonymous if it is to be effective. A good PR person is seen and not heard, working behind the scenes but seldom coming out into the open. This invisibility is especially important during interviews between company officials and reporters.

It is perfectly all right for PR people to sit in on interviews, but they should keep quiet after making the proper introductions. Nothing angers a reporter more than for a PR person to interrupt when a company official is trying to answer a question. The reporter has come to interview the official, not the PR person. Such interruptions will ruin the interview, and possibly the story as well. Very rarely, a PR person will have to step in to correct a major error in a statement by the person being interviewed. But even then, it is preferable to talk to the reporter later about the misstatement than to halt the interview process unnecessarily. "I don't care if PR people sit in," says James Roscow, "but if they jump in, at that point I would have to say, 'I really have to have this from Mr. So-and-so.' They're there because they have to protect against misquotation."

Trying to Buy Off the Press

The days of "freebies" and junkets are over. The press no longer responds well to bottles of wine and whiskey or trips to Las Vegas, as it did in the 1950s and 1960s. Watergate — and its aftermath — has raised the ethical standard and consciousness of members of the press so that they no longer accept even a free lunch from a PR person. Indeed, most publications and television and radio news organizations have written new codes of ethics governing their dealings with PR people, or have started to follow the codes of national journalism organizations like the Society of Professional Journalists and Sigma Delta Chi. "Gifts, favors, free travel, special treatment or privileges can compromise the integrity of journalists and their employers," reads the SPJ, SDX code. "Nothing of value should be accepted." "When I first came to McGraw-Hill, the gifts were fabulous," says Barbara Lamb. "Nothing is free any more. It's not like it used to be. Freebies are gone. Companies no longer pick up the tab. We all pay our own way."

Asking to See a Reporter's Copy

Reporters from most major national publications and a great many regional ones will refuse to submit copy for review by a company official or PR person. Their written or accepted operating methods forbid it, as does long tradition in journalism. It is best not even to try. The absence of the chance to see a story before it goes into print frightens company executives, however. As a result, the PR person can often be caught between the two sides. The best approach is to offer to go over information with a reporter on the telephone before publication, especially if it is of a technical nature. If errors appear in the final story, a PR person should complain and ask for a correction. Such complaints make reporters more careful the next time, and may cause them to accept offers to review copy for errors in advance.

Picking a Fight with the Press

It is impossible to win a fight with a reporter or an editor, or with a publication or television or radio station. In such instances, because of their access to the public, the reporters and editors always win. They always have the last word. No amount of letters to the editor or televised editorial replies can undo the damage done by a shouting match between a company and the press.

Outright errors in reporting must be corrected, of course. But hurt feelings by a member of management treated rudely in an interview, or anger over a cheap shot in an editorial, are no justification for lashing out at the reporter or the publication. The result will be to put the press on the defensive and cause it to lash out in turn, doing damage to the company in the process. Moreover, a PR person should never under any circumstance threaten a reporter with retaliation of any kind.

Handling Television Reporters Separately

"You've got to have a visual story," says George Hobgood of Hill and Knowlton. "They won't show up for talking heads. They've got all that time to fill. The main problem with TV is the need to encapsulate everything in twenty to thirty seconds. You'd better do it for them. If they do it, they may miss the point. Most of them are used to covering murders and rapes. We don't get too many clients like that." Even if a PR person makes the careful arrangements that Hobgood suggests — planning interviews carefully with the visual angle included — the contact can still be a frustrating one. "They [TV people] are the bane of our existence," says R. E. Parr of ARCO. "It's often hard to justify the effort you go to to set up interviews — one minute or forty-five seconds of air time. You try to background a reporter on your business and the issues, but they send someone else from the station the next time, or the person you've filled in moves on. Nevertheless, we must keep trying because television is the chief source of news for a high percentage of the public."

AN UNPREDICTABLE RELATIONSHIP

The best list of rules cannot predict things that still might go wrong in any contact between a company and the press. As noted in Chapter 9, public-relations people must prepare members of management carefully for inter-views. What questions will the reporter most likely ask? Why is this official being interviewed for this story? What is the track record of the reporter and of the publication? Will the interview be hostile? Will the final story be ac-curate? Although a public-relations person cannot answer all these questions, he or she will be able to give the company official involved a fairly good idea about a few of them.

Also, it is important to give the officials being interviewed a short course in the basics of journalism: what a reporter does, what a deadline is, what a publication is in business to accomplish, what the final article will most likely contain. Even with all this preparation, however, the unexpected can some-times happen. "We set up an interview with the president for a reporter from a small weekly," says Vic Pesqueira of Xerox. "She showed up in sandals, blue jeans, and a sweatshirt. Her questions did not go beyond information available to her on the new president's biographical data sheet. It was very embar-rassing."

Another unpredictable aspect of press relations is the hostility a reporter or editor may have for the company and/or public relations in general. The hostility may be based on old encounters for which the reporter is still holding a grudge. There is little a public-relations person can say or do to change that reporter's mind. If he or she has been assigned to write or edit a story, the best thing is to plunge ahead and hope for the best. Perhaps this time it will be different.

Take Robert Henkel of *Business Week*. As the editor in charge of the magazine's industrial coverage, he is in an important position. He decides what stories go into those sections of the magazine and which ones stay out. And he has definite ideas about public relations. "I remember being critical of PR outside New York before I worked here," he says. "New York is the big leagues, it's bush outside, I thought. As a rule, that's not true. PR tends to be practiced in the boonies on a more personal level. Here it is more like selling life insurance. Eastern PR people have a veneer I distrust. There are people in this town I regard as unethical, immoral, and dishonest."

SUMMARY

The single most important public a **PR** person must deal with is the press. Many of the programs they devise rely on newspapers, magazines, and television and radio stations for dissemination. A hostile press that stands between the company and its publics can make the job of a **PR** person difficult, if not impossible, to do. Although **PR** people cannot concentrate exclusively on the press, they cannot ignore it without damage to themselves.

Working with members of the press is not always easy. Some reporters and editors are hostile to public relations and its goals, and they will probably never change their attitudes. There are a number of ways to work successfully with the press: be responsive, be honest, know the press, know reporters personally, explain PR to the press, organize the PR department to help the press, prepare news releases with the press in mind, stay in the background, don't try to buy off the press, don't ask to see copy, never pick a fight with the press.

PR FOCUS: A HORROR STORY

Every reporter has a favorite anti-public-relations horror story in the same way that PR people keep a mental dossier of similarly bad encounters with individual reporters, editors, publications, and radio and TV stations. The stories on the press side are more important here because of the focus of this discussion. When such incidents occur, they build, one upon another, to the detriment of the public-relations people from that time forward.

One such incident exemplifies why some members of the press dislike PR people. An equally damaging example could be found, of course, of what the press does that causes PR people to hate it.

"The worst company I deal with is one that is very large," says Sandra Atchison of *Business Week*. "A couple of years ago I wanted to do a story on the new president's first year. The president was hired in September. I approached the PR man the following June about the story. I never heard from him but called him periodically to remind him we should get started in August. He kept stalling. Finally, he told me the company didn't want a story until January, and that I was in line behind *Forbes*, the *Wall Street Journal*, and somebody else. They apparently had requested the same kind of story before I did. I reminded the PR man I had asked for a general interview with the president the day he was named president — another of those requests that never got answered. Then, he checked his notes and said that actually, on the same day, my request came in behind the same request from *Forbes*, the *Journal*, etc.

"The upshot was that we went ahead and did the story without the company's help. At one point the PR man's boss told me about the amount of advertising the company purchased in *Business Week*. I also received a messenger-delivered letter telling me the company would not jeopardize its relationships with other publications by going against its word to talk to them first.

"The company did not like the story, the president wrote a letter to the magazine protesting it, and under the published letter we wrote a tag saying that if the president had agreed to an interview we would have given his side of the situation. To punish me, I guess, I was cut off the company's mailing list. This company should be in *Business Week* all the time with technical and pollution and corporate strategy pieces, but I have yet to have them suggest a single story idea."

Analysis

The PR man in this case did not do anything that was right. From the start of the contact with Sandra Atchison he was not responsive, honest, or very smart. A PR person does not attempt to play one publication off against its rivals. A correct approach would have been to find an angle for all three publications, if indeed the other two had been promised a story, at the same time or before *Business Week*. If a recalcitrant company president was the problem here, the PR man should have taken Atchison aside and told her the facts. The PR man was foolish to think that the company's lack of cooperation would kill the story.

Atchison's effort to do the story anyway was predictable to anyone with even the most rudimentary knowledge of the thought processes of the press. When the story appeared it was beyond comprehension that a company official hinted at a loss of advertising in the magazine. Most reporters know nothing of the ad side of their publications and could not care less about it. The final retaliation — removing the magazine from the company's mailing list — represents the height of stupidity. Although both the magazine and the company can do without one another, the company can probably use the notice given by an article in a national magazine. Removing itself in this amateurish way is wrong and puts the rest of the press on notice that this is a company to watch out for, this is a company that acts in an unreasonable way.

REVIEW QUESTIONS

1. Why is the relationship between public-relations people and reporters and editors so important?
2. Why does hostility exist between the press and PR?
3. Can a PR person work successfully with the press? If so, what are the ways?
4. Are there times when nothing helps? What can be done then?

ASSIGNMENTS

For Journalism Students

1. You are the public-relations director for a company, and you are preparing your president for his first interview with a reporter. Make a list of things to do to prepare him for the interview, using the material in this chapter and in Chapter 9.
2. Make a similar list for an oil-company president being interviewed by an aggressive, obnoxious energy reporter for a big newspaper that your company cannot ignore.
3. You are a PR person for a company opening a new gambling casino in Atlantic City, New Jersey. You want to bring a large group of press people to cover the opening, but you are worried that codes of ethics will cause them to decline. Tell what you will do in a short PR plan.
4. Draw the organization chart for a press-relations part of a big-company PR department with unlimited resources. What elements should you include?
5. Write a 500-word policy statement that explains public relations to the hostile press in your city.

For Business Students

1. Write an essay on "Why Large Corporations Need the Press."
2. Make a list of ten ways you as a company executive can work with a hostile reporter you must grant an interview to because of the prestige and importance of his or her publication.
3. You are an executive of a forest-products company that has a bad pollution record and a bad press. You have been invited to address the state press association annual meeting on the topic, "How the Press Misunderstands Big Business." Write your 1,500-word speech and deliver it to the class.

CHAPTER **20**

Public relations and other parts of the company

Below the management level are various publics that have a great deal to do with the success of the company but that are not always contacted by people in public relations. It is far easier — and often more important in a survival sense — for PR people to keep in touch with members of management than with general company employees, the sales staff, customers, shareholders, and retirees. But these disparate groups play important roles in the constant battle a company faces to achieve good public relations.

EMPLOYEES

In companies large and small, the general employee group and its opinions about the company are crucial. Each employee touches a broad group of family, friends, and neighbors on a regular basis. If that employee is unhappy about something the company has done — either in general terms or specifically to him or her — that dissatisfaction will be immediately transmitted to the groups noted earlier, which easily total at least 100 people or more per employee.

The biggest failure in employee relations occurs in day-to-day communication. Far too many companies neglect to tell their employees what is going on. Employees read about a major event in the newspaper or hear about it on television along with the general public, and it is a blow to their pride. It is also bad PR if they react negatively to the various groups they touch.

It is much better to let the employees in on the company event ahead of everyone outside. They feel that they have thus been taken into the confidence of management and are "in the know." The information they pass along to the groups they touch is informed and positive as a result. The communication process is reasonably simple and inexpensive. It can take a number of forms.

Company Publications

The most traditional kind of employee communication is the company magazine or newspaper. Published weekly, biweekly, or monthly, the publication is usually inexpensive to produce and is generally well received by its readers (see Chapter 15).

Bulletin Boards

Another traditional means of employee communication is the bulletin board. Few locations should be without such a device because it is a quick and reasonably inexpensive means to reach great numbers of people. Bulletin boards need to be placed in central locations at the office or plant. They also need to be well organized and systematic.

Pacific Power & Light Company (PP&L), a Northwest electric utility, standardized its bulletin boards a number of years ago. Notices are sent out on pre-prepared paper for various categories (benefit information, company news, safety rules, for example) and then placed under headings for each category on the board. Each notice has a time limit so that old information is removed. Colors are also used for different subjects so that they stand out one from another. This orderliness avoids the chaos of many bulletin boards, where current news items are tacked up over old ones, and new and important information is obscured by that which is old and outdated. PP&L issues guidelines for its bulletin boards, and their proper maintenance is checked periodically.

Employee Annual Reports

A newer and more unique form of employee communication is the employee annual report. This publication resembles the more traditional annual report to stockholders but does not have all the financial information. It does contain information about all aspects of the company so that an employee is kept informed in a special way.

PP&L performs this communications task in a special issue of the company monthly magazine, *The Bulletin*. "We are a company of people — not ordinary people who can be replaced by others — but dedicated and competent people who care about service to our customers, the cost and quality of that service as well as the future availability and reliability of power supply," wrote board chairman Don Frisbee in the introduction to the 1979 report. The twenty-eight-page publication went on to feature various company employees in page-long articles that emphasized their contributions to the company. The center spread of the publication detailed income of the company and where the income was spent.

Company Television Programs

Another nontraditional means of communicating with employees is the company television program. Patterned after such documentary "magazine" presentations as CBS's *Sixty Minutes,* ABC's *20/20,* and NBC's *Prime Time Saturday,* such offerings cover news and features about the company or its employees. Bethlehem Steel, for example, produces *Nine Minutes,* a newsreel-type rundown of short items, and *Nine Minutes Plus,* a show that continues for twelve minutes or as long as twenty minutes. Each program is shown once a week at company headquarters during the lunch hour and is later played at thirty-eight outlying locations.

New England Mutual Life Insurance Company does *Video Wheel,* which it thinks of as an employee newspaper on television. Indeed, the biweekly program gets its name from *The Wheel,* the company newspaper. The show is oriented toward employee needs and may feature information on how to care for office plants or a promotion on the annual blood drive. The productions are usually twelve minutes long and are shown in a lounge outside the cafeteria.

Such an approach has its problems, of course. Employees may not watch the programs, which also might be viewed as too much the mouthpiece of management. Content is, by necessity, noncontroversial, detailing plant openings and annual meetings. It is unrealistic to expect management to do otherwise. Such programs are most successful when they involve great numbers of employees. People will watch if they think they will see themselves or someone they know.

These are the mechanisms for transmitting information to employees. How effective are they? The best way for a PR person to find out is to conduct a communications audit, an inventory and analysis of all the various techniques and media that comprise a company's communications system. Hill and Knowlton recommends that such an audit first find out what management expects from its employee communications program, what kinds of communication approaches are used, the content of these approaches, and whether these approaches are doing any good.

Communication with employees should run in both directions. A company also needs to know what its employees are thinking. Hill and Knowlton considers an employee attitude survey a key part of the communications audit. The survey should measure how employees rate the company's present communications, how they perceive the company, and how these perceptions vary from the expectations of management. The attitude survey also allows management to "tune in" to employees and find out what they are thinking about a number of subjects.

Because the tenor of employees communications is set by management, PR people should urge executives to be as familiar as possible about what the people in the ranks of the company think, whether those ranks be 100 or 100,000.

SALES PERSONNEL

A company succeeds or fails by the ability of its sales force. Yet this group is often neglected as a public. Salespeople have special needs for information that can best be fulfilled by special newspapers or newsletters containing information of interest to the sales staff — how to sell, new products, sales figures, sales contests. Feature stories on salespeople are of interest to readers, such as a "salesperson of the month." Articles on sales territories might be helpful as well.

Such a sales newspaper or newsletter can be produced by the public-relations department in a reasonably inexpensive way. It is the thought that counts in such a publication — the company thinks enough of its sales staff to pay for a special newsletter — rather than the lavishness of its production.

Public-relations people also can produce for salespeople special manuals and sales brochures that detail products and procedures of use to salespeople. The layout, design, and writing of brochures is detailed in Chapter 13.

With either sales newsletters or brochures, good design and clear writing are important. As with general company magazines and newspapers, such sales publications compete with slick and sophisticated general magazines, newspapers, and television productions.

CUSTOMERS

Communication with the lifeblood of any company, its customers, is often overlooked. People in this group are often reached through means used for the general public, a segment of which they are definitely a part. They do have special needs, however, and attention to them can pay off in higher sales and general satisfaction.

Again, the route of the special newspaper or newsletter is the least expensive and most effective approach. Articles on subjects of interest to customers and company information of use to them can be included. Suggestions on displaying a product or answering critics of company policies might help a beleaguered store owner and show that the company cares about his or her problems.

As with other kinds of publications, those for customers should be well designed and well written.

SHAREHOLDERS

The people who purchase the shares of stock that finance the company represent another important public. Their special interests and needs should be catered to regularly in publications aimed only at them.

Standard Oil of California has 270,000 stockholders. They each receive *Chevron World,* a slick quarterly magazine that includes articles of more general interest than those in *Standard Oiler,* its monthly employee magazine. A 1979 issue, for example, contained articles on the energy shortage, how the company looks to the press, uranium as a fuel source, a new antimerger bill, the company's centennial exhibit on creativity, and Ninian Central, the world's largest offshore producing platform in the North Sea.

The company has also identified 15,000 of these shareholders as "activists." This group receives two or three letters from the chairman of the board per year dealing with specific issues. The company may eventually produce a special newsletter for them.

Standard Oil, as well as all publicly held companies, also issues quarterly reports to shareholders that detail financial information important to them as investors.

RETIREES

The most neglected of a company's many publics is its retirees. Too often retirees are included off-handedly among its employees or, worse, the general public. Both approaches are mistaken because this group can help a company's public relations if some attention is paid to it. Its members are usually loyal to the company; after all, they have devoted many years serving it and are deriving income from it. Also, they have time on their hands to talk to relatives and friends about issues of the day. If properly informed, these retirees can clear up misconceptions and correct erroneous information about the company.

Standard Oil's 12,000 retired personnel are viewed as important as employees and stockholders. "These people are very clearly employees of the company," says William Jones, manager of corporate communications. "They need some identity when they leave work. They want to defend the company." Standard Oil gives them the information to do so: the employee magazine, a management newsletter, a four-page newsletter for them. They also get copies of "Update Report," Standard's refutation of news reports that are wrong.

Retirees also enjoy being invited to company events like plant openings, retirement ceremonies, or annual picnics.

SUMMARY

Public-relations people have to deal with many publics in a company below the management level. Their skill in dealing with them will have a great deal to do with the success of the company. Some people in PR neglect these publics, however, and concentrate too much on management. Their work would be enhanced if they dealt in special ways with general company employees, sales staffs, customers, shareholders, and people who have retired from the company.

PR FOCUS: STANDARD OIL'S CREATIVITY EXHIBIT

As part of his duties as manager of corporate communications at Standard Oil of California, William Jones had to come up with an idea that would enable all its publics inside and outside that varied corporation to celebrate its centennial. He abandoned the traditional approach of company histories, ceremonies, or, as he puts it, "bands and balloons." His company's many critics simply would not let an oil company do anything that glorified itself.

Jones brought in representatives from J. Walter Thompson, the company's advertising agency, and he and they came up with an idea that seemed to solve the problem: a noncommercial, non-self-serving exhibit on creativity. Although the company was identified as sponsoring the exhibit, the connection was very low key. At first, the exhibit's planners had difficulty isolating and expressing creativity. They finally settled on the process itself of creativity, and the content of the exhibit flamed from there. *Creativity — The Human Resource* opened in May, 1979 at the California Academy of Sciences in Golden Gate Park in San Francisco. The $3.5 million, 4,000-square-foot exhibit was later set up at museums around the country and in Canada over the next three years.

One part shows the achievements of fifteen creative Americans selected by a panel of consultants. Their notebooks, sketches, diagrams, models, videotapes, and audiotapes are included in the exhibit. According to the planners of the exhibit, certain actions and attitudes are common among creative people, who challenge fixed assumptions, discern previously unseen patterns and then see in new ways, make connections where none had seemed possible, take risks, seize upon chance, and form networks of people who interact in creative ways.

Another part of the exhibit deals with the myth that only certain people are creative. Nine computers were programmed with games and exercises that test the creativity of individuals; they demonstrate what the exhibit's designers call the "commonality of creativity."

The third segment of the exhibit is an eleven-minute animated film that reviews periods of high creativity in Western civilization and analyzes what the societies in those periods had in common: institutions that stimulate and support creative effort, an atmosphere where people are free to move about and communicate with one another, tools to facilitate creativity, plenty of resources, and a recognition of the role that audiences have in encouraging creative minds.

The exhibit encourages visitor participation by allowing direct use of the computers and some books on the subject available on the spot.

Analysis

The use of an abstract and interesting idea like creativity as the subject of an exhibit is an excellent way for a company to make an impact on all its publics in an unobtrusive way. A corporation in a controversial field like oil would have been criticized if it had done anything more traditional and predictable. It had the resources to do something different and educate all its publics at the same time it celebrated its one-hundredth birthday. Developing unusual ideas like this one is where public-relations people earn their money.

REVIEW QUESTIONS

1. What are the other publics in a company in addition to management?
2. How can each of them be served by public relations?
3. Should a company newspaper or magazine be the tool of management? Why? Why not?
4. Why are company newspapers important?
5. What means are used to reach other publics like stockholders, retired employees, and sales personnel?

ASSIGNMENTS

For Journalism Students

1. Interview a company publication editor and find out what he or she does. Report your findings to the class.
2. Analyze a company newspaper designed for employees. What does it contain? How effectively does it serve employees?
3. Analyze a slick magazine aimed at shareholders. What does it contain? How effectively does it serve shareholders?
4. Select a group of publications from the same company aimed at different publics — employees, sales personnel, shareholders, retirees. Analyze the contents of each and compare them. How do they differ? How are they similar?

For Business Students

1.   Interview a company president and find out what he or she thinks of the employee publication. How effective is it, what does it contain in the way of regular features? Report your findings to the class.

2.   Analyze a company employee newspaper to determine the kinds of articles contained in it. Which ones serve the interests of management and which ones serve employees? Report your findings to the class.

3.   You are a company president planning a publications program with your public-relations director. Which of your publics do you want to reach, and with what kind of publications? Prepare a publications plan that lists each publication and that justifies its use for the audience intended to receive it.

CHAPTER 21

Public relations, the public, and publicity

To almost everyone in public relations and public information, they are the great unknown, the millions of people "out there," beyond the doors of the company or the agency or the nonprofit organization, toward whom much of their effort is aimed.

The public.

Who are its members? What can be done to make them like the company or the college or the hospital?

After all the publics already discussed in this book are dealt with, there still remain a great number of people who defy such categorization. They live in thousands of towns and cities around the United States, and they work in thousands of jobs in organizations untouched by PR directly. Yet their opinions count for much. As they read about and observe the activities of companies and nonprofit organizations, the members of the general public pass a kind of collective judgment. It may be fleeting and not fully informed, but it is a judgment nonetheless.

Sometimes this opinion can have disastrous consequences for the company or nonprofit organization being judged. The DC – 10 is an unsafe airplane. Oil companies make too much money. Congress is inefficient and slightly corrupt. Hospitals overcharge their patients. The list is endless.

PR people at the companies and organizations being judged have their work cut out for them in reversing such harsh opinions once they have been rendered. The horrible part of the process exists in the fact that PR people never really know about these collectively damning thoughts until judgment has been passed. Nor do they know when — and if — the opinions have been reversed. Sometimes, the task is so monumental — and distasteful — that public relations people may choose to resign instead of attempting to compromise their standards.

THE PUBLIC-OPINION-FORMING PROCESS

The process of forming the opinion of the general public about a company or nonprofit organization begins the moment that people hear things about these organizations. These days, this means reading stories in newspapers and magazines, listening to the radio, and watching television news broadcasts.

The nature of the news-gathering process, however, dictates that what the public hears is generally negative. In all definitions of news, the bad drives out the good more often than not. Thus, information is usually negative before members of the general public even hear it. A company or nonprofit organization can do a great deal of good that will go unnoticed. Let it commit one error, however, and the details will be spread instantly from one part of the country to the other.

Public-relations and public-information people cannot be intimidated by what might happen in this essentially unfair practice. They cannot proceed with their work under the assumption that only the good will emerge. When the bad comes out, they must deal with it and get the public mind back to the good as quickly as possible.

As the PR process goes, the companies or nonprofit organizations issue information about themselves on a regular basis through news releases, special publications, filmed news releases, and public-service announcements sent to newspapers, magazines, and radio and television stations. Once this material goes out, PR people sit back and hope that members of the press will call for more information and run the stories.

When the unusual connotes bad, the public-relations people must go into action with further measures. They need to issue special news releases, hold emergency press conferences, arrange appearances for executives on television and radio talk shows and before the editorial boards of newspapers and magazines, prepare testimony for congressional or legislature hearings, set up speeches for executives all around the country, and prepare appropriate institutional advertisements. Once again, the effect of these means will be difficult to measure immediately.

Sometimes, in unusual circumstances, the feedback might be immediate: letters or telegrams of support for the company or organization after its side of the story has been told. At other times, the result of the PR effort will be increased sales of a product or at least a downward slide brought on by whatever bad news appeared in the first place.

This public-relations process is thus elusive and transitory, maddening and fascinating as other chapters in this book have detailed. The people in the profession spend their days not knowing when the unthinkable will happen, but needing to be ready to deal with it nonetheless.

Elaborate campaigns aimed at the general public are the most difficult to measure in terms of results. There are too many people involved for the PR person to know for certain if the material has hit its mark. How can a PR person tell how many people have read a news release or have watched a PSA on television? It is much easier to assess the effect of the PR programs aimed at smaller publics, for example, stockholders or employees.

Sales of a product go up or down, or an institutional ad campaign might be received favorably, but it is hard to know why with any certainty. Public-opinion polling is one way to obtain an assessment of the effects of PR programs aimed at the general public. It will be discussed in detail in Chapter 22.

PUBLICITY AND "FLACKERY"

Public-relations and public-information people want public notice of a certain kind for their organizations. However, they can get by without it, especially if it is bad.

There are those in the fringe areas of the public-relations profession, however, who want publicity for its own sake. These people do not care if the noteworthiness puts their clients or companies in a good light or a bad one. The important thing for them is to get the individual or company name into print or broadcast at all. These so-called "publicity hounds" want attention at any cost. They combine a "I don't care what you say as long as you spell my name right" attitude with P. T. Barnum-like methods to achieve their goals. In the process, unfortunately, they give the whole public-relations profession a bad name when in reality they are only part of it. They earn the derisive title "flack."

A good example of such a person is the show-business press agent who lives for the day when the names of his or her clients get mentioned in gossip columns. In theory, this public notice leads to interest in the actor or actress involved and the offer of roles in films, plays, and television productions. The process works for the films, plays, and television productions themselves. If enough advance notice — sometimes called "hype" — is generated, more people will buy tickets to the films and plays and turn their television sets to the program.

At one extreme is a press agent like Ed Gifford, who once saved Doug Henning's *The Magic Show* from closing on Broadway after the show got poor critical reviews by hiring thirty unemployed actors to ride up and down all day in elevators at all the big New York department stores and talk about it. The show remained open as box office receipts went up.

At the other end of the press-agent scale are people like Patricia Newcomb of the Pickwick Group, which specializes in promoting films in a non-flamboyant way. Her agency does not "plant" items in gossip columns but relies instead on getting newspapers and magazines interested in a personality or a trend. The approach often results in national coverage. For example, she pitched *Newsweek* with the idea that 20th Century-Fox was making films with women stars — *Julia, Turning Point, An Unmarried Woman*. The idea caught on and the article on the trend featured Jane Fonda in *Julia* on the cover of the magazine.

The agency, which is hired by the distributor, the producer, the director, or the star, insists on being in on the production from the first day. If the set is "open," that is, if the director allows visitors, the Pickwick press agent brings press people and others in regularly to observe progress and, hopefully, to write about it.

Members of the print and electronic media are willing accompanists in this publicity orchestration. They need colorful material to go with the hard news in their pages and on their broadcasts. The unsuspecting public goes along because the product being sold is usually funny and interesting and a good contrast to the real news on most days.

Although most public-relations practitioners view the work of press agents with ridicule and chagrin, the fact remains that there is a market for their work. The public remains fascinated with celebrities, as the success of television talk shows and magazines like *People* indicates. The press agent is just giving the general public what it wants — often by merely spelling the names of their clients right.

THE PUBLICITY CHAIRMAN

The United States is filled with people who are members of hundreds of thousands of clubs and organizations, of high purpose or of no purpose. The aim of most of these organizations is to get a story in the local newspaper or on the local television newscast. Sometimes the item in question is designed to publicize an event the organization hopes that the public will support — a bake sale, an antique auction, a special luncheon or dinner. At other times the publicity is aimed at little more than getting a clipping for the scrapbook, an exercise in vanity for the officers mentioned.

The mechanism for gaining the public notice is the publicity chairman. Untrained, often unskilled, this person — usually a nonprofessional volunteer — has to learn how to get information into the local media to keep organization members happy. Often, the success or failure of the event being publicized will be credited to, or blamed on, the work of the publicity chairman.

Judy Carlson is a longtime publicity chairman for scores of groups in the college town of Corvallis, Oregon. Because it is a high-income community, Corvallis is inhabited by people who have more time on their hands to participate in the activities of clubs and other organizations than residents of a more working-class town.

Carlson went into the publicity chairman "business" as something to do. As the wife of an Oregon State University mathematics professor, she found herself living in a town where there were few opportunities to put her journalism education to work. That journalism degree and some newspaper experience gave her much more background than most publicity chairmen ever have. Because of it, her success in gaining public notice for the groups in her care has been high.

"The key to good publicity is getting a personal relationship going with reporters and editors," she says. "If you've been fair and responsible in your demands of them to run your releases, they will work with you. That's where publicity and public relations mesh. You can't do one without the other."

For Carlson, the process is one of both information (the releases sent to the média) and personal contact. "Some of it is information, the rest is image," she says. "You have to present the right face to the organization you're representing." If publicity chairmen do their job well, the image will be a good one. If they do otherwise, even through no fault of their own, the reverse will be true.

Success in local publicity begins with knowing what a local newspaper or television station wants. They are deluged with hundreds of requests a week for coverage of one event or another. Often, to serve the public and to leave space for real news, newspapers will run such routine information on a calendar page. Such an item lists little more than the name of the organization, the time and place of the meeting, and the topic to be covered, all provided when the publicity chairman fills out a pre-prepared blank in the newspaper office. A publicity person cannot expect a longer story or personal coverage by a reporter for anything so routine. To demand it, in fact, will alienate the city editor and hamper coverage in the future for more important events. The calendar page is not all that bad. Once readers get used to seeing such a page, they will scan it regularly and find the information they are seeking.

More effort is needed, however, when the event to be publicized is on a grander scale, especially one in need of public support to buy tickets. In such cases, the publicity person can fall back on friendships made with local reporters and editors and interest them in publicizing the event in advance and possibly taking photographs.

In such instances, publicity chairmen need to write news releases and deliver them to the newspaper office with a request that they be run, together with possibly other coverage given later. Such releases should be written in a proper news format, typed and double-spaced. "You need the basics — the five w's — who, what, when, where, and why," continues Judy Carlson. "If you have that and the release is typewritten, you're off to a good start. Even in a small town, a release should look good. Even in a small town you have to attempt to bring in some professionalism. Just a basic news story is what a newspaper wants. If you give it enough information to suit its needs, it will be happy. The most important thing is to have paragraphs that it can pick out and use in the paper without losing the story."

With the well-prepared release in hand, Carlson is not pushy in her contacts with the city editor. "In my approach I never make demands that are unreasonable," she says. "If you insist on a certain story being used on a certain day, that's unreasonable. After it has run, it's very rare that I complain that the story is not in a good enough place. You can't do this if you want long-term results. Later, I make a point of thanking editors for running releases or reporters for covering an event. They don't hear that very much." She thinks that such courtesy is particularly important in small towns, where media responsiveness is very important to the success of the publicity person.

But working with the press is not the only concern a publicity chairman has. The organization itself is also expecting often impossible things from the person in that job. Its members are prepared to blame any failure on lack of publicity, even though their own inaction may have been more of a contributing factor. "Some people want miracles," she says. "They are sharks with unreasonable demands."

Carlson thinks a way to avoid this problem is to outline carefully the expectations of publicity in advance. Then people will not be disappointed at what happens.

In addition to writing skills and ability to work with people, she suggests that a variety of other skills are important to a publicity person. "Photography is important," she says. "So often, a photo is needed, time is short, and the media are reluctant to take one. So if you can provide the black-and-white proofs and negatives, the newspaper is more apt to use the photo with the news release. The need for professional quality is important.

"Graphics and brochure layouts and printing processes are important to know about too," she concludes. "So often, in 'PR-ing' an event or a person, we have to stretch in a number of directions to maximize results."

Working with television on a local level is a bit more difficult. Releases can be delivered to the news director, but that director will seldom assign a reporter and camera person unless the event has some substance and is photogenic. Few small organizations have the resources to provide their own film clips, as a company can. As a result, it is best not to try for television coverage unless the event merits it. A routine announcement read by the anchorperson can still get people out to an event. So can a similar mention on the radio. Both radio and television stations need to carry out some public-service announcements to keep their licenses renewable with the Federal Communications Commission.

SUMMARY

The largest public — the general public — is the hardest for PR people to reach. Even when programs are aimed at it, only with difficulty can one measure effectiveness and results because this public is so large and so dispersed. Its members pass judgments on a company and its programs and products nevertheless. The horrible thing for PR people is that they may not know the judgment has been passed until it is too late. A negative public has quit buying the company's products or supporting the programs of a nonprofit organization.

One way to find out how the general public feels is through public-opinion polls, discussed in Chapter 22. If carefully conducted and if the results are used well, such polls can be helpful. One offshoot of public relations — the press agent — will do almost anything to gain public recognition. Although often blatant, the methods of such press agents are effective. At a nonprofessional level, the publicity chairperson also aims his or her work at the general public as he or she tries to get residents of a town to support the programs of a club or organization. Although untrained in sophisticated methods, such people can be effective if they learn the rudiments of the business and are careful in how they work with local newspapers and television and radio news staffs.

PR BIO: HENRY ROGERS, MASTER PUBLICIST

Singer Mac Davis was the cover subject of an issue of *People* magazine. Would shoppers in supermarkets be enticed into buying a copy at the sight of Davis, his shirt off, his personal life delineated in a headline?

The chances are that shoppers would grab the magazine on impulse and throw it in their shopping carts among the hamburger and eggs and bread and cheese. Henry Rogers, chairman of Rogers & Cowan, had thought they would do so eight weeks before, when his associates contacted the editors of *People* about Davis. The singer was good-looking and had been in the news recently over various personal problems. More important for Rogers, however, was the fact that his client had a television special coming up whose ratings might increase if people saw Davis on *People*.

"We tell the editors, 'We have Mac Davis in an important special,' " says Rogers. "If they put him on and sell more magazines that week, our relationship with them is strengthened. Then, we might give them ideas for two or three more covers." (In fact, Rogers had succeeded in getting six of his clients for the cover of *People* in the twelve weeks before Davis appeared.)

"Your relationship with the media depends on the success or lack of success with the recommendations you make to them," Rogers continues. "If you give them a good story, they love you. With Mac Davis, we suggested a story approach. When the editor said OK, we went over all of Mac's background with the editors and arranged his availability for photos and an interview." (The bare chest was the magazine's idea, according to Rogers, with that photo picked from among the many frames taken at the photography sitting.)

The approach Rogers used to get Mac Davis on *People* exemplifies the normal modus operandi for him and his associates. The public-relations counsel that clients get from Rogers, his partner Warren Cowan, and the 100 employees of their agency is not conventional. "We are much more media oriented than the top New York corporate PR firms, which deal more in counseling, industrial relations, employee relations, financial relations, the making up of annual reports," he says. "They do the 101 things one must do to conduct a total PR program. We get into these areas to a point but our principal thing — probably 75 percent of our effort — is media placement. We arrange coverage for our clients on TV, radio, the press.

"Consequently, we are not the complete PR firm like Hill and Knowlton and Carl Byoir," he continues. "They give a much more comprehensive service. I will compete with Hill and Knowlton for a client who is interested in media placement and to whom press, radio, TV coverage is all-important. I will not try to compete with Hill and Knowlton for corporate clients who want the total public-relations services they offer."

Of the accounts at Rogers and Cowan, 65 percent are related to show business. They range from actors like Paul Newman and Robert Wagner, and actresses like Ann-Margret and Joanne Woodward, to musical groups like the Bee Gees and the Village People. The other 35 percent of its business comes from corporate accounts. "Exxon doesn't hire us to do a company magazine," continues Rogers. "It hires us for those projects it feels we are capable of handling."

For example, Exxon and Metropolitan Life Insurance brought in R and C to handle the six-city tour of the Folger Shakespeare Library Exhibition. "We got national media coverage for the exhibit and at the same time made certain our client got proper credit," continues Rogers. "We also coordinated all the promotion and PR activities between the two companies and the Folger Shakespeare Library in Washington."

Although Rogers is best remembered for publicity stunts carried out thirty years ago (he once attracted attention to Jack Benny's TV series by having the late comedian host a black-tie party at one of New York City's automats), the agency's success ($5 million in annual fees) is based largely on a good relationship with the press. "Our knowledge and expertise has been developed over the years," says Rogers. "We have learned what the media are interested in. We don't go to the media unless we're certain something is of interest to them. The media never do, nor should they do, the PR man a favor.

"I've always felt a partnership exists. Let's say I am a newspaperman writing a column. If you, as a PR man, can give me material I can use, in order to do a good job in my column, I will use the material. Your responsibility as a PR man is to give me what will interest me. Contacts are important. They come with experience with a PR man."

Rogers, Cowan, and the agency account executives analyze what various parts of the press need. "We tailor-make our suggestions for specialized media," he says. "Many people deal with the press with a great fear and trepidation. They worry about being rejected. We try to indoctrinate our people with the idea that the press needs us as much as we need them."

Once this friendship with members of the press has been established and the knowledge of what they want and can use has been set, Rogers makes sure that both client and journalist know the purpose of the exchange between them. He also makes sure that the client will cooperate "and talk about what he says he will talk about."

Does this concentration on placement make him a flack or a publicity manager? Rogers rejects such designations or any hint that other, less reputable people in his part of the profession drag everyone in PR down: "I find the majority of press people have a great deal of respect for the PR people they deal with, more for the PR people they don't deal with. When I am asked about ethics in PR, I think of the time I sat with the great PR man Ben Sonnenberg in his magnificent New York house surrounded by all those antiques and works of art. 'I'm so thrilled being here,' I told him. 'Tell me, how did you get started?' 'I started as a Broadway press agent,' he told me."

REVIEW QUESTIONS

1. Why is the general public so hard to reach?
2. How does the general public differ from other publics already discussed in this book?
3. What are the different steps in the public-opinion-forming process?
4. What is a "flack," and why does this term apply to the work of a press agent?
5. How can a publicity chairman work effectively with the local print and electronic press?

ASSIGNMENTS

For Journalism Students

1. Select a current or past press agent, and write a research paper that tells what he or she did and how the methods used were effective in reaching the general public.
2. Interview the publicity chairman of a local club or organization and find out how he or she does the job. Report your findings to the class.
3. Interview the city editor of your local newspaper and find out what he or she thinks of publicity chairmen and their news releases. Do they ever use such information? Why? Why not?

For Business Students

1. When has business turned to the "press agent" approach in reaching the public? Write a research paper on one example in the past.
2. When does business use public-opinion polls? Interview the president of a medium or large company to find out.

SECTION VI

The DOING System

Part iv :

Noting and analyzing results

Part v :

Going ahead or developing new programs

CHAPTER **22**

Conducting a public-opinion survey

Many approaches — elaborate and simple — have been suggested in this book to reach the many publics of public relations. No matter how well-conceived and expensive, however, the programs might not achieve their goals. And, far worse, the agency or company PR people designing the programs may not know that they have failed.

The only real way to find out the effectiveness of a PR program is to conduct a survey of public opinion. This step, which is Part IV, Noting and Analyzing Results, of the DOING system of public relations described in this book, is an important one. It leads naturally into Part V, Going Ahead or Developing New Programs, which brings the work of public relations full circle.

WHAT A SURVEY IS

The American Statistical Association defines a *survey* as "any observation or investigation of the facts about a situation." The same process is sometimes called a *poll*. The word survey is also used to describe a method of gathering information from a specific number of individuals, called a *sample,* to learn something about the larger population from which the sample has been drawn. For example, a survey of voters is conducted before an election to find out how these voters perceive candidates and issues. A manufacturer commissions a survey of the potential market before introducing a new product. A government agency pays for a survey to gather the factual information it needs to draft new legislation. A company wants to know how the residents of a community feel about it before it builds a new plant there.

The American public is too diverse and complex to reach without a prompt and accurate flow of information on its preferences, needs, and behavior. The increasing reliance on surveys is a direct response to this critical need for information by business, government, and nonprofit organizations.

Surveys come in many different forms and have a wide variety of purposes, but they do have certain characteristics in common. Unlike a census of all a population, a survey gathers information from only a small sample of people, businesses, farms, or whatever else is being measured. In a good survey, the sample is scientifically chosen so that each individual in the population has a known chance of selection, thus enabling the results to be projected reliably to the larger public. If a sample is picked in a haphazard way or from volunteers, the results will not be valid.

Information in a survey is collected through use of standardized questions so that every individual contacted responds to exactly the same questions. The participants in a survey are never identified. Their answers are summarized into a statistical profile of the population that is the real heart of any survey. Their random selection makes their individual characteristics less important than their opinions about the subject as combined with all others contacted in the survey.

The sample size required for a survey depends on the reliability needed, which in turn depends on how the results will be used. Thus there is no simple rule for sample size that can be used for all surveys. A moderate sample size is usually sufficient. For example, well-known national political polls generally use samples of about 1,500 persons to reflect national attitudes and opinions. A sample of this size produces accurate estimates even for a country as large as the United States, which has a population of over 200 million.

The value of surveys becomes clear when one simple fact emerges: a properly selected sample of only 1,500 individuals can reflect various characteristics of the total population within a very small margin of error. Surveys provide a speedy and economical means of determining facts about almost any subject as well as the public's knowledge, attitudes, beliefs, expectations, and behavior.

PUBLIC RELATIONS AND SURVEYS

Public relations needs surveys for many reasons. Elaborate campaigns aimed at the general public are the most difficult to measure in terms of results. There are too many people involved for the PR person to know for certain if the material has hit its mark. How can a PR person tell how many people read a news release or watched a public-service announcement on television? Sales of a product may go up or down, or an institutional ad campaign might be received favorably or unfavorably, but it is hard to know without doing something definite to find out. It is much easier to assess the effect of the PR programs aimed at smaller publics, for example, stockholders or employees.

Public-opinion polling is one way to obtain information about the effects of PR programs designed for the general public or for one or more specific publics. Unless a company has trained people in this field, however, it should turn to a public-opinion research firm for help. "When you want to find out what people know or think about an issue or what they're going to do or what groups hold certain opinions, a public-opinion survey is what to use," says Robert Mason, a member of the staff at the Oregon State University Survey Research Center. "Are people hostile to your product or ideas? If so, who are they and why do they feel that way?"

Mason thinks that a public-opinion poll helps a company or anyone else find out, in his words, "what's out there." If set up properly and with enough time, a survey can help. Mason cautions the users of polls to allow sufficient time so that the information obtained from the poll is available early enough to be of help. "Politicians frequently go to pollsters a week before an election and ask, 'Am I going to win?'" he says. "That is too late. It should be three months early so they can intelligently plan a program."

In this instance, a poll obtains opinions that can be included in the final plan of action. "You know what the people sampled think and your plan can mesh with what they'll accept," he continues. When John F. Kennedy was running for U.S. president in 1960, for example, he called in a pollster, got the results, and then actually incorporated phrases from the surveys into his speeches given in places where the polls had been conducted.

Mason advises the use of public-opinion polling if a company lacks confidence in the information needed to develop a public-relations program. "Before you get started, you need to have in mind the purpose of the campaign, what it will achieve, and how well it will likely reach its goals," he says.

The sample polled will be set up based on what the company wants. The sampling method, the type of interview, the analysis — all these details will be determined by the goals worked out in advance, and by the time and budget available. After this, the polling firm will meet with the customer to define the population to be polled, work out the method to be used and the size of the sample, figure out how the sample is to be drawn, determine the interview method, and specify how the data are to be analyzed and used and who owns it.

"The more specific you are in your questions, the better off you are," continues Mason. "The pollster should review the interview schedule with you but you shouldn't sit in on interviews. After the interviewing is finished, you should receive an interpretation and analysis that is well written and that contains a recommended plan of action. There should be no guess as to what the pollster is talking about. The pollster should go back to goals: 'Here's where the client is strong and weak. Judging from the data, here's what you should do.'"

Mason believes in paying attention to the results of polls. "If 20 percent of those polled are dead set against your program, they usually can have quite an effect," he says. "After all, one person can file a court suit and stop the building of a dam."

Once they have the results of a poll, PR people are still not without problems. Others in the company will raise objections to the recommendations, especially if they involve change. They might raise questions about the methodology used in taking the survey and the error rate, which is always a factor in any poll.

"You listen to the recommendations and then ask yourself, 'How important is this problem?' " continues Mason. "Do you want to appeal to the minority and lose the majority? If you do this, what will be the effect on old customers, for example? No amount of data will substitute for good, cogent thinking. The real danger comes in using surveys as a crutch. You use surveys, don't let them use you."

WHO DOES SURVEYS?

The most well-known kinds of surveys are the political ones so prevalent in an election year. Periodically during a presidential campaign, the Gallup Poll and the Harris Survey issue reports that the press uses as a way to tell who is ahead and who is behind. Both these organizations conduct polls throughout the year to gather information and opinion on a wide range of current issues. State polls and metropolitan-area polls, often supported by a local newspaper or television station, are reported regularly. The major broadcasting networks and national news magazines also conduct polls and report their findings.

All political polling firms make most of their money with their less well-known industrial work. None of them could survive with only political clients, who need public-opinion polling done every two or four years. The press attention that comes with the political work, however, brings in the corporations later.

Mervin Field, for example, gets most of his attention from the politically oriented California Poll, but most of his income from the Field Research Corporation comes from clients like Pacific Telephone, Golden West Broadcasters, NBC, CBS, and the Bank of America. Ronald Reagan's pollster, Richard Wirthlin, has a similar business mix with his company, Decision Making Information. Although his noteworthiness comes with his association with Reagan and other Republicans, Wirthlin makes his money doing polling work for General Foods, Ford, Greyhound, and Century 21.

Jimmy Carter's pollster, Patrick Caddell, owns Cambridge Survey Research. He began doing surveys for George McGovern's 1972 presidential campaign and helped Carter in the 1976 and 1980 campaigns. After 1972, Caddell and two partners set up Cambridge Reports, Inc. to provide data for corporations in a quarterly publication based on a large national survey. Caddell's association with Carter cost him some business, but his corporate clients include Exxon, Westinghouse, Shell, and Aetna. In a typical assignment, the firm does market surveys, corporate image work, and studies of government-policy questions. It looks into what the public thinks about such diverse subjects as oil companies, nuclear power, and insurance.

The great majority of surveys are not exposed to public view because they are directed to a specific administrative or commercial purpose. The wide variety of issues dealt with in surveys is exemplified by this list of actual cases compiled by the American Statistical Association:

The U.S. Department of Agriculture conducted a survey to find out how poor people use food stamps.

Major TV networks rely on surveys to tell them how many and what types of people are watching their programs.

Auto manufacturers use surveys to find out how satisfied people are with their cars.

The U.S. Bureau of the Census compiles a survey every month to obtain information on employment and unemployment in the nation.

The National Center for Health Statistics sponsors a survey every year to determine how much people are spending for different types of medical care.

Local housing authorities make surveys to ascertain satisfaction of people in public housing with their living accommodations.

The Illinois Board of Higher Education surveys the interest of Illinois residents in adult education.

Local transportation authorities conduct surveys to acquire information on people's commuting and travel habits.

Magazine and trade journals utilize surveys to find out what their subscribers are reading.

Surveys are used to ascertain what sort of people use national parks and recreation areas.

Surveys of human populations also provide an important source of basic social science knowledge used by economists, psychologists, political scientists, and sociologists. Once gathered, survey information can be analyzed and re-analyzed in many different ways.

TYPES OF SURVEYS

Surveys can be classified in a number of ways.

Sample

One way is by the size and type of sample. Some surveys study the total adult population, while others focus on special population groups, for example, community leaders, physicians, the unemployed, users of a certain product. Surveys may be conducted on a national, state, or local basis, and may seek to obtain data from a few hundred or many thousands of people.

Method of Collection

Surveys can also be classified by their method of data collection: as mail surveys, telephone surveys, and personal-interview surveys. Newer methods involve recording information directly into computers, for example, measuring television audiences by devices attached to a sample of TV sets that automatically record in a computer the channels being watched.

Mail surveys are seldom used to collect information from the general public because names and addresses are not often available and the response rate tends to be low. Such surveys may be very effective with people in a particular group, like subscribers to a specialized magazine or members of a professional association. Telephone interviewing is an efficient method of collecting some types of data and is used increasingly. A personal interview in a respondent's home or office is much more expensive than a telephone survey, but necessary when complex information is needed.

Some surveys combine various methods: using the telephone to find people eligible for a particular survey, and then making an appointment for a personal interview. Some information, like the characteristics of a person's home, may be obtained by observation rather than by questioning. Self-administered questionnaires might also be used as a means to get data from groups.

Content

Content is another way to classify surveys. Some focus on opinions and attitudes (a pre-election survey of voters), while others gather information on factual characteristics or behavior (people's health, housing, or transportation habits). Many surveys combine questions of both types, asking respondents if they have heard or read about an issue, how strongly they feel about the issue and why, their interest in the issue, their past experience with it, and other factual information like age, sex, marital status, occupation, and place of residence.

Types of Questions

The questions in a survey may be *open-ended* ("Why do you feel that way about Senator X?") or *closed* ("Do you plan to vote for Senator X?"). The questions may ask the respondent to rate a political candidate or a product on some kind of scale. They may ask for a ranking of various alternatives. There may be a few questions taking only a few minutes to answer; many questions require an hour or more to complete. Changes in attitude or behavior cannot be reliably determined from a single interview, however, no matter how a survey is organized. As a result, some surveys use a panel design in which the same respondents are interviewed two or more times.

A word about people who work on surveys. An interviewer is usually a woman between thirty and sixty years of age who is skilled at approaching strangers, explaining the survey, and conducting the interview, according to the

American Statistical Association. Women interviewers arouse less fear and suspicion than men, and they can work part-time more easily then men.

HOW TO CARRY OUT A SURVEY

Planning

A survey begins when an individual or organization needs information that is not available or that does not exist. Once this need is discovered, the first step in planning a survey is to work out the objectives of the investigation.

At this point, the person needing the information should consult a polling firm to develop the methodology for carrying out the survey: defining and locating eligible respondents, deciding on how to collect the data, designing a questionnaire and pretesting it, working out procedures for minimizing or controlling response errors, designing and selecting appropriate samples, hiring and training interviewers, making plans for handling instances where there is no response, and planning tabulation and analysis of results.

Questionnaires

The design of a questionnaire is one of the most critical stages in developing a survey. Unless concepts are defined clearly and questions phrased in an unambiguous way, the data that result might contain serious bias. A question must not have a built-in answer. Phraseology must be distinct and the meaning of the question clear. Questionnaires must not be so long that they bore respondents and lead to errors or refusals to answer, yet they need to be long enough to get the desired information. The sequence of questions or sections of questions is also important, as is the decision about whether to use open-ended or closed questions. Instructions must be carefully written. Questions should not be too sensitive or written so they prejudice the respondents or invade their privacy. This creates bias and response errors.

Selecting a Sample

The choice of a proper respondent in a sample unit is a key element in survey planning. If a survey is basically factual, any knowledgeable person associated with the sample unit may be asked to supply the needed information, for example, any member of a household. In other surveys, such a household respondent will produce serious error and invalid information.

The particular type of sample depends on the objective and scope of the survey, including the budget, the method of data collection, the subject matter, and the kind of respondent needed. The first step in deciding on an appropriate sampling method is to define the relevant population, whether it be persons or businesses or institutions, in the entire country or in a single city. Types of samples range from simple random selection of population units to highly complex samples involving many stages of selection.

Whether simple or complex, the most important characteristic of a properly designed sample is that all the units in the target population have a known, nonzero chance of being included in the sample. This feature of a survey makes it scientifically valid to draw inferences from the sample results about the entire population that the sample represents.

A critical element in sample design and selection is defining the source of materials from which a sample can be chosen: a list of housing units, a list of retail establishments, a list of students in a university. If a geographic area with well-defined natural or artificial boundaries is the method chosen, a sample area is picked and an interviewer canvasses the sample area segments and lists the appropriate downtown retail or other units so that some or all of them can be included in the first sample.

Conducting a Survey

All the careful plans in the world are futile if the survey is carried out improperly. For personal or telephone interview surveys, the interviewers must be carefully trained in the concept, definition, and procedures of the survey. The training involves holding practice interviews and giving interviewers a familiarity with the variety of situations that they will likely encounter. Interviewers must also be given ample copies of the questionnaire, a reference manual, and information about the sample unit and where it is located.

Before interviewers go out, survey organizations should send an advance letter to the respondent explaining the purpose of the survey and telling him or her that the interviewer will be calling soon. Interviewers should be told the best time of day to call or visit and the number of allowable "callbacks" when no one is at home.

The American Statistical Association (ASA) cautions against taking shortcuts in surveying that might invalidate the results and badly mislead the user. These shortcuts include (1) failure to use a proper sampling procedure, (2) no pretest of field procedures, (3) failure to follow up nonrespondents, and (4) inadequate quality control.

USING SURVEY RESULTS

The ASA also notes that the statistics gained from a survey rarely correspond exactly with the unknown truth. But the value of a statistic does not depend on its being exactly true. The more important requirement for a statistic is that it be sufficiently reliable to serve the needs of those sponsoring the survey. No general standard of reliability applies to all surveys because the margin of error that can be tolerated in a study depends on the action or recommendations that will be influenced by the data. For example, economists examining unemployment rates consider 0.2 percent as having an important bearing on the U.S. economy. Thus, the government surveys on unemployment try to keep their margin of error below 0.2 percent. In other instances, a high error rate is acceptable.

No general rule on reliability is possible. It all depends on the purpose of the study, how the data will be used, and the effect of errors of various sizes on the action taken based on the survey results. These factors will affect the sample size, the design of the questionnaire, the effort put into training and supervising the interview staff. Estimates of error also need to be considered in analyzing and interpreting survey results.

In any survey, errors of two kinds will result, sampling and nonsampling.

Sampling Errors

In good surveys, sampling errors will be calculated and information about them made available to all users of the statistics. They should also be made a part of any published results. The best way to describe and present data on sampling errors is to note the percentage of likely error when giving the final statistics of the survey (a candidate is ahead of his opponent by a certain percent with the error rate unlikely to be more than 3 percent, or whatever the figure is).

Nonsampling Errors

There is no simple and direct way of estimating the size of nonsampling errors. In most surveys it is not practical to try to calculate the possible effects on the statistics of the various potential sources of error. Nonsampling errors fall into two groups, random errors, whose effect cancel out in large samples; and biases, which tend to create errors and cumulate over the entire sample. With large samples, the possible biases are the principal causes for concern about the quality of a survey.

The main causes of bias — that is, a predisposition to be prejudiced — are sampling operations, noninterviews, adequacy of respondent, understanding the concept, lack of knowledge to answer questions, concealment of the truth, loaded questions, processing errors, conceptual problems when the survey misses the point of the needed information, interviewer error where questions are misread or answers twisted.

All surveys will not have all of these errors. It is considered good practice to report on any of them that have occurred.

Confidentiality

All reputable survey organizations strive to keep survey information confidential. They subscribe to professional codes of ethics that include such safeguards as using code numbers to identify respondents; refusing to give names and addresses of respondents to anybody outside the organization, including the client for whom the survey is being made, destroying questionnaires and identifying information about respondents after responses have been put onto computer tape, omitting names and addresses of survey respondents from computer tapes for analysis, and presenting statistical tabulations by broad enough categories that individual respondents cannot be singled out.

PLANNING A SURVEY

Know Something about Surveys

Any person contacting a public-opinion polling firm should understand the methodology of surveys so that he or she can talk intelligently with people at the firm. Consulting a statistician will help, and so will a basic course on surveying in a marketing, psychology, sociology, or statistics department of a local college.

Prepare a Proposal in Advance

It is important for any company PR person or agency account executive to develop the specifications of what he or she wants to find out before calling in a survey firm. The PR person should have an idea of sample type and size, and of what the goals are. He or she should put these specifications in writing clearly and concisely before calling on a survey firm.

The Price Depends on the Type of Survey

Although some older firms emphasize the face-to-face interview, this approach is very expensive. It is also more difficult now to find good interviewers than in the past. Fewer and fewer people are willing to let a stranger into their homes. For their part, interviewers are increasingly afraid to go into certain parts of town, which results in a whole area and group of people being missed.

Mail and telephone surveys are cheaper than the face-to-face type. It is also easier to monitor interviewers in a telephone survey. A supervisor can listen in on calls and immediately correct mistakes that interviewers make, which is not possible with face-to-face interviews.

Consider the Omnibus or "Piggyback" Survey

Omnibus or "piggyback" surveys combine the interests of many clients in a single interview. Here the respondents are asked a group of questions on one subject, another group of questions on another subject, and so on until all the questions of the various sponsors have been provided. Large polling firms like the Gallup organization do omnibus surveys every two to four weeks throughout the year. Using a standard sample of 1,500 interviews in 300 interviewing areas, Gallup uses personal in-home interviews and reports results by telephone within three to four weeks, with final printed reports available ten days later. An independent sample of individuals is selected for each interviewing period. The sampling procedure is designed to produce an approximation of the U.S. civilian adult population living in private households, excluding those living in prisons, hospitals, or military bases. Survey data can be applied to this population in order to project percentages to numbers of people.

The cost of an omnibus survey is based on the number of questions and whether questions are open-ended or closed, the latter being cheaper. In this way, a company can get national survey results for $10,000 as opposed to several hundred thousand dollars for a survey conducted exclusively for it nationwide. At times the latter approach is necessary, but many times an omnibus will be an ideal way for a company or other organization to get survey results quickly at low cost.

Budget for a Survey Carefully

When applied to a survey, budget applies to time as well as money. A company PR person needs to calculate in advance the need for surveys throughout the year, and set aside money to pay for them. It is equally important to allow enough time for a survey firm to do its work. A brief survey can be done in two or three weeks, but a long and complicated national survey can take months and even a year to complete. It is a good idea for a PR person to work out a flow diagram of all that has to be done in the survey and then keep track of the progress of each of the many parts.

Select a Survey Firm Carefully

Because there are good and bad survey firms in business, it is important to shop around before selecting one to conduct a public-opinion poll. It is perfectly appropriate to ask a prospective firm for a list of clients, and to call these clients to see how satisfied they were with the results. It is a good idea to note how well the firm responds to the proposal. It is important to know what kind of analysis will be used. Everything the survey firm agrees to do should be put in writing; it is a mistake to go by verbal understandings. Survey experts agree that the worst mistake a person can make is to select the name of the first survey firm in the telephone book without knowing anything about it.

SUMMARY

A good way to find out if various public-relations programs are reaching their goals is to conduct a public-opinion survey. Few companies or agencies have the ability to do so on their own, so it is best to contact an outside public-opinion survey firm. Such an organization will conduct a survey in order to get the information desired by the sponsoring company or agency. In the survey, which will be conducted face to face, on the telephone, or by mail, a small group of people, called a sample, are questioned. Because it has been carefully selected by age, location, job, education level, and other factors, this sample provides information that can be extrapolated to the larger population. Surveys can be useful tools for people in PR if they are handled carefully.

PR FOCUS: A SURVEY THAT DID NOT WORK

A national organization interested in influencing congressional legislation wanted to ascertain public attitudes on a number of issues. The purpose was to target its efforts in reaching the public with the organization's policies, goals, and philosophy. The organization's director of information was asked to select a survey firm and work with a committee of the organization's staff to plan the study. This committee met with the survey staff of the firm on several occasions and recommended several policy areas that might be targets of the study. Because of the budget and time constraints, the director of information selected only a few areas and authorized a final summary report. Little additional planning or coordination between the committee and the survey firm took place. Everyone sat back and waited for reports to be submitted.

The result was a disaster. The organization received a series of reports — no more than a few pages long — summarizing some marginal item percents and showing little, if any, analysis of demographic, knowledge, or attitudinal variables. Little information was gained that was not already publicly known. The sample sizes in most cases were so small that additional analysis could not be completed with a satisfactory degree of statistical precision or confidence.

Reviewing this experience, the organization concluded that there had been a number of faults with the study.

1. *The problem was never clearly defined.* No one in the organization under-
    stood the strengths or weaknesses of a sample survey, or the basic stages
    of the survey process, so they were not able to evaluate what the research
    firm was doing. Also, everyone in the sponsoring organization had too
    high an expectation of what a survey could do for them. There were no
    definite plans about how to use the information.
2. *Many of the questions were poorly constructed.* They were not properly
    set up to determine the information the organization really wanted.
3. *The sample was too small to allow a meaningful analysis.*
4. *Many of the conclusions of the survey were useless and could have been
    learned by simple reading.* This literature was readily available and
    would have helped the organization just as much as the survey, at far
    less cost.

What the organization learned was that a public-opinion survey by itself
is no magic answer. The director of information and others in the organization
should have developed a task force within the organization to focus on the
problem or problems already identified. Staff members should have been directed to read the literature. Then, alternative procedures for determining what
they wanted to learn should have been specified and evaluated. Finally, a
decision on conducting a survey should have been made only after everyone
agreed that one was needed and what to do with the results. After that, a request for bids should have been developed specifying the general outline of
the study and sent to a number of firms. Selection of the firm should have
been made on the basis of the specific proposal that was responsive to the bid
request.

The director of information should have monitored the activities of the
survey firm, requiring progress reports so that he would know how things were
going from day to day. The general outline of the final report should have
been agreed upon before the contract was signed. A verbal presentation of
findings and recommendations should have been required as part of the reporting process after a draft of the report with specific conclusions and recommendations had been submitted. If these steps had been followed, much of the
disappointment and acrimony could have been avoided.

PR FOCUS: A SURVEY THAT WORKED

A small private telephone company located in the West was beset with labor
unrest. The firm had been owned by a single family since it began in the
1920s. The head of the firm, the son of the founder, was an engineer; because

of him, the company boasted the most modern equipment in the industry. It had been the first company in the state to install direct-distance dialing, for example, and was proud of adopting other innovations for the industry. Wage rates were equal to, or superior to, those paid in the industry, although workers were not represented by a union.

Despite all this, workers were dissatisfied. Management heard rumblings of this but was not able to find out what was wrong. Wage increases and fringe benefits continued to be offered, but workers were still unhappy. The president finally turned to a commercial opinion-research firm to conduct an employee-opinion survey to find out what was wrong.

The company gave workers compensatory time to complete, in group settings, a lengthy, self-administered questionnaire in which their anonymity was protected.

The results were very revealing. Dissatisfaction did not hinge on wage levels but on unfairness in promotions and seniority rights. The workers viewed management as paternalistic and not allowing workers enough say in decisions affecting their welfare. Many members of individual families were on the payroll, and many had been promoted over those who were more competent and who had been with the company longer. Nepotism had seriously eroded employee morale despite high wage levels and good fringe benefits. As long as the practice continued, the labor unrest would be a problem.

Once these issues had been identified, the president moved to involve workers in management decisions affecting them, including the setting up of a system for promotions that both sides agreed was fair.

REVIEW QUESTIONS

1. What is a survey?
2. What are the different types of surveys?
3. What are the steps in carrying out a survey?
4. How can a survey be scientifically valid?
5. How can public-relations people best use surveys?
6. What is the best way to proceed in using a survey?

ASSIGNMENTS

For Journalism and Business Students

1. You are the public-relations person for a company that makes motor homes. You have had success with some of your publics — stockholders, employees — but not with the general public, which is worried about high

gasoline prices. To help you develop a campaign for the general public, you have decided to hire a polling firm. What do you want it to find out?

2.   Use the same scenario as 1 but substitute airline safety as the subject to be surveyed.

3.   Use the same scenario as 1 but substitute the fruit growers of California plagued by an infestation of the Mediterranean fruit fly as the subject to be surveyed.

4.   You are the PR person for a company that makes motorcycles and a public-opinion polling has just revealed that 20 percent of people polled think your product is unsafe. The board of directors wants to ignore the results, but you think that a new PR safety campaign needs to be carried out. What do you do?

CHAPTER 23

Public relations: The legal and ethical aspects

LAW AND PUBLIC RELATIONS

Public-relations people may not be aware of them, but potential legal problems exist as they conduct even the most routine aspects of their profession. The writing of news releases, especially those about the financial affairs of a company; the preparation of institutional advertisements; the development of internal and external brochures and other publications — all of these reasonably mundane PR activities can get a PR person into legal trouble.

Worse, PR people can be hauled into court just for doing their primary job of advising management in their dealings with the various publics. In effect, they have become victims of their own success as advisers and counselors, the goal that many in the profession have striven to reach for years. As high-level parts of management themselves, these PR people become privy to corporate secrets and strategies of doing business. They give advice on courses of action to be followed, and the advice is followed. If the suggested approach gets the company into legal trouble, the PR person will get the blame.

Two major areas present the most common sources of legal difficulty: government agencies, and other laws dealing with libel, invasion of privacy, and copyright, the last three faced by anyone in journalism.

Government Agencies

The Securities and Exchange Commission (SEC) is the watchdog agency for all corporations whose stocks are sold on national stock exchanges and over the counter at brokerage firms. The commission, established in 1934, requires these companies to file registration statements with it, as well as annual reports to update the statements. It also polices brokerage houses and regulates the over-the-counter market. The problems for public-relations people come in getting SEC clearance for the wording of annual reports and news releases about all financial aspects of a company. The SEC also requires that news releases ap-

374

pear at certain times; for example, one announcing earnings must come out at the same time a company files its annual report on form $10 - K$.

Court decisions in two landmark cases affect public relations and the dealings of the company with the SEC. The 1968 *Texas Gulf Sulphur* case, detailed in Chapter 8, made it illegal for corporate insiders to engage in securities dealings on the basis of material, nonpublic corporate information. Such material corporate information should be disclosed to the investing public via a news release unless there is a legitimate reason for withholding it. Companies have a responsibility to disclose information to the investing public, said the SEC, and the courts agreed.

The *Arvida* case dealt with public offerings of corporate stock. When a company is "in registration," that is, preparing to offer shares of stock for sale to the public, the SEC keeps careful control of publicity from that company lest such publicity seem to mislead or promote stock sales. In 1958, Arthur Vining Davis formed the Arvida Corporation and then transferred several large tracts of land in Florida to the new company. Two Wall Street firms agreed to underwrite a public offering of stock later in the year. A news release and press conference followed soon after, and the story got wide play.

The SEC, however, was not pleased. It said that the news release read "precisely like a letter which a distributor would send to a prospective purchaser in an effort to persuade him to invest in the enterprise. The only thing it does not do is specifically ask the reader to send in his order." After hearing the publicity, investors asked their brokers and dealers about the stock, understandable under the circumstances but before a registration statement had been filed with the SEC for the securities. The SEC soon charged the Arvida Corporation and its underwriters with violation of the Securities Act of 1933, which makes it illegal to offer to buy or sell any security unless a registration statement has been filed. Although the company had acted in good faith, the law had been violated.

These two instances provide good examples of the tightrope a company and its public-relations people must walk in dealing with the SEC. The intricate rules of that agency make it imperative that a careful clearance process be set up for news releases or any other printed publication dealing with financial matters. This process should include appropriate corporate officers and the legal department.

The Federal Trade Commission (FTC), which regulates competition and controls unfair or deceptive practices in interstate commerce, also passes judgment on advertising and news releases. If the FTC decides that an ad or a release contains false or misleading information, it can take the offending company to court. Congress has sought to reduce its power in recent years, but the FTC is still operating under the broadened authority given to it in the Magnuson-Moss Act. Accordingly, the commission began to issue trade-regulation rules on various subjects affecting areas within its jurisdiction.

One of these rules contained a definition of advertising: "Any written or oral statement, illustration or depiction, which is designed to affect the sale of any [product], or create interest in the purchase of such product, whether the same appear in a newspaper, magazine, leaflet, circular, mailer, book insert, catalogue, sales promotional material, other periodical literature, billboard, public transit card, or in a radio or television broadcast or in any other medium."

In commenting on the definition in *Public Relations Journal,* lawyer Morton J. Simon notes that the definition is not limited to a paid communication or "advertisement" as that term is normally understood. Nor are PR or publicity statements exempted in an accompanying FTC staff report. Using this language, Simon says, a commission staff member might make a case against a company if a press release or other "statement" contained deceptive or unfair claims, even though its original purpose was not to sell products directly.

Given this FTC penchant to sue, company PR people should avoid putting claims about products in news releases unless those claims have been authenticated. Exaggeration should be avoided in all news releases anyway (see Chapter 12), but especially since such language might get the company in trouble with the FTC.

But institutional advertising can be just as worrisome as product advertising. The use of such advertisements to improve company images increased greatly in the 1960s and 1970s. The ads were particularly prevalent among oil, chemical, and other companies accused of polluting the environment. Consumer groups, the Environmental Protection Agency, and individual congressmen and senators complained about companies that stated too strongly that they had not been guilty of damaging the environment. The FTC took no immediate action but started following a balancing test, according to Simon, that took into consideration "whether the dominant appeal and likely effect of the advertisement is commercial."

When the FTC begins an investigation, by the way, it requests copies of all ads, news releases, company magazines, and other publications.

Other Laws

Public-relations people are subject to a number of other laws that apply equally to journalists or anyone else communicating publicly.

Libel is a malicious, false, and defamatory statement issued in printed form, and it can subject anyone guilty of it to civil and, occasionally, criminal action. A person in public relations can libel an individual or a company in a news release or other printed publication. Care and attention — and, when necessary, legal advice — should be paid to the preparation of all material issued by a company or by a PR agency in the name of a client.

Libel has four defenses: truth; fair comment and criticism (where what was written was restricted to the work of another and without malice); privilege (where material of an official nature is immune to libel action); and the *New York Times* Rule (in which the U.S. Supreme Court in 1964 ruled that public officials cannot collect libel damages unless they can prove that what was written about them was a malicious and deliberate lie). This ruling was extended to private individuals involved in matters of public interest in *Rosenbloom* v. *Metromedia* (1971). In the *Gertz* decision (1974), the *Firestone* decision (1976), and the *Hutchinson* and *Wolston* decisions (both in 1979), the court gave more protection to private individuals (*Gertz*) and public figures (the other three) in libel cases, thus increasing the risk for journalists and others like PR people.

Invasion of privacy applies to public relations because a picture, name, letter to or from, or a direct quote of a person cannot be used in publicity or advertising without the written consent of that person. If something of that nature is used in a news release, brochure, annual report, or company magazine, the PR person responsible and the company can have legal problems without the written release. The problem usually surfaces most often in advertisement, although PR people can run afoul of the privacy laws if they use the name or the words of a person without that person's consent in an institutional ad. Sometimes the violation results from the use of a voice sounding like that of another person. For example, the actress Katharine Hepburn once sued a fish company for using someone imitating her easily recognizable voice in a commercial. The words were read by someone else, but they sounded like her. The court agreed, and she won her case.

The U.S. Supreme Court has seldom ruled in this area of the law, and local rulings vary from state to state. In general, a PR person will be on safe ground by getting a signed release for both words and pictures from those involved. The release need not be elaborate; often, if the need arises frequently, a preprinted form can be prepared. The person signs the original and keeps a copy. Releases are seldom looked at after being put in a file drawer, but it is essential to have them in the rare instances when they are needed.

The release itself should specify the material for which the permission is sought (interview, photograph, speech, excerpt, letter), where this material will be used, the name and address of the PR person, and a place to sign at the bottom as well as address and date. A photo release form is equally simple. It grants permission to use the photographs taken of the person on a specific date, at a specific place, to the PR person and his or her company, for use in a specific publication. A release for general use may also be obtained. If a minor is involved, his or her parent must sign the form as well. It is also a good idea to get releases signed by employees too. They may not work at the company forever, and at a later date they might deny that they gave oral permission.

In the area of privacy, particular care must be taken for those in hospital public information. The privacy of patients and of their medical records must be preserved. In Oregon, patients must give their written consent before a hospital will allow interviews and photographs. If the patient is a minor, the permission of a parent or guardian must be obtained as well. The physician on the case must be informed of the request too. For each specific request for photographs, the hospital should require a completed, dated, and signed patient consent form for its records and protection prior to the picture taking. This consent form should then be filed as a permanent part of the patient's record. Requests to interview or photograph a patient under arrest or custody should be referred to the police department or government agency with jurisdiction.

The hospital spokesperson may decline to grant permission to interview or photograph a patient if such actions interfere with the patient's well-being or with the delivery of patient care. In any interview, the public-information person should stay with a patient throughout to help him or her and to protect his or her rights. Those persons who are suffering from severe illness or injury are rarely interviewed. A hospital spokesperson can give out basic information on a patient (name, residence, sex, age, occupation, whether the patient is unconscious, plus a statement of condition and a general description of injuries) in, for example, those cases reported by fire or police departments. In cases not on the public record, these facts will be released if the patient or the family give permission.

Such protection is eased a bit when the patient is a prominent person. Such people give up some rights to privacy, usually at their own request. When a prominent person is hospitalized, the hospital will cooperate with the patient, family, and physician to provide information about the patient's illness and to protect his or her privacy where possible. If the prominent person has a spokesperson, all requests for information should be directed to him or her. When the prominent person is in serious or critical condition, the hospital should arrange for medical bulletins to be issued on a regular basis. These bulletins should be issued through the physician and with the consent of the family.

The hospital public-information person can give the general nature of the accident or illness but not the specific circumstances. Further medical information dealing with specific situations can be given on fractures, injuries to the head, skull fractures, internal injuries, unconsciousness, shooting or stabbing, burns, poisoning, battered children, and rape, whether the person is famous or not.

Standard definitions should be used to describe a patient's condition:

Good — Vital signs, such as pulse, temperature, and blood pressure, are stable and within normal limits. The patient is conscious and comfortable.

Fair — Vital signs are stable and within normal limits. The patient is conscious; however, he or she is uncomfortable and may have minor complications.

Serious — Vital signs may be unstable or outside normal limits. The patient is acutely ill.

Critical — Vital signs are unstable or outside normal limits. There are major complications.

In giving such a statement of condition, a hospital spokesperson should never offer a prognosis. In case of death, not usually announced by a hospital, a spokesperson can reveal that fact if the next of kin have been notified. If the next of kin have not been notified, the press can be told that and given the name of the attending physician. In the case of the death of a prominent person, the hospital has the responsibility to contact the press after notifying the patient's relatives. Information of cause of death can be given only by the physician with the approval of the family, or by the family itself. If the death is the subject of a medical examiner's investigation, inquiries should be directed to that office. The name of a mortician can be released. The fact that a person committed suicide or attempted it should not be announced by the hospital.

Medical records are always confidential and are never revealed except by a patient or a family.

Most states have a set of guidelines similar to that in Oregon, prepared by the Oregon Hospital Public Relations Organization.

Public-information persons at hospitals can still have occasional problems. There are so many gray areas that are impossible to anticipate in a code applying to general situations.

Ken Niehans, former director of public information at the University of Oregon Medical School, once announced that a child had died when she was still being kept alive on a machine. "The resident said, 'She'll be dead by morning,'" he recalls, "but she lived two or three more days and the doctors couldn't agree on whether she was dead." In the meantime, the girl's family had held a memorial service for her. "That was the one time I could have been sued," says Niehans.

Copyright grants its owner the exclusive right to print, publish, or reproduce an original literary, musical, or artistic work for a certain number of years. The federal government has the authority to grant a copyright, which must first be registered by following a set procedure that includes filling out the appropriate form (obtained from the Register of Copyrights, The Library of Congress, Washington, D.C. 20559); printing the word "Copyright," the abbreviation "Copr" or the © symbol with the name of the company on the title page of the publication to be copyrighted; and sending the form, a fee, and two copies of the publication to the Register of Copyrights.

A PR person will not need to copyright everything produced in his or her office. Only if something is unique and distinctive — for example, a booklet on a subject that seems of real use to its readers and is not just self-serving to the company — should it be copyrighted. Only an entire publication or advertisement can be copyrighted, but not a slogan, an idea, or a symbol. Permission must usually be secured to reproduce a trademark.

Public-relations people need to consider copyright, however, as it applies to the works of others. They must be careful not to use copyrighted material in their publications beyond the limitations allowed. What the copyright law calls "fair use" is permitted. This allows a writer to use a reasonable amount of material from a published work if proper credit is given, for example, less than 150 words of a textbook. But material from trade books, letters, speeches, news articles, feature stories, syndicated materials, illustrations, and all photographs except those of public personalities must not be used without permission. A simple form will suffice in granting this permission, similar to that discussed earlier for people interviewed and photographed. Something in the public domain (all government publications), never copyrighted, or now out of copyright, needs no permission. A revision of the copyright law took effect on January 1, 1978 that extended the duration of a copyright to a term lasting for the author's life, plus an additional fifty years. In the old law, dating from 1909, the maximum amount of time for a copyright was fifty-six years.

With care and discretion, and after checking with the legal department, the public relations person can avoid difficulty. In extremely fractious situations, the corporate attorneys often take over, telling the PR people what to release.

ETHICS AND PUBLIC RELATIONS

Ethics in public relations is governed by two factors: the Code of Professional Standards published by the Public Relations Society of America (noted in Chapter 3), and the conscience and training of PR people themselves. The Declaration of Principles that accompanies the code pledges professionalism, the improvement of individual competence, and adherence to the code, which deals with a number of potential ethical problems and how to avoid them. (Copies of the complete declaration, code, and interpretations can be obtained from PRSA, 845 Third Avenue, New York, New York 10022.)

Public-relations people who belong to PRSA and those who do not have probably worked within such guidelines all their professional lives. If not, they could not keep their jobs very long. An unethical person is soon revealed by his or her actions; if not in a first job, the unscrupulousness will come out in the second one, and the person will soon be unemployable. Violators can also be drummed out of PRSA after a proper hearing.

Ethics generally becomes so ingrained in a PR person's soul that its practice is second nature, an automatic extension of the way a person has conducted himself or herself. That is not to say that unethical people do not work in PR. There are some of them, as in any large field. They do not last very long, however. Co-workers and clients and employers will not long work with them.

Ethical pressures abound, in spite of the code and whatever the backgrounds of the PR people themselves. Corporations have been undergoing their own pressures since the early 1970s from environmental and consumer groups and from revelations of illegal corporate political contributions and bribery to gain business overseas. It was only natural for corporate officials, in turn, to seek help from their PR people. Could they lessen the damage by hiding the truth or at least putting the best face on the negative information revealed about the company? Some PR people would try, but others refused to do so.

A number of officials regularly ask PR people to do other things that compromise their ethics. Can they comply? For some, the requests to write news releases that deliberately mislead, to delay bad news, to lie to reporters and investors, and to cover up things are impossible to fulfill. If they refuse, they may have to quit. If they comply, they may have trouble living with themselves. The process leads to pressure and stress, so much of it, in fact, that a federal occupational health report in 1978 ranked PR positions sixth among jobs showing the highest admission rates to mental-health institutions, according to the *Wall Street Journal*.

PR people have their own opinions on ethics, formed from years of experience.

"For me, ethics are not an issue," says Victor Pesqueira of Xerox, "because it never occurs to me not to be ethical, other than, perhaps in a procedural sense. Do you have separate press conferences for print and radio-TV? Do you give one magazine a break on an announcement? Most weekly magazines need breaks to be competitive. Their deadlines won't always coincide nicely with your announcement date. Knowing to whom to give a break and knowing when to give it is a judgmental risk that is part of this business."

"Ethics come into play in representing competing accounts," says John Pihas, president of Pihas, Schmidt, Westerdahl in Portland. "We have a number of real-estate accounts that we have to keep separate. You also have to ask yourself and the client on occasion, 'Is this really a news story? We can take your money, but why don't you send out a letter to employees?' Things have changed a lot in regards to ethics. You can hardly take a reporter out to lunch any more. Christmas creates a few ethical problems. We usually don't do anything but we used to give a bottle of wine. We'll announce a press party to distribute a press kit for a client over dinner and drinks. A number of people we invited will call back and ask, 'What is this all about?' All you can do is buy a guy a drink or send him a note about a nice job of covering something."

"The professional people who have lasted are as ethical as in any other profession," says Joan Dolph, formerly with West Point Pepperell. "It's just good business. You have to have a token for everything that's offered. A good newsperson is as interested in a good story as you are. If they respect you and you respect them, you don't have to be unethical in your dealings with them."

SUMMARY

Potential legal and ethical problems confront the public-relations person every day. Most of the time, however, the problems can be avoided by knowing that they exist and, in the case of the legal ones, consulting company lawyers for help in avoiding them. Legal difficulties lurk for PR people doing their daily jobs in dealing with government agencies like the Securities and Exchange Commission and the Federal Trade Commission, and in following court rulings and laws dealing with libel, invasion of privacy, and copyright. Ethical problems are more ephemeral and elusive. They arise daily but can be dealt with not with law and regulation but with background, experience, common sense, and principles like those promulgated by organizations like PRSA.

PR FOCUS: ETHICAL HYPOTHETICALS

Franklin James has had a reasonably lucrative public-relations firm for ten years, but the really big success he had dreamed about in college had eluded him. He has thrived on a number of small and medium real-estate accounts. One day the telephone in his office rings, and the caller proposes a deal he cannot refuse. If he will represent a new client in the area, that client will assure him a substantial income for the rest of his life. The caller represents some Arab interests who want to buy all the land around a nearby lake and develop it into small estates, condominiums, a shopping mall, and an industrial park. James does not commit himself on the telephone, but he is elated at the prospect of handling the new account. The problem with the proposal, however, is that the new venture will likely put all his real-estate accounts out of business. They have long handled the sale of small vacation lots and cottages at the lake, as well as business and residential sales in town. The new venture will leave them little to handle. What should Franklin James do in light of points 4 and 8 of the PRSA code?

What if Dolores Morris had known that her promise to Imperial Oil was a lie? The possibilities present in her acquisition of the oil company account was worth the risk. She had promised to get the state Sierra Club to call off its opposition to Imperial's new refinery next to the game preserve. After all, she had represented the club *for free* for five years as a public service, and even served on its board, for God's sake. What harm would a bit of lobbying do on behalf of Imperial? All those new jobs would help the economy of the entire region. Some of those new jobs might be in her own agency. What should Morris do? Has she even read points 2 and 13 of the PRSA code?

If Robert Martin could only get the press on the side of Edgar Hastings, the old man would set him up for the rest of his life. Martin had been PR director of Hastings' umbrella company, the 20/40 Group, for only six months. So what if Hastings was eccentric and right-wing? Weren't all billionaires supposed to be that way? At least he was presentable, not like Howard Hughes, lying around those moldy hotel rooms with matted hair and long fingernails. Hastings wanted to be liked by the press and was sick of those stories that called him "reclusive" and "unscrupulous." He also wanted to be seen in a better light by the public and its representatives in Congress. You see, he was buying both an airline and an aircraft manufacturing company next month, and he would probably have to go before a Senate antitrust committee to explain his actions. Martin had about decided to go through with his plan. After all, Hastings had given him unlimited money to do the job. He would send every aviation and business writer a round-trip ticket to Las Vegas, $2,000 in silver dollars, arrange for their hotel and food, even get them girls if they wanted them. At the appropriate time, they would all be flown by helicopter to Hastings' ranch for a get-acquainted session with him. What did it matter if some sections of the PRSA code were violated? He needed to cement his future.

REVIEW QUESTIONS

1. What kind of potential legal problems exist for people in PR?
2. How can legal problems be avoided?
3. What is the best way to deal with the Securities and Exchange Commission?
4. What is the best way to deal with the Federal Trade Commission?
5. How great a problem is libel for PR people?
6. How can invasion of privacy be avoided as a PR problem?
7. What measures are necessary to avoid violating copyright laws?
8. How do ethics apply to public relations?
9. What good is a code like that of the Public Relations Society of America?
10. What are some of the ethical problems PR people face daily?

ASSIGNMENTS

For Journalism and Business Students

1. Research the SEC rules that apply to printed materials, and write a report on them.
2. Research the FTC rules that apply to institutional advertising, and write a report on them.
3. Examine the U.S. Supreme Court decisions that apply to libel, and write a report that analyzes their possible impact on public relations.
4. Research recent court decisions in the privacy area, and analyze in writing their application to public relations.
5. Research the new copyright law, and write a research paper that analyzes its application to public relations.

6.   How ethical are the public-relations people in your town? Interview five of them and ask them how they feel about the principles in the PRSA code. Then ask reporters on local papers and radio and TV stations how closely the PR people you interviewed follow the PRSA principles. Report your findings to the class.

CHAPTER 24

Public relations: A future and a career

A Route to the Top
Self-Consciousness and Feelings of Inferiority
What Makes a Good PR Person?
Summary
Review Questions

Public relations.

The words themselves contain the answer to any questions about the survival of the profession. As long as there are *publics* to be *related* to, public relations will hold its distinctive place in the world.

The profession has grown steadily in size over the years of its existence. PR has thrived in boom times and has been cut back in the Depression and numerous recessions, only to reemerge unscathed when conditions improved. The power of PR has grown as well. More and more corporations and non-profit organizations are realizing that they must tell their side of the story, both to the outside world and to their own employees. While far too many company presidents still avoid turning to PR people until it is too late for them to help, an increasing number of companies are including PR in the decision-making process at all times. Each year, public relations is represented at the vice presidential level of more and more companies in the United States and abroad.

A ROUTE TO THE TOP

This high-level access has made public relations a good vehicle for reaching top management, a thing deemed impossible only a few years ago, when PR was only beginning to emerge as a profession. Today, troubled as they are by hostile consumer groups and demanding labor unions, companies need more help than in the past. They are turning to PR people for help, paying them more and listening to what they say.

The much pilloried "flack" has now become a high-level counselor. Public relations has become a true profession for which people train and prepare in much the same way they would for medicine and law. No longer do people enter the ranks of PR because they cannot get another job. They become PR people because of the challenges and rewards it offers as a good career.

"Public relations is a career that if an individual approaches properly can lead to more than PR," says Ted Weber, executive vice president of

McGraw-Hill and its former PR director. "A good PR person is a generalist and a generalist is a problem solver that PR needs very badly."

Adds Gwil Evans, chairman of communication of the Oregon State University Extension Service: "I think PR has changed its own image. When I was a student, PR was viewed askance, as the flack. The quality of the practice is higher than before; we've learned a lot. The principles stay the same. They are fundamental. But techniques change constantly. The biggest challenge facing PR professionals today is to maintain some kind of reasonable balance between being good in the things that don't change and keeping up with the technical changes that come ever faster. There is a risk of feeling left behind if you don't pay attention to technical changes."

John Pihas of Pihas, Schmidt, Westerdahl in Portland, Oregon sees even bigger changes for public-relations people in the immediate future. "PR is going to change dramatically," he says. "What you're getting is PR with marketing, consumer affairs and sales promotion under it. Every ad you run has an impact on sales. As society gets more complex problems and people are less inclined to take things at face value, public relations will be more important. PR has got to quit being so self-conscious."

SELF-CONSCIOUSNESS AND FEELINGS OF INFERIORITY

Such self-consciousness goes back to the days when people inside and outside companies and nonprofit organizations thought of PR people as unprofessional hacks who could not succeed elsewhere.

"As soon as you say you're in PR, people think immediately it's shaky," says Jeff Clausen of Marx, Knoll & Mangels, Inc. "A lot of people — PR people — are around who don't know anything about PR. A lot of companies change the name to corporate communication or public affairs because of the bad connotations of the term. I consider myself to be ethical and honest. But you worry about the image."

"PR people spend a disproportional amount of time proving they are professionals," continues Ted Weber. "It's like an inferiority complex, a perception of what exists. A career with that mind set is not satisfying. The inferiority complex might come from the fact that PR people come from journalism. They have turned their backs on a career that is professional. PR people, rather than standing up and being identified with management, seek refuge in the aura of their former profession. This gets in their way in PR."

WHAT MAKES A GOOD PR PERSON?

Anyone contemplating a career in public relations should measure his or her own abilities and interests with the demands of the profession. A good PR person must:

Be a Good Listener

"I've found one of my biggest frustrations in the administrative meetings I go to are people who don't listen," says Gwil Evans. "I'm impatient with those people. They've never learned how to listen. If I'm going to give someone counsel, it's very important that I listen to them and take copious notes of what they say."

Know the Media

Since PR people depend on the press and electronic media to help them do their jobs, they should know how the various parts operate. This knowledge should best come from a few years of personal experience on a weekly or daily newspaper or a radio or TV station. This experience has become less important in recent years because of the increase in public-relations courses and majors. "The best communicators are those who are still thrilled when their news release is picked up in a paper or their PSA is used on television," continues Evans. "You need to see the kind of impact media has on an audience, and you realize you can never take it for granted."

Be a Good Problem Solver

As PR people have risen in management, so has the need for them to be able to tackle company or organizational problems and help solve them. The ability to conceptualize things and then list the ways to proceed is invaluable. "Here is the problem; this is what we should do in five steps," or ten or whatever it takes. The good PR counsel will come up with a suggested course of action.

Possess Good Communications Skills

The ability to write, edit, take photographs, make speeches, assess layout and design, and produce material for radio or TV are all important in public relations.

Like to Work with People

All the publics in PR contain people, and PR practitioners will have to deal with one or more of these groups every day. Anyone who hates meeting new people and encountering new situations will dislike PR. Outgoing, friendly individuals do well in PR.

Be Comfortable in the Profession

"Public relations is a matter of advocacy and it bothers me," says Ted Michel, director of investor relations at Levi Strauss. "My previous editorial training was to be objective. I've never been comfortable with the advocacy role." A person should not take a PR job unless he or she believes in the company and its products. To do otherwise is to prostitute oneself and sell out.

Have Initiative

In a good company or nonprofit organization with a well-defined public-relations role, a person will have a great deal of room to come up with new ideas and programs. "There is a lot of room for initiative," continues Michel. "If you're not generating things as a PR man, you're either tired or there's something wrong."

Be Articulate

"I would recommend PR as a career only if someone is articulate," says Vic Pesqueira of Xerox. "A PR man is like a lawyer. He does for the company what it would do for itself if it knew how. In our business, that requires knowing the language, but more to the point, how to use it with skill."

Enjoy Variety

"PR never gets dull," says Thomas Nunan of Burson-Marsteller. "I am dealing with five or six clients a day, each with totally different programs and markets. You're using broadcast, videotape, and seminars to deal with employees, the outside world, government. The practice has broadened considerably in terms of what can be done." This variety necessitates that a person be able to do more than one thing at once. People who like to finish one project before they start another had best look elsewhere for employment. A PR person is always doing a number of things at once, from writing a news release to supervising a graphic designer working on a brochure to setting up a press tour to fifty other things. People with one-track minds do not belong in PR.

Handle Stress Well

"When the phone rings, it's not someone calling to give you good news," says Ken Niehans, former public-information director at the University of Oregon Medical School. "They've got a problem. You're constantly dealing with other people's problems. That's what makes PR so exciting, but it also makes it more difficult than other kinds of jobs." PR is no place for nervous, excitable, overly sensitive people. They will not survive. Neither will someone who does not have good health.

Dress Carefully

Personal appearance is very important in PR. The initial impression a public-relations person makes on those he or she deals with daily is often as important as the tangible work to be done. A badly dressed person will not last long in PR, a profession where personal image ranks with corporate image in the scheme of things.

What kind of a future exists for public relations and those who choose it as a career? All signs indicate nothing but continued growth and enhanced job possibilities.

"As we get into a more sophisticated and complicated society, there is a greater need for interpretation of technical material," says Ken Niehans. "This has led to a more specialized kind of PR because nobody can inform the public about all things. It's changed so much. They still call it PR but it's really public information, not gilding the lily as much as providing channels for clients to tell a story. PR people need to continue to stress to management, however, that you can't change a bad product or bad service no matter what you say. And you also have to be kept informed. You can't put out a fire if you don't know what caused it."

SUMMARY

Public relations has increased in importance throughout the years of its existence as a profession. Recently, more and more companies are turning to PR people for help in solving the complex problems of modern society. They are paying such people well and giving them more power. People in public relations still have a tendency to feel inferior, however. Some of this comes from their own feelings about the field when they were journalists. Some of the attitude results from the unqualified hacks who used to predominate in PR. In order to succeed in PR, a person should be a good listener, know the media, be a good problem-solver, possess good communications skills, like to work with people, be comfortable in the profession, have initiative, be articulate, like variety, handle stress well, and be conscious of personal appearance.

REVIEW QUESTIONS

1. Why has the stature of public relations increased in recent years?
2. Why do some PR people feel inferior to those in other professions?
3. Why do PR practitioners need to like people, be good listeners, appreciate the value of PR, and like variety?
4. Why is a good PR person someone with good communications skills, a good appearance, and a strong physical constitution?
5. Having read this book and these characteristics, are you ready to answer the big question? Do you belong in public relations? If so, get busy. It's there waiting for you.

Glossary and Bibliography

Glossary

account — the company or individual hiring the services of a public-relations agency; also called a *client*.

account executive — a member of the **PR** agency staff who is the liaison between the account and the agency, and who is in charge of all work connected with this relationship.

advance — a news story about an event that appears before the event takes place.

advertising — a means to sell products to potential buyers through use of prepared announcements that stress advantages of the product and reasons to buy it in print or broadcast advertisements whose placement is paid for by the company manufacturing the product (see also *institutional ads* and *PR ads*).

agency — an organization that performs public-relations (and advertising) services for the account that pays a *fee*.

alignment — the proper arrangement of elements on a page so that they look pleasing and are not crooked.

AM — a morning newspaper.

annual report — a printed report issued once a year in which a company or other organization reveals financial and other information about itself; required for all companies issuing stock.

art — illustrations used in printed publications.

ascender — the part of a lowercase letter that goes above the body of the letter (b, f, h).

assignment — the instructions a reporter gets on what to cover.

attribution — the source of a story, usually appearing in the first paragraph.

audience — the group of people at which the messages of **PR** are aimed; can be as varied as the many publics of **PR**.

audio — the sound element of radio and television.

background — information that helps a reporter write a story but that might not appear in the story.

beat — the part of a publication's service area covered by a reporter on a regular basis.

bleed — a picture that runs off the edge of a page.

body type — type that is used for the text portion of a printed piece as opposed to type used for headlines.

booklet — a multipanel publication that is held together with staples.

brainstorming — a planning meeting in which the staff of a PR agency or an in-house PR department "think out loud" in an effort to come up with new ideas.

brochure — a multipanel publication that is folded; used a great deal in public relations to convey information.

by-line — the name of a reporter who wrote a story, usually noted directly over or under the headline or title.

campaign — the systematic organization of activities to accomplish a specific purpose, usually to influence one public or another.

caption — the small amount of words used to identify a photograph.

center spread — the two pages of a publication that face each other.

channel — a frequency band wide enough for one-way communication from a radio or television station.

circular — a one-page printed publication that is inexpensive to prepare.

circulation — the number of subscribers a newspaper or magazine has.

civil libel — printed and published defamation of a person, written maliciously and falsely, that results in those responsible paying damages.

classified advertisements — small ads sold by the square inch to people wanting to sell, buy, and get jobs or other goods.

client — the company or individual hiring the services of a public-relations agency; also called an *account*.

clipping service — a company that clips out all newspaper and magazine articles about the organizations that pay a fee for the service; clippings can also be obtained on any subject; a useful way to keep up on what is being written about a company or a specific subject.

close-up — a photograph or televised picture of an object seen at close range.

coated paper — paper that has an enameled coating that gives it a smooth, hard finish ideal for good photo reproduction.

cold type — typesetting by computer or photographic means, a part of offset printing.

collaterals — extra things like printed materials that are produced for an agency client beyond the standard fee.

composition — setting written material into type.

condensed — type that is narrower than the standard width.

copy — the stories written for a publication; the text for a brochure or other printed piece; the material for a news release.

copy block — that part of a printed piece in which the main part of the message is conveyed, as opposed to the headline.

copy editor — an editor who edits reporters' stories and writes headlines for them.

copyright — the exclusive right, granted by law for a certain number of years, to make and dispose of copies of a literary, musical, or artistic work.

copywriter — the employee of an agency who writes the words for brochures, other printed publications, and advertisements.

correspondent — a reporter for a publication who works out of town; a part-time reporter for a company publication who covers the factory or office in which he or she works.

cover — the front and back pages of a magazine, used to attract attention and give an idea of what is contained inside.

cover — to gather the facts about an event in order to write a story.

cover stock — paper designed to be used for covers of magazines or annual reports because of its durability.

criminal libel — printed defamation that results in a breach of the peace; it can send those guilty of causing it to jail.

cropping — eliminating elements of a photograph or other illustration to improve the photo or illustration, or changing the shape of a photo or illustration to fit it to a page design.

cutline — a caption appearing under a photograph to identify it.

deadline — the time when the final version of a story, release, or any other product of journalism or public relations is due at the editor's desk or at the printer; deadlines must be met if the work of journalism and PR is to proceed.

demographics — statistics on the age, sex, occupation, and education of a particular market; used to plan PR and advertising campaigns.

descender — the part of a lowercase letter below the body (j, p, y).

dummy — the plan of how a publication is to be arranged in rough form.

editorializing — inserting opinion in a news story or a feature story as opposed to an editorial that is clearly labeled; a thing to be avoided in PR news releases, if they are to be creditable, as well as in newspaper and magazine journalism.

ethics — the accepted standards of behavior for public-relations people as established by organizations like the Public Relations Society of America.

external publication — a company magazine or newspaper that goes to an audience outside the organization.

Federal Trade Commission (**FTC**) — the federal agency empowered to prevent misleading, deceptive, or fraudulent advertising in interstate commerce as well as unfair competition.

fee — the amount charged by an agency for its services to clients.

filmed releases — filmed stories about a company or nonprofit organization that are sent free to television stations with the hope they will be used on the air.

financial public relations — a specialized part of public relations that deals with writing news releases about financial matters and preparing annual reports.

First Amendment — the amendment to the United States Constitution that ensures freedom of the press.

follow-up — a story that appears after a news event to provide new information.

font — the full range of a type of one size and style.

freebies — gifts given to reporters, editors, and others outside a company or organization in order to win their good will.

free lance — a writer or article who is not a full-time employee of an agency or company but who is available to work on an ad hoc basis.

galley proof — the first printing of a column of type, to be read for errors.

glossy print — a photograph with a smooth and shiny surface; used most often in **PR** to send to newspapers and magazines where it must be screened before it can be printed.

grain — the direction of the fibers in a sheet of paper; papers fold best with the grain.

graphics — design of printed material as well as lettering, artwork, and visual displays in broadcasting.

gutter — the separation between two facing pages.

hand-out — a news release.

hard news — news that is current, happening today (the opposite of *soft news*).

headline — a title in large, bold type appearing over text material.

hold for release — a date, usually printed at the top of a news release, before which the information in the release cannot be printed or broadcast.

home towner — a news release, usually prepared by a college or university, about certain students or faculty that is sent to, and only of interest to, a hometown newspaper.

hot type — type set by a Linotype or similar machine using molten metal to cast lines of type; a part of letterpress printing.

house magazine — another name for a company magazine; also called a house organ.

image — the opinion everyone has of a company or organization.

initial letter — a design technique in which a large letter is used at the start of various paragraphs scattered throughout the page to break up the monotony.

institutional ads — advertisements that aim to create good will and build image rather than to sell a product.

internal publication — a company magazine or newspaper that goes to employees only.

invasion of privacy — the violation of a person's privacy by writing or photographing that person without his or her permission.

investor relations — another term for financial **PR**.

italic — type with letters and characters that slant forward for variety and emphasis.

junkets — free trips given to reporters and editors to influence coverage.

justification — aligning lines of type to the same length in a column.

lead — the first paragraph of a story or a news release.

lead — the space between lines to make reading easier (1 point leading is average, although 2 points is sometimes used; no leading is called "set solid").

letterpress — a printing method in which the raised surface image goes directly onto the paper.

libel — a malicious, false, and defamatory statement by printed means; can be of a civil or criminal type.

Linotype — a machine that casts lines of type from hot lead; used in letterpress printing.

logo — the symbol of a company used on all its printed material; short for logotype.

mailing list — a list of names to which all company publications can be mailed.

make-up — the arrangement of all elements of a publication page: headlines, copy block, illustrations.

mug shot — a photograph of a person's head and shoulders.

network — a broadcast link of two or more stations.

news peg — the reason to publish a story or put out a news release, the thing that makes it newsworthy.

newsprint — a rough-finish paper that is relatively inexpensive, used for newspaper printing.

news release — a story, written by a company to give its view of an event, that the PR people hope the publication will publish; also called a *press release*.

news source — the people who give reporters their story ideas and stories.

not for attribution — information whose source cannot be revealed in the story but whose substance can be included; not to be confused with *off the record*.

off the record — material from interviews that serves only as background and cannot be used in print; not to be confused with *not for attribution*.

offset lithography — an indirect printing method based on the principle that grease and water do not mix; the image goes from a plate to a rubber blanket to the paper.

pamphlet — a small brochure.

paste-up — the process of preparing the final page of a publication: all headlines, copy blocks, and illustrations have been attached to a layout sheet with wax or rubber cement (dummy) and are ready to be photographed and printed (mechanical).

photojournalism — using photographs to tell a story.

pica — a printer's measure, 12 points or approximately one-sixth of an inch.

PM — an afternoon newspaper.

point — a unit of measurement for type, approximately 72 points to an inch.

poll — a survey of opinions and beliefs of a carefully selected sample of people; also called a *survey*.

press conference — a meeting to which reporters are invited in order to hear about a development at the company or nonprofit organization that is newsworthy.

press release — the "release" of information to the press by written means; also called a *news release*.

principles of design — the design of any printed page should be carried out with five principles in mind: balance, proportion, sequence, unity, contrast.

privacy — the public's right to be let alone; the reporter's right to cover people involved in news events without fear of legal action.

public — of or for the people as a whole but including many portions of this group for public relations purposes, i.e., employees, customers, reporters, stockholders, etc.

public information — programs designed to inform publics about a nonprofit organization.

public relations — promoting goodwill toward a company by printed or other means; also known as **PR**.

PR ads — advertisements designed to improve an image with facts.

public-service announcement (**PSA**) — pre-prepared television or radio spots that inform and entertain the audience as well as get the name of the sponsoring organization across to it.

sanserif — type with no serifs.

screening — processing photographs in order to build up a tiny dot structure on them that will retain ink and enable them to be printed.

Securities and Exchange Commission (**SEC**) — the federal agency that regulates the sale of stock.

serif — a small stroke at the outer edges of printed letters.

slander — a malicious, false, and defamatory statement or report by oral, not printed, means.

soft news — stories that are not always timely but are interesting and informative nevertheless; features are usually soft news, while news stories are *hard news*.

style — the way publications want their stories to be written in terms of abbreviation, spelling, capitalization, etc.

style book — the details of a publication's style compiled in a book for easy access by those writing for that publication.

subhead — headlines of a type size smaller than that for the main head, used to break up a long copy block into more easily read segments.

survey — a poll of opinions and beliefs of a carefully selected sample of people; also called a *poll*.

tabloid — a newspaper page half the normal size.

thumbnail — a rough, preliminary sketch of a publication done in miniature.

trade publications — magazines and newspapers whose editorial content and advertisements are aimed at a particular audience.

type — printed letters and characters of various sizes and styles used for printing headlines and copy blocks.

type classifications — there are six type classifications: text, roman, sanserif, square serif, scripts and cursives, novelty and decorative.

typeface — a particular style or design of type.

Video display terminal (**VDT**) — a kind of "electronic typewriter" consisting of a keyboard and video screen; operators type stories using the keyboard and edit them on the screen electronically using a *cursor*.

X-height — the body of a letter without descenders and ascenders.

Bibliography

Adams, A. B. *Handbook of Practical Public Relations*. New York: Thomas Y. Crowell, 1970.

Anderson, Walter. *Handbook of Business Communications*. Box 243, Lenox Hill Station, New York, NY 10021, 1975.

Ashley, Paul P. *Say It Safely: Legal Limits in Publishing, Radio and Television*, 4th ed. Seattle: University of Washington Press, 1969.

AP Broadcast News Stylebook. New York: Associated Press, 1977.

AP Stylebook and Libel Manual. New York: Associated Press, 1977.

Ayer Directory of Publications. Philadelphia: Ayer Press, annual.

Bacon's International Publicity Checker. Chicago: Bacon, annual.

Bacon's Publicity Checker: Magazines, Newspapers. Chicago: Bacon, annual.

Bernays, Edward L. *Biography of an Idea*. New York: Simon & Schuster, 1965.

Bernays, Edward L. *Public Relations*. Norman: University of Oklahoma Press, 1970.

Bernstein, Theodore M. *The Careful Writer: A Modern Guide to English Usage*. New York: Atheneum, 1975.

Bittner, J. R. *Mass Communication*. Englewood Cliffs, NJ: Prentice-Hall, 1977.

Bloom, M. H. *Public Relations and Presidential Campaigns*. New York: Thomas Y. Crowell, 1973.

Blumenthal, L. R. *The Practice of Public Relations*. New York: Macmillan, 1972.

Boettinger, H. M. *Moving Mountains: The Art and Craft of Letting Others See Things Your Way*. New York: Macmillan, 1969.

Broadcasting Yearbook. Washington, D.C.: Broadcasting Publications, annual.

Burger, Chester. *The Chief Executive: Realities of Corporate Leadership*. Boston: CBI, 1978.

Burton, Paul. *Corporate Public Relations*. New York: Reinhold, 1966.

Center, Allen. *Public Relations Prospectus: Case Studies*. Englewood Cliffs, NJ: Prentice-Hall, 1975.

A Manual of Style. Chicago: University of Chicago Press, 1969.

Cutlip, Scott, and Allen Center. *Effective Public Relations*. Englewood Cliffs, NJ: Prentice-Hall, 1978.

Darrow, Ralph. *House Journal Editing*. Danville, IL: Interstate Printers, 1975.

Drucker, Peter. *Management: Tasks, Responsibilities, Practices*. New York: Harper & Row, 1974.

Editor & Publisher Yearbook. New York: Editor & Publisher, annual.

Encyclopedia of Associations. Detroit: Gale Research Co., annual.

Fortune Double 500 Directory. New York: Time-Life, annual.

Gebbie Directory of House Organs. New Platz, NY: Gebbie, annual.

Gebbie Press All-in-One-Directory. New Platz, NY: Gebbie, annual.

Gordon, G. N. *Persuasion: Theory and Practice of Manipulative Communication.* New York: Hastings House, 1971.

Greenfield, Stanley, R., ed. *National Directory of Addresses and Telephone Numbers.* New York: Bantam Books, 1978.

Grey, David L. *The Writing Process.* Belmont, CA: Wadsworth, 1972.

Hiebert, Roy. *Courtier to the Crowd.* Ames: Iowa State University Press, 1966.

Hiebert, Roy. *Political Image Merchants: Strategies in the New Politics.* Washington, D.C.: Acropolis, 1971.

Hill & Knowlton. *Critical Issues in Public Relations.* Englewood Cliffs, NJ: Prentice-Hall, 1975.

Hudson's Washington News Media Directory. Washington, D.C., annual.

Lesly, Philip. *The People Factor: Managing the Human Climate.* New York: Dow-Jones Irvin, 1974.

Lewis, H. G. *How to Handle Your Own Public Relations.* Chicago: Nelson-Hall, 1976.

Lippmann, Walter. *Public Opinion.* New York: Macmillan, 1960.

Marston, John. *The Nature of Public Relations.* New York: McGraw-Hill, 1963.

Martin, Dick. *Executive's Guide to Handling a Press Interview.* New York: Pilot Books, 1977.

Monaghan, Patrick. *Public Relations Careers in Business and the Community.* New York: Fairchild, 1971.

National Directory of Newsletters/Reporting Services. Detroit: Gale Research Co., 1978.

Newson, Doug, and Alan Scott. *This is PR: The Realities of Public Relations.* Belmont, CA: Wadsworth, 1976.

New York Times Manual of Style and Usage. New York: McGraw-Hill, 1977.

Nolte, L. W. *Fundamentals of Public Relations.* New York: Pergamon Press, 1974.

Norton, Alice. *Public Relations: A Guide to Information Sources.* Detroit: Gale Research Co., 1970.

Public Relations Guides for Nonprofit Organizations: (1) Planning/Setting Objectives; (2) Using Publicity to Best Advantage; (3) Working with Volunteers; (4) Making the Most of Special Events; (5) Measuring Potential/Evaluating Results; (6) Using Standards to Strengthen Public Relations. New York: Public Relations Society of America, 1977.

Public Relations Register. New York: Public Relations Society of America, annual.

Rivers, William L. *Finding Facts.* Englewood Cliffs, NJ: Prentice-Hall, 1975.

Rivers, William L. *Writing: Craft and Art.* Englewood Cliffs, NJ: Prentice-Hall, 1975.

Schmidt, Frances, and Harold M. Weiner. *Public Relations in Health and Welfare.* New York: Columbia University Press, 1966.

Simon, Morton J. *Public Relations Law.* New York: Appleton-Century-Crofts, 1969.

Simon, Raymond. *Perspectives in Public Relations.* Norman: University of Oklahoma Press, 1966.

Steinberg, Charles. *The Creation of Consent: Public Relations in Practice.* New York: Hastings House, 1975.

Stephenson, Howard. *Handbook of Public Relations.* New York: McGraw-Hill, 1971.

Strunk, William, and E. G. White. *The Elements of Style.* 3rd ed. New York: Macmillan, 1979.

Ulrich's International Periodical Directory. New York: Bowker, 1978.

United Press International Stylebook. New York: United Press International, 1977.

Washington Representatives of American Association & Industry. Washington, D.C.: Columbia Books, annual.

Working Press of the Nation. Burlington, IA: National Research Bureaus, annual.

Zinsser, William. *On Writing Well.* New York: Harper & Row, 1976.

Index